AF478291

con il patrocinio di

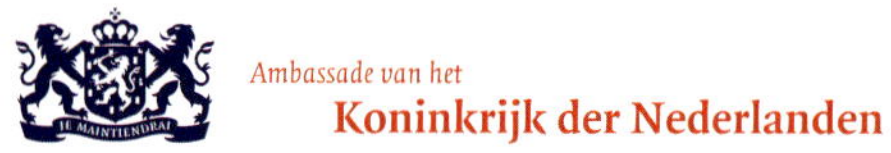

Musei Vaticani

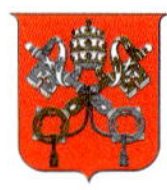

Carla Hendriks

Northern Landscapes on Roman Walls
The Frescoes of Matthijs and Paul Bril

with essays by

Angela Negro and *Louisa Wood Ruby*

edited by

Bert W. Meijer

Centro Di

Carla Hendriks
Northern Landscapes on Roman Walls.
The Frescoes of Matthijs and Paul Bril
Edited by *Bert W. Meijer*

Translations:
Yvette Rosenberg (texts Carla Hendriks)
Ursula Creagh (texts Angela Negro
and Francesco Buranelli)

Layout and Design:
Manola Miniati (Centro Di)

With the contributions from:

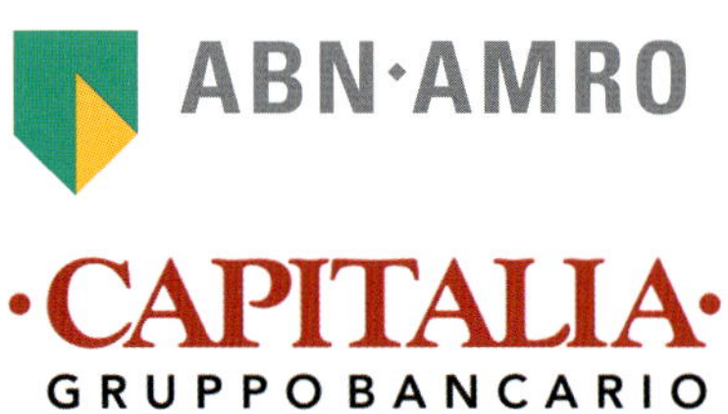

The publication of this volume was made possible
also by a generous contribution from the
Soprintendenza Speciale per il Polo Museale Romano

I am truly delighted that the results of the research conducted on the frescoes of the most important Dutch landscape painters in Rome, are now brought together in this volume. This beautifully executed publication does justice to the key role played by the Bril brothers in the development of Italian and Dutch painting in the sixteenth and seventeenth century. The Embassy has gladly lent its support to the publication of this important book.

This is the first study dedicated exclusively to the frescoes by Matthijs and Paul Bril. Both artists were highly regarded in their time, witness the many commissions they received from popes, cardinals and members of the Roman nobility. Thanks to careful conservation and restoration by the Italian authorities and by the Vatican, most frescoes can still be admired in a number of places in and around Rome. Thus, today's spectator can make sure of the quality of the works by both masters and of the wealth of detail that lies hidden therein.

The authors have succeeded in mapping practically the complete body of works of the Bril brothers, including illustrations in colour of most frescoes. This work documents an important element of the Dutch cultural heritage in Italy; moreover, it meets the keen Italian interest in northern landscape painting and in the influence which northern painters exerted on Italian painting in general.

I sincerely hope that the dialogue between art historians, artists and art lovers of both countries may receive a new impulse through this publication.

In conclusion, I should like to thank all those whose support has been indispensable for this undertaking: first of all the two initiators of the project – art historian Carla Hendriks and Jan E. Boeles, former Counsellor for Press and Cultural Affairs at the Netherlands Embassy in Rome; the co-authors Louisa Wood Ruby and Angela Negro; Professor Bert W. Meijer, Director of the Dutch University Institute for Art History in Florence; Professor Claudio Strinati, Soprintendente Speciale per il Polo Museale Romano; Francesco Buranelli, Director of the Vatican Museums; Ginevra Marchi, Centro Di Publishers, Florence; and, last but not least, ABN AMRO and CAPITALIA GRUPPO BANCARIO whose generous financial contributions have been crucial for the realisation of this project.

Ronald H. Loudon
Netherlands Ambassador to Italy

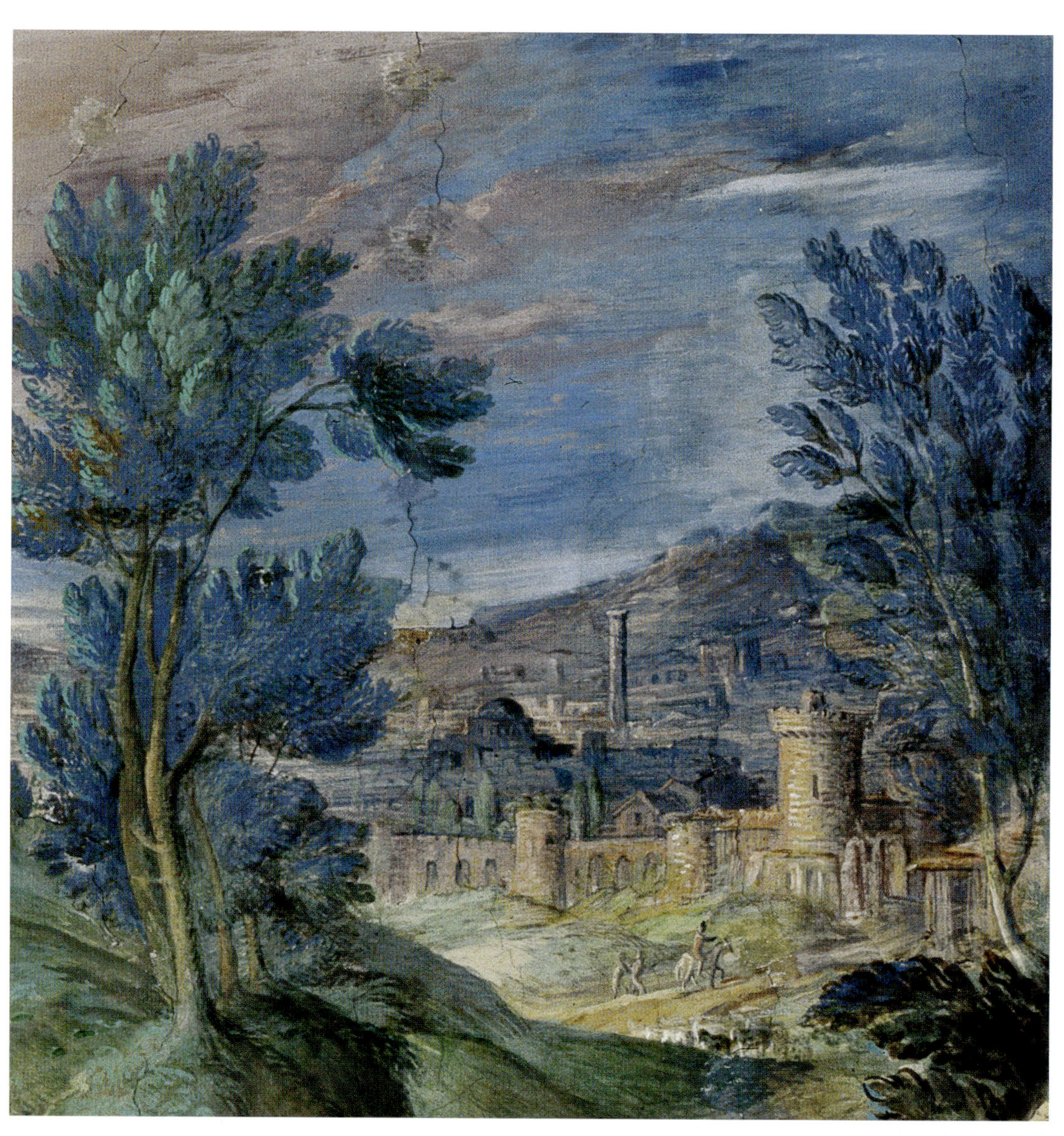

This volume establishes the extreme importance of the work of the Flemish painters and brothers, Matthijs and Paul Bril, to a better understanding of the major developments which had such a profound impact on the future of painting, at that crucial period between the late 16th and the early 17th centuries. While Matthijs's artistic career was cut short by his untimely death, the career of the equally gifted Paul was so long, varied and successful that in the eyes of contemporary art historians the artist has become an essential reference point in the history of landscape painting.

The Bril brothers were originally from Antwerp and this volume presents their artistic works in Rome, focusing particularly on their fresco painting, their chief activity and one in which they both achieved a high degree of excellence. In fact, frescoes constitute the major body of the work of both Matthijs and Paul, so that today's scholars can trace their artistic position and follow the evolution of their style of painting through a study of their Roman mural paintings alone.

Moreover, the learned author of this volume, Carla Hendriks (supported by Angela Negro and Louisa Wood Ruby) has adopted an interesting methodological approach, full of insights, to trace the path which enabled the two brothers to give landscape painting the all-important and highly eminent position it was later to occupy for centuries.

The particular talent of the Bril brothers lay in their ability to adopt appropriate styles for both religious and lay painting, lending support to the previously little considered thesis of the conceptual and spiritual scope of landscape painting, freed from the purely decorative role it had occupied during the Cinquecento, a movement which began at the time of their major fresco works.

As the author makes clear, this is the more remarkable since in their own country the two brothers would never have had the opportunity to learn the technique of fresco painting, it being little practised in the Netherlands, so that it was their time in Italy, and particularly in Rome, which led them in this direction. Yet in the eyes of their contemporaries (and ours to a certain degree) the Bril brothers are the very epitome of the northern-European school which, with Paul, became gradually assimilated with the Italian style of painting.

This latter fact becomes clear from a close study of Paul Bril's life, from which it emerges that although he was closely involved in life in Rome, becoming virtually 'Roman' himself, he always kept in close touch with artists and intellectuals in his home country and far from wishing to renounce his native land he defended it proudly.

This volume of critical biography traces the Bril brothers' activity in the service of papal commissioners, and their works are skilfully illustrated. The photographic documentation is rich in splendid images and in details which were virtually unknown even to the experts (expressly produced and made available by the Vatican Museums), making it a precious and indispensable source for a deeper understanding of these two painters.

Matthijs made his debut in Rome with fresco paintings in the Torre dei Venti, built during the pontificate of Gregory XIII, while Paul was engaged on various occasions in the Vatican, making it possible to follow the development of his work and style through a study of his paintings in the Vatican and in buildings which still today fall within the provenance of the Holy See, including the *Palazzo Apostolico Lateranense*, the *Patriarcale Basilica di Santa Maria Maggiore* and the *Scala Santa*. Paul Bril produced some of his finest frescoes in the latter building and we should take the occasion of this book's publication to mention that the project to restore the complete cycle of frescoes in the Sistine Chapel of the *Scala Santa* is now fully under way. This will be a splendid opportunity to fully restore important works by artists who include, among others, Cesare Nebbia and Giovanni Guerra, and there is little doubt that the restoration will cause Paul Bril's elegant and accomplished painting to re-emerge in all its glory.

This will be a tangible result of that essential fusion of scientific research, conservation, scholarship and restoration, closely correlated in the unified and well-informed study and conservation of the immense artistic legacy that has been handed down to us over the centuries.

Francesco Buranelli
Director of the Vatican Museums

Table of Contents

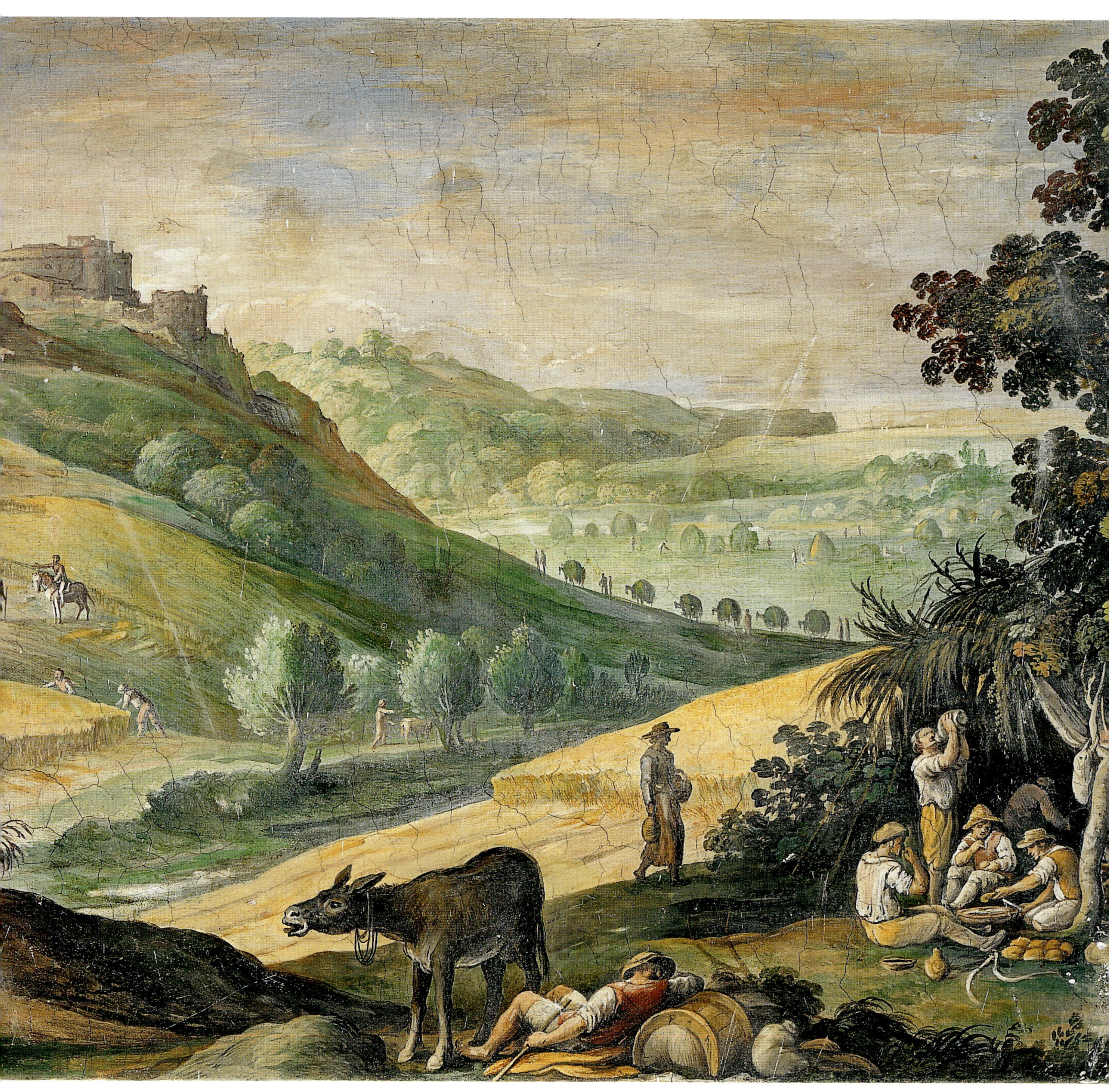

Preface

In the history of European painting, the representation of landscape has long been considered primarily a field of Netherlandish expertise, to which only relatively few Italian painters have made significant contributions. Moreover, in the hierarchy of pictorial genres, landscape was for a long time seen as one of the minor categories, and distinctly inferior to narrative painting with multi-figure compositions, in which the Italians excelled. For that reason, it was not a problem for Italian artists and critics to leave the palm of primacy in landscape to Northern painters, particularly since Titian was recognised as a notable exception to the rule of Northern superiority.

In a well-known letter written around 1620 by the great collector Marquis Vincenzo Giustiniani to his Dutch friend Dirck van Ameyden, the Roman Curia lawyer, Giustiniani not only ranked landscape as seventh on the scale of genres, but he also distinguished two styles in landscape painting: a grand manner, represented (according to Giustiniani) by Raphael, the Venetians, the Carraccis, and Guido Reni; and a more diligent, precise way of painting, whose leading proponents were mainly of Netherlandish origin. Of these, Civetta, Brueghel, and Paul Bril were the better known names in Italy. However, the more classical and, in some instances, more painterly Italian current and the fresh Northern landscape style influenced each other and mixed fairly regularly. This was also the case with the easel and fresco paintings by Paul Bril, the foremost landscape painter in Rome during the more than forty years of his successful Roman career.

The short-lived Matthijs Bril, and particularly his younger brother Paul, played a fundamental role in the development of landscape painting in Italy and Northern Europe. It was not so much the great quantity of the latter's production as his convincing representation of nature, its flora and fauna, and an almost unlimited variety of different human manufactures and activities set in their natural surroundings that must have been perceived as something novel, arousing great admiration.

The importance of this richly illustrated volume lies in the fact that it is the first book to bring together the frescoes of the Bril brothers, offering art lovers and art historians a hitherto unavailable visual panorama of the wall-paintings executed by the Brils and their workshop (or workshops). It will allow us to understand the full scope and character of their fresco production and also to gain knowledge about the creative process, through a study of both the preliminary drawings and their fresco technique.

Paul's official role as *principe* in the Accademia di San Luca, as well as certain of his commissions, indicate that the younger of the two Brils raised the status of the landscape painter to a level of recognition and dignity comparable to that of the important 'history' painters of his time. With the increased production of autonomous and other landscape paintings in the seventeenth century, and with the official appreciation of a painter such as Bril, the perception of the importance of landscape, and of what was required to become a good landscape painter, was changing. In 1642, sixteen years after Paul's death, the Dominican friar Francesco Bisagno published his *Trattato della Pittura* in Venice. The chapter dedicated to landscape painting testifies to this changed perception: "Although many unwise people consider that landscape painting is very simple and of little value, nonetheless they are seriously misleading themselves, because painting landscapes with *artificio*, if attempted according to rules of science, is one of the most difficult arts embraced by painting, and what I say is so true that in order to do it well, one needs a special grace and a divine gift...".

But the history of the struggle of landscape painting and painters for greater respect was far from over. It was only in the nineteenth century that landscape achieved parity with other categories of painting. The production of the two Brils, and particularly Paul, and the rank acquired by the latter were essential steps in this direction. With the publication of the present book, the underlying reasons for the improvement of the situation, and the work by the Brils that encouraged it, can now be more easily appreciated.

Bert W. Meijer

This book rounds off a comprehensive study of the frescoes in Rome and Latium of Matthijs and Paul Bril, and will be followed shortly by the publication of my dissertation on their work.

The brothers' drawings and landscapes in fresco and Paul's easel paintings have enjoyed considerable attention for some time. Though the spotlight has generally fallen on Paul, the younger of the two brothers, the fresco landscapes Matthijs painted in Rome before his untimely death at the age of thirty-three are also of great importance. In the period of approximately ten years that he worked in Rome, he executed several fresco series in both sacred and secular buildings, in Rome itself and in the nearby town of Monterotondo, north of the city. Matthijs paved the way for his brother and laid the foundations for his long and immensely successful career as a landscape painter in Rome.

The earliest printed publication on the lives and work of Matthijs and Paul Bril is Karel van Mander's *Schildersboeck*, dating from 1604 and written during Paul's lifetime. [1] Van Mander is believed to have obtained his up-to-date information on the brothers' work from Willem van Nieulandt, who studied under Paul in Rome around 1600 and returned to Amsterdam in 1603. A few years later, in 1621, Giulio Mancini published new facts about Paul Bril in his *Considerazioni sulla pittura*. [2] A third important source on the brothers' work in Rome is the brief biography by the painter Giovanni Baglione (1649), who had worked with Paul on several projects. [3] But the first monograph on Paul Bril appeared only in 1910. The author of the work, Anton Mayer, presented an analysis of Bril's style, and concluded that his main influence had been the German Adam Elsheimer rather than Italian painters such as Annibale Carracci. Mayer's illustrated study is far from complete, especially as regards the frescoes, but even today it remains a valuable source of information and offers the earliest overview of Bril's drawings, prints, paintings and frescoes. Rudolf Baer's study of Paul Bril, which followed in 1930, was intended, according to the author, to inspire further study of the evolution of landscape painting. [4] Baer also challenged Mayer's theory about the extent of Elsheimer's influence on Bril's work, basing his diverging views mainly on the frescoes and drawings.

A major contribution to our understanding of Paul's work came in the form of an article by Giorgio Faggin (1965), which focused mainly on the artist's cabinet paintings. [5] Faggin ascribed to Paul a number of frescoes which had previously been regarded as the work of Matthijs and whose attribution even today remains controversial. [6]

1990 saw the publication of Nicola Courtright's dissertation on the Torre dei Venti in the Vatican, which examines the frescoes and analyses the decoration in relation to the ideas of the Counter-Reformation. [7] Courtright pays particular attention to the landscape frescoes, all of which she attributes to Matthijs. Her study was followed in 1993 by Andrea Berger's thesis focusing mainly on the easel paintings. [8] A revealing discovery in the Mattei family archive in the form of a contract with Paul Bril was published by Francesca Cappelletti and Laura Testa in 1994. [9] The frescoes Bril painted in Palazzo Mattei (now Caetani) in 1599 were published for the first time. Following a restoration project in Rome in 1996, Angela Negro reported on her comprehensive study of the Casino del Patriarca Biondo (known today as the Loggia della Pergola), where Bril painted his most mature landscapes and a pergola with vines and animals. [10] Louisa Wood Ruby published her dissertation on Paul Bril's drawings in 1999, establishing yet another milestone in the study of his work. [11] Luuk Pijl has studied Bril's paintings and published several works on the subject. [12] So far, the frescoes of Matthijs and Paul Bril have never been published in full. The present book marks a step towards filling that gap. It concerns the frescoes whose attribution can be established on the basis of documents or stylistic analysis. [13] Louisa Wood Ruby's contribution examines drawings that Matthijs and Paul Bril may have used as preliminary studies. The chapter by Angela Negro sheds light on Paul Bril's painting technique in the Casino del Patriarca Biondo.

The authors hope their efforts will contribute further to the growing body of knowledge on these two pioneers of landscape painting.

1) Van Mander 1604, fol. 291v and 292r.
2) Mancini 1621 (1956-1957), vol. 2, p. 260.
3) Baglione 1649, ed. 1924 (reprint 1986), vol. 1, p. 18.
4) Baer 1930, p. 5.
5) Faggin 1965.
6) *Ibid.* 1965, pp. 21-22. Based on a comparison between a seascape with galleys in the Torre dei Venti in the Vatican and a drawing by Paul Bril in Leiden, see figs. 16 and 43.
7) Courtright 1990.
8) Berger 1993.
9) Cappelletti, Testa 1994. Francesca Cappelletti wrote a dissertation on Paul Bril in 1995, which I have unfortunately been unable to consult.
10) Negro 1996. The restoration presented an opportunity to study Bril's technique. See Angela Negro's essay in this volume.

11) Ruby 1999. Her *catalogue raisonné* attributes 109 drawings to him.
12) See the Bibliography. Pijl has traced about 140 paintings and is currently preparing a thesis on Paul Bril's cabinet paintings.
13) My dissertation on the frescoes of Matthijs and Paul Bril and the function of landscape painting in religious and secular buildings in Rome and its environs around 1600, due to be published in 2003, will include a complete *catalogue raisonné*.

Note: Technical datas of drawings and easel paintings by the Bril brothers are mentioned in the captions of the illustrations; those of frescoes are included in the *Repertory of the Frescoes* in this volume.

Acknowledgements

A book of this kind could not have been written without the assistance of many individuals and organisations. In particular I would like to mention the research departments of the Dutch Institute in Rome and the Dutch University Institute for Art History in Florence, whose generosity has enabled me to work in Italy on several occasions. I am also grateful to all the staff of the libraries, photograph libraries, museums and records offices in Rome, Paris, Antwerp and Breda, who guided me through labyrinths of information to material on Matthijs and Paul Bril.

For giving me their time and shedding new light on the frescoes during my visits to Rome, I would like to express my sincere gratitude to Alessandro Zuccaro, Nicola Courtright, Christoph Merzenich, Francesca Capanna, Judith Verberne and Angela Negro. I am also deeply indebted to my Dutch friends in Rome for their kindness and support over the years.

My fellow Bril scholars, Louisa Wood Ruby and Luuk Pijl, have stood by me and encouraged me right from the start. I am grateful to have this opportunity to record my appreciation to them for their willingness to share with me their expert knowledge of the two painters. A special word of thanks is also due to Professor Anton W.A. Boschloo for his invaluable advice throughout my research.

The publication of this book would have been impossible without the assistance and support of the Netherlands Embassy in Rome. I would like to send my thanks in particular to Ronald H. Loudon, Jan Boeles, Madeleine Mansvelt Beck, Marion Penninck and their staff.

I would also like to record my personal gratitude to my principal sponsors ABN AMRO and CAPITALIA GRUPPO BANCARIO for enabling me to publish such a richly illustrated book, and also to Francesco Buranelli, Director of the Vatican Museums, who made it possible for us to obtain a significant part of the photographic repertory. Many thanks, too, to my translator Yvette Rosenberg, whose optimism spurred me on. I also owe a debt of appreciation to the Dutch University Institute for Art History in Florence for allowing me to use their photographs and to the Soprintendenza Speciale per il Polo Museale Romano in the person of Professor Claudio Strinati for its contribution.

Finally, I would like to say a very special word of thanks to Professor Bert W. Meijer for his invaluable advice on the concept of the book and his critical reading of my manuscript.

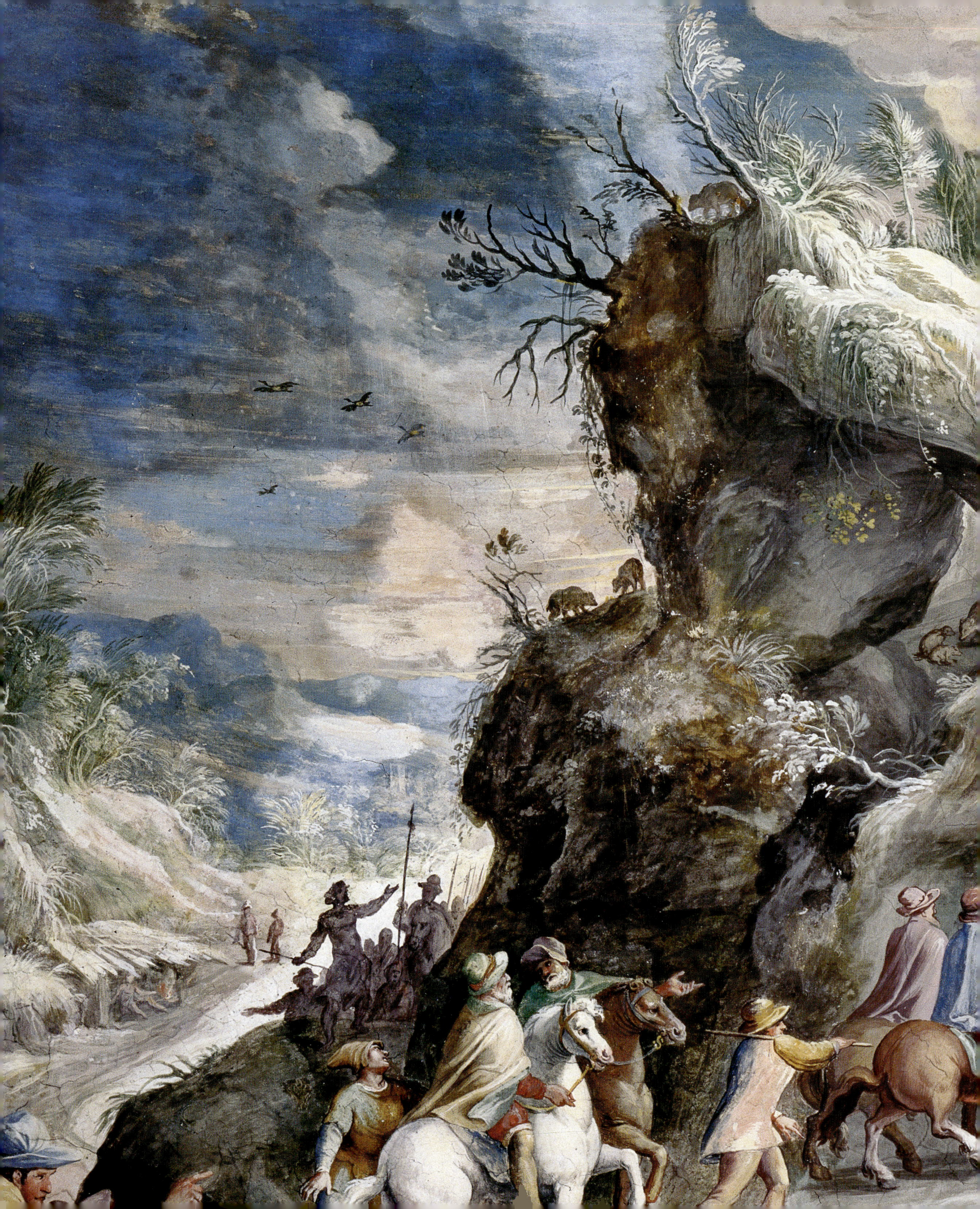

The painters Matthijs and Paul Bril were born in the Southern Netherlands in the middle of the sixteenth century (figs. 1 and 2). Matthijs was born in Antwerp, probably in 1550 and his younger brother Paul in Antwerp or Breda in 1553 or 1554. Neither their dates nor their cities of birth have been firmly established.[1] Both, however, died in Rome, Matthijs in 1583 and Paul in 1626.[2]

A brief biography in the *Schilderboeck* (1604) by the painter and writer Karel van Mander (1548-1577) notes that they came from Antwerp.[3] However, documents found in the archives of Breda show that the Bril family was living in that city.[4] A deed in Breda's municipal archive refers to the father as "Mathijs Baermaker Janszone, known as Bril, the painter". Another document in Breda, dated 1558, names all the Bril children including "Matthijsken" and "Pauwelsken".[5] A seventeenth-century document refers to father Matthijs and son Paul as "Mathijs Bril of Breda, a fine painter of fruit and grotesques, and Pauwels Mathijsen his son, at an early age the finest landscape painter in Rome".[6] As far as is known, no work by Matthijs Bril the Elder has survived, nor does his name appear in the archives of the Antwerp painters' guild.

Matthijs and Paul Bril, as well as their brothers Hans (Jan) and Jacob, probably received their first painting lessons from their father. Hans and Jacob subsequently pursued their studies in Antwerp, where they were registered with the guild of St Luke in 1569.[7] The guild archive however contains no reference to either Matthijs or Paul, although it does record the painter Damiaen Wortelmans, whom Karel van Mander describes as Paul Bril's teacher.[8] It is not known whether Matthijs Bril the Younger had a teacher in Antwerp and, if so, who it might have been. Van Mander writes that Paul Bril worked for Wortelmans, painting the lids of harpsichords and other musical instruments in tempera. This is how he earned his livelihood at the age of fourteen.[9]

The two brothers left for Italy in the early 1570s, Matthijs Bril slightly earlier than Paul who, according to Van Mander, spent some time in the French city of Lyon in 1574 before continuing his journey to Rome.[10] Lyon was popular with artists and merchants passing through on their way to Rome and other parts of Italy. Dutch and Flemish travellers coming from Antwerp, Brussels and Paris stopped off in Lyon and many remained there for some time.[11] It is impossible to say how long Paul Bril stayed in Lyon, but as a young novice he would presumably have joined an artists' collective.[12] Whether Matthijs also visited Lyon on his way to Italy is unknown. Once in Rome, Matthijs found employment fairly quickly, possibly with the help of fellow countrymen working for Pope Gregory XIII (1572-1585).[13] His arrival in

Rome was timely, as the Holy Year 1575 was approaching and the celebrations to mark the event brought a great deal of work for artists. According to archival documents, Matthijs was living in the Campo di Marzio quarter: he is first referred to as "Mastro Mateo fiamengo pitore" in the accounts of the Accademia di San Luca, dating from 1580.[14] His marriage to Clara Scocchi on 30 August 1582, which was registered in the *Libri Matrimoniorum* of the parish of San Lorenzo in Lucina, suggests that he was intending to settle in Rome permanently. Interestingly enough, the name of his brother Paul does not appear on the list of witnesses.[15] In the event, the marriage was shortlived, as Matthijs died suddenly the following year. The death register of Santa Maria dell'Anima, the church attended by the Flemish and German

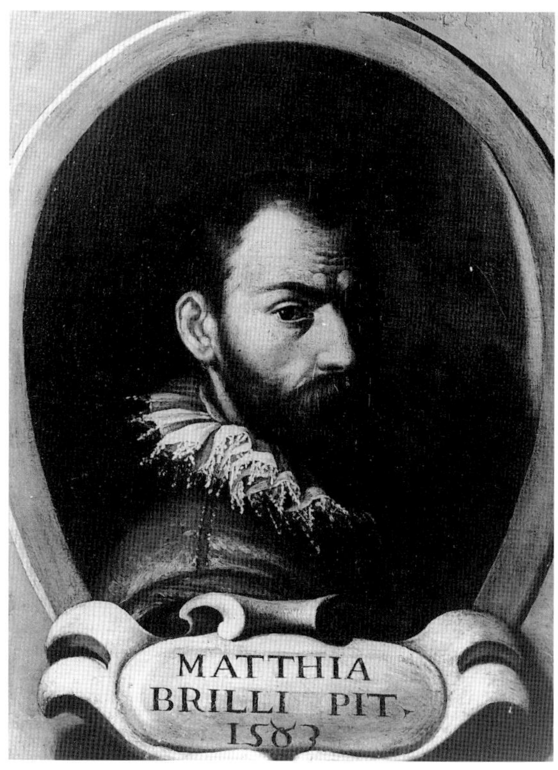

1. Anonymous, *Portrait of Matthijs Bril*,
oil on canvas, 71 x 52 cm. Rome, Accademia
di San Luca, inv. no. 2030.

communities, gives the date of his death as 8 June 1583.[16] Both Matthijs and Paul are buried in the church.

It is uncertain when Paul Bril arrived in Rome. He left Lyon to join Matthijs,[17] and spent his first few years in Rome working with him. And though he is not recorded as having attended Matthijs' wedding in August 1582, a few weeks later, on 17 October, their names appear together in the ledger of the Accademia di San Luca, the *Libro degli introiti*. They had contributed money for the feast of St Luke, the patron saint of painters. Matthijs' name also appears in the ledger in 1580 and 1581.[18] Both were therefore enrolled at the academy. The first record of Paul after the death of his brother dates from 1584, when he received a fee for his work in the

Collegio della Compagnia di Gesù (Collegio Romano). This was probably his first independent commission. [19] "Mastro Paolo Fiamengo" was paid in instalments between 11 August and 26 October for two landscapes "dipinti in sala". Though the frescoes no longer exist, the account book gives an idea of the nature of the commission, the fee and the amount of time he spent on the project. [20]

Paul Bril was one of a team of painters who worked for Pope Sixtus V (1585-1590). His landscapes formed part of almost every decoration programme commissioned by the pope, among them those for the Santa Maria Maggiore, the Lateran, the Vatican Palace and Scala Santa. From then on, his career as a landscape painter flourished. He received commissions for frescoes not only from the pope's successors, but also

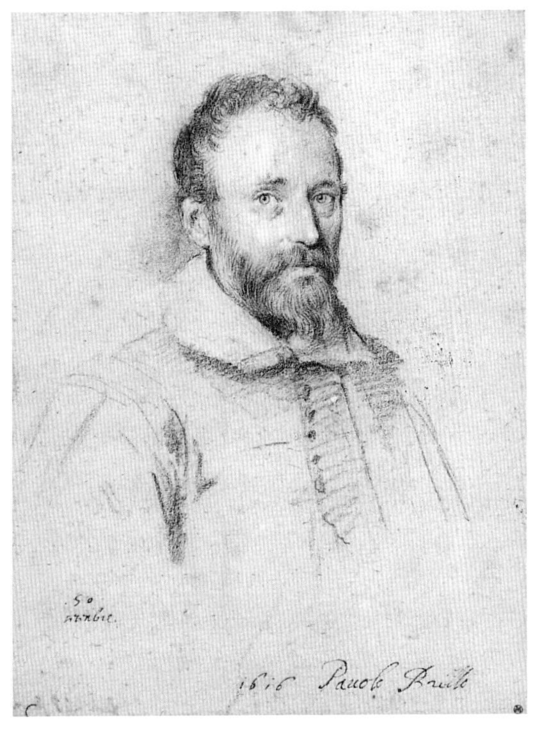

2. Ottavio Leoni, *Portrait of Paul Bril*, black chalk with white heightening, 230 x 170 mm. Paris, Musée du Louvre, Département des Arts Graphiques, inv. no. 3332.

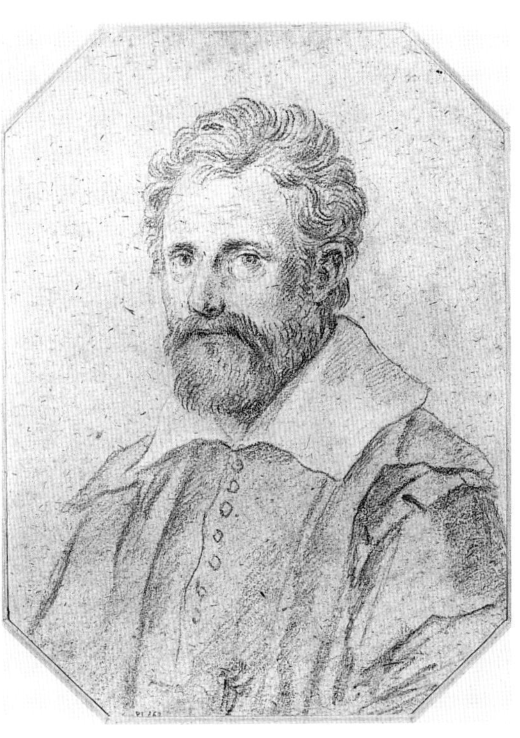

3. Pier Leone Ghezzi, *Portrait of Paul Bril*, black chalk with white heightening, 274 x 183 mm. Lille, Palais des Beaux-Arts, inv. no. Pl. 262.

from high-ranking prelates and distinguished Roman families. In the 1590s he also started painting landscapes on canvas, copper and panel. About one hundred and forty of his paintings and several designs for prints are known. [21]

The parish archives in Rome are a rich source of information on the life of Paul Bril after his late marriage, in 1592, to Ottavia Sbarra, the daughter of a Florentine goldsmith. The couple's first son was born that year, and their second, Matthijs, was christened on 21 April 1594. Barely a year later they gave birth to a third child in their home in Strada Paolina, now the Via del Babuino. [22] Only three of their eight children reached adulthood: a daughter Faustina, and two sons, Luca and the evidently unruly Ciriaco, both of whom heaped misfortune on their father. At his death,

Paul Bril bequeathed his estate to his wife and three surviving children. [23]

Many of the Brils' neighbours were artists from northern Europe, among them Willem II van Nieulandt (Guglielmo Terranova), who may have been Karel van Mander's source of information on Paul Bril and a companion of his, Pieter van Houte (Pietro de Lignis). The German painter Adam Elsheimer and his family lived seven houses away. [24] Bril was closely acquainted with Elsheimer and was a witness at his marriage on 22 December 1606. [25]

Though Bril married an Italian, spoke and wrote the language fluently, and worked for Italian patrons, he nevertheless maintained close ties with his former compatriots. He attended meetings at the home of an expatriate pharmacist from Delft, Hendrik de Raeff (1567/68?-1639/40, also called Corvinius). [26] A patron of the arts, De Raeff received other painters at his home in the Vicolo del Pavone, among them Rubens, Jan Brueghel the Elder, and Adam Elsheimer. Jan Brueghel the Elder, who lived in Rome from 1591 to 1595, befriended Paul Bril and sometimes worked in his studio. He copied drawings by various artists, including some by Matthijs, which Paul had acquired after his brother's death. [27]

From 1593 on, Paul Bril's name occurs frequently in the accounts of the painting academy. As a member, he donated money for the Feast of St Luke on several occasions. In 1593 the academy elected the painter Federico Zuccari (c. 1540-1609) as its first *Signor Principe*. Its patron was the influential cardinal and art collector Federico Borromeo (1564-1631), who bought a considerable number of cabinet paintings from Bril. [28]

The academy's archives contain several documents concerning Paul, including an assessment he had made for the painter Giovan Battista Ricci in 1604 in the palace of *Signore* Giuliano Cesarini, and a receipt for transferring the fee he received to the treasurer of the guild. [29] In June 1605 he was charged one *scudo* for declining to accept the office of *primo rettore*. [30] In 1607 the academy elected him as *camerlengo* (treasurer) in which capacity, according to the *Libro degli introiti*, he collected many *baiocchi* from his later biographer Giovanni Baglione and other painters. [31] In 1620 Bril was given the honour of representing the Accademia as *principe* (chairman). The appointment was unusual in that he was the first Northerner and the first landscape painter elected to that position. [32] A new chairman was elected every year. In 1623 Bril occupied the office of *secondo consigliere* and in the following year that of *primo censore*. [33] The last document he signed as "io Paolo Brilli primo censore mano propria", approving a number of receipts, is dated 24 February 1624. [34]

These records show that Bril continued to serve the academy until he reached an advanced age. The same is true of the various fraternities he belonged to, such as that of Santa Maria in Camposanto dei Tedeschi, where he is known to have attended a meeting on 12 July 1626. [35] A few months later, in September of that year, he took ill and drew up a will, which is now in the Archivio di Stato in Rome. [36] As mentioned before, Bril left his entire estate to his wife and three surviving children, Faustina, Luca and Ciriaco. His drawings, prints and paintings went to his son Ciriaco only after his mother's death in 1629. Under the terms of the will, Ottavia Bril Sbarra was allowed to sell her husband's paintings if necessary to provide for the family. Ciriaco, who had also trained as a painter, received all his father's unfinished

paintings. He may have completed some of them, but as far as is known no autograph works have survived. Paul Bril bequeathed part of his parents' home, which
he had apparently inherited from his father Matthijs Bril the Elder, to a nephew of
his in Breda, the son of his brother Peter. On 7 October 1626 Paul was buried beside
his brother Matthijs in the Santa Maria dell'Anima, the church founded by the
Flemish community. According to a document in the archive of the Camposanto dei
Tedeschi, on 6 October of that year members of the fraternity received payment for
carrying Bril's coffin, which was draped with the pall of the congregation.[37] His wife
had an epitaph inscribed on the pilaster between the second and third chapels in the
left nave, but unfortunately it has not survived. The text however is still known:
"ambo hi fratres / Etate impares / Pari pingendi laude / Topographiaeque artis /
Peritia admirabili / Et quae raro concordia / Clauere / Ottavia Barra Rom".[38]

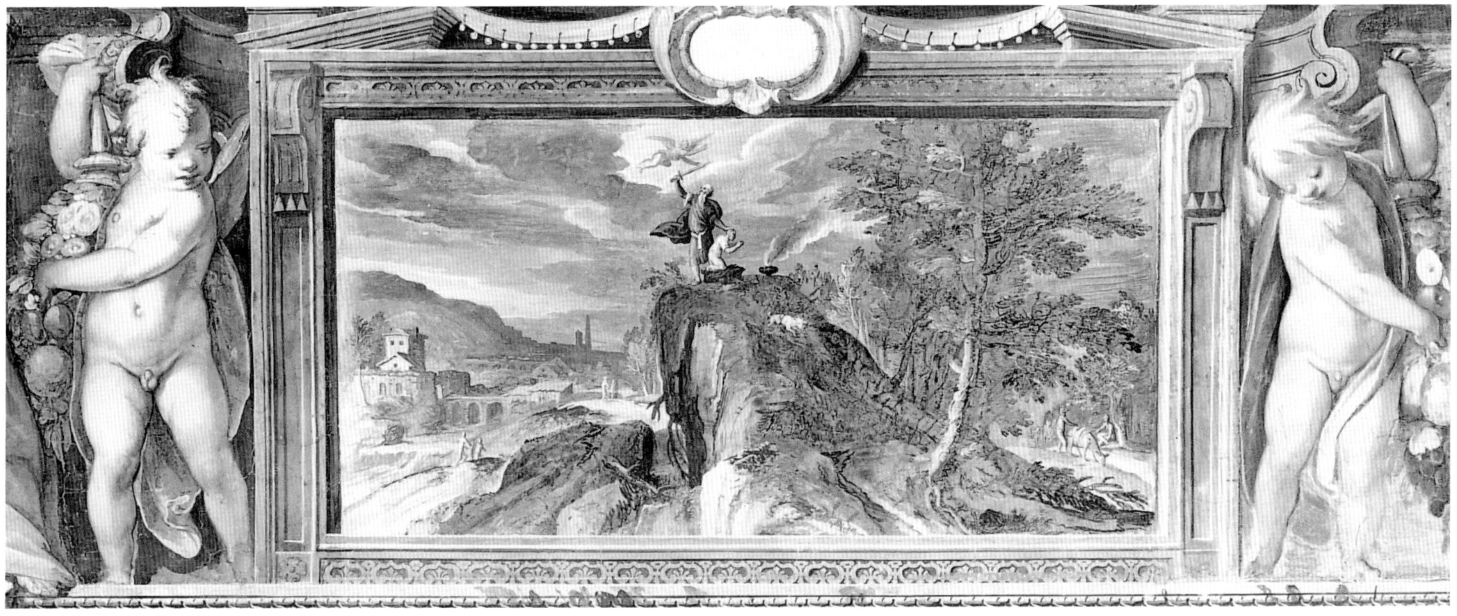

4. Matthijs Bril, *Landscape with the Sacrifice of Isaac*, fresco. Rome, Palazzo
Apostolico Vaticano, Torre dei Venti. Room of the Old Testament Patriarchs.

On 15 October 1629, following Ottavia's death on 30 September of that year, an
inventory was drawn up of the Bril family's property.[39] Paul's son Ciriaco, who
inherited his father's workshop equipment, is mentioned in several documents, more
of them court orders concerning brawls than records of his activities as a painter.
Ciriaco died in 1654.[40]
Paul Bril's estate, as documented in 1629, included two portraits of Paul himself
and one of his brother Matthijs.[41] The Accademia di San Luca has a portrait of
Matthijs Bril (fig. 1) by an unknown seventeenth-century Roman painter.[42] An edge
of the canvas was detached from the wooden frame at the back to reveal the inscription: "Paolo Brilli Principe donò // alla [...] Accademica // l'anno 1622".[43] Paul Bril
has been proposed as the author of that work, but the attribution seems unlikely. No
portraits by him are known, although in 1694 the collection of the Marquis Alessan-

dro Rondanini was said to include a portrait of Bril, allegedly "from his own hand". A portrait in a drawing attributed to Pier Leone Ghezzi may have been executed after that work (fig. 3), [44] but the portrait itself has not been traced. Paul's portrait is also missing from the collection of the Accademia di San Luca, where it was customary for the *principe* to present the academy with a self-portrait on completing his term of office. Paul gave them a portrait of his brother instead, presumably to honour Matthijs' name for the sake of his children, [45] and to keep his memory alive. Matthijs and Paul Bril studied painting in the Netherlands. But what they probably

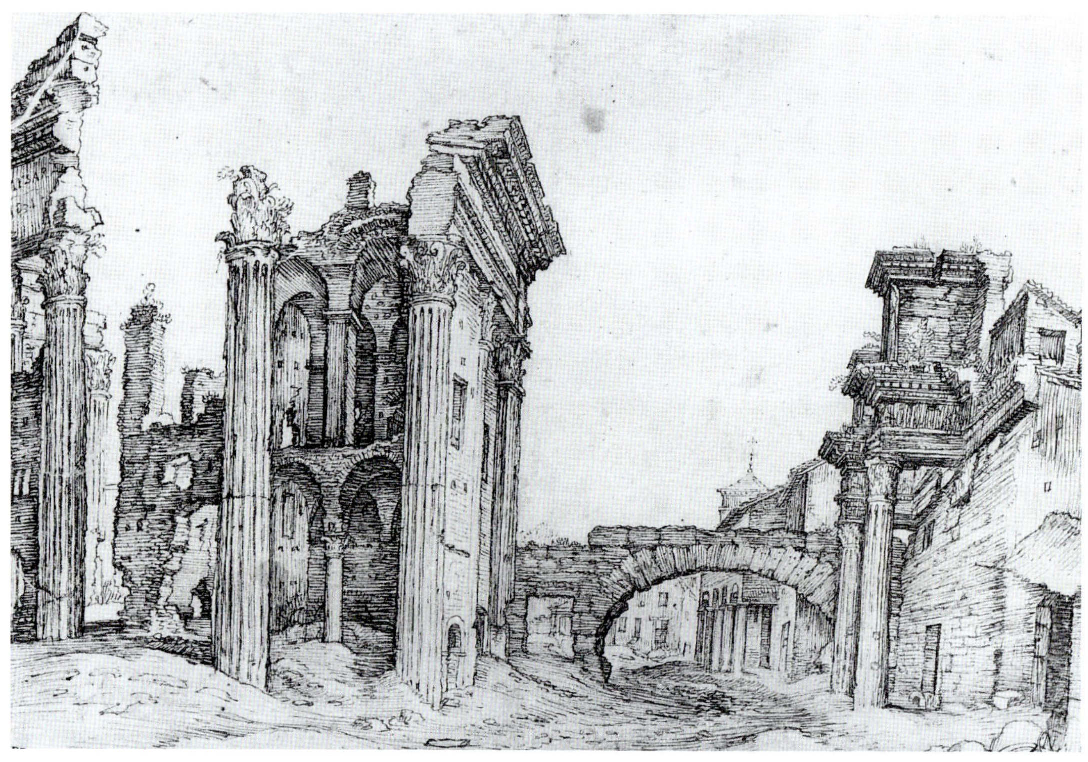

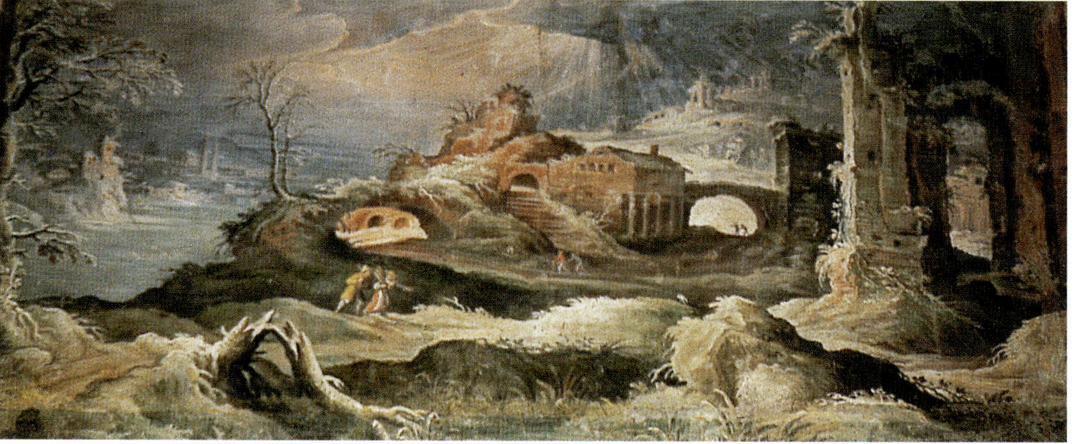

5. Matthijs Bril, *Temple of Minerva in the Forum of Nerva*, pen and brown ink, 220 x 422 mm. Paris, Musée du Louvre, Département des Arts Graphiques, Lugt 359, inv. no. 20.958.

6. Matthijs Bril, *Winter Landscape with Ruins*, fresco. Monterotondo, Palazzo Comunale (formerly Orsini), first floor, first room.

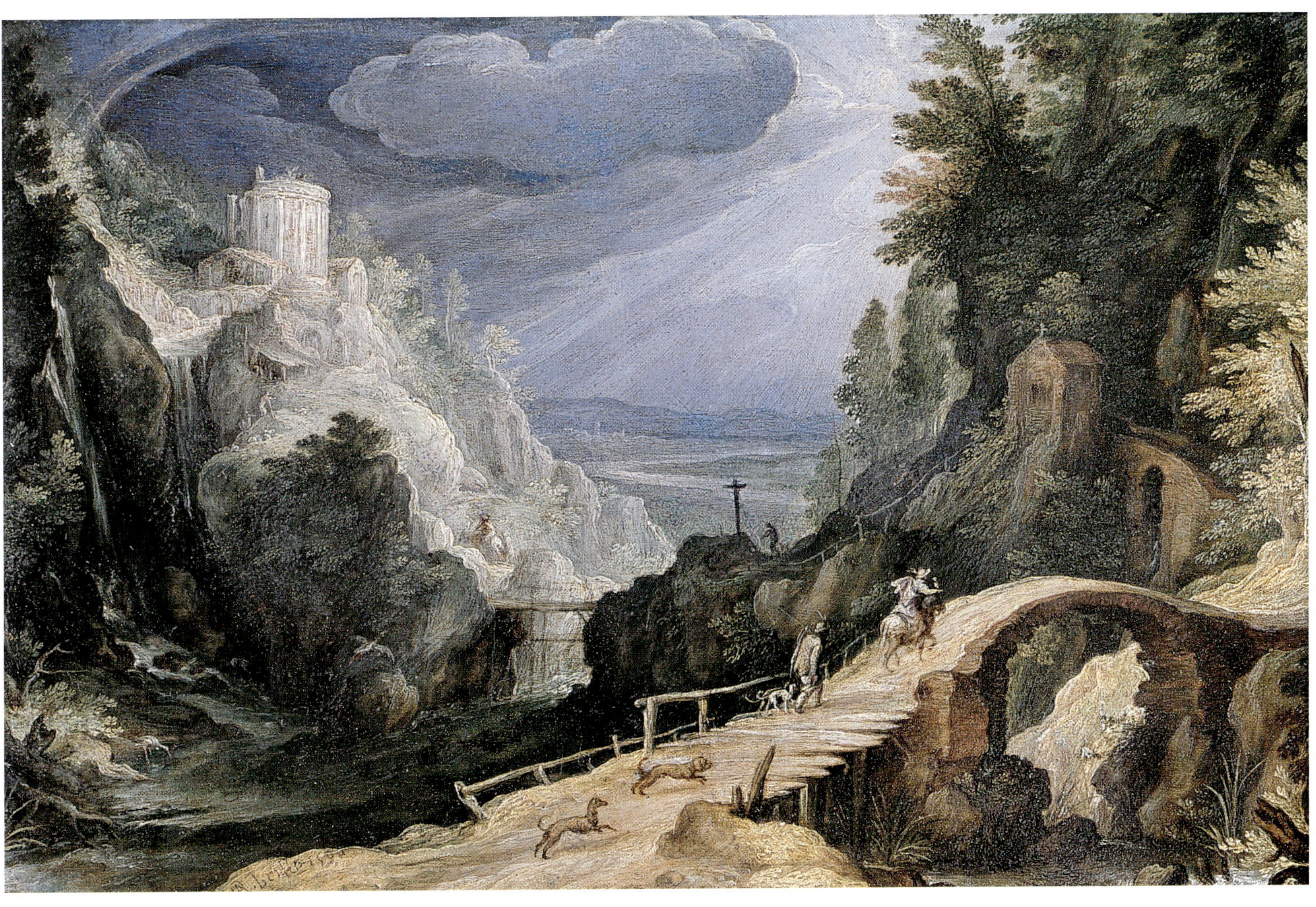

7. Paul Bril, *Landscape with the Temple of Sibyl*, oil on copper,
11.8 x 17.5 cm, signed and dated "PA Brillo 159 [...]".
Cologne, Wallraf-Richartz-Museum, inv. no. 3178.

did not learn there was the art of fresco. Paintings applied to a wet ground would
not last in the dampness of northern Europe, so the technique never gained a
foothold in the Low Countries. Matthijs and Paul, however, embarked on their
careers in Rome as members of a team engaged to paint frescoes for the pope.
Dutch and Flemish artists enjoyed a good reputation in Italy as highly qualified
landscape painters. Even so, Matthijs must have started off as an apprentice in
Rome with Italian or expatriate Netherlandish painters. He probably worked in a
studio or team before receiving his first independent commission to decorate the
walls of the Vatican with landscapes. It is also reasonable to assume that Matthijs,
who was already in Rome by the time his brother arrived, would initially have
engaged Paul as an assistant, thereby giving him an opportunity to learn the technique of fresco painting and the rules for painting landscapes in perspective high on
a wall – some of them four metres above floor level.
The contracts and accounts of patrons, such as popes, cardinals and noblemen,
rarely name all the artists involved in a project. The fee was usually paid to the

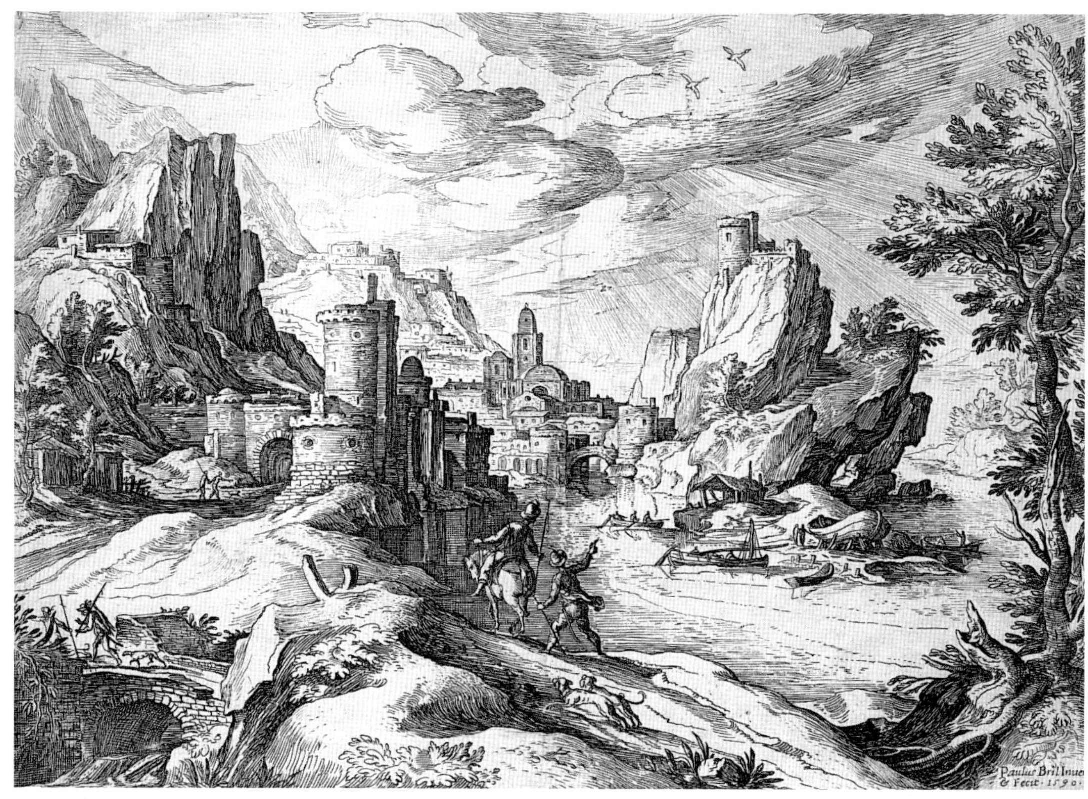

8. Paul Bril, *View of the Coast of Campania, River Landscape with Travellers*,
print, signed and dated "Paulus Bril Invent.& Fecit 1590", 208 x 280 mm.
Amsterdam, Rijksmuseum, Rijksprentenkabinet, inv. no. A 662, Holl. 1:III.

painter who supervised the work and it was his name that appeared in the accounts.
He would then remunerate the other artists and craftsmen. Occasionally both
Matthijs and Paul Bril are named in such documents, in some cases with the suffix
"fiamengo" or *"fiammingo"* instead of their surname. These references confirm their
involvement in a number of commissions.
Matthijs' name first appears in an archive document in connection with a commission to paint frescoes in the Torre dei Venti for Pope Gregory XIII (1580-83; fig. 4).
He is referred to as "Matteo fiamengo Ecc.mo nel far paesi".[46] According to
Baglione's *Vite*, Matthijs worked at the Vatican under the supervision of the Bolognese painter Lorenzo Sabbatini, whom the Bolognese Pope Gregory XIII had
appointed to oversee the decoration of the palace. Sabbatini died in 1576,[47] which
means that Matthijs Bril must have been working for the pope by that time. Possibly through the right connections, his career in Rome got off to an excellent start
and he soon received several commissions. He painted six series in the Vatican for
Gregory XIII, and one in Monterotondo for the Orsini family.
Though drawings and frescoes by Matthijs Bril have survived, none of his paintings
are known. A few however are described in household inventories.[48] His topographical drawings attest to a keen eye for historical buildings and their surroundings.
There are nine extant drawings from nature of Roman ruins (fig. 5).[49] Ruins are also
the subject of many of his frescoes, such as those in the Torre dei Venti and in Palaz-

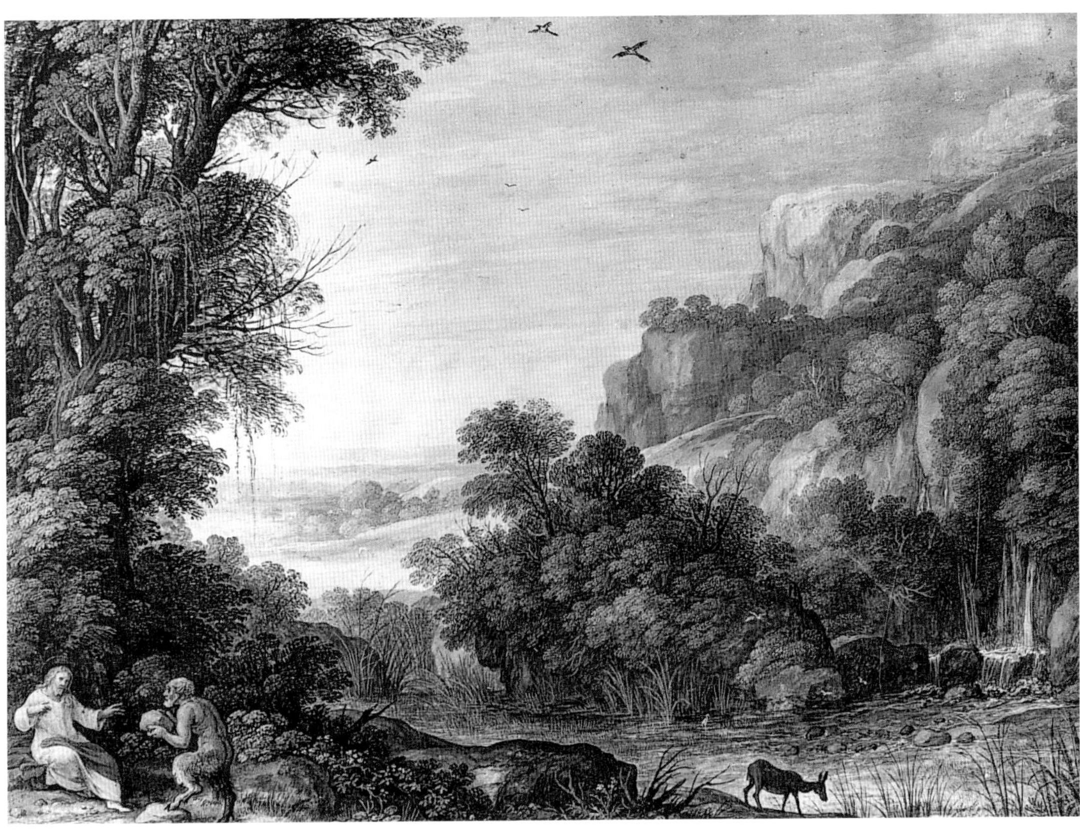

9. Paul Bril, *Landscape with the Temptation of Christ*, 1613,
tempera on vellum, 228 x 273 x 31 mm. Enschede, Rijksmuseum
Twenthe, inv. no. 0050.

zo Orsini in Monterotondo (1581; fig. 6). In addition, he drew seascapes and forest
scenes full of craggy rocks, and mostly with a tree on one side of the drawing, and
a path or river running diagonally into the distance. He used the tree motif to close
off the composition and lead the observer's eye into the picture. His winding paths
or rivers have a similar effect, directing our gaze over the landscape in the manner
prescribed for artists of his day.[50]

Though there is no documentary evidence that Matthijs and Paul worked together,
Paul probably assisted his brother when he first arrived in Rome. Their styles were
so similar that even now, some four hundred years later, it is difficult to distinguish
between them.[51] In the early large projects the older, more experienced Matthijs
must have done the lion's share of the work, but certain passages and details can be
ascribed to Paul.

After his death, Matthijs' drawings went to Paul, who drew inspiration from them
all his life.[52] As a result, his early work corresponds closely to Matthijs', if only
because they were both specialised in landscapes. Paul occasionally based frescoes
on his brother's drawings, as explained elsewhere in this book.[53]

Karel van Mander's biography of Paul of 1604 may give the impression that he was
not entirely convinced of Paul's skill during his early years in northern Europe.[54] He

says that Paul was slow to make progress, but the point was that he himself had little regard for the type of work Paul was doing: at that stage he was decorating musical instruments. As far as Van Mander was concerned, his work, notably his landscapes, improved substantially only after he had moved to Rome.

Paul's career lasted far longer than his brother's. He lived to a respectable age and continued to paint all his life. From the above-mentioned receipt of 1584 for landscapes in the Collegio della Compagnia di Gesù, we know that he continued to paint frescoes for Gregory XIII after Matthijs' death. Under his successor Sixtus V (1585-1590) he was involved in numerous decoration programmes for the pope, including those in Santa Maria Maggiore, the Lateran Palace, the Vatican Palace and Scala Santa. He also executed landscapes in the Vatican Palace for Pope Clement VIII (1590-1605) and Pope Paul V (1605-1621). The cardinals Paolo Emilio Sfondrati (1561-1618), Girolamo Mattei (1547-1603), Scipione Borghese (1576-1633), Ludovico Ludovisi (1595-1632) and others, among them the most important patrons and collectors of their day, commissioned cabinet paintings and engaged him to decorate their titular churches – Santa Cecilia, for one – and their palaces in Rome. Though his landscapes in their palaces have no religious connotations, those he painted for Cardinal Sfondrati in the Church of Santa Cecilia, inhabited by saints and hermits, were of a different order.

Not until the early 1590s did Paul Bril turn his hand to painting on canvas, copper and panel. These small landscapes were extremely popular both in Italy and abroad and found their way into museums and private collections all over the world (fig. 7). In his later years he painted fewer frescoes and produced more for the art market. In 1621, however, at the age of 68, he painted one last landscape on the wall of Casino Ludovisi. He also produced prints after his own work, such as a lunette in the Lateran Palace (fig. 8). [55]

Paul Bril was a celebrated landscape painter in Rome and beyond. He received numerous commissions and must have had a fairly large workshop with assistants and pupils to help him. His pupils enabled him to work on several assignments simultaneously, but as a result some of the frescoes, such as those in the Lateran Palace, are of rather indifferent quality. Besides Willem II van Nieulandt, who is mentioned above, Balthasar Lauwers and possibly Bril's son Ciriaco were members of his workshop. [56]

The many commissions Bril received throughout his long career from popes, other church dignitaries and the Roman elite attest to his popularity and prestige. The esteem accorded to him is confirmed by the public offices he held. Besides his work for the Accademia di San Luca, he was a member of several congregations such as that of the Compagnia di San Bernardo (from 1597 to 1603) and San Giovanni dei Virtuosi al Pantheon (1620), [57] which were both religious and humanitarian. From January 1624 to January 1625 he held the highest office, as guardian, in the brotherhood of Santa Maria in Camposanto dei Tedeschi (Teutonico). [58]

Not only Van Mander but other contemporaries – art historians, painters and art lovers – heaped praise on Paul Bril and his work. The page devoted to Matthijs and Paul Bril in a biography of artists by the Italian painter Giovanni Baglione (1571-1644) is an important source of information about their work in Rome. [59] Baglione and Paul Bril were among the painters who worked for Pope Sixtus V. Some time earlier, the art lover and physician to the pope, Giulio Mancini, had described Paul in his dissertation on painting (1621) as the leading landscape painter of his time.[60] And his praises were sung far beyond Rome. A German aristocrat and art dealer Philip Hainhofer spoke admiringly of Bril as the best landscape painter. In a letter written in 1610, when Bril was at the height of his career, he said: "After Brueghel [Jan Brueghel the Elder], Bril was more famed for his landscapes than any other painter alive at the time".[61] In another letter, Hainhofer, who collected art for his client Duke Philip II von Pommern-Stettin, mentions that a "small painting on copper" (*Küpferlein*) had cost him two hundred *scudi*.[62] In 1612 he wrote a letter saying he intended to ask Bril for a small landscape on vellum for the duke.[63] Like Hans Bol before him, Bril had mastered the technique of painting in watercolour on vellum. His *Landscape with the Temptation of Christ* (1613), now in the collection of the Rijksmuseum Twenthe in Enschede, is a fine example of this kind of work (fig. 9). The few surviving details concerning Bril's fees show that cabinet paintings were more lucrative than frescoes. In 1584 his two landscapes in fresco in the Collegio della Compagnia di Gesù brought in a meagre "4.85 scudi".[64] In 1599 he received 255 scudi for all the frescoes in the principal room of Palazzo Caetani (formerly Mattei) – nine large and ten small landscapes – but that amount included fees for the artists who had painted the allegorical figures, grotesques and putti in a frieze.[65] The accounts for the two fresco projects for Scipione Borghese are still in the archive. Bril received 60 scudi for painting the four seasons in Casino dell'Aurora[66] and the handsome sum of 700 *scudi* for the work in Casino del Patriarca Biondo (Loggia della Pergola).[67]

The English painter and art theorist Edward Norgate visited Bril in 1622 and spoke of him in the highest terms: "In a word, the most generall and absolute rule and vniversally to be observed in landscape was taught mee by the most excellent Master in this kind now dwelling in Rome, Paulo Brill".[68]

1) Van Mander 1604, ed. Miedema 1994, vol. I, pp. 424-427. There was unrest in both cities, which were under Spanish rule at the time. Parish archives were either not kept or not preserved.

2) Rome, Archive of Santa Maria dell'Anima, *Totenbücher*: "1583 8 Junij, Mattheus Bril Antwerpiens", "1626 Sepultus est ante altare Sanctae Barbarae Paulus Brilli, pictor, ex parochia Sancti Laurentii in Lucina, die 7 octobris 1626".

3) Van Mander 1604, fol. 291v.

4) Cerutti 1960 p. 17. For instance, Bril Sr. (Matthijs Bril the Elder) is said to have rented part of Onze Lieve Vrouwe Convent in Antwerp in 1546, and bought two houses in Breda in 1550 and in 1564.

5) *Ibid.*, p. 18. Guardians were appointed for the Bril children, who received an inheritance from their mother's side.

6) *Ibid.*, p. 41 note 98, refers here to a note by Adriaan Havermans, who was registrar in the city of Breda in 1637 and interested in Brabant's history.

7) Rombouts, Van Lerius, s.a., p. 242.

8) Karel van Mander (1604, fol. 291v) dismisses this Wortelmans (also referred to as Ortelmans) as a painter of little importance. No work by him is known. In 1534 he was registered with the Antwerp painters' guild as a pupil and in 1545 as a master. Wortelmans evidently died in 1588 or 1589; his date of birth is unknown. See Van Mander 1604, ed. Miedema 1999, vol. VI, p. 11.

9) Wortelmans was related to the famous Ruckers family of harpsichord builders in Antwerp. As an apprentice, Paul Bril probably decorated

instruments with simple flower or animal motifs, but once established as a landscape painter he may occasionally have received more challenging commissions. His name is listed in several household inventories along with artists who decorated harpsichords. See D.L. Sparti, *Le collezioni dal Pozzo. Storia di una famiglia e del suo museo nella Roma seicentesca*, Modena 1992, p. 189, no. 360.

10) Van Mander 1604, fol. 291v.

11) Ternois 1976, pp. 3-23, 25-42. Most of them remained in the city for periods ranging between twelve months and three years before continuing their journey to Italy. A few settled there permanently. Lyon's municipal archives show that the Northerners formed their own little "colonies".

12) Van Mander 1604, ed. Miedema 1994, vol. I, pp. 424, 36: "waer hij eenen tijt langh woonde" ("where he lived for some time"). Ternois (p. 46) reports that Paul Bril was living in Lyon around 1573, but this information is based only on Van Mander, who says he left for France at the age of twenty. See also Audin, Vidal 1918-1919, vol. 1, p. 131. Much of Lyon's archive material has not yet been studied.

13) See Meijer in *Brussels, Rome* 1995, pp. 324-325. Jan Soens and Denijs Calvaert were both working in the Vatican around 1574.

14) Rome, Archive of Accademia di San Luca, *Libro degli introiti dall'anno 1534 fino all'anno 1653*, V2, fol. 87v. See also Hoogewerff 1913, p. 26. Matthijs Bril's name appears on five occasions, once in 1580, three times in 1581, and once in 1582.

15) Hoogewerff 1942, p. 169. The witnesses were Joanni Donato Simonetta of Treviso and Petro Hardicole. Paul's absence does not necessarily mean he had not yet arrived in Rome.

16) Archive Rome, Santa Maria dell'Anima, *Totenbücher*.

17) Van Mander 1604, fol. 291v.

18) Rome, Archive of Accademia di San Luca, V2, fol. 87v. See also Noack 1927, p. 105, who quotes from fol. 103v of the *Libro*, which refers to a "Mattheo fiamingo" employed by "Signor Gio. Giorgio Cesarini". Hoogewerff (1913, p. 26) wonders which Matthijs is meant. He believes that this folio number dates from around 1600, by which time Matthijs Bril was no longer alive. Paul Bril was assisted by Giuliano, son of the aforesaid Cesarini.

19) Bertolotti 1880, pp. 57-58.

20) *Ibid.*, Paul Bril spent "7 giornate" painting the landscapes there, and earned a total of 48.50 *giulii* (= 4.85 *scudi*). For the value of the currency in that period, see Reinhardt 1984, p. XIV.

21) See Berger 1993. Luuk Pijl is writing a monograph entitled "Paul Bril. The Paintings". The prints have not yet been fully examined or inventoried. However, see Hollstein 1949-, pp. 221-222, notably under the engravers Willem van Nieulandt, Aegidius Sadeler, Jan and Raphael Sadeler.

22) The family subsequently moved to the Via della Croce, then returned to the Strada Paolina before finally settling in the Selciata della Trinità, on the hill between Piazza di Spagna and Santa Trinità dei Monti, now the site of the Spanish Steps.

23) See Bertolotti 1880, p. 379, and a reference to the document in Archivio di Stato di Roma (ASR), Not. Pizzuti, *Testamenti 1625-26*, fol. 706-708.

24) Hoogewerff 1943, p. 83. Parish data from 1609-1610.

25) *Ibid.*, p. 170.

26) The author is grateful to Judith Verberne (Rome) for this information. Corvus is the Latin word for raven.

27) Bedoni 1983, pp. 31-34.

28) The cardinal was an enthusiastic art lover and collector. In the 1590s he started buying paintings by Paul Bril, whom he had presumably met at the academy. On Borromeo, see Jones 1988b and 1993.

29) Rome, Archive of Accademia di San Luca, V42, 1593-1627, fol. 19v.

30) See Hoogewerff 1912, p. 244.

31) Rome, Archive of Accademia di San Luca, *Libro degli introiti...*, V42 1593-1627, fol. 19v-167r.

32) Hoogewerff 1912, p. 244.

33) *Ibid.*

34) Rome, Archive of Accademia di San Luca, *Libro degli introiti...*, V42 1593-1627, fol. 167r.

35) Hoogewerff 1913, vol. II, p. 372.

36) See Bertolotti 1880, p. 379.

37) Hoogewerff 1913, vol. II, p. 255.

38) For the full text of the epitaph, see Forcella 1873, vol. 3, p. 480. In translation it reads as follows: "Though different in age, these brothers were equally famous for their painting and their admirable skills in topographic art, and their affinity in outlook is attested to by Ottavia Sbarra", etc.

39) ASR 30 *Notai Capitolini, Ufficio 19, notaio Tranquillus Pizzutus*, 1627-1632, fol. 351r.

40) Bertolotti 1880, pp. 102-104, see also ASR, Notai Capitolini, Uff. 19, Not. Pizzuto, testamenta, 1627-1632, fol. 347r and v, 348r.

41) ASR 30 *Notai Capitolini, Ufficio 19, notaio Tranquillus Pizzutus*, 1627-1632, fol. 361v. There were eight portraits in all; besides the two of Paul and one of Matthijs, there were also two of his children.

42) Incisa della Rocchetta 1979, p. 32, n. 52, inv. no. 757.

43) *Ibid.*

44) Luuk Pijl kindly brought this drawing to my attention, see Pijl 1997, p. 174 and notes 17, 18.
45) This must have been a different portrait from the one referred to in the estate of 1629.
46) Biblioteca Apostolica Vaticana (BAV), Boncompagni D5, fol. 240v. See also Courtright 1990, p. 20.
47) Baglione 1649, ed. 1924 (reprint 1986), vol. 1, p. 18.
48) The inventory drawn up in 1598 by Paul Bril and others of the paintings of the late Cardinal Bonelli includes "Quatro quadri de paesi, di mano di Mattheo Fiamengo, a guazzo", and states more specifically, "In uno l'historia di Abraham, nell'altro Tobia, nell'altro la Tentatione nel Deserto di Nostro Signore et nell'altro un giardino, stimati: scudi 100". Orbaan 1920, pp. 489-494, notably p. 489.
49) See Louisa Wood Ruby's essay in this volume.
50) Van Mander 1604 (ed. Miedema 1973), pp. 130, 202-218, 535ff.
51) For different opinions on Matthijs and/or Paul Bril's contributions to the frescoes in the Torre dei Venti, see Courtright 1990, pp. 22-25 and note 100, and Limentani Virdis, Pietrogiovanna 1995, pp. 69-71, 73-77.
52) Neither these drawings nor any paintings by Matthijs are mentioned in Paul's will.
53) See Louisa Wood Ruby's essay in this volume.
54) Van Mander 1604, fol. 291v.
55) Hollstein 1949-, vol. III, p. 219, "Paulus Bril Invent. & Fecit".
56) Van Mander 1604, fol. 292r. Miedema 1999, vol. VI, p. 16. Hoogewerff 1943, p. 233 describes Karel Philips Spieringh (Carlo Filippo Spiringh, d. 1639) of Brussels as a pupil of Bril's in 1623-26. The archive of the parish of Santa Maria del Popolo (Hoogewerff 1943, p. 83), contains a reference to Giovanni Fiamengo as living with the Bril family. It is impossible to establish whether this was Bril's brother Hans (Jan), who was also a painter. There is no evidence of his having been in Rome. Nor is anything known about the work of Ciriaco Bril. It is possible that he completed his late father's unfinished works. See also in this volume Hendriks, *The Frescoes*.
57) Bertolotti 1880, pp. 58 and 183.
58) Corvinius, who was mentioned earlier, is named in conjunction with Paul Bril in the archives of the Confraternita del Campo Santo: at a meeting held on 5 January 1614, Corvinius and Bril were nominated to represent the Flemish community. See Hoogewerff, 1913, vol. 2, p. 363, fol. 73v.
59) Baglione 1649, ed. 1924 (reprint 1986), vol. 1, p. 297. He unfortunately neglected to name all the painters involved in a given project, the Lateran Palace being a case in point.
60) Mancini 1621 (1956-57), vol. 2, p. 260.
61) See Doering 1896, on Hainhofer, p. 41: "der Brill hat in Landschaften de ruem uber alle Mahler, die disser Zeit leben, nach ihme der Brügel".
62) *Ibid.*, p. 40. So far, the archives have yielded few receipts for payments made to Bril himself.
63) These may have been less expensive.
64) See also note 20.
65) See Cappelletti, Testa 1994, p. 16 and 20, note 31.
66) Archivio Segreto Vaticano (ASV), Archivio Borghese, 308, *Fabbricati a Roma*, Titoli diversi III, fol. 393r. The workmen who erected the scaffolding, for instance, received 13.65 *scudi*. See also in this volume Hendriks, *The Frescoes*, note 110.
67) *Ibid.*, fol. 393v. This amount included the putti by Reni. In the Casino a total of 85 days were spent on the pergola and 20 on the landscapes. See Martelotti in Negro 1996, p. 135.
68) Ogden, Ogden 1955, p. 10. From Bril Norgate learnt the following rule to suggest depth in a painted landscape: "His observation was only this, that a good workeman must be suer ever to place light against darke and darke against light. His meaning was that the only way to remove the ground, and to extend the prospecte farr off was by apposing light to shadows, yett soe as euer they must loose theyre force and vigoure proportionally as they remoue from the eye, and the strongest shadows euer nearest hand, and (as they caule it) on the first ground".

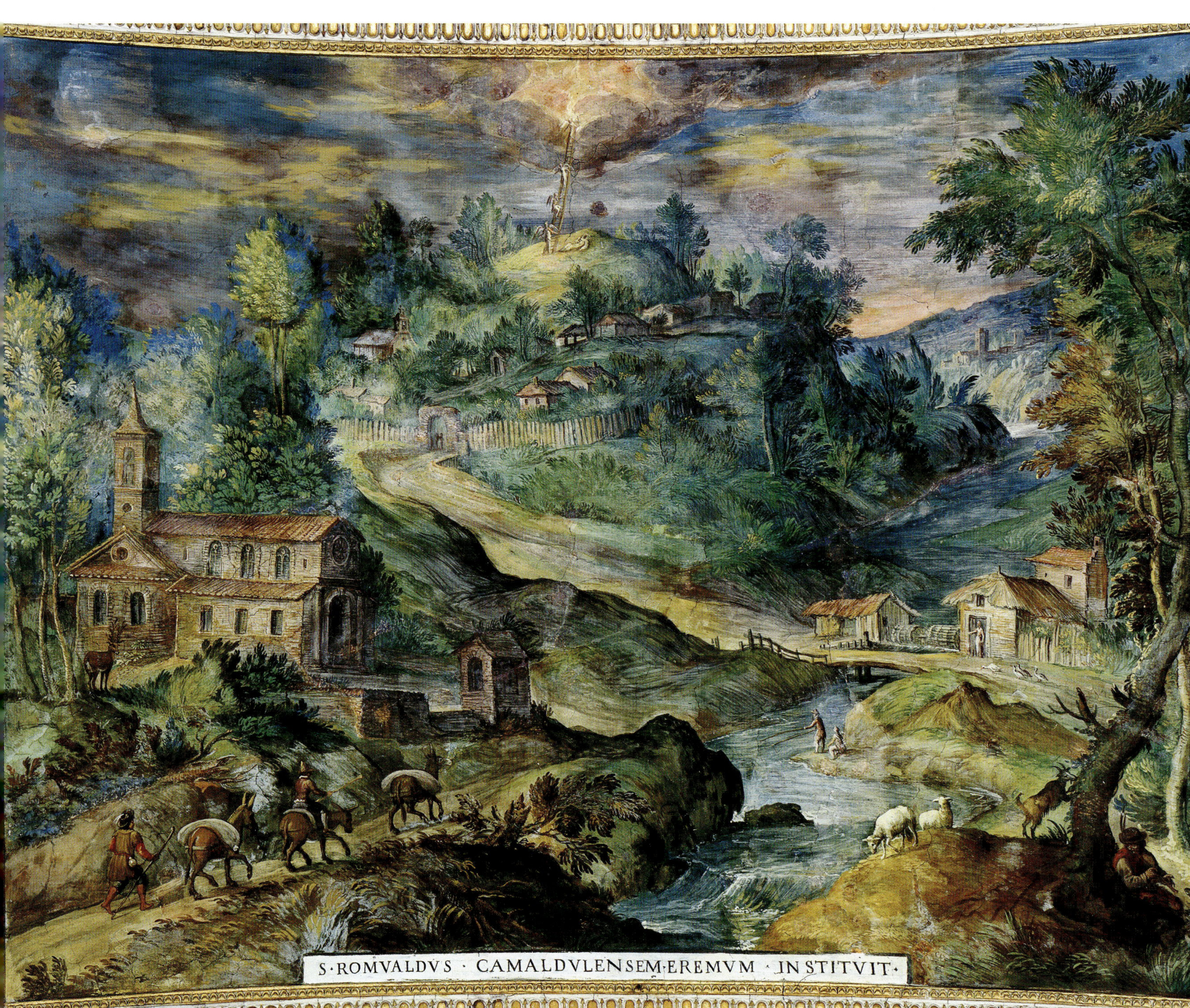
S·ROMVALDVS · CAMALDVLENSEM·EREMVM · INSTITVIT·

THE FRESCOES

Matthijs and Paul Bril made an inestimable contribution to the development of the painted landscape in Rome and its environs. This is true of Paul Bril in particular, who started off working with his elder brother and, after his death in 1583, continued as an independent master for over forty years. The brothers' numerous paintings of both religious and profane subjects in Rome, the Vatican and the surrounding Latium bear witness to the leading position they occupied and the prestige they enjoyed.

Their landscapes on walls, ceilings and vaults appear in a variety of shapes, decorations and frameworks. Some cover an entire wall, but most are painted in friezes, several of which extend over all the walls of a room. Others are painted in small panels, forming part of a larger decoration. They are horizontal, vertical, round or oval, or in the shape of lunettes, cartouches and *tabulae* (classical inscription plaques), and the borders around them therefore vary equally in shape. There are simulated paintings in trompe-l'œil frames (*quadro riportato*); vistas through windows with painted stone sills, complete with shadows on the window frame cast by light entering through the window; panels or views of imitation painted tapestries (*arazzi finti*), and vedute between the columns of illusionistic loggias and fantastic painted architectural frames (*quadratura*). The surrounds were painted first and the landscapes filled in subsequently.

Both Matthijs and Paul used fairly strong contrasting colours to bring their pictures to life. Their skies, often blue with pink-tinged orange sunsets, are one of the hallmarks of their work. However, the frescoes that were originally outdoors have faded as a result of exposure to light and moisture, and today little remains of the sparkling colours, the once bright yellows and greens and brilliant blues.

Matthijs' landscapes can be distinguished by their compositions built up in diagonal planes, with high horizons, gnarled trees and rocks, a wealth of detail and sharply contrasting colours. Most are painted in friezes as panels or windows, and in one case they cover the walls from floor to ceiling.

A nocturnal landscape with a view of a town in a frieze in the Sala Ducale is believed to be one of Matthijs' earliest works (1575) for Pope Gregory XIII (no. VI a, fig. 10). It differs from the other three landscapes in the cycle, where a dragon, the emblem of Gregory XIII, descends among ruins in the Roman countryside. In the left foreground an elephant, symbolising perseverance, stands in a moonlit river. In view of the prominence of the architecture here, the fresco is attributed to Matthijs.[1] The landscape resembles an engraving of a similar composition with a square tower on a river bank, by Hendrik Hondius (1611-13) after a drawing by Matthijs Bril.[2]

A few years later Matthijs painted four fresco landscapes in a frieze in the First Sala dei Foconi in the Vatican Palace (no. VI c). [3] They are fairly animated scenes in rectangular fields, with water playing a prominent role. The rocks with trees perched precariously on top are common motifs in Matthijs' work. He used gradations of light and dark in the different planes and a range of greens for the trees. Human activity is prevalent in all but the third fresco (fig. 11). The landscapes are dotted with figures riding, sailing, fishing and walking. Architecture too is an important element in these scenes, which include classical ruins, farms, houses, bridges and churches with the spires typical of northern Europe. Rustic wooden fences and animal staffage are also a standard part of the repertoire, though his animal figures tend to be weak. [4]

Apart from landscapes, in two locations he painted frescoes of entirely different subjects. In the Vatican Palace he painted three pergolas with a variety of animals, harking back perhaps to his first lessons with his father, a painter of fruit and grotesques (no. VI b). [5] The pergola motif was not unprecedented in sixteenth-century painting. In 1519 Giovanni da Udine painted pergolas with creepers, birds and other animals in the Loggia of Leo X in the Palazzo Apostolico Vaticano. Other extant examples include Raphael's pergola in the Loggia di Psiche in Villa Farnesina (1517) and one attributed to Pietro Venale da Imola in the semicircular loggia in Villa Giulia (1552). [6]

The second group of works with other subjects, also commissioned by Pope Gregory XIII Boncompagni, is the series of frescoes in the Third Loggia of San Damaso Court in the Vatican Palace (no. VI d). [7] Here, Matthijs worked in collaboration with Antonio Tempesta (1555-1630), who painted the figures in ten scenes depicting a procession that was held on 11 June 1580. [8] These pictures of a contemporary event – Gregory XIII transferring the relics of his illustrious predecessor, St Gregory of Nazianzus, from Santa Maria in Campo Marzio to St Peter's Cathedral, against the background of the city as it looked at the time –, offer a unique, almost photographic view of Rome in the late sixteenth century. Matthijs portrayed the streets and buildings with meticulous precision and undoubtedly based them on sketches. The recently completed façade of the Santa Maria dell'Anima, which was still under construction at the time, shows just how up-to-date these pictures were. The Piazza Navona in the third scene, with Pasquino's small sculpture and the figures of Peter and Paul on the bridge over the Tiber, is still one of the city's most famous landmarks. And even today, we can follow nearly the entire route taken by the procession more than four hundred years ago.

One of the more striking scenes in the series is the view of Castel Sant'Angelo, partly because of the sharply diagonal and therefore less static angle from which it is observed, and partly because the wide prospect over the bridge and the Tiber afforded a view of St Peter's with its unfinished dome (fig. 12). [9] A *View of Castel Sant'-Angelo* showing the unfinished dome of St Peter's Cathedral is the only known drawing that could have served as a study for the fresco (fig. 40). [10]

Matthijs Bril and Antonio Tempesta included a wealth of detail in their frescoes,

10. Matthijs Bril, *Nocturnal Landscape with Elephant*.
Rome, Palazzo Apostolico Vaticano, Sala Ducale.

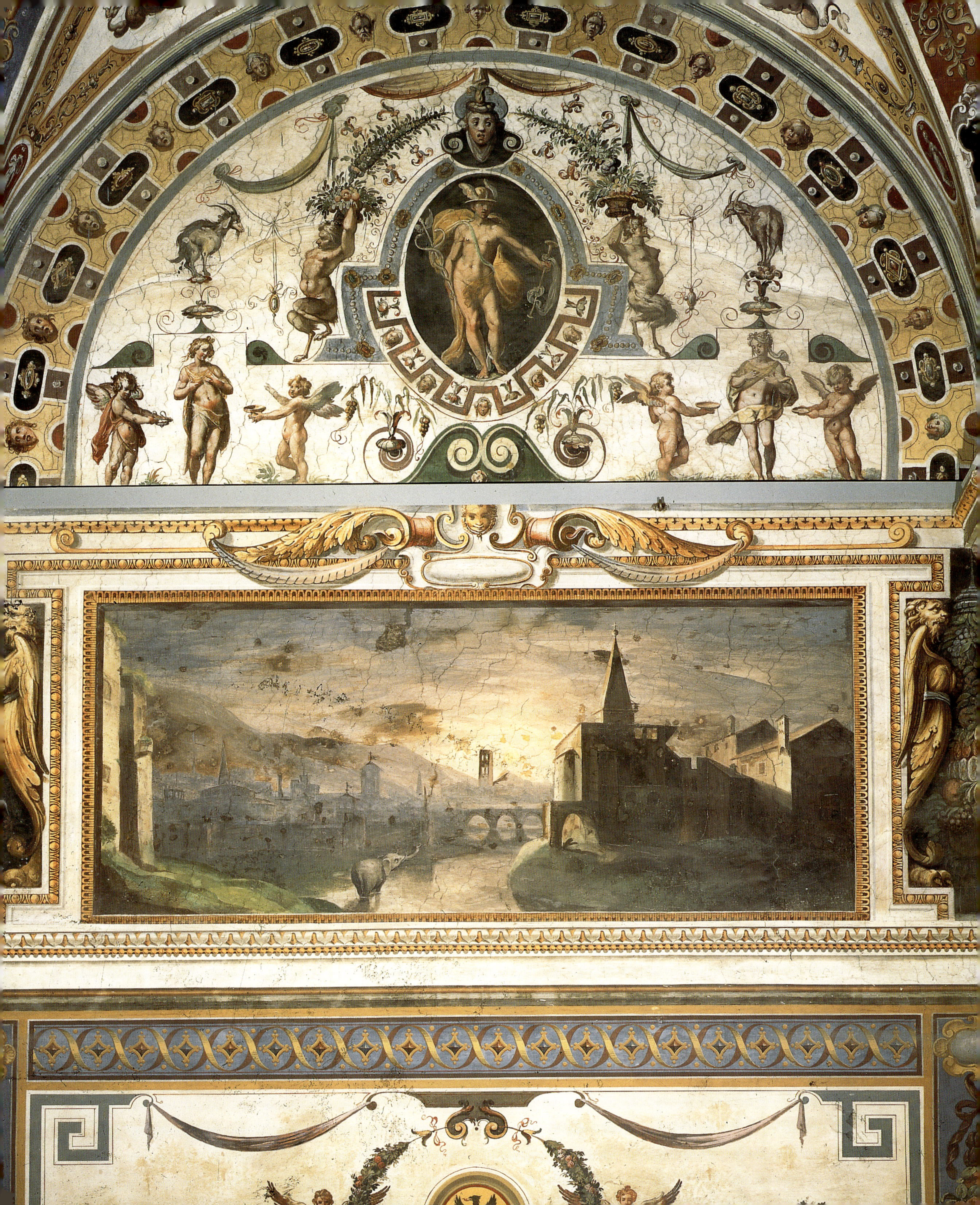

apparently indifferent to the fact that, high on the walls, they would have been barely perceptible to anyone below. One of the painters, for instance, probably Matthijs,
depicted hams and sausages hanging out to dry in the open loggias at the tops of the
buildings along the Tiber. In the Via della Scrofa Matthijs painted the *scrofa* (sow)
on the signboard of an inn by that name. And among the people in St Peter's Square,
Tempesta painted a vendor selling doughnuts. He also rendered the costumes of the
Swiss guards in detail.

But Matthijs' largest and most important project, and one that contains all the characteristic features of his work, was the cycle of landscapes and vedute that Gregory
XIII commissioned for the Torre dei Venti, in different formats and different sub-
stantive and formal contexts (nos. VI e-k). Bril spent the years from 1580 to 1583
painting religious scenes in landscapes as well as purely decorative views of Rome
and the Roman countryside, in seven rooms on the three storeys of the tower, behind
and adjoining the Vatican palaces. [11] The series comprises a total of sixty-eight paintings as well as the backgrounds of the frescoes in the Sala Meridiana.

In four of the seven rooms he portrayed biblical scenes in landscapes on friezes. They
are surrounded by painted architectural borders and separated from one another by
garlands, grotesques, allegorical figures, putti, roundels and cartouches, also depicting episodes from the Bible (nos. VI f, g, j, k). The illusionistic architectural frames
and cartouches were probably executed by a specialist. Interestingly, however,
Matthijs painted the figures as well as the landscapes, which was not the case in the
Loggia of San Damaso Court series. Many of the figures are slightly elongated, and
those in the background silhouettes, probably to compensate for distortion, as the figures are high overhead. In any event, they are less detailed than his buildings. The
eyes are dark dots and the hands fairly rudimentary, often with a finger extended.
But viewed from a distance, the poses and gestures are effective and lifelike (fig. 13).
By and large, the same applies to the animal figures in his biblical scenes – Matthijs
was indeed better at landscapes and architecture than animal or human figures.

Most of his trees look like oaks, with feather-shaped foliage. The dark green leaves
in the foreground brighten to a yellowish green further in the distance, heightening
the illusion of depth. Many of the scenes include a couple of tangled trees or a tree
trunk on an overgrown river bank in the foreground, adding contrast, depth and
liveliness to the composition. Craggy rocks are also a recurrent motif. Each of these
friezes represents a particular biblical cycle. According to Courtright (1990), Gregory XIII intended them to proclaim the Catholic Church the only true church. [12]

Of an entirely different order are Matthijs' topographical and imaginary vedute cov-
ering the walls of the mezzanine. They are the largest landscapes he painted. The
observer imagines himself to be in the open loggia of a belvedere, looking out past
caryatids and columns. The horizons are high and the landscapes dotted with ruins,
trees, bridges, boats and fortresses. In the distance are towns with soaring towers.
The scenes are filled with people hunting, fishing, strolling and ploughing, feeding
animals and putting them out to pasture. The landscapes recall classical examples
that Matthijs may have seen in Rome, in Domus Aurea, for instance. Be that as it
may, in content and appearance they correspond to descriptions of classical wall
paintings by Vitruvius and Pliny the Elder. [13]

The two views of Rome in this room again reveal Matthijs' skill as a topographer. Here, the pope could show his guests the Pantheon, the Torre delle Milizie, and St Peter's Cathedral under construction, which in reality were on the other side of the tower walls (fig. 14).

It is uncertain whether Paul assisted his elder brother Matthijs in this monumental project. I would venture that he had only a small hand in some of the larger landscapes. His contribution can be illustrated by comparing two motifs of a peasant ploughing with oxen. One, in a frieze depicting *Esau and Jacob and the Mess of Pottage* (Genesis 25:34), can be firmly attributed to Matthijs. The other is in the seascape with galleys on the mezzanine (fig. 16). In both scenes the figures and animals are in exactly the same positions and poses, but the two examples differ in quality. The peasant and oxen in the large landscape are far truer to life than those in the scene of Esau and Jacob, and were therefore probably painted by Paul.[14] It is

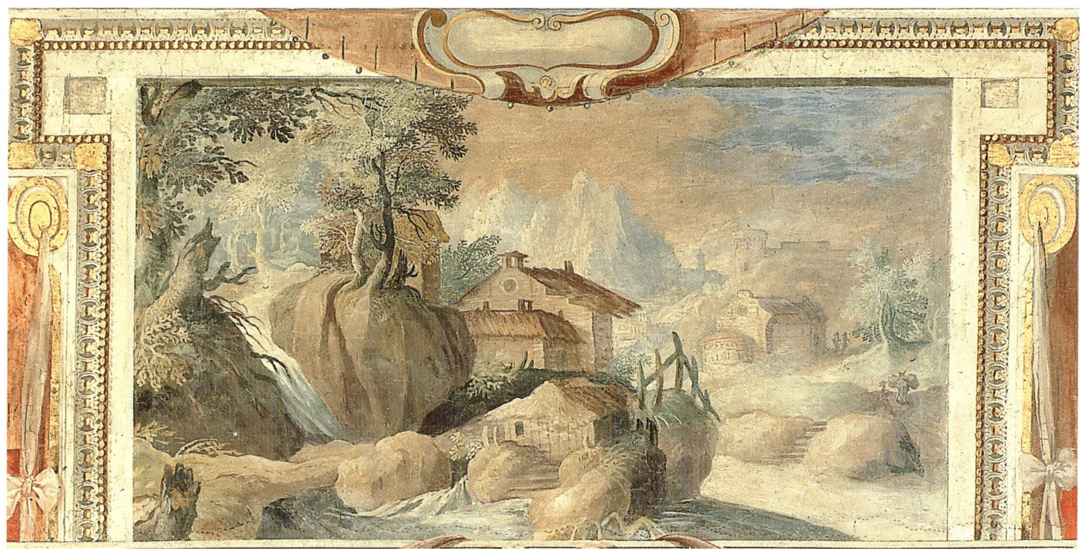

11. Matthijs Bril, *Rocky Landscape*. Rome, Palazzo Apostolico Vaticano, First Sala dei Foconi.

difficult to judge the extent of Paul's contribution to these paintings. He may however have helped his brother on the technical side as well, for instance by preparing the ground in fresco for Matthijs to apply his mixture of wet chalk and pigment, or by sketching the underdrawing on the wet ground.

The paintings here are not true frescoes. The extravagant building projects commissioned by popes, prelates and Roman families in the second half of the sixteenth century created a great deal of work for decorators. Pressed for time, they gradually abandoned *buon fresco*,[15] which was time-consuming and costly. In any event, it is doubtful whether many of them possessed the knowledge and skills it demanded.[16] They opted instead for the *mezzo fresco* technique, applying their colours to a relatively dry and therefore less permeable plaster. This allowed them to work more quickly and cheaply, and it required less technical skill.

By and large, they applied most of it in *fresco*, adding the details once the plaster

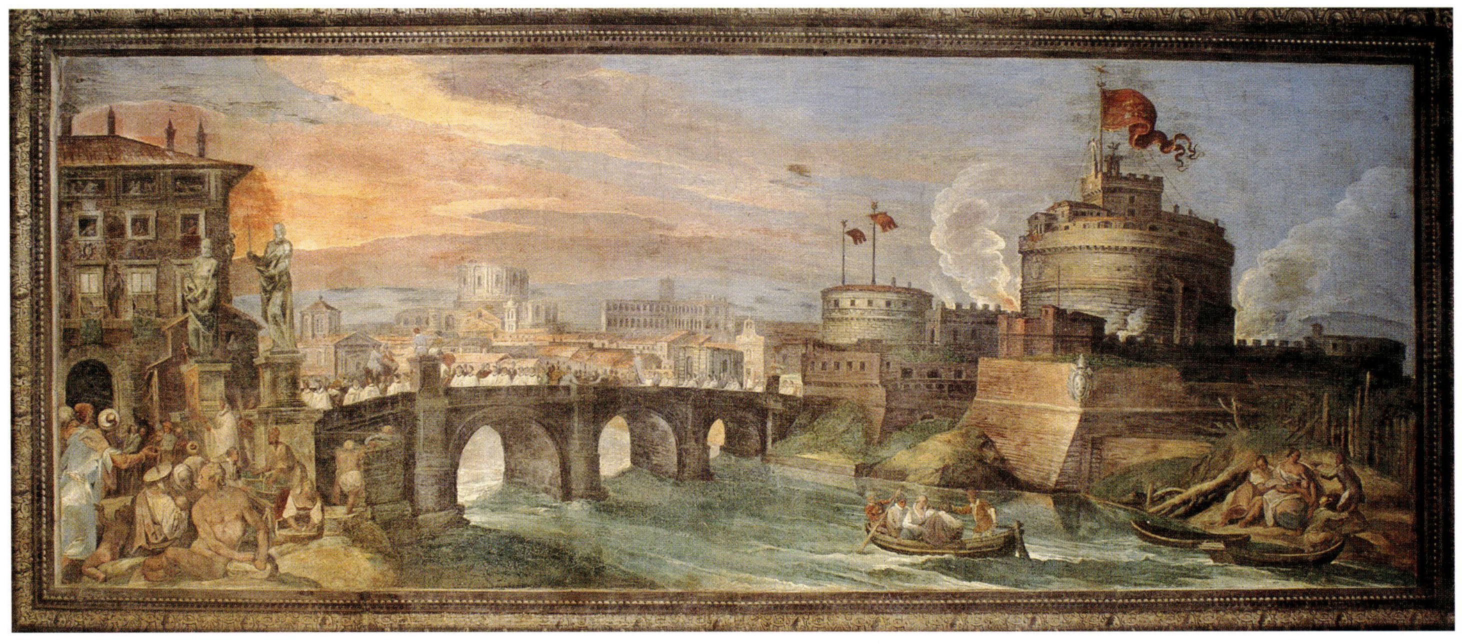

12. Matthijs Bril and Antonio Tempesta, *The Procession
on the Bridge by Castel Sant'Angelo*. Rome, Palazzo Apostolico
Vaticano, San Damaso Court, third Loggia.

had started to dry. They could also paint on a completely dry ground, generally using tempera (egg white) or oil to bind the pigments together instead of fusing them into the wet plaster. As several painters often worked together on the same wall, their work was retouched to achieve a more uniform style.

Recent restorations have shed light on the techniques that Matthijs and Paul Bril employed. [17] Viewed from close up, the pastose paint and brushstrokes in the large vedute in the Torre dei Venti stand out almost in relief from the wall or plaster. [18] Older restorations, however, which often involved overpainting in *secco* or even oils, make it difficult to reconstruct their procedure.

Matthijs worked on *Christ Calms the Storm* and *Paul Shipwrecked on Malta* in the Sala Meridiana of the Torre dei Venti in close collaboration with Niccolò Circignani, who executed the figures and the boats at sea. Matthijs, however, painted the landscape elements in the backgrounds of the painted tapestries (fig. 17). The sea, with wild, foaming waves, recalls the seascapes with galleys in the Torre dei Venti (fig. 16) and in the Room of Hunting Scenes in the palace in Monterotondo. [19] The design and colours, the high horizon, the trees clinging to rocks, the overcast sky and the herdsman with swine are unmistakably the work of Matthijs. The trees are rendered in a different manner from those in the other rooms. They are far sturdier than the feather-like trees in his smaller scenes. The looser, less compact foliage recalls the trees Paul Bril painted years later in Palazzo Caetani, Santa Cecilia and Sala Clementina. It is thus a forerunner by Matthijs of similar work by Paul.

Presumably while working for Pope Gregory XIII in the Vatican, the brothers were invited to decorate two rooms of a country palace in Monterotondo belonging to the wealthy Orsini family of Rome (nos. I a and I b). [20] In the first room, they painted eight landscapes in a frieze, as vistas in painted tapestries separated from one another by garlands and cartouches bearing the arms of Orsini and the later owner of the palace, Barberini. They are very similar in style to the landscapes in the Torre dei Venti. Matthijs' three columns in a landscape, for instance, can also be seen in the Room of the Apostles and the Room of Tobias. [21]

This frieze includes one of Matthijs' few winter landscapes. [22] Not all the landscapes were equally successful, as the compositions are sometimes weak (cf. nos. I a, 1 and 7). In some, the animal and human figures are more compact than in others, such as the winter landscape and the landscape with ruins and a horseman and servant. It is possible that Paul assisted his brother here. The unusual obelisk resembles a similar structure in a drawing by Paul Bril in Washington, although it is viewed from a slightly different angle. [23] The architecture, too, reveals Matthijs' fastidious eye for detail. The coffered ceiling in the landscape with Roman ruins and a fountain, and the Roman masonry exposed under the marble in the architecture are painted with great finesse (fig. 18).

A frieze of hunting scenes and a view of Monterotondo extends along the four walls in the second room. In form, this animated frieze is unique in Matthijs' *œuvre*. It is signed with a pince-nez and dated (1581). Matthijs brought continuity and coherence into the succession of images by extending the undulating landscape and the sea with outcrops of rocks almost to the top of the wall. Trees whose tops disappear behind the edge of the wooden ceiling separate the scenes from one another. The landscapes are enlivened by figures running, shooting and riding, by quarry fleeing and hounds giving chase. In the background of one, the scene with the falcon, is the hill that overlooks Monterotondo and the lands in the vicinity of the town (fig. 19). The representation of different types of hunt appears to have been inspired by drawings by Antonio Tempesta (fig. 20), with whom Matthijs had in all likelihood

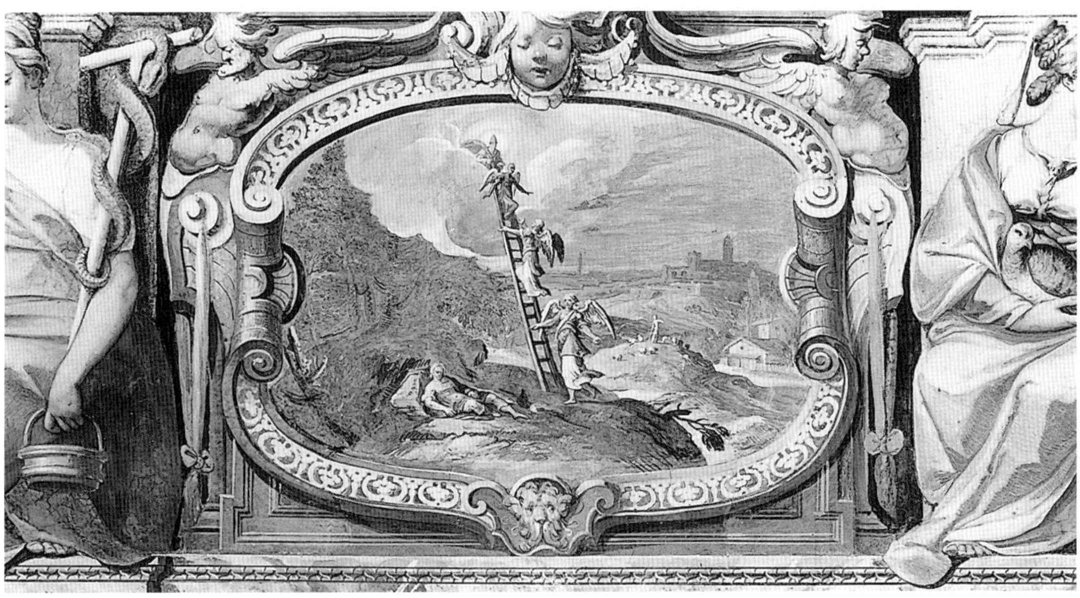

13. Matthijs Bril, *Jacob's Dream*. Rome, Palazzo Apostolico Vaticano, Torre dei Venti, Room of the Old Testament Patriarchs.

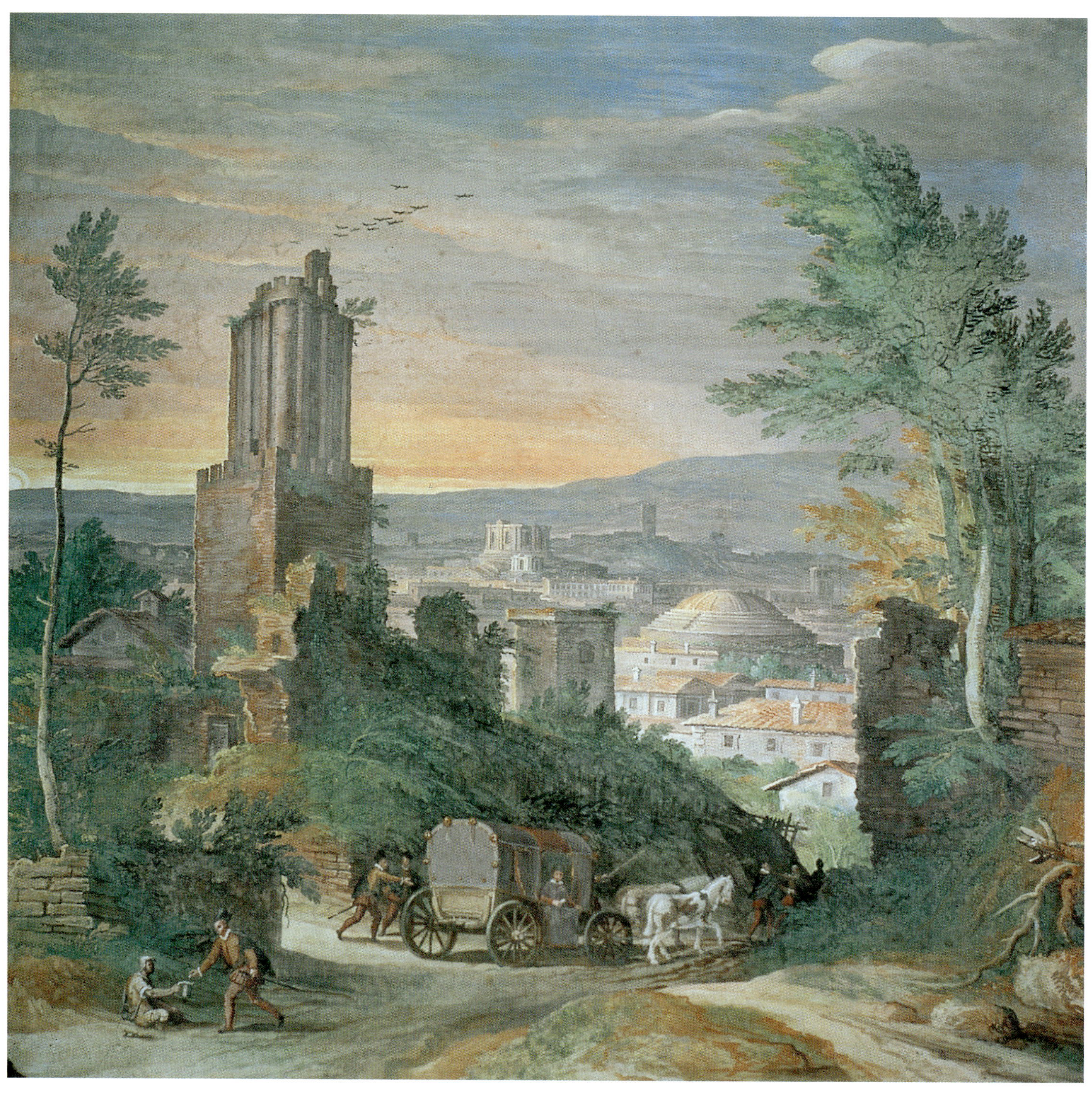

14. Matthijs Bril, *View from the Viminale*. Rome, Palazzo Apostolico
Vaticano, Torre dei Venti, mezzanino, Room with Topographical Views.

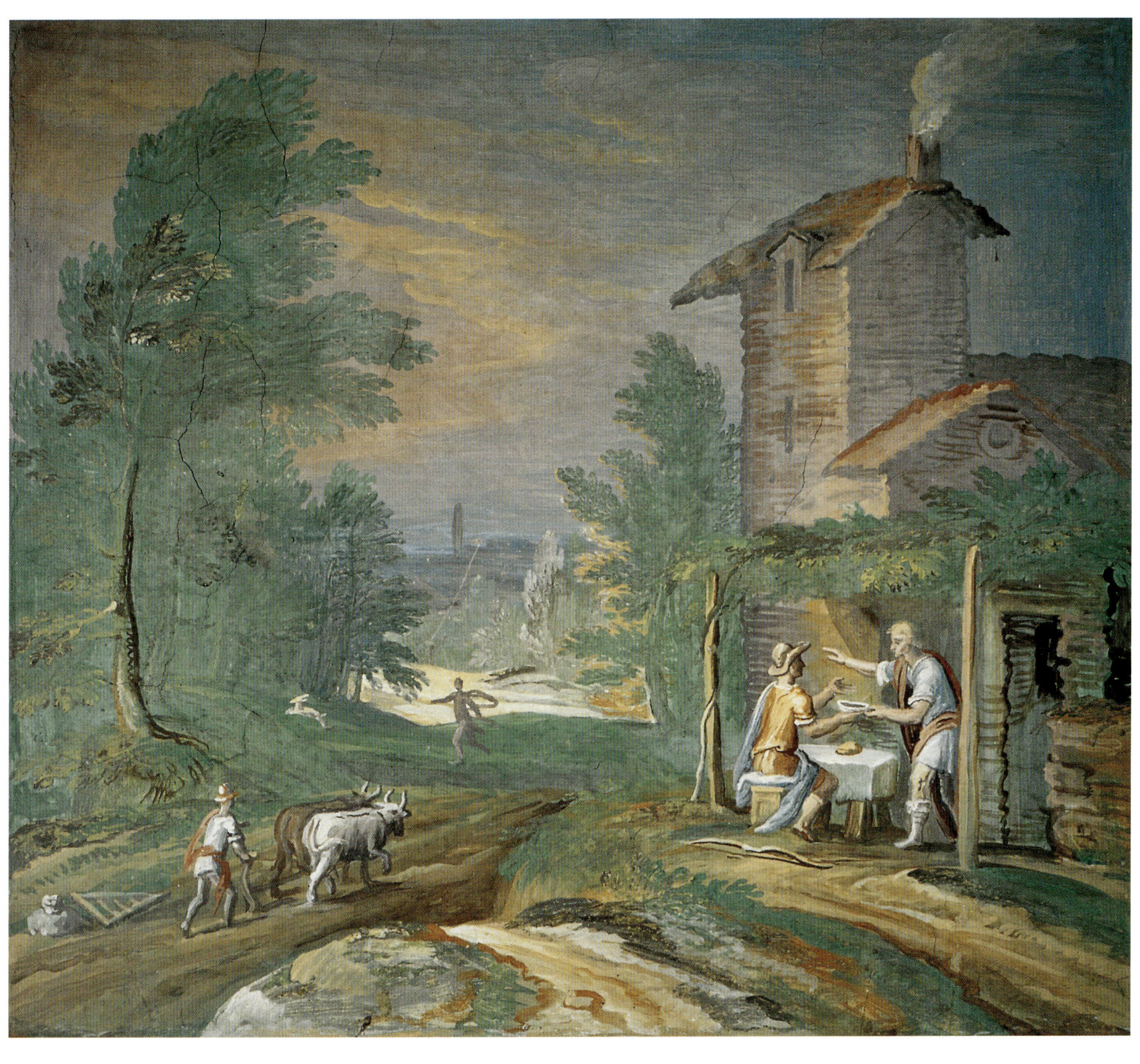

15. Matthijs Bril, *Esau Gives Jacob his Birthright*. Rome, Palazzo Apostolico Vaticano, Torre dei Venti, Room of the Old Testament Patriarchs.

worked in the Loggia of Pope Gregory XIII.[24] Matthijs depicted hunts of every conceivable type: fowlers laying nets, hunts with falcons, and hunts for hare, deer, boar, hedgehog, porcupine, badger and tortoise.[25] On one side of the room are allegorical figures representing the winds, and seascapes with Roman ruins on the coast. The frescoes on either side and above the windows in the opposite wall are badly damaged.

Because of the pince-nez signature the frieze is attributed to both Matthijs and Paul Bril – *bril* being the Dutch word for a pair of spectacles.[26] But its stylistic resemblance to the landscape, figures and animals in the Torre dei Venti and in Monterotondo suggests that here too Matthijs painted the lion's share, with Paul as his assistant.

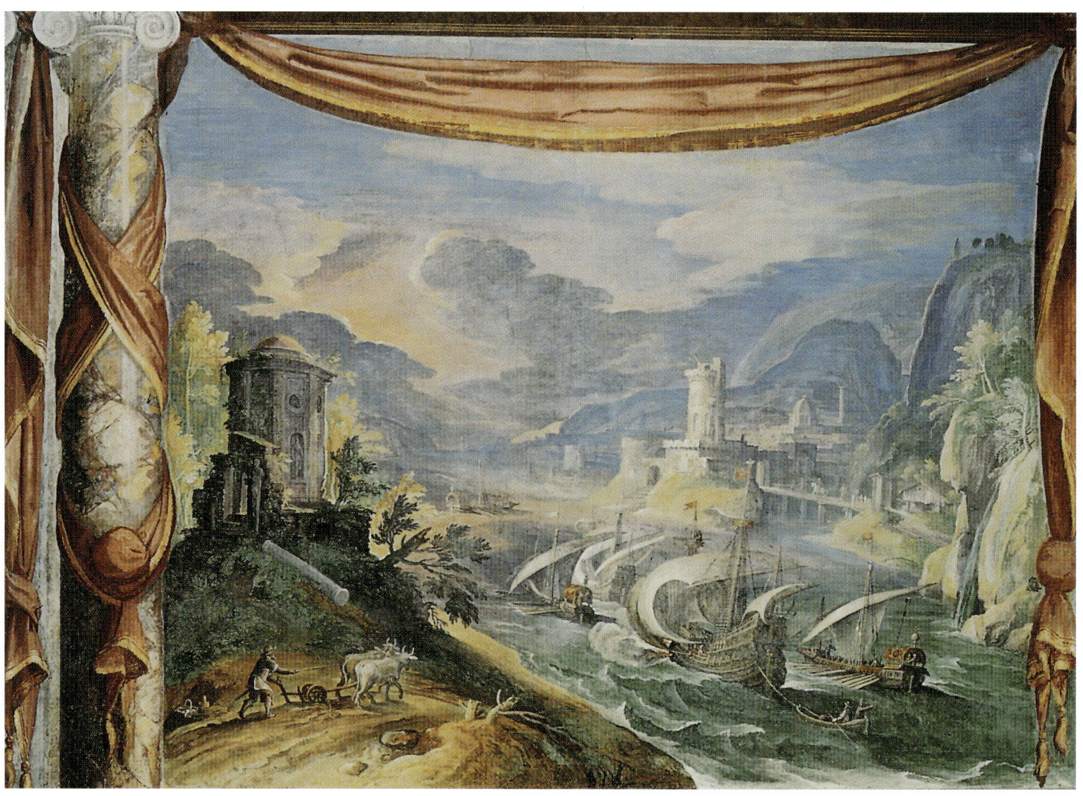

16. Matthijs Bril, *View of a Coastal Landscape with Galleys*. Rome, Palazzo Apostolico Vaticano, Torre dei Venti, mezzanino, second room.

A far smaller commission and one of a different order was the project in the Galleria delle Carte Geografiche (1580-82). At the request of Gregory XIII, Matthijs and Paul painted small landscapes on maps by Egnazio Danti (no. VI l).[27] The lower sections of the maps presumably looked bare and the landscapes were intended to add interest. The green paint of the trees shows that they were superimposed on the maps: some of the green has turned black, and patches have peeled away, apparently because the paint had not fused with the plaster. Besides trees, the pictures include scenes of herdsmen and animals, game, hunters with hounds, and a small bridge over a river.

The frescoes for the vault of this *galleria* were designed by Cesare Nebbia and exe-

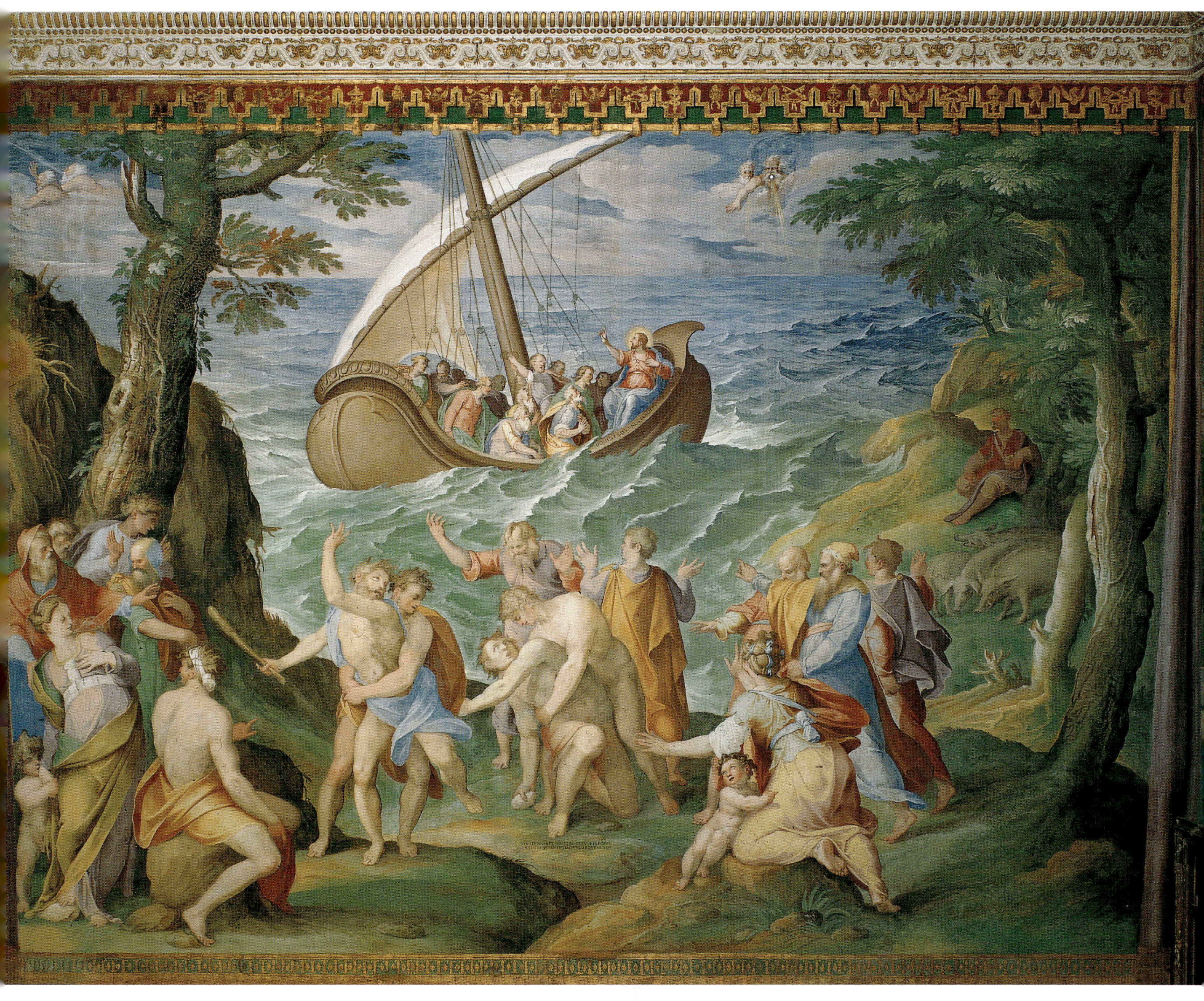

17. Matthijs Bril and Pomarancio (Niccolò Circignani), *Christ Calms the Storm*. Rome, Palazzo Apostolico Vaticano, Torre dei Venti, Sala Meridiana.

cuted by a team of painters under the supervision of Muziano. The background landscapes in twenty biblical and historical scenes were painted by Matthijs, assisted by Paul (no. VI m). [28] For this assignment they probably had less say in the type of landscapes they depicted. A number of extant drawings by Nebbia show not only the figures in the compositions but elements of the landscapes as well. Matthijs copied the cottage in the drawing quite literally (fig. 21). [29] These background landscapes incorporate all the features described in detail above.

In short, the style of Matthijs Bril's landscapes changed little in those years. All the work described above is more or less similar in quality. Matthijs had developed a formula of his own, which he varied by altering his foregrounds and backgrounds, by rearranging trees and staffage, and by creating different effects through light and dark. His untimely death in 1583 brought an end to his promising career. In a relatively short time, he had managed to secure a prominent place among the painters working for Gregory XIII and complete several prestigious projects. His reputation and experience enabled him to give his younger brother a good start. Paul continued to work on commissions for the pope, building a career that was to last for more than forty years. It is of course futile to speculate about the course their careers might have taken, had Matthijs not died so young. After 1583 Paul had to prove that he too had "una bella, e sicura maniera in saper adattare l'invenzione del paese". [30] In the first few years, particularly, his landscapes bore a close resemblance to his brother's. He presumably relied heavily on the drawings he acquired after Matthijs' death.

Unfortunately, nothing remains of Paul's first independent assignment, the paintings for the Collegio Romano, described above, which Pope Gregory XIII commissioned in 1584. [31] Paul completed numerous projects for Sixtus V Peretti, the Franciscan who succeeded Gregory XIII on 24 April 1585 for a brief five-year term. Sixtus V had an ambitious programme. His dream of making Rome the leading Catholic centre of the world left an indelible mark on the city. His legacy remains, for instance, in the street plan designed under his aegis. [32] He dismissed the painter Muziano, who

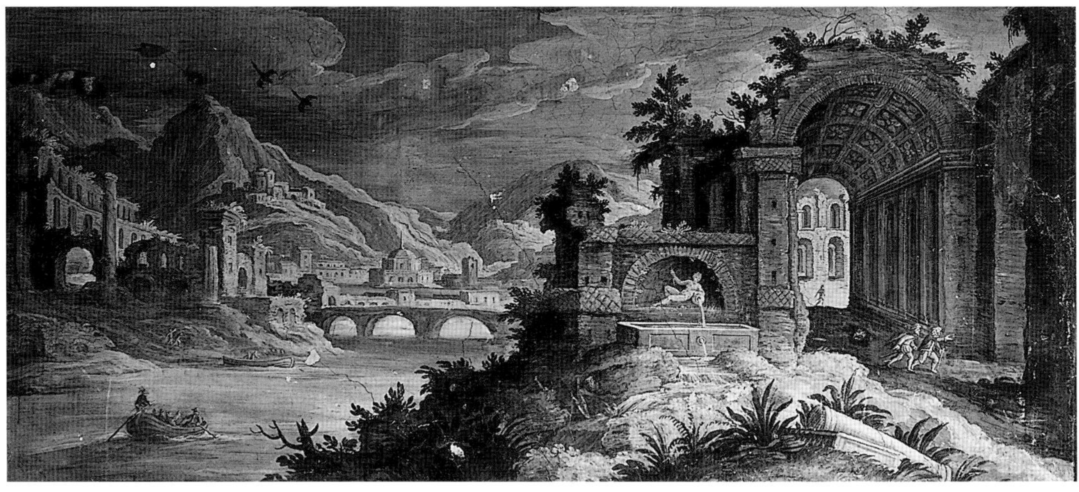

18. Matthijs Bril assisted by Paul Bril, *Landscape with Roman Ruins and a Fountain*. Monterotondo, Palazzo Comunale (formerly Orsini).

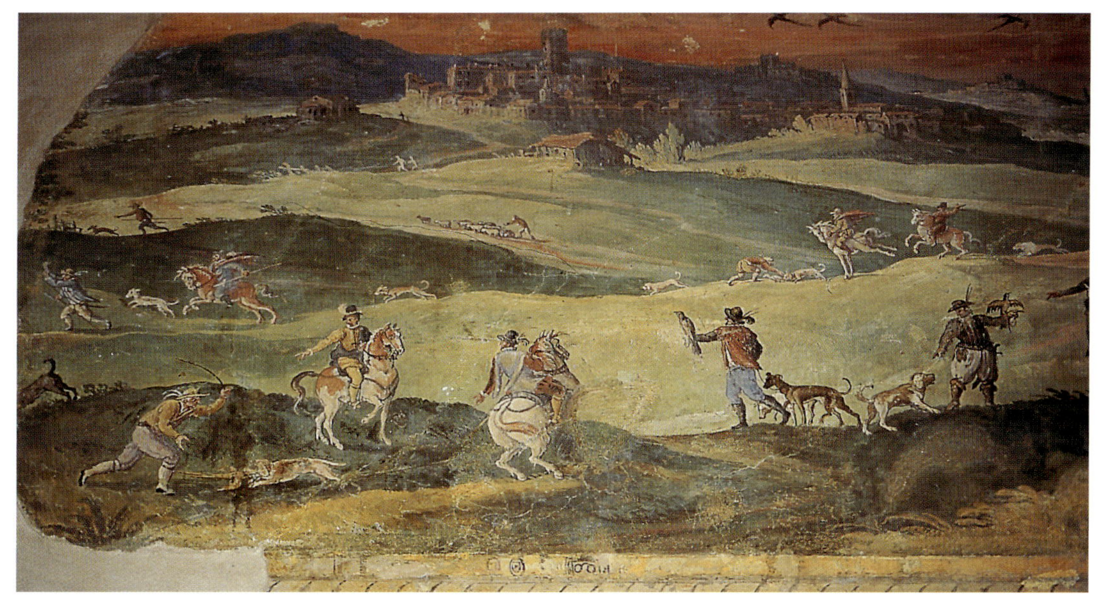

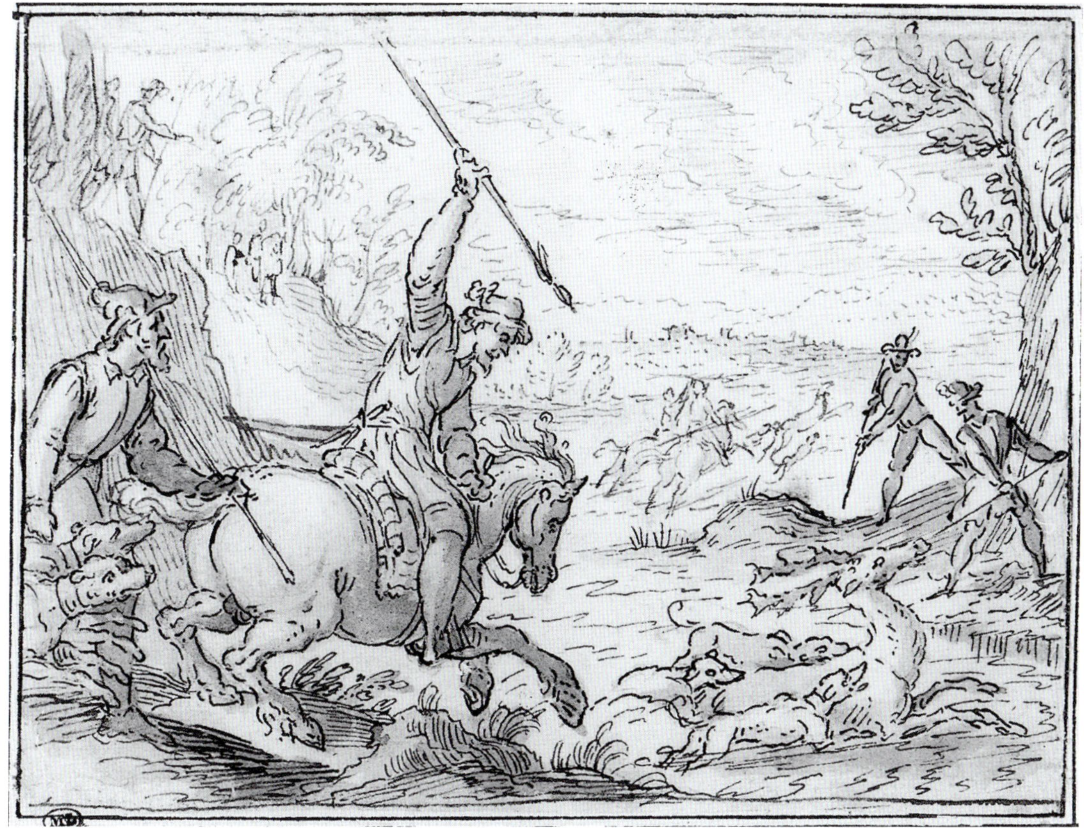

19. Matthijs Bril assisted by Paul Bril, *Hunting Landscape*.
Monterotondo, Palazzo Comunale (formerly Orsini).

20. Antonio Tempesta, *Deer Hunt*, pen and brown ink, brown wash
over traces of black chalk, 115 x 149 mm. Paris, Musée du Louvre,
Département des Arts Graphiques, inv. no. 1870.

had occupied a leading position under Pope Gregory XIII, and appointed Cesare
Nebbia and Giovanni Guerra to head his team of painters. Landscapes are a major
feature in almost every decoration project executed under the pope's auspices.[33] Sixtus V was primarily concerned with the content of paintings and the message they
conveyed, particularly those in cycles to which pilgrims had access, and conse-
quently adopted a functional rather than aesthetic approach to decoration.[34] Zuccari (1992) points out that Bril's landscapes are inhabited by figures of humble
stock, such as shepherds, fishermen and, in the landscape with a crucifix, a pilgrim.
Above the six paintings in the sacristy, which are discussed below, are pictures of the
Church Fathers. If that is not coincidence, and it certainly is not, Zuccari suggests
that the landscapes with figures correspond precisely to the representation in the
vault: the Church Fathers above what might be called the church of the humble.[35]
In January 1584 Peretti, while still a cardinal, had the first stone laid for his family chapel in the Santa Maria Maggiore by his architect Domenico Fontana.[36] In 1587
Paul Bril painted six landscapes in lunettes on the three walls of the sacristy of this
Cappella Sistina (no. XI).[37] Lunettes, often decorated with painted landscapes, are
common in Sistine architecture.[38] It is a shape that Matthijs Bril, unlike Paul, never
quite managed to work with. The sacristy is no longer in use. One of the windows

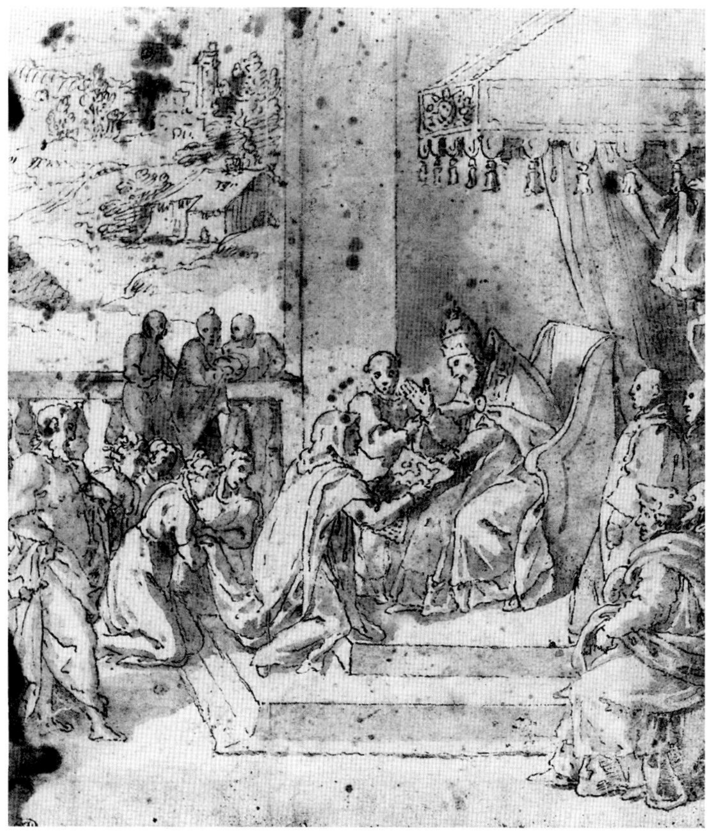

21. Cesare Nebbia, *Mathilda of Canossa Donates
her Possessions to the Church*, pen, black chalk
and brown wash on cream laid paper, 275 x 262
mm. Paris, Musée du Louvre, Département
des Arts Graphiques, inv. no. 11579.

22. Matthijs Bril, *Mathilda of Canossa Donates
her Possessions to the Church*. Rome, Palazzo
Apostolico Vaticano, Galleria delle Carte
Geografiche.

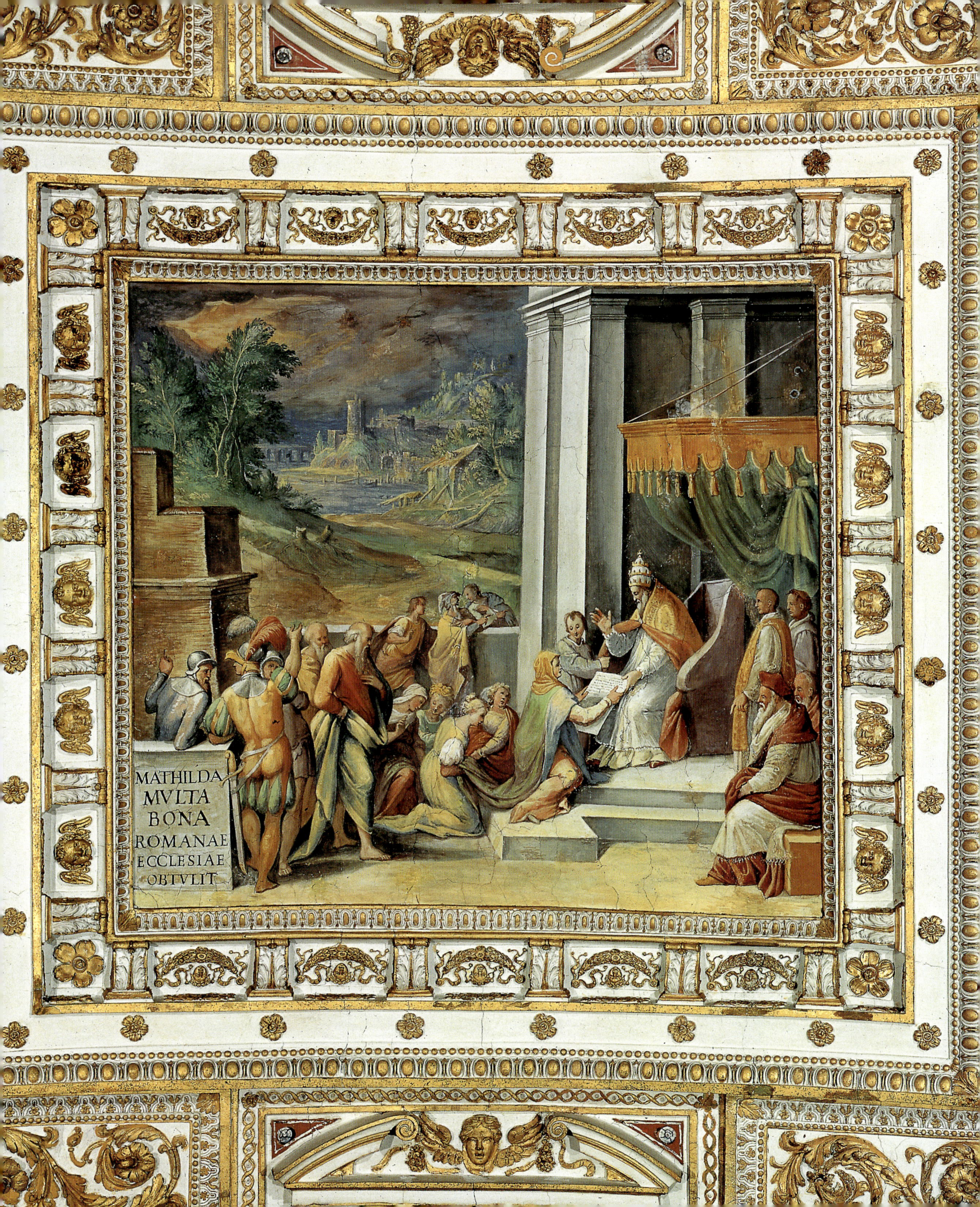

MATHILDA
MVLTA
BONA
ROMANAE
ECCLESIAE
OBTVLIT

beside the first lunette on the south wall (XI: 1) was broken for many years. The frescoes are in poor condition and two have been partly overpainted. [39]

What do these early landscapes by Paul Bril look like? Here, he painted decorative woodlands, rugged landscapes, stretches of coastline and rivers, with human figures, animals, boats and buildings serving as humble staffage. The landscapes are built up of diagonal planes which contrast in light and shade. The observer looks into the distance from a high vantage point. Bril extended the landscapes up to the edge of the picture plane and applied a border of shadow to create the illusion of looking out at the landscape through a window. [40] Many of the pictures are closed off by a tree or an outcrop of rock. Like his brother, Paul often depicted oak-like trees, bridges, fences and distant towers. His use of colour was also similar to Matthijs': browns and greens in the first plane, occasional patches of bright yellowish green, and shades of pink, lilac, orange and bluish grey on the horizon. The pictures are dotted with colourful details, such as a red roof or flower or jacket, although the colours have lost some of their crispness through exposure to light and grime. Bril often painted sunsets in overcast skies. In some pictures the sun's rays are covered by looming clouds. In all six lunettes the observer's eye is drawn into the landscape along diagonal planes in gradations of light and dark. [41]

In the first lunette, showing a landscape with a bridge, Paul appears to have drawn inspiration from one of the landscapes in the Torre dei Venti (VI h: 1, 2). The two are similar in composition, although there is no waterfall in the lunette. In the Room of Hunting Scenes in Monterotondo, the brothers painted a precarious wooden bridge very similar to the one here.

The second lunette shows merchants driving heavily laden mules over a stony path heading into the mountains. In the distance on the right are the ruins of a tower. The spruce-like trees in the centre are unusual for Paul, whose trees are mostly deciduous. The seascape with galleys and a town in the distance (fig. 23) in the third lunette is one of the best known pictures in the series. It bears a certain resemblance to Paul's earliest known drawing, dated 18 April 1587, which is now in the Print Room of Leiden University (fig. 43). [42]

The composition and staffage of the fourth painting, a river view with a herdsman and animals, recall frescoes by Matthijs. The twisted trunk of the tree on the river bank, the view of a town in the distance, and the herdsman and animals can be seen in his work in the Torre dei Venti. [43]

The fifth lunette is badly damaged and appears to have been partly overpainted. Bril's distinctive trees and foliage can still be seen quite clearly on the left, but little remains of the river or the rocky landscape.

The sixth lunette has been almost entirely overpainted.

These landscapes are the only images in the sacristy that have no specific religious theme. [44] They are conspicuous in the decoration as a whole because of their subject matter – humble figures in landscapes – and their colours, which distinguish them from the other paintings in the vault, executed by Italian artists. [45] The same is true of work by the Brils in other locations.

The next major assignment for Sixtus V's painters was the decoration of the Palazzo Apostolico Lateranense. [46] The frescoes started to deteriorate soon after being

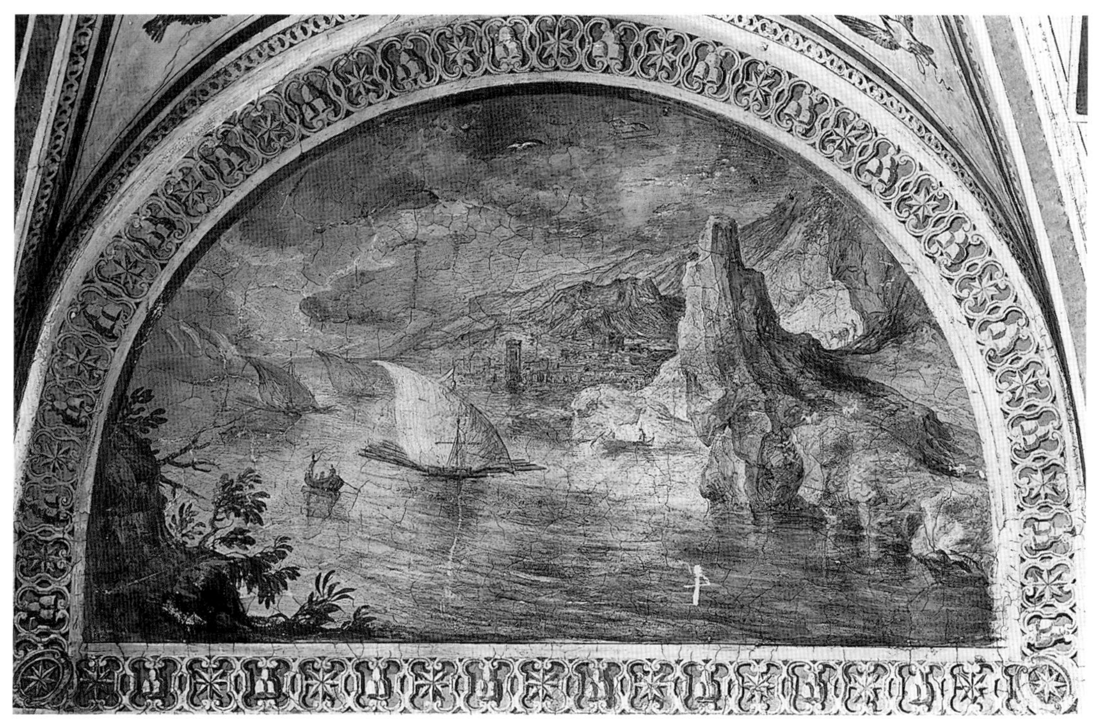

23. Paul Bril, *Seascape with Galleys and a Town in the Distance.*
Rome, Santa Maria Maggiore, Cappella Sistina, Sacristy.

completed and have undergone several restorations. Some of the landscapes appear to have been substantially overpainted and are therefore difficult to attribute. [47] Documents show that the Scala Pontificale in the palace was painted as early as 1586. [48] Here, in the corners of the vault on the first floor at the top of the staircase, are four landscapes executed as framed illusionistic paintings (no. V a, fig. 24), two of which (no. V a: 1, 2) can be firmly attributed to Paul Bril. He may have based V a: 1 on a drawing in Stockholm (fig. 25): the diagonal composition with a tree growing on a rock on the left, and the galleys and rock in the background are almost identical. [49] Bril included his ubiquitous little fence on the rock and added a figure to the painting. The greens of the trees, the sea and the rose-tinged blue sky were distinguishing features of his landscapes, as they had been in Matthijs' *œuvre*.

Given the haste in which the project had to be completed, and possibly the limitations of the artists involved, it is hardly surprising the paintings are not all of the highest standard. [50] Their shortcomings are especially obvious in the lunettes the pope instructed his team to paint on the first floor of the west and south loggias in the courtyard of the Lateran Palace (no. V b). [51] Most of the surviving sixteen lunettes (they were painted in 1588-89) appear to have been executed by Paul Bril, but they are rather mediocre. The compositions recall examples in the Torre dei Venti and Monterotondo. Some of the lunettes were painted by assistants, at least two of whom can be distinguished. [52] As a result the landscapes vary in style and quality. One assistant's style was far sketchier than Bril's (assistant A; nos. V b: 9, 14, 15), the other's slightly more delicate (assistant B; nos. V b: 11, 12).

One of the landscapes has become quite widely known through an engraving Bril made after the fresco in 1590 (figs. 26 and 8). It is a beautiful example of his early work and shows how much he still relied on his brother's examples. The horseman and dogs, the town and towers in the distance, the weather-beaten rocks and Bril's use of colour echo those in the large imaginary landscapes in the tower of Gregory XIII. In the second lunette we find another of several examples in this series of the way Paul Bril drew on landscapes by Matthijs. In this case, his source was the fresco of an imaginary landscape in the second room of the Torre dei Venti. This too is a hilly landscape rich in detail, with trees, animals, herdsmen, cottages and ruins, and a pink-tinged orange, overcast sky.

Sixtus commissioned a remarkable number of landscapes in his palace. There are at least sixty, painted in a variety of settings by different artists, among them Paul Bril and his assistants. [53] In the Sala di Costantino on the main floor, Sixtus instructed Bril to paint four rectangular panels high on the walls, three depicting landscapes and one a seascape with galleys (no. V c). [54] The composition of the first landscape, with a man hunting duck, is strongly reminiscent of one of the landscapes in the sacristy of Santa Maria Maggiore. Here too, Paul Bril divided the landscape in two by means of a tree on a wooded bank; to the left is a little stream crossed by a bridge, and to the right, through the trees, a view of a houses in the distance. A couple of monks stroll along a path through the forest behind the wooded bank. The other two landscapes are of indifferent quality, and though the compositions look like Bril's, they are not very well balanced. They may have been overpainted or perhaps executed by assistant B under Paul's supervision.

Of a different order and definitely executed by Paul is the seascape with Sixtus' galleys engaged in battle (fig. 27). A beautiful lighthouse and a town with an obelisk can be seen in the background. The diagonal composition, closed off by a tree-covered rock on the left and affording a good view of the fleet, was used in other works by Matthijs and Paul Bril, in the Torre dei Venti and Santa Maria Maggiore, for instance. While working in the Lateran Palace, Paul painted a similar picture in Sixtus' library in the Vatican.

Another project Paul Bril executed for Pope Sixtus V in 1588 was a series of landscapes in a loggia in Villa Montalto, near Santa Maria Maggiore (no. XIV). [55] However, the frescoes he executed in collaboration with the young landscape painter Giovanni Battista Viola (1576-1622) were lost when the villa was demolished. [56] The English painter and theoretician Edward Norgate had seen these works by Bril "in Fresco and in oyle both in the Pallace of Cardinall Montalto by Santa Maria Maggiore". [57]

Paul Bril's most important commission from Sixtus was for several paintings in the Scala Santa, the pope's grand project around the Sancta Sanctorum, and the staircase in the house of Pontius Pilate, which Christ had mounted several times on the day he was condemned to death (no. XII a). Sixtus chose subjects he considered appropriate for this public building, scenes from the Old and New Testaments that

24. Paul Bril (with assistants), *Four landscapes* (in the corners). Rome, Palazzo Apostolico Laterano, Scala Pontificale (vault).

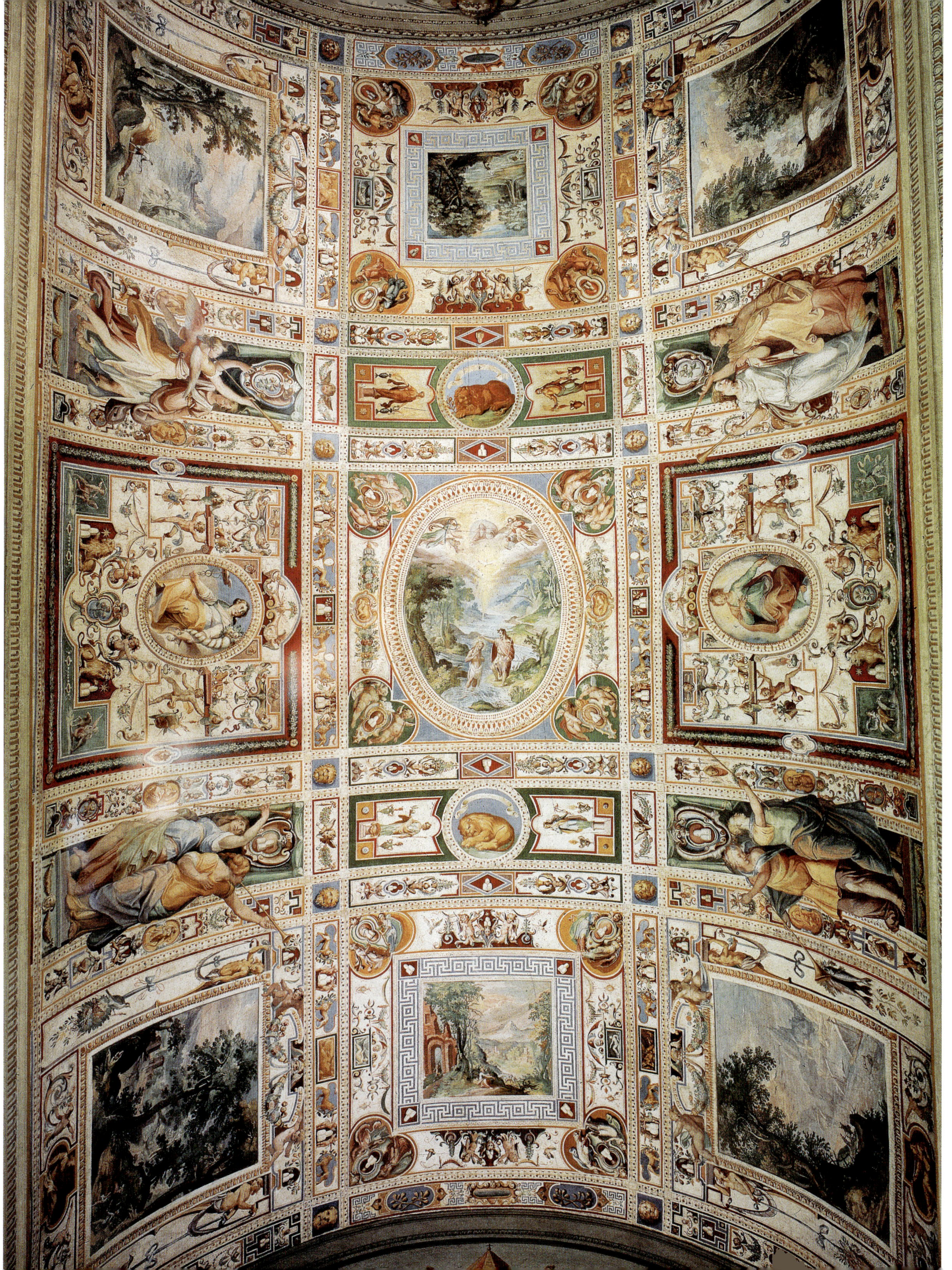

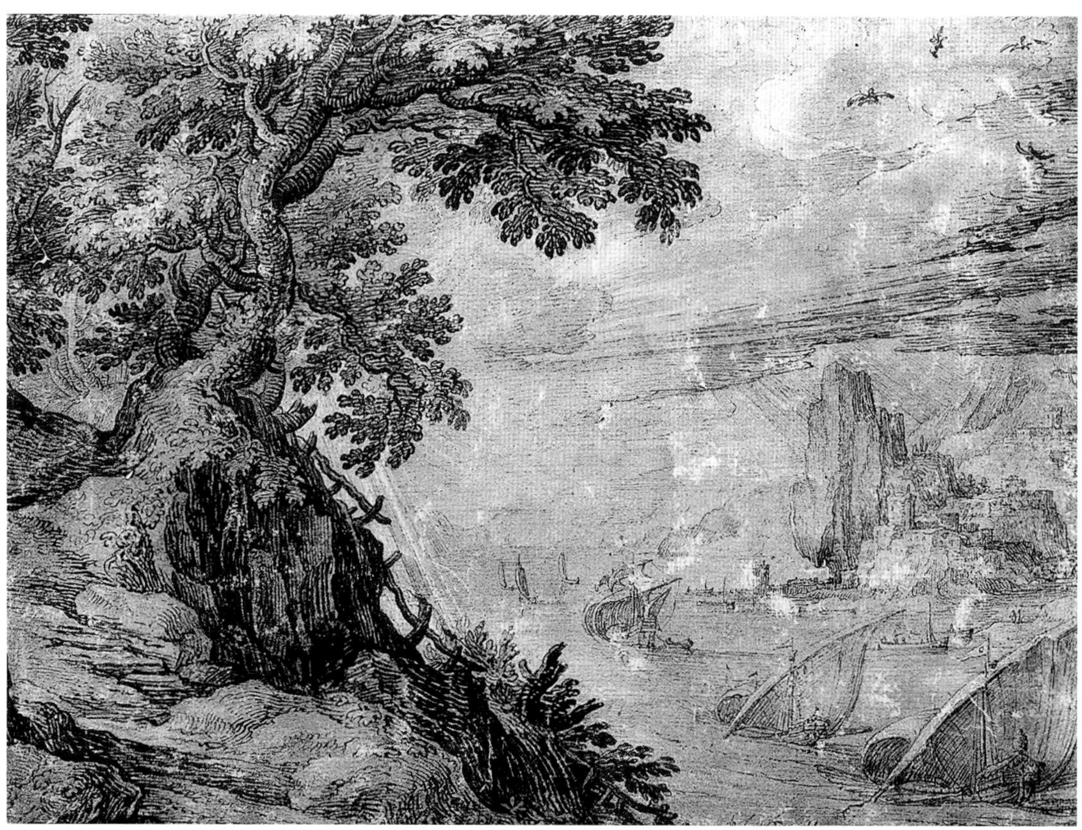

25. Paul Bril, *Seascape*, pen and brown ink and brown wash with white heightening, 194 x 264 mm, annotated at lower right in pen and brown ink: "Paul Brill". Stockholm, Nationalmuseum, inv. no. Z379/1957.

were to be both didactic and devotional. [58] Like the projects in the Vatican, Santa Maria Maggiore and the Lateran Palace, this enterprise executed by around twenty painters was supervised by Guerra and Nebbia. [59] Organising it must have been a logistical nightmare. Scaffolding had to be erected and moved – the painters worked in day shifts (*giornate*) from top to bottom and needed plasterers on standby. [60] The way these large commissions for Pope Sixtus were carried out, with teams of painters working side by side, makes it difficult to attribute work to individual artists. Painters deliberately toned down their personal style to achieve a degree of uniformity, developing what is known as the *stile sistino* (the predominant artistic style during the papacy of Sixtus V). [61] The same applied to Bril and other landscape painters, albeit to a lesser extent. The attribution of the Scala Santa frescoes is further complicated by their poor condition. Much of the work is concealed under a thick layer of grime that has accumulated over the years. [62]

This project too was executed at great speed. Domenico Fontana probably started construction work in the summer of 1586. [63] By May 1587 some of the frescoes were ready, and the walls and vaults of the three central staircases were completed within a year. [64] The decorations in the chapels of San Silvestro and San Lorenzo were completed in 1589. [65] In the vault and on the right wall of the right-hand staircase Paul painted two episodes from the story of Jonah (figs. 28, 29). The one in the vault is based on a drawing by Matthijs and his own reworked version of it. [66] He portrayed the harrowing moment when Jonah is about to be cast overboard. A huge fish, which bears little resemblance to a whale, opens its cavernous jaws and prepares to devour him. In his characteristic manner, Bril embellished the bare facts related in the Bible to heighten the dramatic tension. He painted a storm at sea with a lowering sky, foam-capped waves and a ship listing, its mast broken and sails thrashing. In the background he painted his gnarled rocks and a town with a tower in the distance. The love of detail that Paul shared with his brother is evident here in the small figure walking along the rocks, seemingly oblivious to the impending disaster at sea.

The sequel to the story is depicted on the right wall of the staircase, where the fish violently disgorges Jonah on to the rocky beach. In the distance – behind the still slightly airborne Jonah – Paul painted a splendid city with towers, obelisks and a round temple, against a mountainous background. Although the entire picture is attributed to Paul, he probably lacked the skill to have painted such a large figure. Moreover, the figure is quite different from the small Jonah above it in the vault, which can indeed be attributed to Bril. In that scene Jonah is portrayed as an elderly man with a grey beard, totally unlike the clean-shaven young man on the wall. Examined under floodlight, the lines scored into the wet plaster reveal that the figure was painted in a different *giornata* and therefore not at the same time as the landscape.

Though Paul Bril was assigned a number of surfaces in the Scala Santa to cover with complete paintings of his own, he was generally commissioned to paint appropriate background landscapes in figure scenes (no. XII a). He painted several landscapes, including that in the *Earthly Paradise* in the left staircase, that was engraved by Giovanni Guerra for Pope Sixtus V. [67] An outstanding landscape is that in the pic-

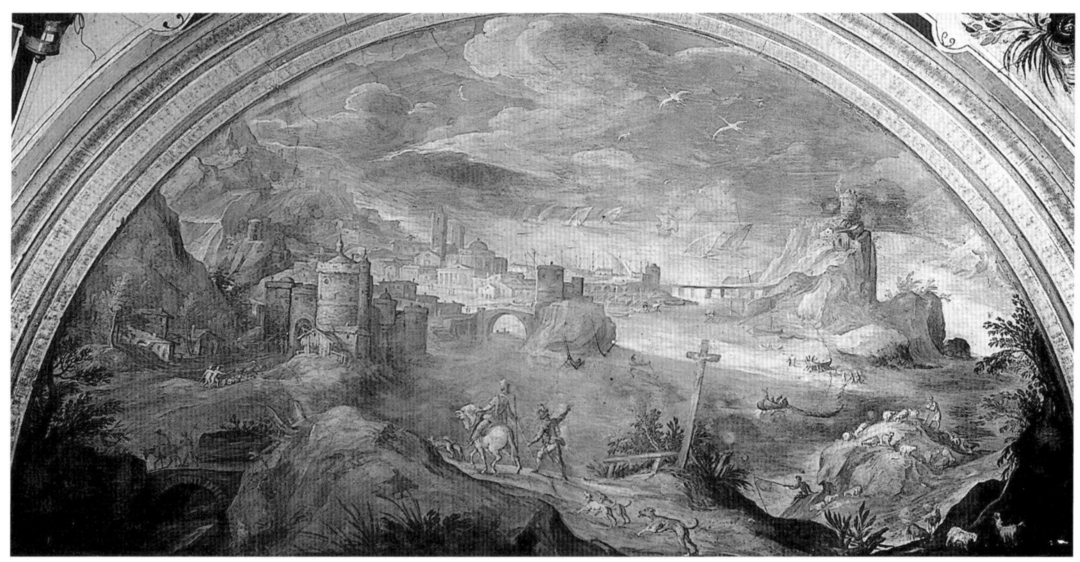

26. Paul Bril, *Coastal Landscape with a Man on Horseback, Hounds,*
a Cross, Herdsmen and Fishermen with a Town on a Bay,
Rome, Palazzo Apostolico Lateranense, loggias.

ture of *Adam and Eve Cast out of Paradise*. The right section is filled with a hilly landscape in contrasting colours, bushes, tree stumps and a path leading into the distance. A wrathful angel emerges from a sky covered with dark pink clouds. *The Flood* strongly recalls the painting of the same subject in the Sala Meridiana, which has the same green sea and high, white-crested waves (fig. 17).

Bril painted a beautiful, chequered landscape in *Jacob's Dream* in the vault. The tree under which Jacob sleeps divides the picture space in two, which allowed Bril, or whoever designed the composition, to paint a high landscape on the left and a view into the distance on the right, where a solitary wanderer – who does not feature in the biblical tale – heads in the direction of a tower on a hilltop. Here, and in similar landscapes, Paul's style still bears a close resemblance to Matthijs': Matthijs painted the same episodes from the Bible in the Torre dei Venti, where he executed the figures as well as the landscapes. Paul was given a similar opportunity only once, in some of the frescoes in the Scala Santa.

The chapels of San Lorenzo (fig. 30) and San Silvestro in the same building were decorated some time later (1589; nos. XII b and c). Here, Paul was again engaged to paint landscapes in lunettes, as he had done in Santa Maria Maggiore and the Lateran Palace. The quality of the lunettes has been discussed above. The four landscapes Bril painted for the chapel of San Lorenzo – three on the exterior wall and one above the entrance to the Sancta Sanctorum – are likewise embedded in the context of Church Fathers, angels and allegorical figures. When last restored, the frescoes were not cleaned and they are therefore difficult to see.

The four landscapes bear all the hallmarks of the 'early' Paul Bril, incorporating a panoramic view, a high horizon and a great deal of variation in the different planes. The original colours would undoubtedly have been brighter, though even now they are distinctive of Bril, down to the red details of the garments. There is human activity in all four: horsemen and hunters make their way through the countryside with a frolicking dog at their side; a merchant and his mule trudge into the hills; a man carrying a basket of fruit passes a beggar. In the landscape above the door to the sanctuary, Bril painted two artists with sketchbooks on their laps, drawing the rugged landscape around them. In one lunette a tree closes off one side of the composition, whereas in the other, two serve as *repoussoirs* on either side. The landscapes differ considerably in height. The pink, cloudy skies apparently appealed to Norgate (1623-26): "The best and most pleasing kind of Landscape are those that represents the morning or the evening. For a rising or setting sun affoard such varietiee and beauty of colours, by reason of those Blushing reflexions upon nearer clouds".[68]

Though the lunettes in the chapel of San Silvestro have turned completely black, it is still possible to discern the outlines of a landscape on the right wall, which included a motif of herdsmen tending their animals in a woodland. In the vault Bril painted another two *tabula*-shaped landscapes, but the figures have been severely damaged by cracks running over the entire ceiling (no. XII c).

27. Paul Bril, *Seascape with Papal Galleys and Fort and Town in the Distance*. Rome, Palazzo Apostolico Lateranense, Sala di Costantino.

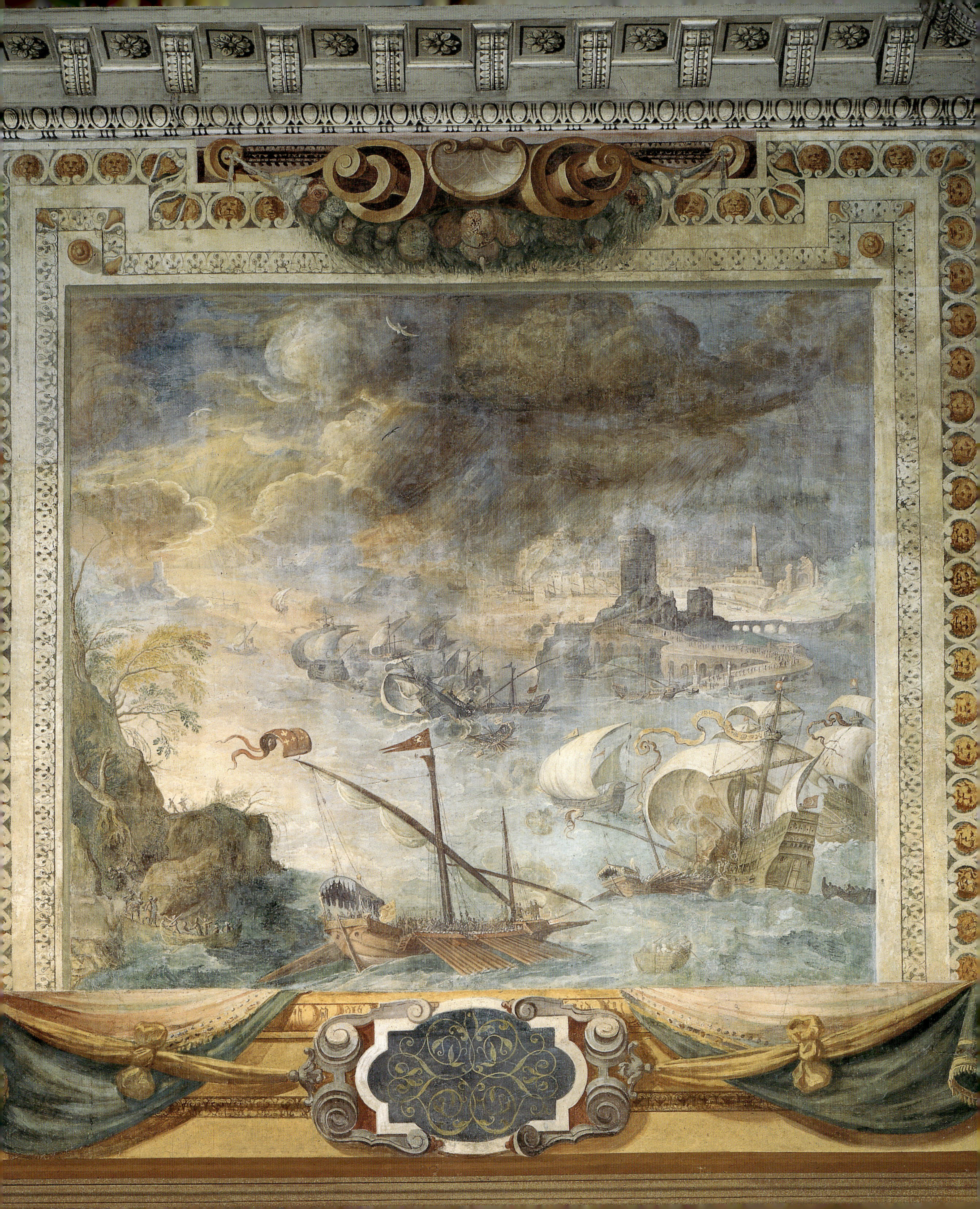

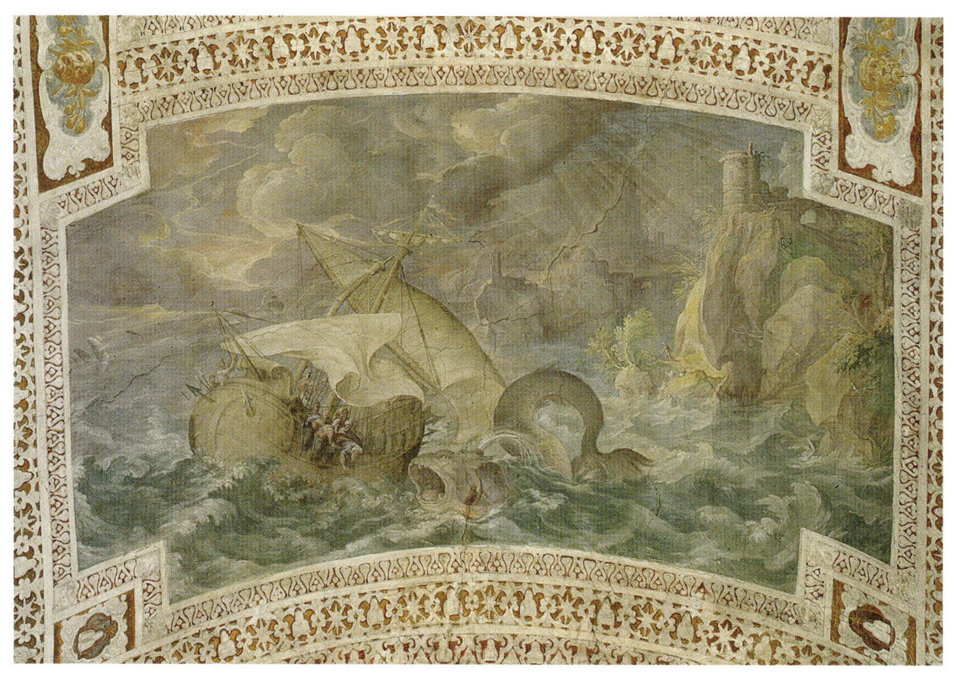

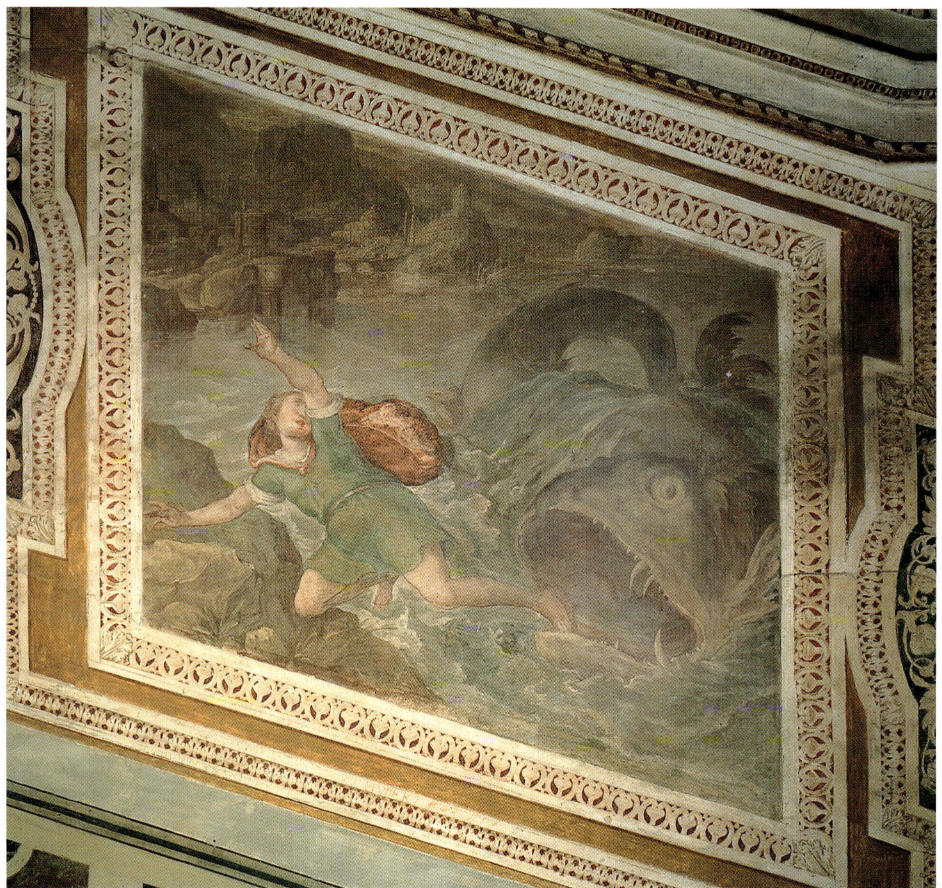

28. Paul Bril, *Jonah and the Whale*. Rome, Scala Santa, Staircases.

29. Paul Bril (and Andrea Lilio?), *The Whale Disgorges Jonah*.
Rome, Scala Santa, Staircases.

He also painted a number of background landscapes for Sixtus V in the Vatican Library (Salone Sistino, 1588-89) in another project involving a large team of painters (no. VI n).[69] He painted at least six landscapes in scenes depicting the most famous libraries in the world, all with his distinctive rosy orange sunsets. These landscapes are purely functional supports for the scenes in the foreground, such as the Tower of Babel in the picture of the library of Babylon. Another of Bril's frescoes is in the vault on the north side of the library. It shows the pope's fleet and in front of it, Roma with Romulus and Remus. The diagonal composition, the frothy waves, the white sails and the ships behind the pope's galleys recall paintings in the Sala Meridiana, the lunette in Santa Maria Maggiore, the fleet of ships in the Lateran Palace and a scene in Palazzo Caetani (formerly Mattei), which is discussed below.[70] Sixtus V instructed the architect Fontana to build a staircase in the Vatican Palace that would enable him to move between the Sistine Chapel and St Peter's without being observed. Payments were made to the architect and his two foremen in 1586 and 1587.[71] The pope's coat of arms was painted by different artists in the vault of the staircase. Guerra and Nebbia engaged Paul Bril to paint the four lunettes above the doors at the top and bottom of the stairs (no. VI o). The two landscapes at the upstairs entrance to the Sistine Chapel are strongly reminiscent of those in the Room of Landscapes in Monterotondo. There are bright planes in the foreground, weather-beaten rocks, log cabins, bridges, a profusion of human and animal figures and, on the high blue horizon, a town on a river, basking in the glow of the setting sun. The composition of one of the landscapes at the bottom of the stairs, a scene with the ruins of a tower on the left, is generally more tranquil. The planes are more undulating and the only figure is a solitary wanderer. The scene in the fourth lunette, with a hunter and two figures walking, is more animated and there is more contrast between the foreground and background.

How can we summarise the commissions Paul Bril completed for Pope Sixtus V? Firstly, the pope's decoration programmes included very many landscapes – his Franciscan background may have inculcated in him a love of pastoral themes.[72] Sec-

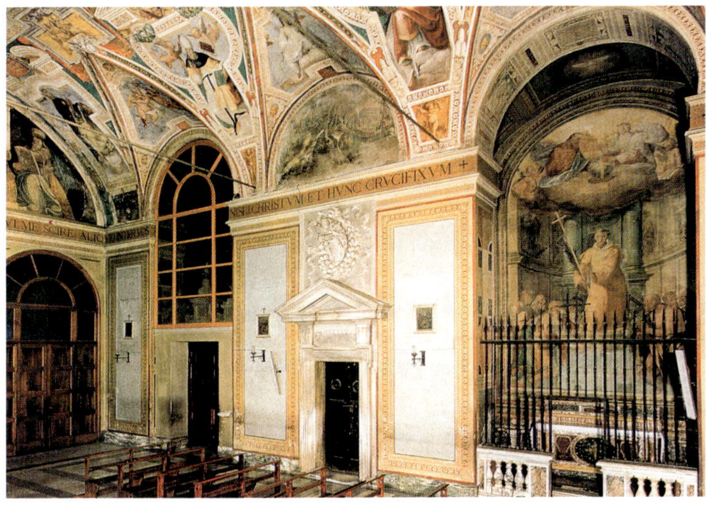

30. View of the Chapel of San Lorenzo.
Rome, Scala Santa.

ondly, Paul Bril, along with a number of other landscape painters, was engaged to work on the majority of those projects, generally to paint landscapes in lunettes. His style evolved slowly in this period. His landscapes became less panoramic and less cluttered than Matthijs', but they never changed fundamentally.

After the death of Sixtus V in 1590 the demand for fresco painters abated for a while. In 1593-94 Bril painted two landscapes for a *Creation of Adam and Eve* and a *Last Judgment* in the Chiesa Nuova, of which Paris Nogari painted the figures. Both are unfortunately lost (no. III).[73] In these years, Bril turned his hand to painting landscapes on copper, demonstrating his skill as a true master of detail. Giovanni Baglione's brief biography of him mentions that in 1598 Bril was also commissioned by Pope Clement VIII (1592-1605) to paint landscapes in the transept of the San Giovanni in Laterano (no. X). Baglione, who was himself involved in the project, observes that Paul Bril already had a good reputation: "E come era Pittore di chiarissimo nome, cosi in tutti li lavori principali fu adoperato; e nelle pitture fatte fare dal Pontefice Clemente VIII in S. Gio. Laterano egli in quelle storie da diversi formati vi accompagnò con ogni esquisitezza i paesi, & aggiunse pregio a quelli grandi opere".[74]

The most striking of Bril's landscapes in this series is the one in the scene of Sylvester ascending Mount Soracte, on the right wall in the right transept. The composition and subject matter of the right section, which is decorated with plants and rocks, is to some extent comparable to the landscape with St Peter of Murano in the vault of Galleria delle Carte Geografiche.

Barely a year later, in 1599, Paul Bril received two interesting assignments, which attest to his growing reputation. In May 1599 he signed a contract with Cardinal Girolamo Mattei, agreeing to paint a frieze with a cornice beneath it and grotesques around the windows of the principal room in the cardinal's new palace, now Palazzo Caetani (nos. VII a and b).[75] This important find in the archive gives us some idea of the terms that were laid down in a contract of this kind. Bril was to produce a design; the dimensions of the frieze were agreed. He was responsible for engaging

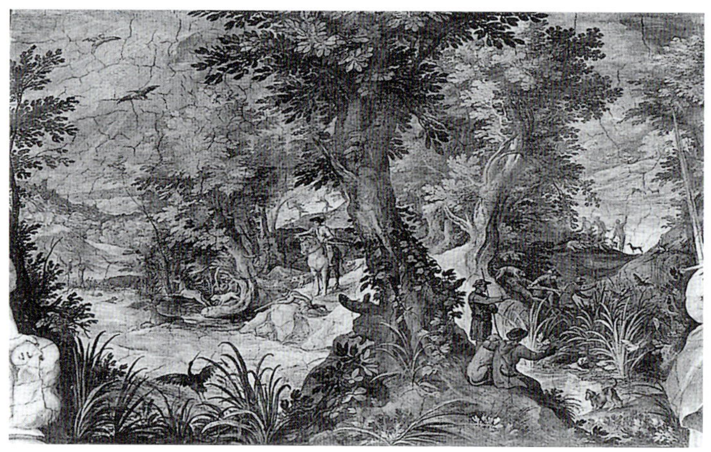

31. Paul Bril, *Landscape with Hunting Scenes*. Rome, Palazzo Caetani (formerly Mattei).

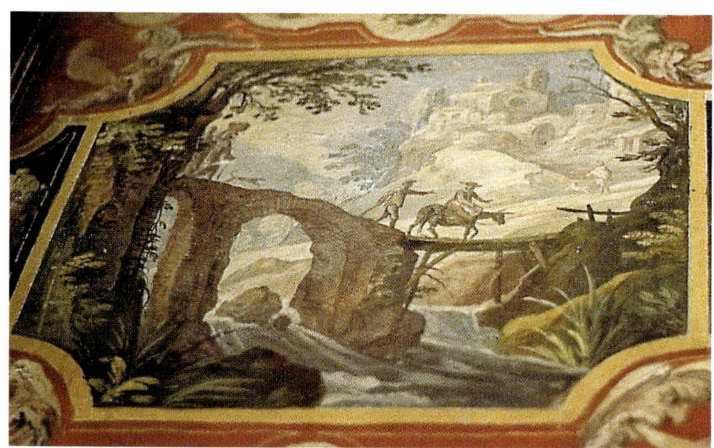

32. Paul Bril, *Landscape with Man and Woman on a Donkey crossing a Bridge*. Rome, Palazzo Caetani (formerly Mattei).

suitable assistants and all payments, as was customary, would be made to him as the master in charge. The project was to be completed in October 1599. [76]

Paul painted nine large landscapes on three walls of the room. He based some of them on earlier compositions, which apparently met with the cardinal's approval. The cycle included wooded landscapes with herdsmen tending their animals, hunting landscapes, a view of a harbour, and galleys at sea. [77] One scene (fig. 31) was based on the landscape with hunters in the Sala di Costantino of the Lateran Palace. In both frescoes, a group of men out on a duck shoot stand or lounge around the foot of an ivy-covered tree. Bril made a few changes in the sections on either side of the tree, which extends to the top of the picture space and divides the composition in two. He added more hunters, a horseman and quarry pursued by hounds.

For the galleys at sea in a storm he again seems to have drawn on the seascape he had painted for Sixtus V in the Sala di Costantino a few years earlier (fig. 27). However, he reversed the composition, possibly because of the picture's position on the wall. [78] Between the landscapes are paintings personifying the Virtues. [79] For the ten small landscapes between the grotesques on either side of the windows, Bril confined himself to a smaller format. He painted beautifully detailed, chequered landscapes in 'windows' (VII b; fig. 32).

On 20 October 1599, workmen in the Church of Santa Cecilia in Trastevere discovered sarcophagi containing the remains of several martyrs, among them those of St Cecilia. Hers were of particular interest, as favourable conditions in the catacombs

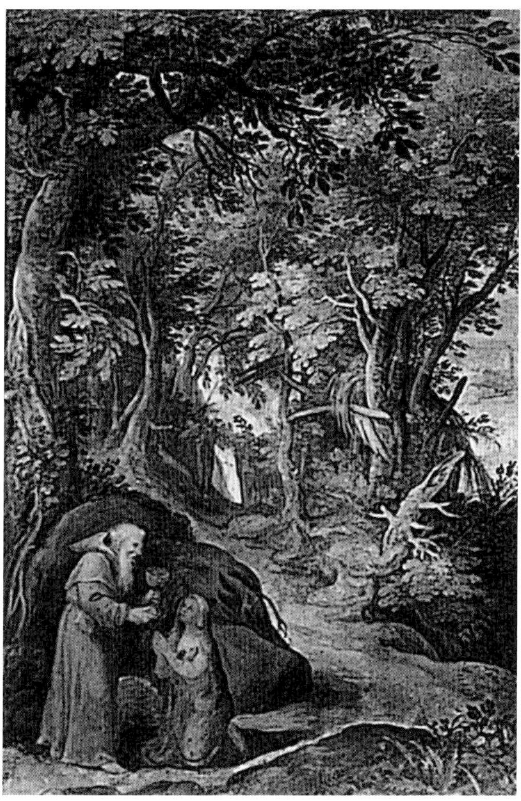

33. Paul Bril, *Maria Egyptiaca and Zozimos.*
Rome, Santa Cecilia in Trastevere.

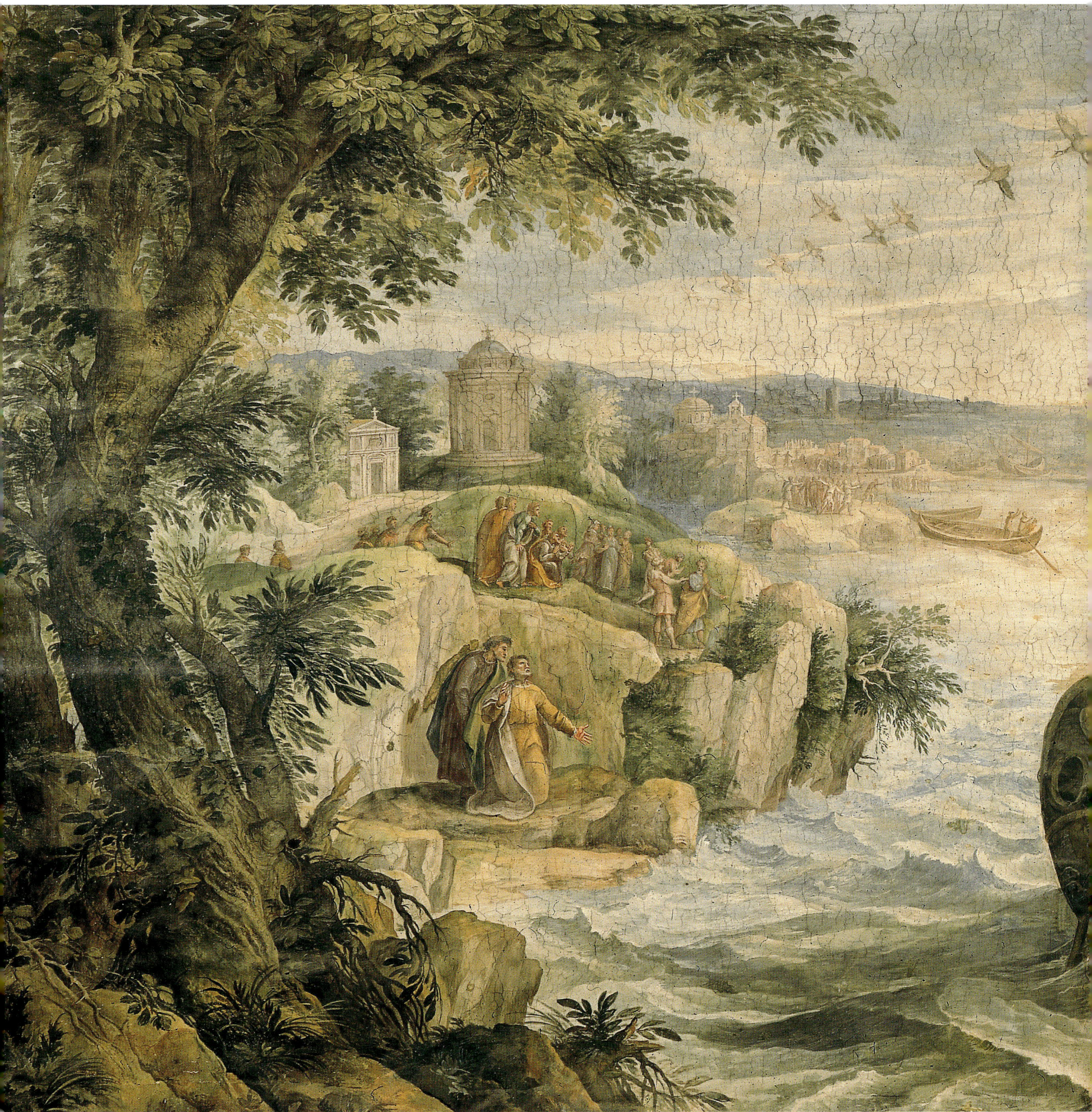

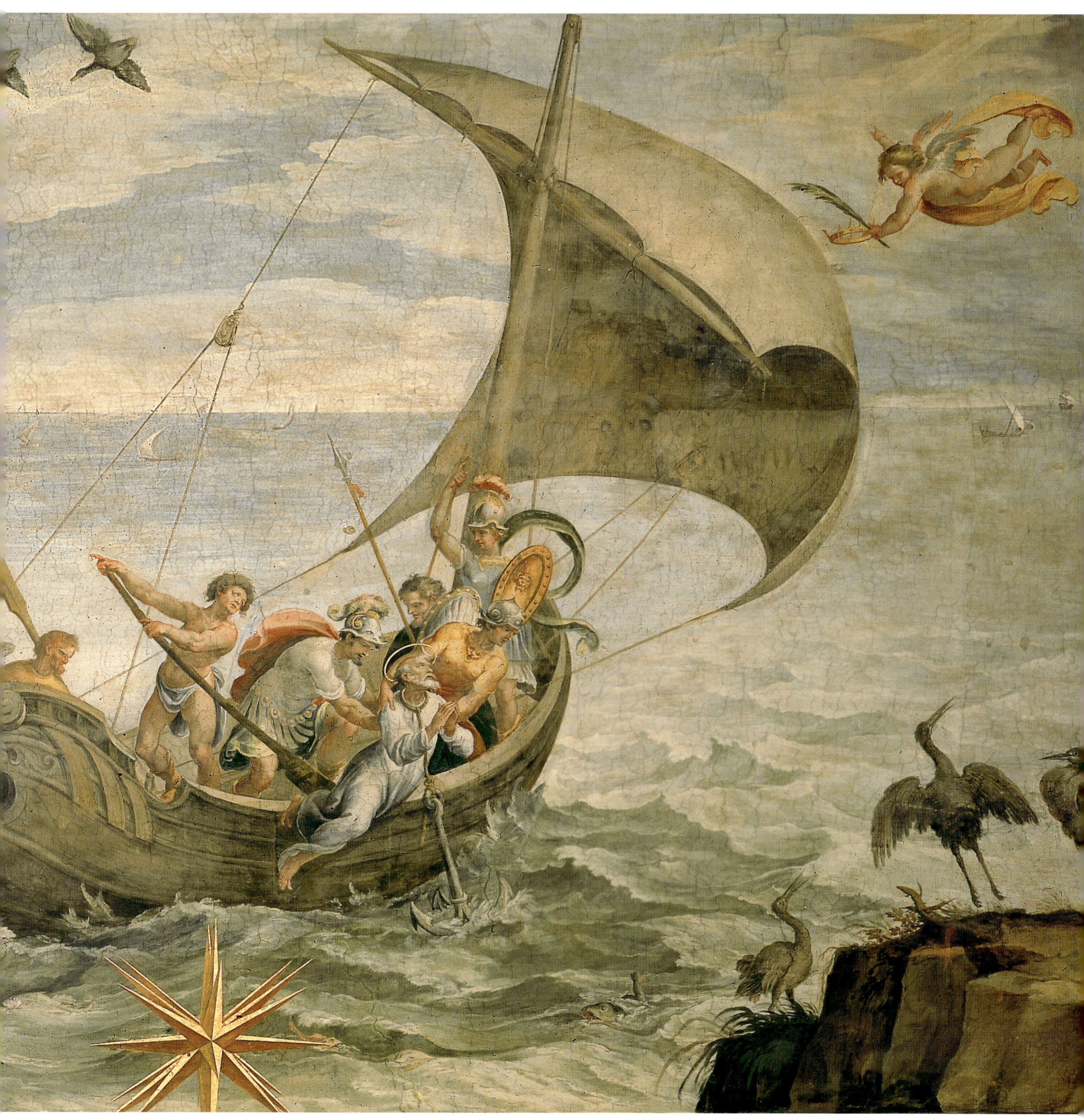

34. Paul Bril (with Cherubino and Giovanni Alberti), *Seascape with the Martyrdom of St Clement*. Rome, Palazzo Apostolico Vaticano, Sala Clementina.

where she had originally been buried had kept the body intact. Cecilia's sarcophagus had been brought to the church built on the site of her home as early as the ninth century. The find was opportune for the titular cardinal of the church, Paolo Emilio Sfondrati (1561-1618), occurring shortly before the Jubilee of 1600. On 22 November 1599, Cecilia's coffin was buried in the crypt in an elaborate public ceremony attended by Pope Clement VIII and many members of the Curia. The cardinal took this opportunity to order four new altars and engaged a team of artists to renew the main altar.

Paul Bril was commissioned to paint frescoes of saints in landscapes on the walls, lunettes and the vault of a corridor which leads from the right aisle to a chapel on the site of the *calidarium*, where Cecilia was said to have been tortured (no. IX; fig. 33). [80] On the walls he painted saints in three large and three narrow landscapes. They are portrayed as men and women who have renounced the world to do penance in the wilds of nature. In most of these paintings Bril gives us a distant glimpse of the abject world they have abandoned. The large frescoes are panoramic and rendered with high horizons. They gave Bril an opportunity to demonstrate his skill at painting trees and foliage, tree stumps, bark, calabashes and various species of birds. His figures, however, are rather schematic and stiff.

The frescoes on the walls differ in style from those in the vault, particularly the landscapes in the two lunettes. Restorers working on the aisle in 1995-96 discovered that Bril had used preparatory cartoons for the lunettes, whereas reddish-brown drawings were found under the other landscapes. Bril must have worked with an assistant here, although the compositions of the two lunettes suggest that he designed them himself. The direct precursors for these frescoes of saints in landscapes are prints of saints engraved by Cornelis Cort after Muziano and engravings of hermits by Jan and Raphael Sadeler after drawings by Maarten de Vos. [81] Sadeler's prints also influenced the work of Jan Brueghel the Elder, who became acquainted with Paul Bril during his stay in Rome from 1591 to 1595. [82] Both artists painted hermits in landscapes after prints from Sadeler's *Solitudo* series for Cardinal Borromeo. [83]

Under the pontificate of Clement VIII (1592-1605), Paul Bril was involved in a number of projects in the Vatican Palace. The largest fresco he ever painted is in the magnificent Sala Clementina (no. VI p; fig. 34), [84] whose walls and vault were decorated with illusionistic paintings by the brothers Giovanni and Cherubino Alberti. Here, Bril painted the seascape of the monumental, illusionistically framed *Martyrdom of St Clement*. Macioce (1990) offers an interesting iconological analysis of the work, interpreting the boat as a symbol of the Church of Rome. This would have been all the more reason for the pope to display his predecessor so prominently opposite his throne in this room. [85]

The wide brown imitation-wood frame around Bril's large seascape jars with the Alberti's elegant work. Prominent in the picture is the ship with Pope Clement I on board. He has an anchor around his neck and is being cast overboard by Roman soldiers. The diagonal composition and the waves of a cold, Northern sea recall the frescoes in the Sala Meridiana (Torre dei Venti) and the Jonah in the Scala Santa. The tree on the left, the rocks, the tree stumps and white sails on the high horizon

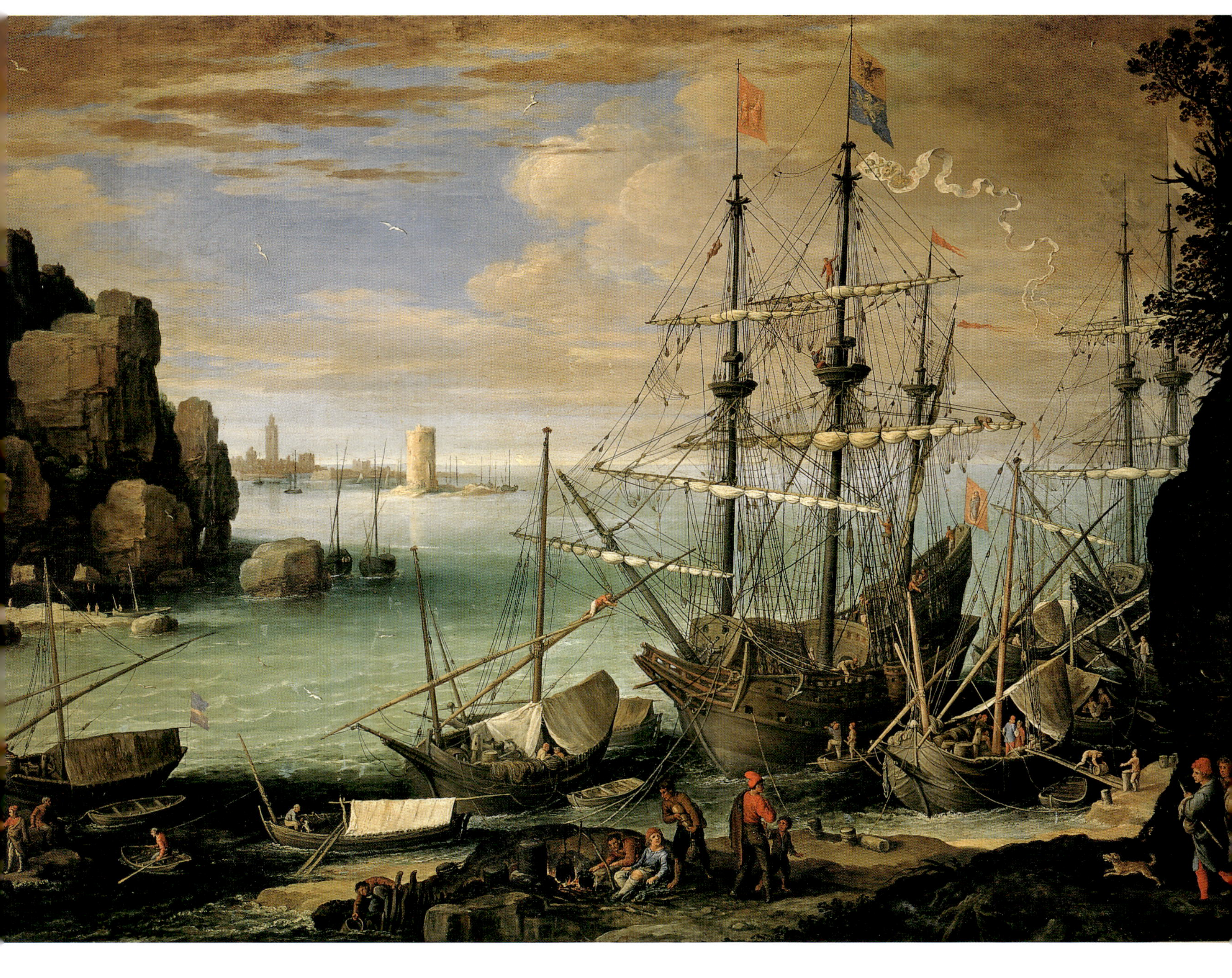

35. Paul Bril, *Harbour View*, 1611, oil on canvas, 107 x 151 cm.
Rome, Galleria Borghese.

are features of earlier works by Bril, such as those in the Torre dei Venti and Santa Maria Maggiore (figs. 16, 17 and 23).[86]

The fresco is not in very good condition, nor is it a successful composition. The ship is disproportionately large in relation to the background, but this was undoubtedly intentional, since the ship is of course the central motif and therefore the most important part of the composition. The rendering of the martyr's followers huddling on the rocks in the background also lacks finesse. The tree, forming a rather heavy *repoussoir*, is abruptly truncated by the frame. The flight of ducks is also out of proportion. The waves, on the other hand, are true to life in both form and colour. A small detail which is strongly reminiscent of the scene of Jonah in the vault of Scala Santa (fig. 28) is the fish, supposedly meant to represent the whale, swimming near the anchor. Also interesting is the *repoussoir* on the right, consisting of three cranes which appear to have been inspired by the three birds in the tapestry representing the *Miraculous Draught of Fishes* that Raphael designed for the Sistine Chapel (now in the Pinacoteca Vaticana).

In 1602 Paul painted a frieze depicting seven well-known monasteries in Italy, in a frieze in the Sala del Concistoro, the room adjacent to the Sala Clementina in the Vatican Palace (no. VI q). The smallest (c. 1.80 x 1.60 m) and most beautiful in the series is the monastery of Montecassino.[87] It looks as if Bril painted the hilltop monastery from the crest of a hill on the opposite side. The observer first looks into a cavernous valley, then along two tortuous paths winding up the precipitous slopes to the monastery perched on top. In the left foreground are Paul's distinctive trees and tree stumps on an outcrop of rock, forming a beautiful contrast against the pale background. The composition as a whole recalls the paintings Bril made for the Mattei family in 1601, which Karel van Mander wrote about in 1604. They are similar in subject matter too, as both show the family's estates.[88] Bril would certainly have made drawings for this commission – as Pijl suggested for the Mattei canvases – but in neither case are any such drawings known. The frescoes of the other monasteries are of inferior quality, and the compositions far less compact.

Paul V Borghese was elected pope on 8 May 1605, following the death of Leo XI, the successor of Pope Clement VIII, twenty-seven days after taking office. Like Sixtus V, Borghese was an unstinting patron of the arts, who engaged architects, sculptors and painters to execute numerous projects. Not long after assuming office he had several rooms to the south and east of the Sala Clementina decorated with landscape friezes. They too are of variable quality.[89] Given the number of commissions Bril was receiving and the fact that he engaged assistants, like most independent masters he must have trained a number of pupils in his studio.[90] At least one of them presumably worked in these rooms. Bril's hand can be distinguished in only a few of the landscapes in the Sala degli Scultori, though he probably designed the whole series himself (no. VI r). Framed trompe-l'œil paintings of hermits in landscapes with ruins, rivers, panoramas and woodlands are separated from one another by allegorical figures and putti. The style of the woodland scene with a hermit at a stream corresponds to Bril's wall frescoes in Santa Cecilia (fig. 33).

The four landscapes in the Sala dei Papi have all the hallmarks of Bril's hand (no. VI s). The first, which is painted in an illusionistic frame, is a lovely view of a river with two walkers resting. Here, his work seems to have changed: the trees no longer extend all the way up to the cornice, the river meanders gently to the horizon, the horizon itself is lower, and the mountain in the background is aglow in the setting sun. These features, along with the two resting figures, make the picture tranquil and atmospheric. The coastal landscape with the ruins of a tower is similar in this respect, although it includes more human activity.[91]

In the adjacent room, appropriately called the Sala dei Pittori, the pope gave instructions to have the Borghese coat of arms painted prominently in the corners (no. VI t). The arms consist of a black eagle on gold in the uppermost field; the lower field is blue with a winged dragon. Beside the devices, which are borne by plump putti, are two long, narrow landscapes and four in illusionistic frames. They feature hermits, a subject Bril had already painted on previous occasions. One of the two large landscapes, which gives a wide view over a flat stretch of land, is closed off on the right by a subtle *repoussoir* consisting of a tree growing on a bank with a bright yellowish green thicket behind it. Here, too, pink and orange clouds hover above the low the horizon. A comparison of the frescoes in Santa Cecilia with those of similar subjects in the rooms described above shows how Bril's style gradually changed. He may have been inspired by Annibale Carracci, Cavalier d'Arpino, Adam Elsheimer and other painters, who in turn would have been influenced by Bril, the foremost landscape painter in Rome at the time.[92] In his *Considerazioni* (c. 1620) Mancini says: "Pauol Brillo … vedendo le cose dei Carracci, e del Cav. Giuseppe, ha nelle figure fatto assai passaggio, et nel paesaggio lasciato quello sten-to fiammengo, accostandosi più al vero".[93] This can be seen, for instance, in the sim-ilarities between the compositions and figures in Bril's fresco in the second lunette in the Casino del Patriarca Biondo, showing a landscape with boats on a river (fig. 36), and those in a *Landscape with the Flight into Egypt* by Annibale.[94]

The animated panoramic landscapes on the walls of Santa Cecilia (fig. 33) have given way in these rooms to far simpler compositions, where movement and detail

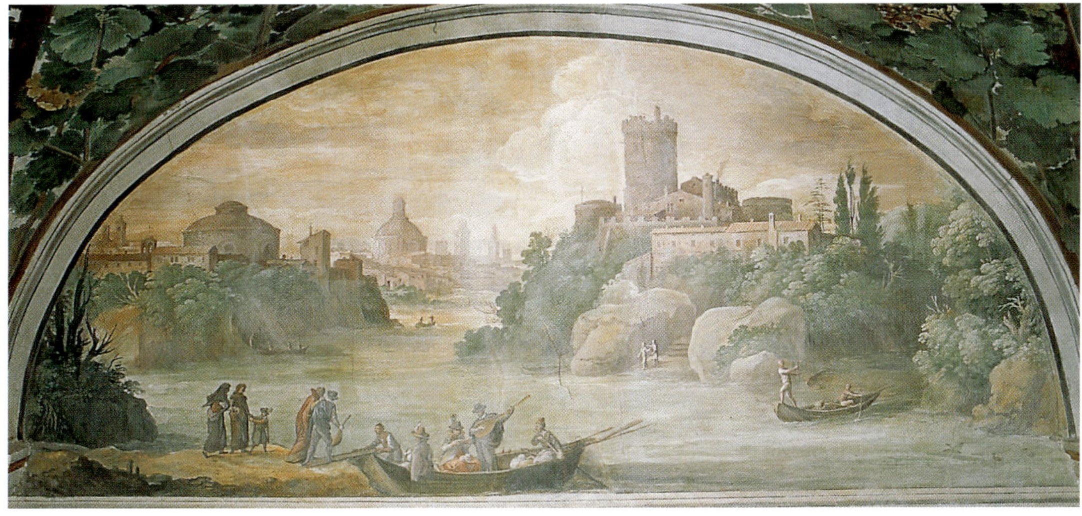

36. Paul Bril, *View with Boats on a River*. Rome, Palazzo
Pallavicini Rospigliosi, Casino del Patriarca Biondo.

have been reduced to achieve a more balanced whole. A comparison of these frescoes and Matthijs' landscapes in the friezes in the Torre dei Venti highlights the differences between the brothers' styles. Matthijs' complex constructions have been transformed into more natural compositions and softer colours.

In 1611 Paul was commissioned to paint frescoes for Cardinal Scipione Borghese (1576-1633),[95] the son of Paul V Borghese's sister. Born Scipione Caffarelli, he was adopted in 1605 and made a cardinal by his devoted uncle, whose name he subsequently bore. In 1611 Bril had painted a *Harbour View* on canvas for Paul V, with galleys displaying the Borghese family arms (fig. 35).[96] Scipione was another ardent patron of the arts and one of the most remarkable collectors of his day. He had numerous churches, palaces and villas built by the architect Flaminio Ponzio (1560-1613) and his Utrecht-born pupil Jan van Santen (c. 1550-1621), known in Italy as Giovanni Vasanzio.

In 1611 and 1612 Scipione engaged Guido Reni and Paul Bril to decorate a loggia in the Casino del Patriarca Biondo of the palace (now Palazzo Pallavicini Rospigliosi; no. VIII a; fig. 36).[97] This commission from such a prestigious patron and his association with the famous Reni attest to the esteem Bril enjoyed in those years.[98] Documents concerning the fees paid for this commission are still in the family archive. There are also a few drawings that Paul used as models for his landscapes.[99] He worked in close collaboration with Reni, who painted putti on vases of flowers, in the Casino (also known as Loggia della Pergola). The loggia was restored in 1996, yielding an abundance of new information.[100]

Interesting views have been expressed regarding the interpretation of the decoration of the Casino. Angela Negro (1996) draws a link between Scipione Borghese and Apollo, and relates certain features of the decoration to the sun god, such as the "golden" flowers (the marigold, for instance) on the south wall, among tame and nocturnal animals. The putti, too, look more playful.[101] Bril painted not only landscapes here, but also a pergola with vines and animals.[102] Though this is the only example that occurs in his *œuvre*, it is related to some extent to the genre his father specialised in and to his own earliest work, decorating musical instruments with flowers and animals. The pergolas with flowers and animals in the Second Loggia of Gregory XIII, attributed to Matthijs Bril, can also be seen as a forerunner of Paul's work. Birds and other animals are common motifs in Paul's paintings and frescoes.[103]

Under Scipione, aptly nicknamed "la delizia di Roma", the loggia was painted as an outdoor room.[104] It is no longer open. The *treillis* consists of ingeniously woven twigs and vine leaves, affording a glimpse of white summer clouds against a pale blue sky. The large birds in the openings – a peacock, a heron, a falcon, a turkey, a chicken and a cock – are remarkably lifelike, as are the smaller species, which include a hoopoe, parrots, sparrows and tits.

Bril painted landscapes in six lunettes, the first of which recalls the hunting landscape in Monterotondo.[105] It includes many of the same motifs: a gnarled tree in the centre extending up to the painted frame, hunters on horseback, their servants carrying lances and, in particular, frenzied hounds pursuing a deer. The following five lunettes are of a different calibre (fig. 36). The compositions are more horizontal, the colours less contrasting, and human activity more restrained. The landscapes –

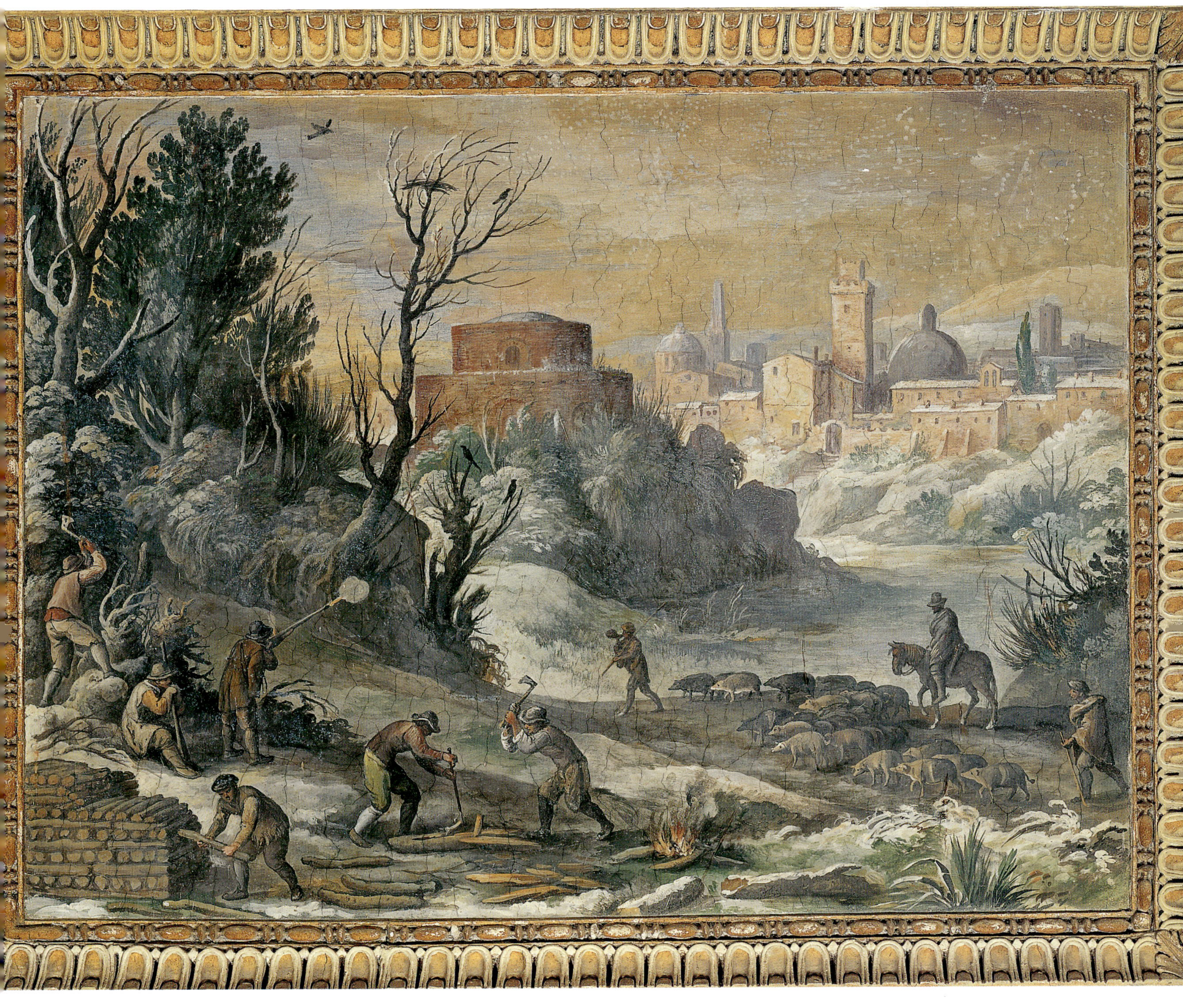

37. Paul Bril, *Winter*. Rome, Palazzo Pallavicini Rospigliosi,
Casino dell'Aurora.

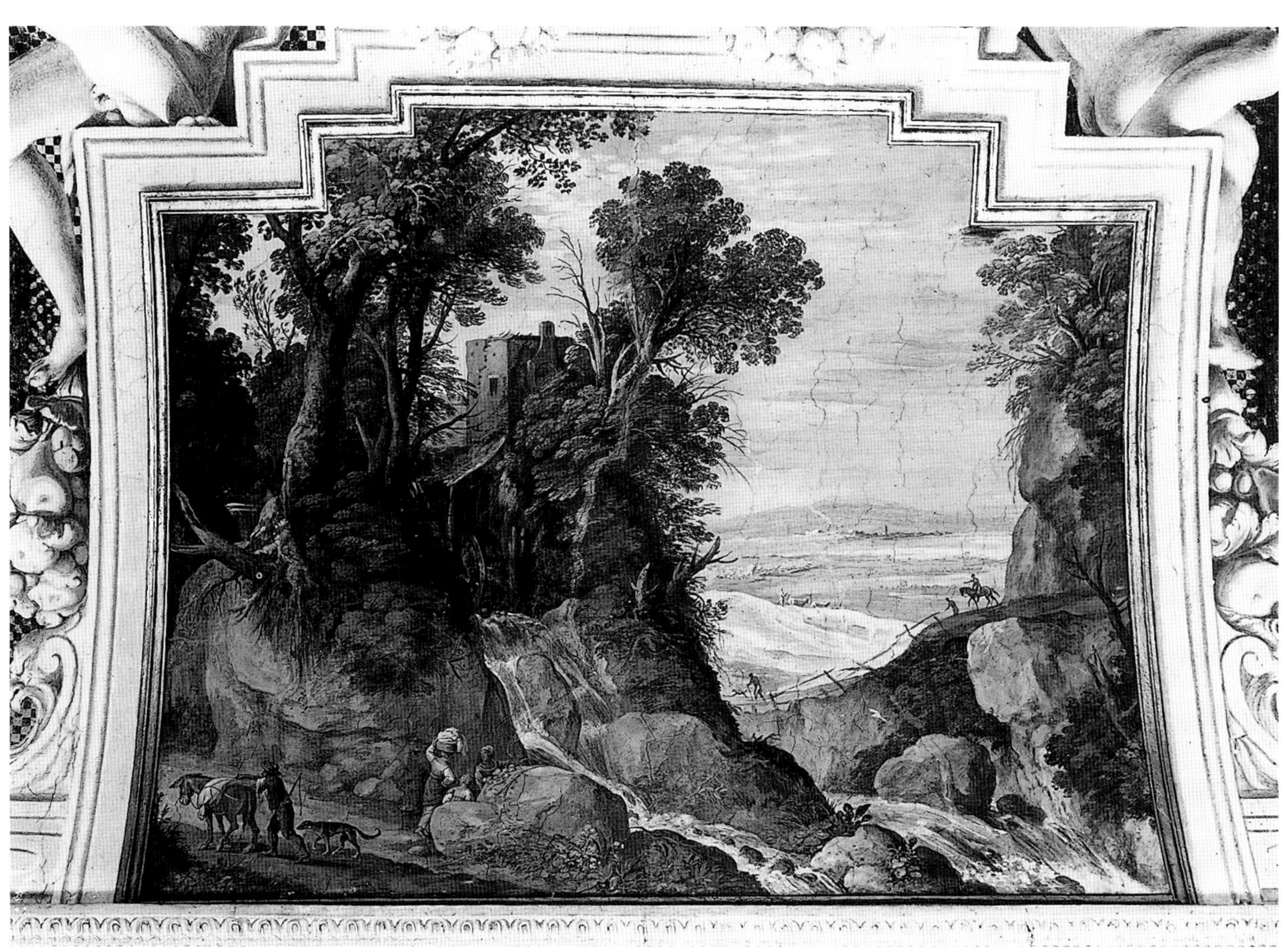

38. Paul Bril, *Rocky Landscape with a Bridge and Figures Walking*.
Rome, Casino Ludovisi, Stanza dei Paesi.

the most balanced of all in Bril's frescoes – mark the culmination of an evolution in the artist's style, which had first become discernible around 1600. [106] Landscapes of this kind had an immeasurable impact on the development of Romanist landscape painting. All Bril's landscapes are characterised by a wealth of detail, which distinguishes his work from that of Italian painters such as Annibale Carracci.

The landscapes in the loggia show people in a boat making music, while others fish in the background. We see men lighting a fire on a beach, travellers making their way through the countryside, and a herdsman driving his animals. But here, they are details in far grander, more majestic landscapes. The architecture, the water, the sky, and the subtle colouring of the foliage are rendered with superb finesse. [107]

The remaining seven lunettes, also depicting landscapes, are clearly not from Bril's hand. [108] However, a drawing by Bril, which is closely related to other designs for these frescoes, may have served as the model for one of them. [109] Now restored to their former glory, these frescoes are among the most beautiful in Bril's entire *œuvre*. Shortly afterwards, Bril received another commission for landscapes, once again in collaboration with Guido Reni and Antonio Tempesta. They were to decorate Cardinal Borghese's second Casino (dell'Aurora), built by Jan van Santen after a design by Carlo Maderno. The Casino belonged to the same palace and was graced with a hanging garden (no. VIII b; fig. 37). It is named after Reni's celebrated fresco of *Aurora* on the vault, which, according to archive documents, was painted between 1613 and 1616. [110]

The wall on the garden side of the long, narrow loggia was originally open. On the wall opposite the entrance, where the light falls in, Bril painted *Spring* and *Summer*. On the darker wall facing it he painted *Winter* opposite *Spring* and *Autumn* opposite *Summer*. The drawings for the project have survived. Bril illustrated in great detail the activities associated with each of the seasons. In the winter landscape the cold is almost palpable and visible in the dark, snowy sky, while languid sunshine and freshly mown hay conjure up the delights of summer. Like Bril's works in the other Casino, these landscapes in 'frames' contain a wealth of detail in Bril's delicate style. Once again, as the English painter Norgate observed, he alternated light and dark to correspond with foreground and distance. [111]

Now advanced in years, Bril was to climb the scaffolding once more to paint what is believed to have been his last fresco. On 15 February 1621, following the election on 9 February of Alessandro Ludovisi (Gregory XV) as the successor of Pope Paul V, Gregory's favoured nephew Ludovico (1595-1632) was made a cardinal. In the same year, Ludovico acquired the vineyard near the Porta Pinciana. He commissioned Guercino (Giovan Francesco Barbieri, 1591-1666) to paint an *Aurora* on the vault of the hall on the ground floor of the Casino Ludovisi. For the four landscapes in a smaller adjoining room he engaged the most distinguished landscape painters in Rome: Guercino, Domenichino (Domenico Zampieri, 1581-1641), Giovan Battista Viola (1576-1622) and the elderly Bril. These four landscapes, all featuring water and framed in gilt stucco, are totally different in style (no. II; fig. 38). [112] Bril's is the first one sees on entering the room, its prominent position possibly a tribute to the master. He created a landscape which incorporates all the ingredients of his standard repertoire, now infused with new life. He paraphrased his theme, guiding the observer past trees growing on rocks, a waterwheel, a man with a donkey and a dog, a woman carrying a washing basket on her head, a rickety bridge, a man on horseback, and a sparkling river, into a magnificent low, blue vista with the outlines of a city in the distance. Alongside his young colleagues, Bril took this final opportunity to demonstrate his "gran prova del valor suo" and show that his landscapes were worthy of the most celebrated figure painters in Rome. As a Northerner, he was certainly their match. Bril's landscapes had gradually evolved into more classical and natural compositions, which were admired both in Italy and beyond. They influenced Roman landscape painting of the late sixteenth and early seventeenth centuries and, along with the prints made after them, were famed throughout Europe.

1) Mayer 1910, p. 7 note 1 has reservations about the attribution to Matthijs; Baer 1930, p. 27 attributes the work to Bril on the grounds of an engraving by Simon Frisius after Matthijs. Considering the prevalence of architecture and the way Matthijs painted moonlight, Baer sees clear similarities with Frisius' engraving. See also Vaes 1928, pp. 295-305 and Hahn 1961, pp. 308-323. The frescoes are extremely faded and in poor condition.

2) Mayer 1910, pp. 15 and 16, no. 5 and fig. V. According to Mayer, this sheet bears the signature "Matthias Bril inventor H. Hondius excudit". The print belongs to a series of five and is in the Print Room of the Rijksmuseum in Amsterdam.

3) Vaes 1928, p. 310. He uses the room's former name (Camera dei Fuochi), and describes the landscapes as the first complete autograph compositions.

4) In general, Paul was better at painting animals than Matthijs, but in this instance it is impossible to discern whether Paul assisted Matthijs. Nor is it certain that Paul had arrived in Rome by the time Matthijs executed these paintings.

5) Hess 1936, pp. 161-166; Courtright 1990, p. 584; Negro 1996, p. 52.

6) For more examples, see Negro 1996, pp. 49-52, figs. 31-40. Negro, p. 51, mentions Pliny's *De re rustica* (L. III,5) as a model for the pergola. In the light of Christian symbolism, the pergola could allude to Earthly Paradise or Paradise in general.

7) Van Mander 1604, fol. 291v.

8) Ciappi 1596 (Biblioteca Apostolica Vaticana, BAV), pp. 17-21, describes the solemn procession and the firing of artillery on the Castel Sant' Angelo, just as Matthijs painted them.

9) The procession is unaccountably illustrated in reverse sequence, heading towards Santa Maria in Campo Marzio.

10) See Louisa Wood Ruby's essay in this volume, fig. 40.

11) See, for example, Mancinelli 1980, pp. 13-22, who distinguishes the work of two different artists in the landscapes, and Courtright 1990, pp. 565-566, for the attribution to Matthijs based on documents. *Ibid.* on style, pp. 20-25, p. 225 note 100.

12) Courtright 1990, pp. 109-121.

13) Vitruvius 1991, *De Architectura libri decem*, p. 333 and Pliny 1961, *Naturalis Historia*, XXXV, pp. 116-117.

14) Opinions differ regarding Paul Bril's contribution to these frescoes. Both Van Mander and Baglione say that both brothers were working in the pope's loggia and galleries, but offer no further details. Mayer 1910, pp. 19-20 doubts that Paul ever collaborated with Matthijs. Baer 1930, p. 23 does see a relationship between Paul's early work and Matthijs'. Faggin (1965, p. 22) regards Paul Bril's Leiden drawing as evidence of his collaboration in this seascape. Courtright (1990, p. 252 note 100) considers Matthijs the author of all the landscapes in the tower.

15) On the technique of fresco painting, see, for instance, Cennini, ed. Daniel V. Thompson jr., 1933, pp. 42-57; Bensi 1990, pp. 86-90.

16) See New York 1968, pp. 19-24 and 45. Procacci 1975, pp. 7-33.

17) On Paul Bril's techniques, see Angela Negro's essay in this volume.

18) The paint was coarse because sand was mixed into it, causing it to carbonise far more slowly than a *buon fresco*. As the paint dried more slowly, artists could work with it for a longer time.

19) See Mancinelli 1980, p. 28 and Courtright 1990, pp. 513-561.

20) On the restoration, see Mignosi Tantillo 1982, pp. 124-125; Pagliara 1980, pp. 235-278; and Marchetti 1984, pp. 185-198.

21) Though it is unknown which paintings were executed first.

22) Matthijs and Paul Bril also painted a winter

landscape in the Galleria delle Carte Geografiche. In the snowy landscape on the left a man under a thatched roof warms himself at a fire. See no. VI m.16.

23) Washington, National Gallery of Art, inv. no. B.26.773, as Paul Bril. See Louisa Wood Ruby's essay in this volume, p. 74, fig. 42.

24) Louvre, Département des Arts Graphiques, inv. no. 1812 and 1870. Published in *Inventaire Général des Dessins Italiens*, III, *Dessins Toscans*, I, 1988, nos. 432 and 433.

25) See Marchetti 1984, p. 194.

26) Mignosi Tantillo 1982, p. 124. Tantillo was in charge of the restoration in Monterotondo in 1978-81, when the signed and dated frescoes were discovered. Paul Bril used this signature in several drawings and paintings.

27) Van Mander 1604, fol. 291v; Baglione 1649, ed. 1924 (reprint 1986), vol. 1, p. 296; Pinelli in Gambi, Pinelli 1994, vol. 1, pp. 64-65. Limentani Virdis 1999, pp. 67-72. See for all figs. of the maps Gambi, Pinelli 1997.

28) See, for example, Van Mander 1604, fol. 291v; Baglione 1649, ed. 1924 (reprint 1986), vol. I, p. 296; Baldinucci 1681-1738, vol. 3, p. 26; Hoogewerff 1912, p. 240; Baer 1930, p. 23; Courtright 1990, pp. 22-24, note 100; Gambi, Pinelli 1994, vol. I, p. 24; Limentani Virdis 1999, pp. 67-72. See for all figs. Gambi, Pinelli 1997.

29) For other drawings by Nebbia, which Bril used as examples for these landscapes, see Gambi, Pinelli 1997, p. 214, fig. 2; p. 215, figs. 3 and 4; p. 220, fig. 7.

30) Baldinucci 1681-1738, vol. 3, p. 26.

31) See in this volume Hendriks, *The Lives...*, pp. 17-18, and note 19 and 20.

32) For a comprehensive overview of all these works, see Madonna 1993, and the small catalogue, *Roma di Sisto V. Arte, architettura e città fra Rinascimento e Barocco*, published for the major exhibition (Rome, Palazzo Venezia, 22 January to 30 April 1993).

33) See Mandel 1991, p. 26ff.

34) The iconographic message was more important, see Ostrow 1987, pp. 382-283. Zuccari 1993, p. 643.

35) Zuccari 1992, p. 16 and fig. VI.

36) For more information, see Schwager 1961, pp. 324-354, and Ost 1978, pp. 279-303; Ostrow 1987, especially on the iconography of the decoration of the Sistine Chapel, and Zuccari 1992, pp. 33-46.

37) Baglione 1649, ed. 1924 (reprint 1986), vol. 1, p. 296; Mayer 1910, pp. 48-51; Baer 1930, pp. 36-40; Zuccari 1992, p. 16.

38) The lunettes are approximately 1.70 m wide and 0.80 m high.

39) The landscapes were restored in 1870, see Baer 1930, p. 37. The foliage of the tree in lunette 6 was evidently completely overpainted.

40) The lunette is the same shape as the windows of Roman baths.

41) Around 1625 Norgate described a conversation with Paul Bril, who explained how he made his landscapes *"caminare"* (wanderings), referring to his use of different colours for different planes. For a verbatim account, see Pijl 1995, p. 39.

42) See Louisa Wood Ruby's essay in this volume, for a detailed description of this drawing.

43) Ruby 1999, the tree on the bank seems to have been based on a drawing by Matthijs in Berlin, see p. 260, fig. 18.

44) Zuccari 1992, p. 16: "Sia il tema del paesaggio che l'indentità dei personaggi non sono casuali, ma rappresentano l'ambiente e la Chiesa degli umili posta in perfetto accordo con quella dei Dottori".

45) See Zuccari 1992, pp. 16, 21-24, figs. VI, VII, VIII.

46) See, for instance, Mandel 1991 and 1994; Mandel in Madonna 1993, pp. 94-103, no. 4; Torchetti in *ibid.*, pp. 103-105, no. 4a, on Scala Pontificale; Zuccari 1992.

47) The frescoes were in poor condition by the seventeenth century. They were restored in 1691-1700 and 1831-46. The most recent restorations were carried out in 1961-69 (see Madonna 1993, p. 94).

48) Torchetti in Madonna 1993, pp. 103-105, no. 4a.

49) See Louisa Wood Ruby's essay in this volume and Ruby 1999, pp. 77-78, fig. 4. These drawings bear a certain resemblance to one of the imaginary landscapes in the Torre dei Venti, see fig. 16.

50) Mandel in Madonna 1993, p. 95. In 1589-90 Sixtus V commissioned his regular team of painters to decorate not only the Lateran Palace but also the Vatican Library, the Scala Santa and Villa Montalto.

51) Mayer 1910, pp. 23-26, refers to 28 lunettes, six of which (including lunette 13) he considers different from the others. Baer 1930, p. 95 identifies the same six lunettes as Mayer (nos. XVII-XXII).

52) For different assistants, see nos. V a, V b and V c.

53) Van Mandel, 1994, appendix 1. The names of the other landscape painters are unknown.

54) See Barroero in Pietrangeli 1991, pp. 217-221. Nothing more is said about the attribution of the landscapes to Bril.

55) Baglione 1649, ed. 1924 (reprint 1986), vol. 1, p. 173; Massimo 1836, p. 42; Epp in Madonna 1993, pp. 152-153 and Torchetti in Madonna 1993, p. 153, floor plan of the villa on pp. 154-155. From the descriptions by Massimo, Epp and Torchetti, it is impossible to say for certain

that these landscapes were painted in lunettes.

56) Villa Montalto was demolished in the 1870s. Thanks to the detailed descriptions given by its last owner, Principe Vittorio Massimo, we know what the paintings looked like. See Massimo 1836.

57) Ogden, Ogden 1955, p. 10.

58) Zuccari 1992, pp. 106-121.

59) See Baglione 1649, ed. 1924 (reprint 1986), vol. 1, p. 296. Scavizzi 1959, pp. 196-200; idem, 1960, pp. 111-122 .

60) Overlaps between the *giornate* can be seen quite easily, sometimes from a thick edge, sometimes from differences in colour. The restoration might help us to understand how Nebbia and Guerra divided the work among to the artists involved in the project.

61) See Morello in Madonna 1993, p. 349.

62) The building was originally open; doors and windows were added much later. All the frescoes will be restored as part of a major programme launched in the summer of 2002.

63) Ippoliti in Pietrangeli 1991, p. 121.

64) See Barroero in Madonna 1993, pp. 127-135. Bril's share was limited, according to Baglione, who mentions only two scenes of Jonah.

65) Barroero in Madonna 1993, p. 127.

66) See Louisa Wood Ruby's essay in this volume on both drawings.

67) Stefani in Madonna 1993, pp. 30-31 and app. I, fig. 34. The print is in the Biblioteca Angelica in Rome.

68) Norgate cited in Hardie's edition of 1919, p. 48, describing "Rowland Savery" as an excellent artist in this genre.

69) See Zuccari 1992, pp. 47-61, Zuccari in Madonna 1993, pp. 59-76 and Böck 1988. The landscapes in the small hall behind the library, which are often attributed to Paul Bril, are in fact the work of an unidentified pupil.

70) The landscape in the background has been badly damaged by moisture and may have been overpainted.

71) Cosmelli in Madonna 1993, pp. 92-93. The landscapes were restored in 1999.

72) Zuccari 1992, p. 16.

73) Baglione 1649, ed. 1924 (reprint 1986), vol. 1, p. 296.

74) *Ibid.*

75) Van Mander 1604, fol. 292r. Testa in Cappelletti, Testa 1994, pp. 15-16, note 27 gives the full text of the contract.

76) Testa in Cappelletti, Testa 1994, p. 20 note 31.

77) Dirt on the frescoes hides much of the original bright colouring.

78) The seascape in Palazzo Caetani is on the short wall on the left, opposite the fireplace.

79) See Testa in Cappelletti, Testa 1994, pp. 16-17 for an explanation about this style of decorating.

80) Baglione 1649, ed. 1924 (reprint 1986), vol. 1, p. 296 mentions eight landscapes by Bril. See also Macioce 1990, pp. 130-131.

81) On De Vos and Sadeler, see Jones 1993, pp. 131-133 and figs. 35 and 36.

82) On Brueghel's stay in Rome, see Bedoni 1983, pp. 29-88.

83) See Jones 1993, Brueghel figs. 33, 34, Jan and Raphael Sadeler figs. 35, 36 and Bril figs. 68 and 69.

84) See Macioce 1990, pp. 111-112. The measurements estimated on site are approximately 12 m wide and 4 m high.

85) Macioce 1990, pp. 187-193.

86) Macioce 1990, p. 192. The huge tree is said to symbolise Fidelity and Religion.

87) Martin 1990, p. 94, has identified all the monasteries.

88) Van Mander 1604, fol. 292r. See Cappelletti, Testa 1994, pp. 97-98, 434-440, figs. 96-99b; Pijl 1995, p. 39, note 11 and fig. 3 and Ruby 1999, p. 36 and notes 248 and 249.

89) Baglione 1649, ed. 1924 (reprint 1986), vol. 1, p. 296 and Baer 1930, p. 49 note 68, pp. 91 and 95.

90) Van Mander 1604, fol. 292r. Baer 1930, p. 61, who suggests that Balthasar Lauwers (Antwerp 1578-1643/45) was employed in Bril's workshop in the 1590s and may have assisted Bril in these rooms.

91) For a similar composition, see, for example, the coastal landscape, oil on canvas, 86 x 116 cm, inv. 1890 no. 1052 at the Uffizi in Florence. Mayer 1910, fig. XXXVIb and Berger 1993, p. 211 as a copy after Bril. Pijl (by e-mail of 28 August 2002) is in no doubt that the canvas, executed only in 1617 for Carlo de' Medici, is autograph.

92) See, for example, Ruby 1999, p. 53 on the way these artists influenced one another, a view I support without any reservation. Mancini 1621 (ed. 1956-57), vol. 2, p. XVI names Bril, Carracci and Domenichino, among others, as the most important landscape painters of their time.

93) For Mancini's manuscript, see BAV, Barb. Lat. 4315, fol. 127v.

94) Rome, Galleria Doria Pamphilj, oil on canvas, 122 x 230 cm. See fig. 5, p. 41 in *I capolavori della Collezione Doria Pamphilj da Tiziano a Velázquez*, Milan 1996. Carracci's landscape belongs to a series of six lunettes commissioned for the chapel of Pietro Aldobrandini's palace on the Corso in 1603-04.

95) See, for instance, Baglione 1649, ed. 1924 (reprint 1986), vol. 1, p. 296, Mayer 1910, pp. 46-48.

96) The painting is in the Pinacoteca of the Galleria Borghese, inv. 354.

97) For detailed information about this Casino,

see Negro 1996 and Angela Negro's essay in this volume.

98) The fees paid to the three artists show that the work and/or the type of work done here by Reni and Tempesta was more lucrative, see note 110.

99) For the payments made to Bril, see Negro 1996, p. 25 note 47 and p. 49. For the drawings, see Louisa Wood Ruby's essay in this volume and Ruby 1999.

100) See Angela Negro's essay in this volume and Negro 1996.

101) Negro 1996, pp. 113-128.

102) Mancini 1621, BAV, Barb. Lat. 4315, fol. 127v: "…in particulare in alcuni animali condotti à fresco, con grandiss. fine, e senza stento".

103) See, for example, Bril's cranes in the Sala Clementina and the ducks, geese and herons depicted in the various hunting scenes.

104) Hibbard 1964, p. 164.

105) There are five large lunettes on the inside wall and a small one on the wall opposite the door.

106) Blankert 1978, pp. 49-56 and figs. 4 and 5. Ruby 1999, pp. 53-58.

107) When studying the frescoes from the scaffolding during the restoration of 1996, I was surprised by the tiny details in Bril's figures, gestures, boats and trees. Everything is rendered minutely.

108) For the attribution of three of the lunettes (one of which is lost) to P.P. Bonzi, see Negro 1996, pp. 62-67 and in Angela Negro's essay in this volume.

109) See Louisa Wood Ruby's essay in this volume and fig. 51.

110) Archivio Segreto Vaticano (ASV), Archivio Borghese, 308, *Fabbricati in Roma*, Titoli diversi III, fol. 393r. On 24 September 1616 Reni received 247.54 *scudi* (200 *d'oro*) for Aurora and the sun chariot; Tempesta received the same amount for his two friezes, but for his four seasons Paul Bril received a mere 60 *scudi*. For a brief description of the Casino, see Giovanna A. Buffalini, *Il Casino dell'Aurora Pallavicini. Percorsi, Immagine, Riflessioni*, Rome 1985.

111) Pijl 1995, p. 39 and note 14, see also notes 41 and 68 above.

112) Felici 1952, see figs. XVb and XVId. However, Felici's attribution of the landscapes is incorrect: the work he attributes to Bril is in fact by Domenichino, and the fresco he attributes to Domenichino is by Paul Bril.

Note: The roman numbers between brackets in the text refer to the numbering of the frescoes in the repertory.

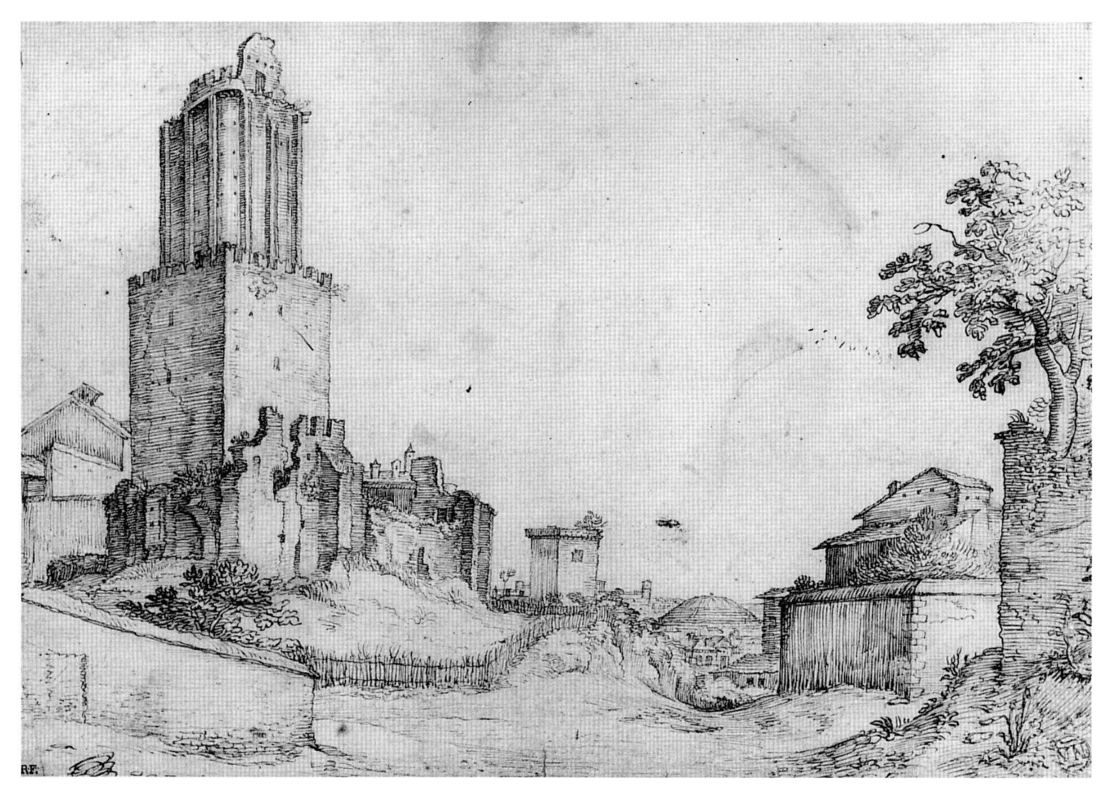

39. Matthijs Bril, *Torre delle Milizie*, pen and brown ink, 195 x 275 mm.
Paris, Musée du Louvre, Département des Arts Graphiques, Lugt 358,
inv. no. 20.959.

Before the Frescoes: the Drawings

Louisa Wood Ruby

Unlike frescoes, which are usually large, finished, public works, drawings are mostly smaller, more intimate, often unfinished thoughts, meant only to be seen by the artist who created them, a few students in the workshop, or a single collector. In studying an artist's drawings, we learn more about his or her ways of thinking and working, and thus achieve a greater understanding of the creative process. The following examination of a number of drawings for the Bril brothers' frescoes will illuminate aspects of the working methods of the Bril studio in Rome from the late 1580s until the late 1620s and thus broaden our knowledge and improve our understanding of their wall paintings.

While many drawings in print cabinets throughout the world have been attributed to Matthijs Bril, only very few are actually by him. The largest number by far are in the Louvre, in Paris, where the greatest concentration of drawings by Paul Bril can also be found.[1] It is from the drawings in the Louvre, as well as a number of studies for prints after Matthijs, that we can get the clearest idea of his *œuvre*, which consists not only of landscapes very close in style to those of his brother, but also of a series of topographical drawings of ruins.[2] The drawings of ruins (eight in the Louvre, one in the Institut Néerlandais in Paris, one in a private Dutch collection) are attributable to Matthijs based on the inscription on the back of one of them: "Dit is een van die besste desenne die Ick van Mathijs mijn broeder nae het leeven hebbe" (This is one of the best drawings from nature that I own by my brother Matthijs).[3] Only two of Matthijs' extant drawings of ruins were used as models for elements in his fresco work. A drawing in the Louvre of the *Torre delle Milizie* in Rome (fig. 39) was used for his fresco including the same subject on the second floor on the south wall of the first room (The Room with Topographical Views) of the Torre dei Venti from the early 1580s (fig. 14).[4] Although the angle of the tower is somewhat different, the acute detail with which the fresco is worked out clearly came from the knowledge gained from sitting in front of the monument with a sketch pad and transcribing what he saw directly onto paper.

Matthijs' drawing of the *Ponte Sant'Angelo and Castel Sant'Angelo* (fig. 40) is even further removed from the fresco it resembles than the previous drawing.[5] Again, the viewpoint in the fresco, in the Loggia of Gregory XIII (from the late 1570s) on the third floor of the Vatican (fig. 12), is slightly more from the left than in the drawing, so that only three arches of the Ponte Sant'Angelo are visible. The viewer's standpoint is also slightly closer in, and figures have been added on the left and in the boat in the water. That the fresco is from a later date than the drawing may be indicated by the fact that the cupola of St Peter's Basilica is higher, perhaps indicating more work had been done to finish it.[6] This also indicates that Matthijs looked at the cupola again when he was executing the fresco and updated his drawing accordingly, a sign of his desire to be accurate when depicting reality. [7]

Of Matthijs' landscape drawings, at least three appear to have been used as models for elements in his frescoes. One of these landscapes is in the Louvre (fig. 41), and is closely connected to the small fresco in the south-west corner of the first room on the top floor of the Torre dei Venti (The Room of the Old Testament Women) in between the cycles of Deborah and Jael and Ruth. [8] The drawing differs from the fresco in small ways: Matthijs finished off the ruined tower in the fresco, took out the bridge on the left side, and slightly altered the hut, water and boulder. Unfortunately, the fresco is in such bad condition that a complete list of comparisons is difficult to make. It is also possible that a few other drawings in the Louvre may have originally been used for the Torre dei Venti as well, although no corresponding frescoes have been found. [9] They are of a similar size and execution.

The second landscape drawing by Matthijs that served as a model for a fresco in the Torre dei Venti is in the Fitzwilliam Museum in Cambridge. [10] This drawing is a model for a fresco in the second room on the top floor (The Room of Tobias), and depicts *Raphael on his Journey to Claim Tobit's Money from Gabael*. [11] The fresco differs slightly from the drawing in the background and on the left side, omitting some bushes and adding figures that tell the story of Tobias. The drawing is done with a loose, free hand that is reminiscent of the penmanship in five other drawings with the same inscription in the same hand: "P. BRIL". [12] Neither the signature nor the drawings are by Paul, and all but one are most likely by Matthijs. [13] The inscription probably reflects the inclusion of these drawings in the same collection, where they were thought of as by Paul Bril. We know that Paul willed all of his and Matthijs' drawings to his son Ciriaco at his death, [14] so it is possibly Ciriaco's handwriting that mistakenly identifies them.

Another landscape drawing by Matthijs (with the same "P BRIL" inscription) is not closely linked to any particular fresco, but has a monument in it that is similar to monuments depicted in several of the frescoes in the Torre dei Venti. This drawing, in the National Gallery in Washington (fig. 42), does have a few similarities with another fresco in The Room of Tobias, entitled *Tobit Leaves the Feast Table to Remove the Body of the Murdered Jew*, and one on the first floor, in The Room of Apostles, entitled *Bartholomew Exorcises King Polymius' Lunatic Daughter*. [15] A monument somewhat like the one in this drawing can also be found in the first room of the frescoes in Monterotondo. [16]

These five drawings appear to represent the only extant drawings used as models for elements in frescoes by Matthijs, although it is also possible that more exist. More work must be done on Matthijs before this can be determined conclusively. [17] Since these five drawings are relatively finished works, it seems that Matthijs probably did not make them with the express purpose of using them in the frescoes. Nonetheless, it seems he did make use of them, almost as reference tools, once he had the fresco commissions in hand and was actively painting. Perhaps future research will uncover more drawings used in this way, or even a few whose sole purpose was as studies for frescoes. [18]

The earliest surviving drawing by Paul Bril is a seascape with a town in the distance

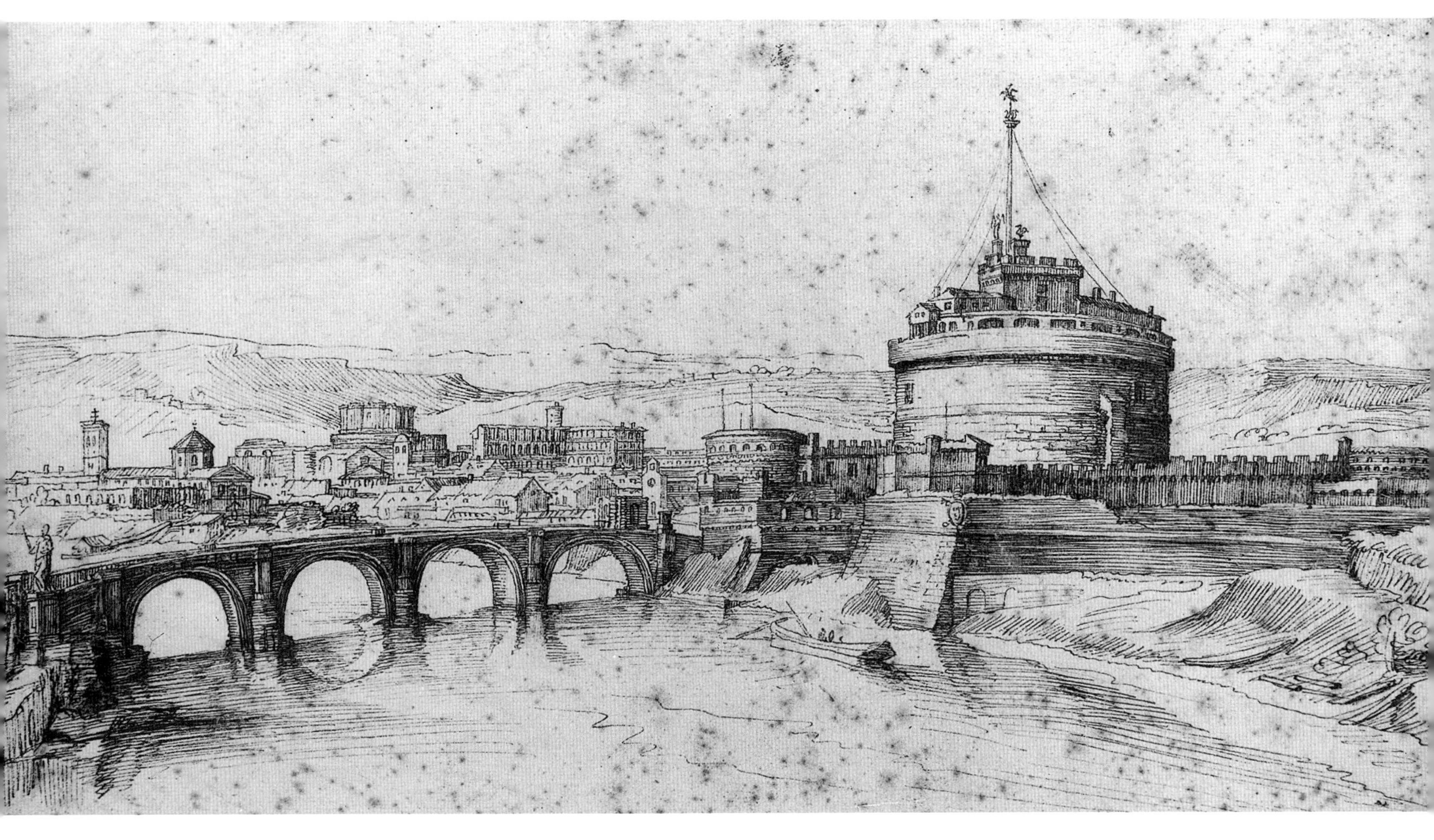

40. Matthijs Bril, *Ponte Sant'Angelo and Castel Sant'Angelo*, pen
and brown ink, 220 x 422 mm. Paris, Musée du Louvre, Département
des Arts Graphiques, Lugt 365, inv. no. 873.

in Leiden dated 1587 (fig. 43). [19] In many ways it is similar to one of the six frescoes in the Sacristy of the Sistine Chapel of Santa Maria Maggiore from 1585-90, (fig. 23), and has often been considered as a study for that fresco. Although it may have been the basis for that fresco, however, upon closer inspection it becomes clear that it is not an exact precursor, but rather an autonomous drawing used as a general model. The idea of a bay with ships is the same, and the boat, buildings and towering rock cliff are all similar. But these elements are rearranged in the fresco, creating a deep sense of space that is not evident in the drawing.

The drawing of *Jonah and the Whale* in the British Museum (fig. 44) is the earliest known sheet by Paul that can actually be classified as a study for a fresco. [20] This fresco, in the Scala Santa (fig. 28), is one of his most well-known and can be dated to the late 1580s. The drawing, dating from slightly earlier, is very closely connected to a drawing by Matthijs in the Louvre (fig. 45). [21] Although Paul's drawing has sometimes been considered merely a copy of either Matthijs' drawing or the fresco in the Scala Santa, the lively lines, skilful depiction of ship and sails, and presence of black chalk underdrawing belie any notion that this drawing is a copy. [22] On clos-

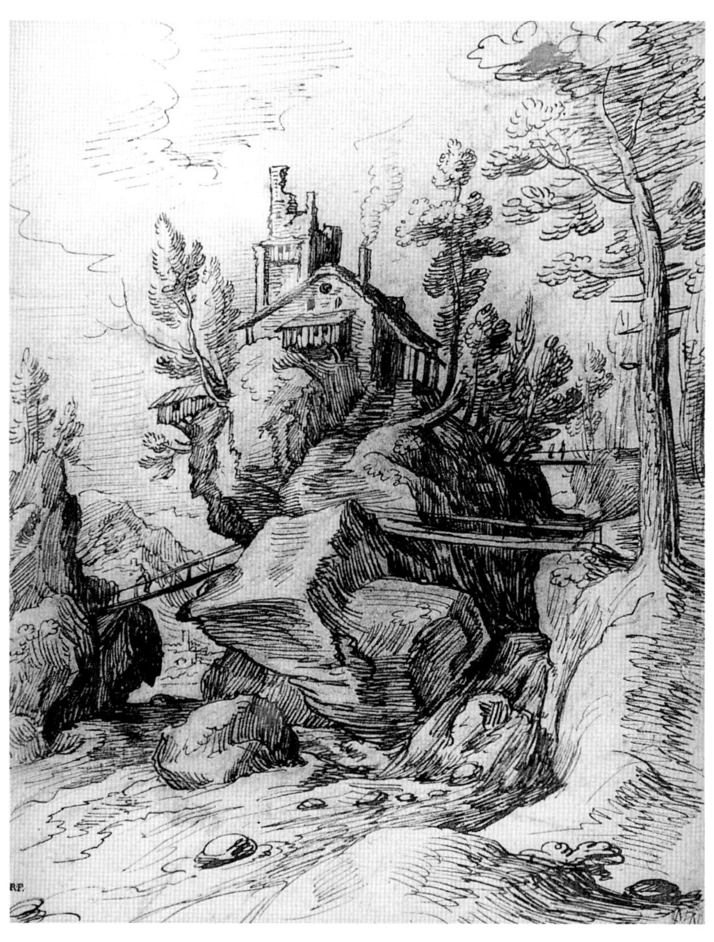

41. Matthijs Bril, *Cottage on a Hill*, pen and brown ink, black chalk, 265 x 205 mm. Paris, Musée du Louvre, Département des Arts Graphiques, Lugt 366, inv. no. 19.787.

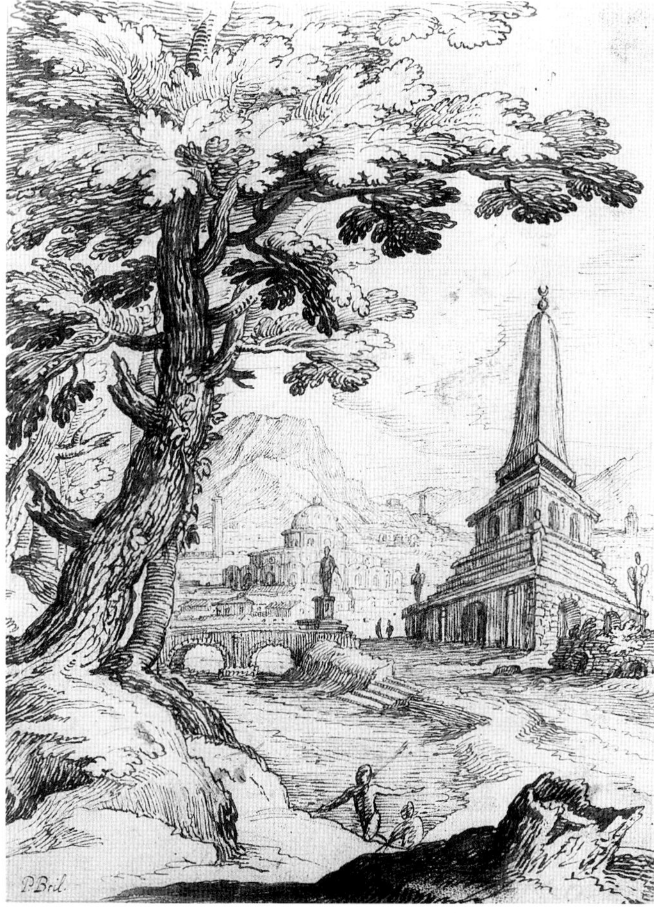

42. Matthijs Bril, *Landscape with Monument*, pen and brown ink over black chalk, 271 x 193 mm. Washington D.C., National Gallery of Art, inv. no. B 26.773.

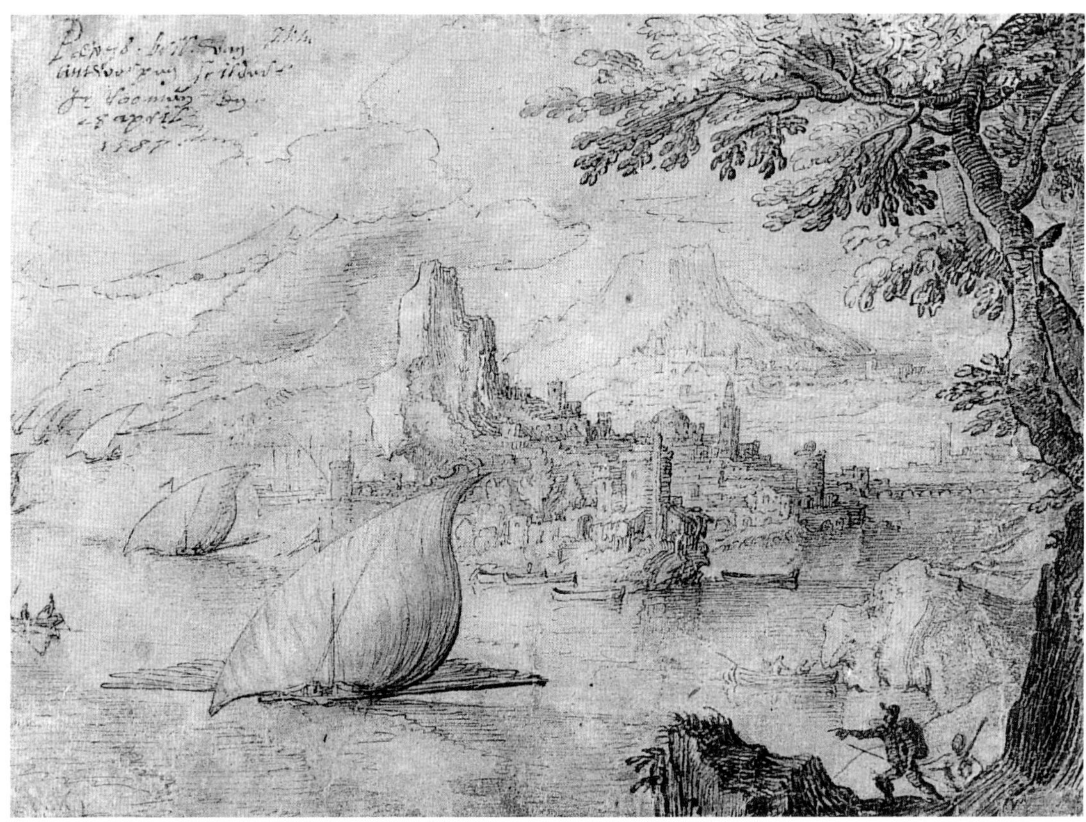

43. Paul Bril, *Bay with Galleys and a Town in the Distance*, pen, brown ink
and brown wash, touched up by a later hand in reddish-brown ink,
144 x 191 mm. Leiden, Prentenkabinet Universiteit Leiden, inv. no. AW 1001.

er inspection, it appears that Paul actually only used Matthijs' drawing as a spring-board. The latter is a fairly simple view of a ship on a stormy sea by the coast. Paul took this basic view, brought the boat in closer, enlarged it, added figures and a whale and thus changed Matthijs' seascape into the story of Jonah. [23] Although the lines in Paul's coastline are hesitant, this is not surprising, given that is where he followed Matthijs most closely. [24] Paul then used his own drawing as a study for the fresco of *Jonah and the Whale* in the Scala Santa. For the fresco, Paul changed the shape of the whale, added a number of ships and altered the relationship of the landscape elements in the background to each other as well as making them more prominent in relation to the ship and whale.

Although Paul executed numerous fresco series between 1590 and 1610, there are no extant drawn studies for any of these, nor any autonomous drawings that were used as models for them. The next frescoes for which there are extant studies are the extensive Palazzo Pallavicini Rospigliosi frescoes from 1611-13. By this time, Paul had undergone a transformation in his drawing style, from tightly executed moun-tainous landscapes with precipitous drops and dramatic lighting effects to a more relaxed, looser, more Italian style of draughtsmanship. This change is gradual from about 1606 on, when Bril first saw Annibale Carracci's Aldobrandini lunettes, and is fully reflected by the time he began work on the six extant studies for three of the ten Pallavicini Rospigliosi frescoes. These drawings are therefore quite different

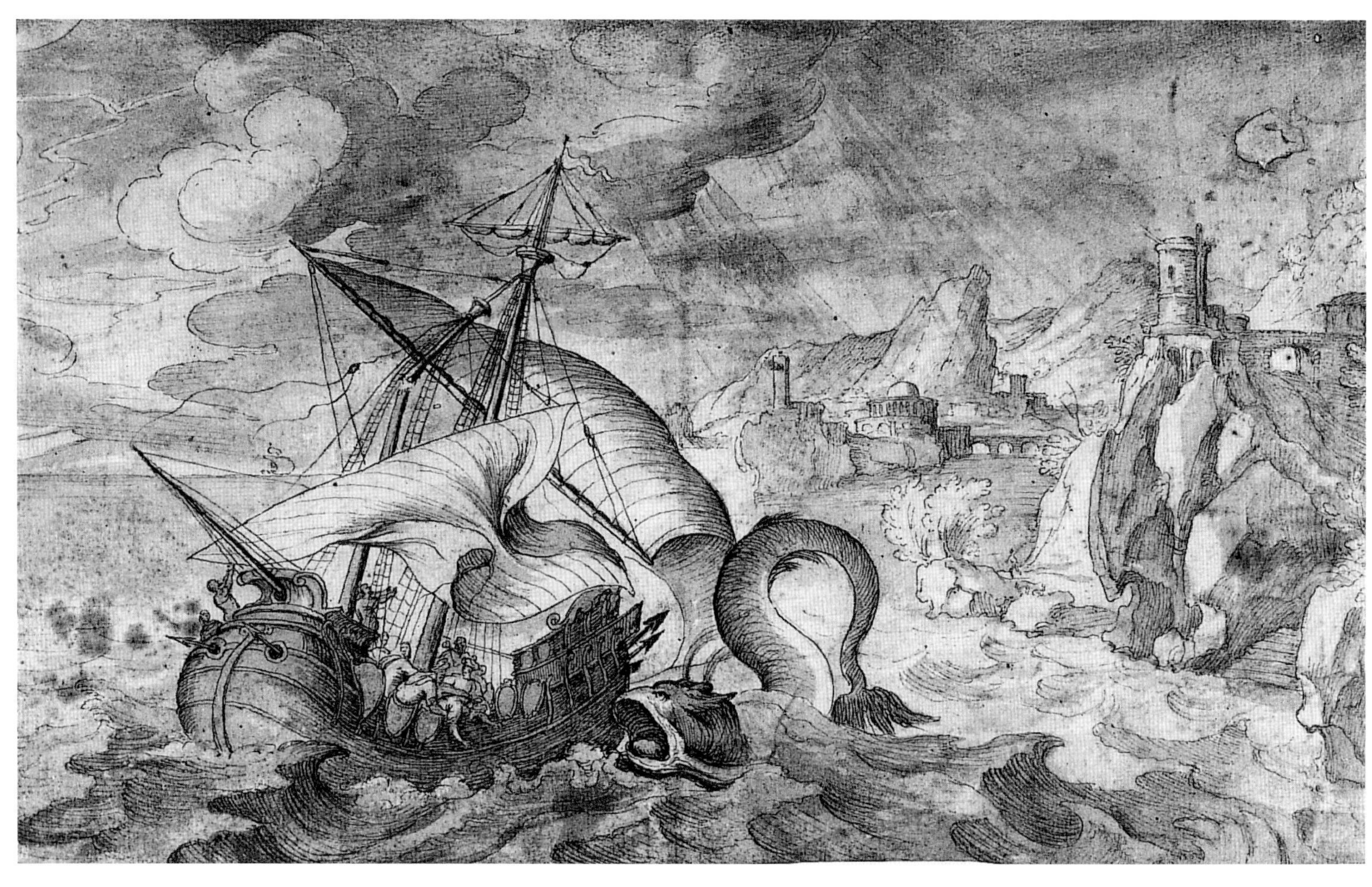

44. Paul Bril, *Jonah and the Whale*, pen and brown ink over traces
of black chalk, and brown and blue wash, 228 x 356 mm. London,
British Museum, inv. no. 5214-233.

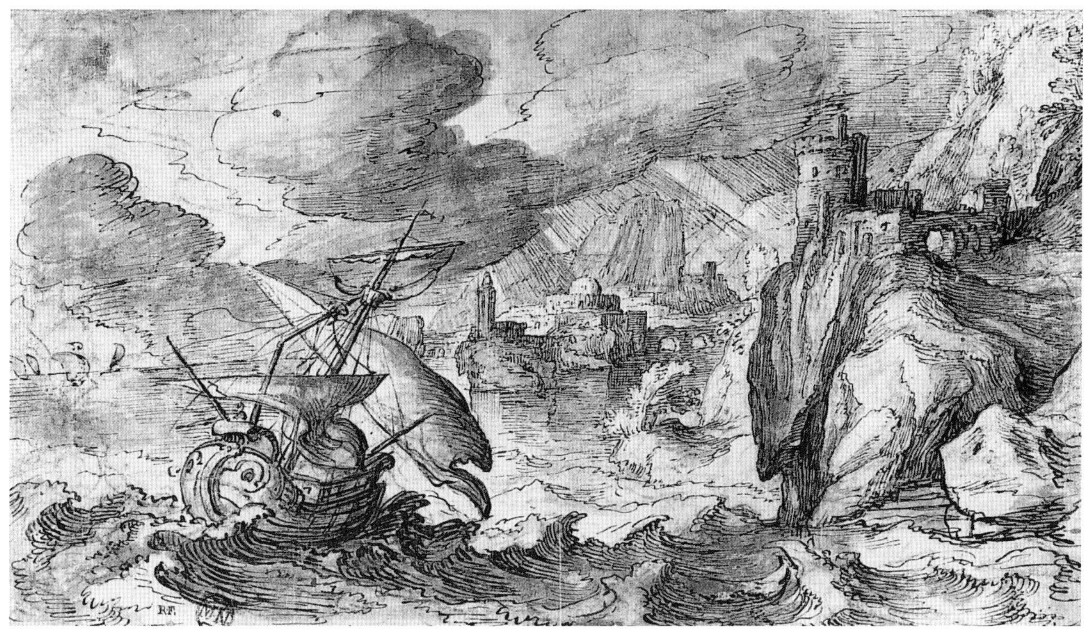

45. Matthijs Bril, *Tempest*, pen and brown ink, 163 x 279 mm. Paris, Musée
du Louvre, Département des Arts Graphiques, Lugt 355, inv. no. 19.819.

from the studies for the Scala Santa fresco or the early drawing in Leiden that
served as a precursor to one of the Santa Maria Maggiore frescoes. They are freely
sketched studies in which the general ideas are adumbrated and details are not
included. The outlining of the figures and landscapes is loose and assured, in stark
contrast to most of his earlier, more tightly controlled, highly finished drawings.
Although lights and darks are still contrasted against one another, there is less dis-
tinction between them, thus giving a serener, more overall tonal effect. This is
achieved for the most part with the use of brush and grey wash, materials that never
appeared in Matthijs' drawings and only began to be more significant in Paul's at
this later point in his career.[25]

Although the drawings appear to be rapidly executed first thoughts for the frescoes,
a number of them were actually second or third versions made for the same frescoes,
indicating that Paul was trying to work out the best design. Two drawings in the
Louvre (figs. 46 and 47) are both studies for the same fresco in the Casino del Patriarca Biondo (Loggia della Pergola).[26] Although the tighter execution and more elaborate detail might make one think that figure 47 was the final version of the composition, it lacks the lunette shape of figure 46 and is further from the fresco in several significant details, such as the trees and buildings. It is therefore more likely
that Paul executed this drawing first, perhaps as a finished sheet, and then made
figure 46 as a direct study for the fresco, using elements from the first sheet but fit-
ting them into a lunette shape, changing the buildings and the trees. For the fresco,
Paul seems to have reverted to the original figures found in figure 47.

Another drawing in the Louvre for a fresco in the Casino del Patriarca Biondo in the
Palazzo Pallavicini Rospigliosi also has the same arched top (fig. 48).[27] For the fresco (fig. 36), Paul widened the space between the buildings and added more build-

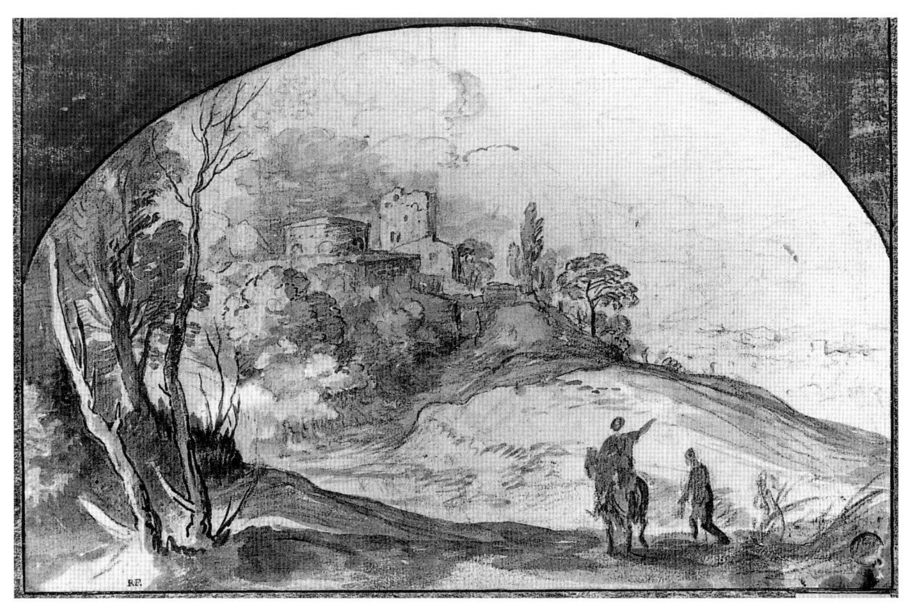

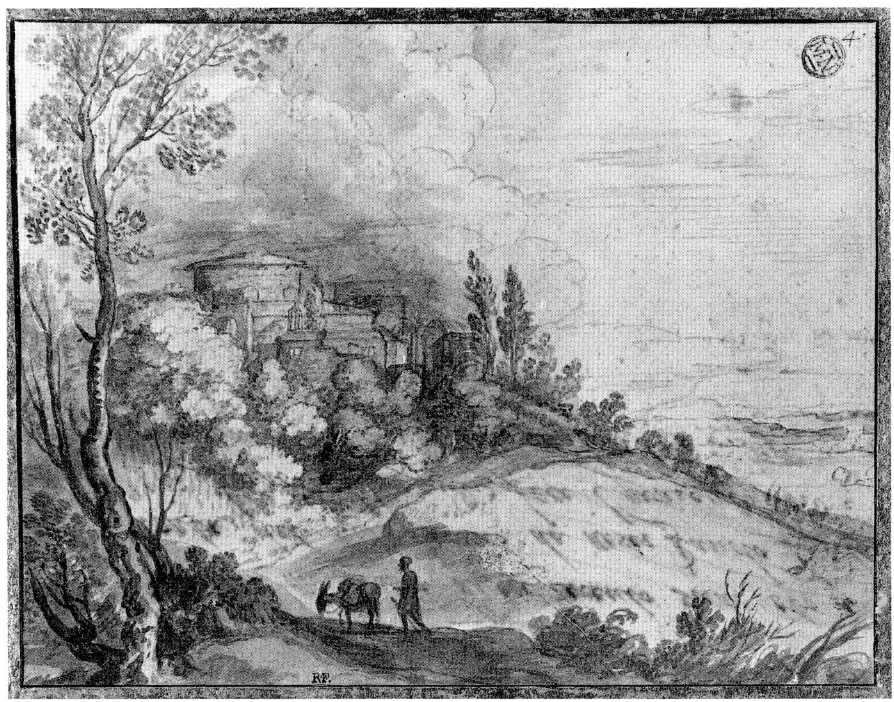

46. Paul Bril, *Landscape*, brush and black ink over black chalk,
180 x 270 mm. Paris, Musée du Louvre, Département des Arts Graphiques,
Lugt 414, inv. no. 19.810.

47. Paul Bril, *Landscape*, pen and black ink, 156 x 200 mm. Paris,
Musée du Louvre, Département des Arts Graphiques, Lugt 415, inv. no. 19.807.

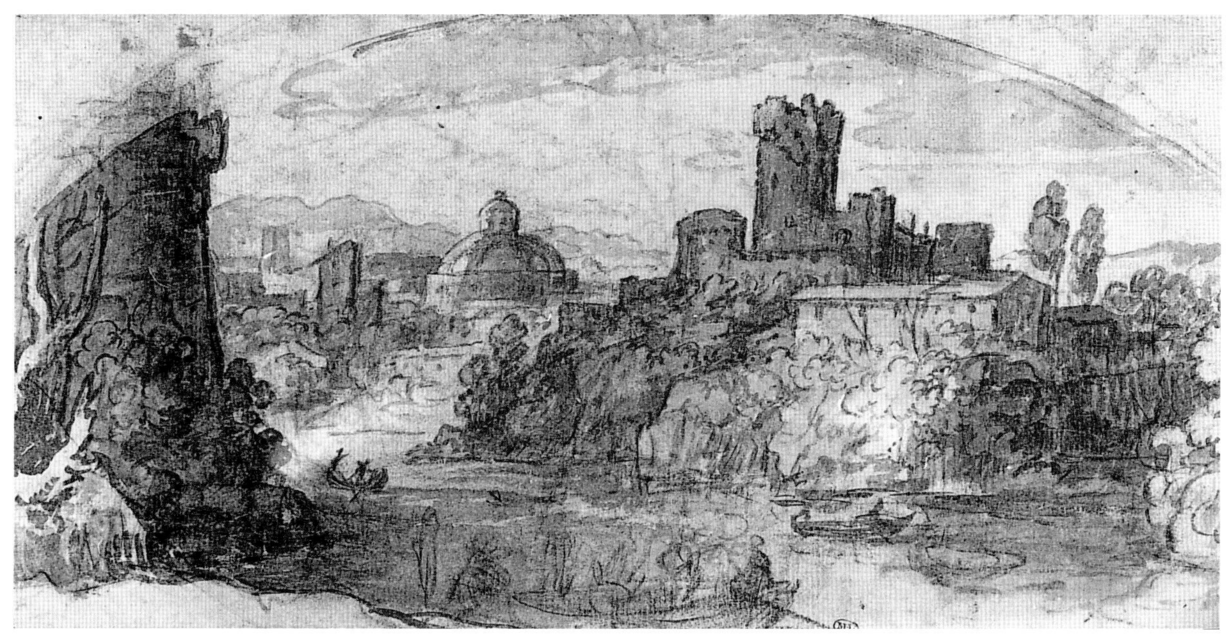

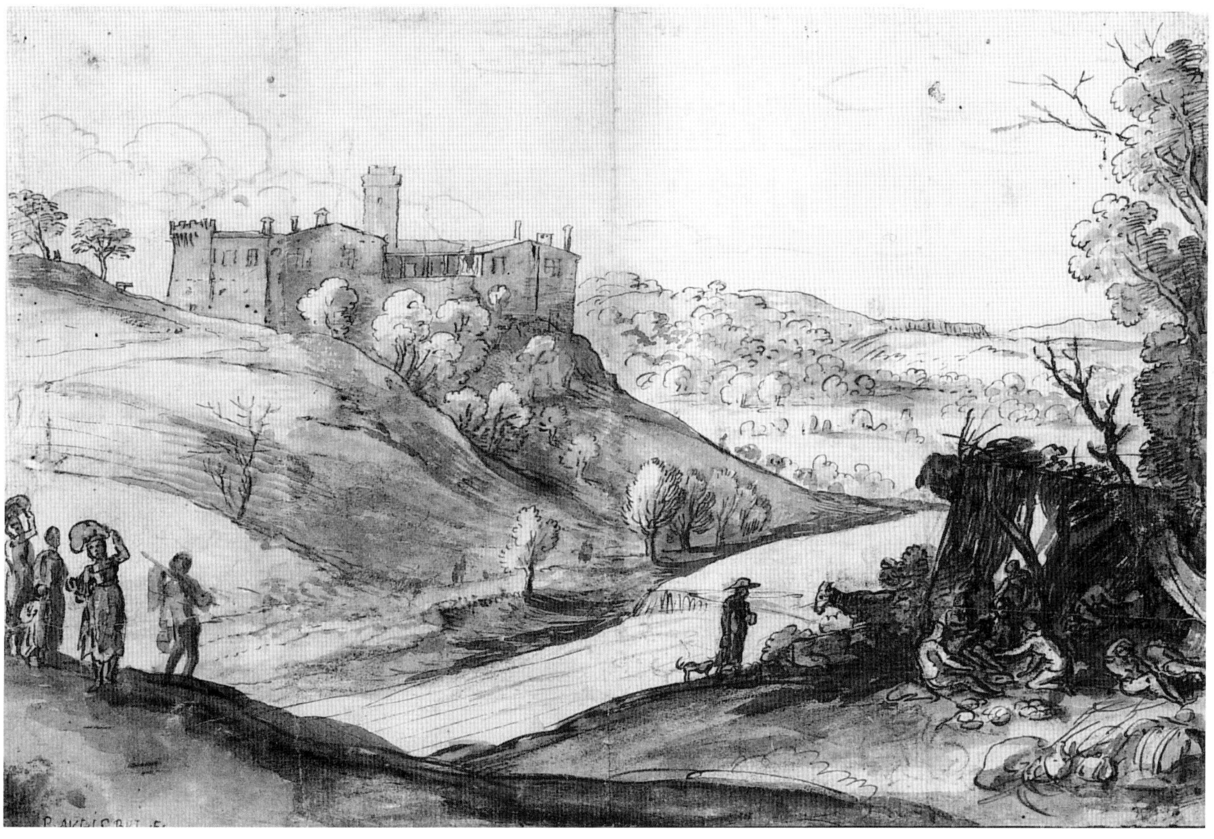

48. Paul Bril, *Landscape*, brush with black ink and wash over black chalk, 134 x 256 mm. Paris, Musée du Louvre, Département des Arts Graphiques, Lugt 413, inv. no. 21.739.

49. Paul Bril, *Landscape*, pen and brown ink and grey and black wash over black chalk, 187 x 272 mm. Munich, Staatliche Graphische Sammlung, inv. no. 1028.

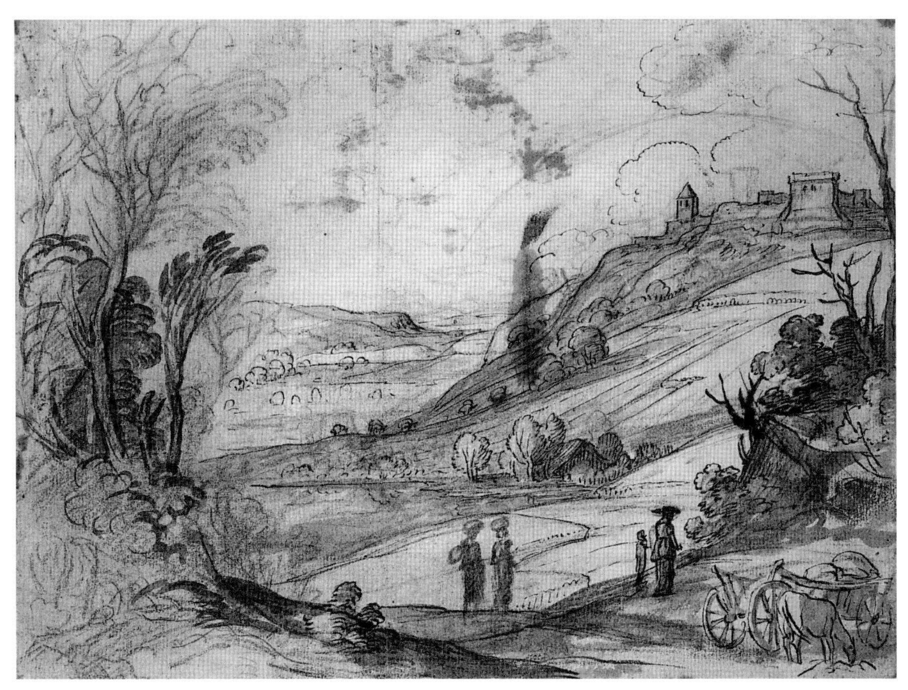

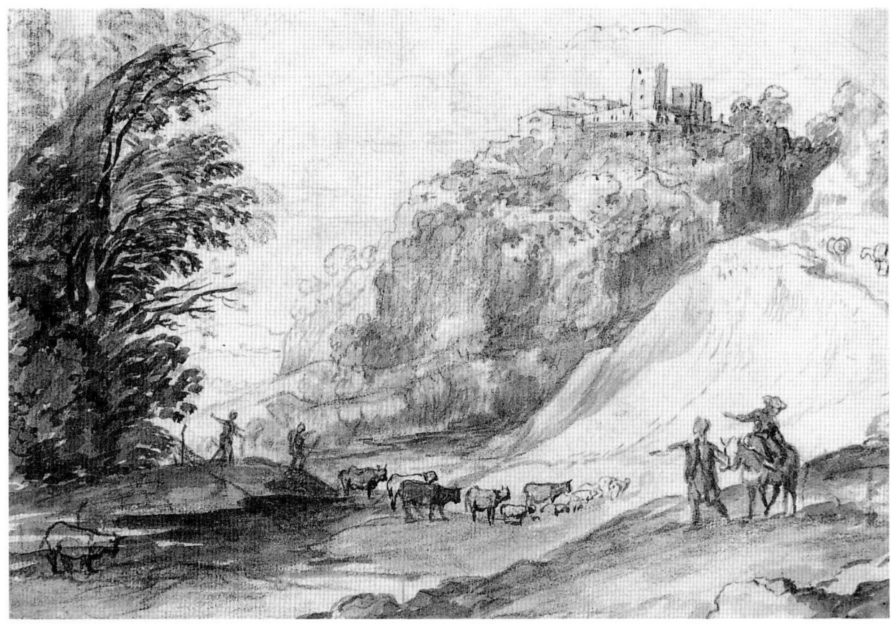

50. Paul Bril, *Landscape*, pen and brown ink over grey chalk
with grey wash and traces of brown wash and red paint,
205 x 277 mm. Dresden, Kupferstichkabinett, inv. no. C3779.

51. Paul Bril, *Landscape*, brush and grey wash over black chalk,
178 x 257 mm. The Netherlands, Art Market.

ings in the distance. He also removed the tower on the left and more carefully filled in the people entering the boat in the foreground. This sheet has been cut down at both the top and the bottom, but otherwise would be of similar dimensions to the other study with a lunette shape in the Louvre.

A drawing in Munich (fig. 49) is a study for one of the four season frescoes by Paul that accompany Reni's masterpiece, the *Aurora*.[28] In the fresco of *Summer*, there is no tower, the building is different and more distant, and the space is more open. In addition there are figures harvesting hay in the left middle ground; a child, not a man, in the left foreground; an extra man in the foreground; different figures under the shack; and rows of donkeys carrying hay in the right middle ground. The figures are very characteristic for Paul, quite similar to figures in his early series of season drawings in the Louvre.[29] The compositional layout of the Munich sheet was probably derived from a sheet now in Dresden (fig. 50), though in reverse.[30] The speed and energy of the brush stroke in the Dresden drawing indicate it was a quick study. He began this drawing with broad, quick wash strokes and then filled in the necessary details with pen and brown ink.

Although there is no extant fresco related to a drawing currently in the art market (fig. 51), the strong similarities of this drawing in both technique and compositional structure to the one in Dresden indicate that it is from the same time, c. 1613.[31] In addition, the use of brown and grey wash at the top left and black chalk at the top right suggest a lunette shape and thus indicate this drawing probably was a study for a fresco in the Palazzo Pallavicini Rospigliosi that was never executed. It is not clear why this was so – perhaps Paul made more studies than were necessary, either miscalculating the number of frescoes needed or perhaps to have a few to choose from. It is possible that he showed the patron, Cardinal Scipione Borghese, a number of the studies, and only a certain number were eventually accepted.

Other than these few drawings, no more studies for frescoes by Paul Bril are extant. The fact that drawings for frescoes were lost is attested by a note in the contract for frescoes executed for Cardinal Girolamo Mattei. The contract states that the frescoes must conform to the drawings by Paul Bril, indicating that such drawings did, in fact, exist: "…et la pittura deve essere conforme al disegnio dato da esso ms. Paolo…".[32] Not only does this show that studies for drawings have been lost, but it indicates that Bril was, at least occasionally, in the habit of making contract drawings for his patrons. Contract drawings could be used in two different ways: first, to suggest certain compositions to the client, then to serve as 'contracts', as here, so that the client could be assured of the works that he was going to get when the frescoes were finished. Since we have evidence that he made these drawings for Cardinal Mattei, the likelihood that the Pallavicini Rospigliosi drawings served the same purpose is much higher.

While it is unfortunate that no more of these contract drawings, or even studies for frescoes, survive, it is not surprising. The appreciation of the process of creating a work of art had not yet been fully developed, and as a result, studies were not handled with the same care by artists or collectors. It is also quite possible that neither Paul nor Matthijs made study drawings for their frescoes of the 1580s and 1590s. These early frescoes were executed with great haste, as part of a large number of frescoes being created for popes, who probably had little or no contact with the Brils. There was probably little time or need to create studies in such an atmosphere, where many of the frescoes were of similar subjects, so that they would have had a lot of practice in painting. Further study of the frescoes may even reveal preliminary drawings for the frescoes in the plaster layer. On the other hand, the Brils' use of autonomous drawings as models for frescoes reveals their highly practical natures. Finished drawings could serve not only as models for frescoes, but for prints and paintings as well. In addition, such works could later be sold to eager collectors.[33] It is therefore not surprising that autonomous drawings are the predominant category of drawing in both of the Brils' extant *œuvres*.

1) See catalogue by Frits Lugt, 1949.

2) For more information on Matthijs' *œuvre*, see Ruby 1999, p. 11.

3) On the back of Louvre, inv. no. 20.955, pen and brown ink, 207 x 275 mm, Lugt 1949, no. 356, illus., Louvre 1978, no. 137.

4) Louvre, inv. no. 20.959, pen and brown ink, 195 x 275 mm, Lugt 1949, no. 358, illus., Louvre 1978, no. 141. Fresco in Courtright 1990, p. 497, fig. 109.

5) Louvre, inv. no. 873, pen and brown ink, 220 x 420 mm, Lugt 1949, no. 365, illus., Ruby 1999, pp. 11, 139, n. 108. I have some doubts as to Matthijs' authorship of this drawing: it seems somewhat too carefully done, as if it were a copy of a lost original by Matthijs. I have included it here because either way, an original by Matthijs did exist that he most likely used in the fresco.

6) As Bert Meijer kindly pointed out, sometimes artists such as Pieter Stevens drew buildings at greater or lesser stages of development than they were at the time of the execution of a drawing, but I do not think this was the case here. All of Matthijs' drawings of ruins update earlier versions of the same sites, indicating his interested in accurate representation of reality. See Ruby 1999, p. 11.

7) Another fresco related to this drawing is in the Torre dei Venti, first room, second floor, The Room with the Topographical Views, with the Castel Sant'Angelo, cupola and bridge from the other side. See Courtright 1990, p. 487, fig. 107.

8) Louvre, inv. no. 19.787, pen and brown ink over traces of black chalk, 265 x 205 mm, Lugt 1949, no. 366, illus., Louvre 1978, no. 64. Fresco in Courtright 1990, pp. 454-455, fig. 75.

9) Louvre, inv. no. 19.802, pen and brown ink over traces of black chalk, 264 x 200 mm; Louvre, inv. no. 20.991, pen and brown ink over traces of black chalk, 266 x 206 mm; Louvre, inv. no. 20.990, pen and brown ink over traces of black chalk, 264 x 204 mm; Lugt 1949, nos. 366a, illus. and 367, 368; Louvre 1978, nos. 71, 87, 88.

10) Cambridge, Fitzwilliam, inv. no. P.D. 198-1963, pen and brown ink over traces of black chalk, 192 x 267 mm, Jeudwine 1956, p. 192, fig. IV.

11) See Courtright 1990, p. 469, fig. 94.

12) Paris, Institut Néerlandais, inv. no. 589, pen and brown ink over traces of black chalk, 194 x 272 mm, Boon 1992, vol. 1, pp. 48-51 and vol. 3, plate 210, no. 29, illus.; London, Courtauld Institute, inv. no. 676, pen and brown and grey wash over traces of black chalk, New York 1986, no. 5, illus.; Hannover, Niedersächsisches Landesmuseum, inv. no. N 148, pen and brown ink over traces of black chalk, 191 x 266 mm; Washington, National Gallery, inv. no. B 26.773, pen and brown ink over black chalk, 271 x 193 mm, Washington 1974, no. 45, illus.; Manchester, Whitworth Art Gallery, inv. no. 1936.19, pen and brown and grey wash over black chalk, 191 x 262 mm, Manchester 1983, no. 51, illus.

13) The penmanship in the Courtauld drawing is too rounded and neat to be by Matthijs and is probably a copy.

14) Bodart 1970, App. 1 and n. 9.

15) Washington, National Gallery, inv. no. B 26.773; see above for literature. For the frescoes, see Courtright 1990, pp. 461 and 415, pls. 88 and 66.

16) Thanks to Carla Hendriks, e-mail, June 2000.

17) No *catalogue raisonné* of Matthijs' drawings exists to date, although I am planning an article in the near future.

18) With the publication of the frescoes in this book, it will be possible to study more details.

19) Leiden, Prentenkabinet Universiteit Leiden, inv. no. AW 1001, pen and brown ink and brown wash, touched up by a later hand in reddish-

brown ink, 144 x 191 mm, Ruby 1999, cat. no. 1, illus.

20) British Museum, inv. no. 5214-233, pen and brown ink over traces of black chalk, and brown and blue wash, 228 x 356 mm, Ruby 1999, cat. no. 2, illus.

21) Louvre, inv. no. 19.819, pen and brown ink over traces of black chalk, 163 x 279 mm, Lugt 1949, no. 355, illus., Ruby 1999, p. 77, illus.

22) Gerszi 1982 and verbally, 1992, indicated she thought the drawing was a copy.

23) Close comparison to drawings by Maarten de Vos indicate that Paul could have used one of that artist's drawings of *Jonah and the Whale* for the whale. See for example, Antwerp, Plantin Moretus Museum, Delen 1938, no. 101, of 1585, pen and brown ink, 65 mm diameter.

24) Gerszi's suggestion that Paul's drawing is a copy of the fresco must be rejected because of many areas in which the drawing is closer to Matthijs' version than the fresco.

25) The washes in his earlier drawings were not the predominant medium the way they are in these drawings.

26) Louvre, inv. no. 19.810, brush and black ink over black chalk, 180 x 270 mm, Lugt 1949, cat. no. 414, Ruby 1999, cat. no. 71, illus.; Louvre, inv. no. 19.807, pen and black ink, 156 x 200 mm, Lugt 1949, cat. no. 415, Ruby 1999, cat. no. 72, illus.

27) Louvre, inv. no. 21.739, brush with black ink and wash over black chalk, 134 x 256 mm, Lugt 1949, cat. no. 413, Ruby 1999, cat. no. 73, illus.

28) Munich, Staatliche Graphische Sammlung, inv. no. 1028, pen and brown ink and grey and wash over black chalk, 187 x 272 mm, Ruby 1999, cat. no. 75, illus.

29) Louvre, inv. no. 19.786, pen and brown and black ink and brown and grey wash over black chalk, 196 x 339 mm; Louvre, inv. no. 19.791, pen and brown ink with traces of black chalk in center, 187 x 334 mm; Louvre, inv. no. 19.784, pen and brown ink and white heightening and brown, grey and blue washes with a trace of green paint, 207 x 339 mm; Louvre, inv. no. 19.789, pen and brown ink and brown and grey wash 200 x 341 mm; Louvre, inv. no. 19.792, pen and brown ink and brown and grey wash, 200 x 339 mm; Louvre, inv. no. 19.788, pen and brown ink and grey wash, 198 x 343 mm; Leiden, Prentenkabinet Universiteit Leiden, inv. no. AW 1171, pen and brown ink with brown wash over black chalk, 198 x 338 mm, Ruby 1999, cat. nos. 23-29, illus.

30) Dresden, Kupferstichkabinett, inv. no. C3779, pen and brown ink over grey chalk with grey wash and traces of brown wash and red paint, 205 x 277 mm, Ruby 1999, cat. no. 74, illus.

31) Brush and grey wash over black chalk, 178 x 257 mm, Ruby 1999, cat. no. 76, illus.

32) See Cappelletti, Testa 1994, p. 15.

33) The great 18th-century collector of drawings, P.J. Mariette, discussed the popularity of Bril's drawings amongst collectors in his *Description sommaire des dessins...* of 1741, p. 109.

Note: All drawings are on cream laid paper.

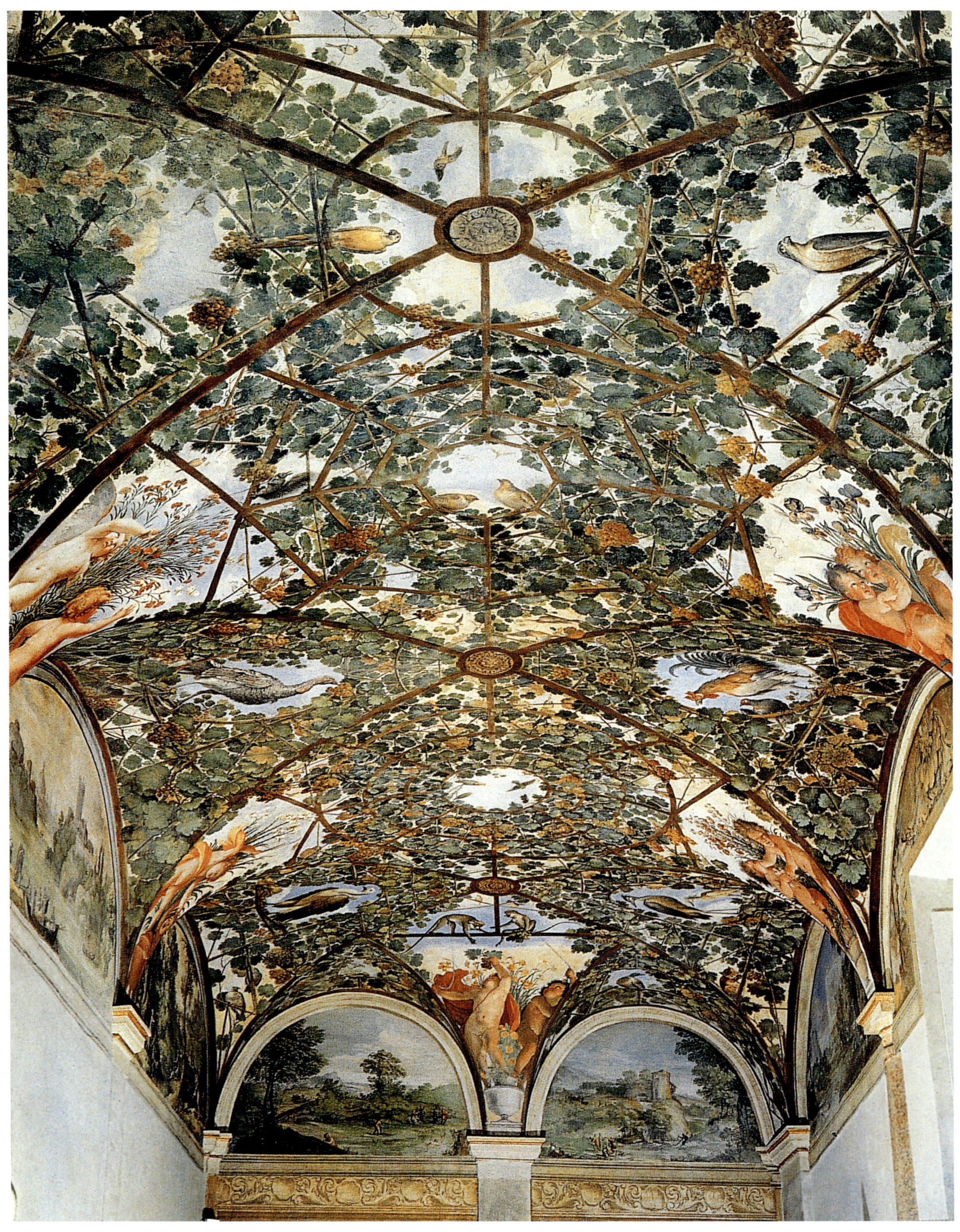

Paul Bril and Guido Reni in the Loggia della Pergola in Palazzo Pallavicini Rospigliosi

Angela Negro

One of the most charming decorative complexes that Paul Bril produced in Rome during his extremely long career is undoubtedly the Loggia della Pergola, today part of the Palazzo Pallavicini Rospigliosi, where he painted the walls with a series of landscapes in lunettes and the ceiling with a network of interwoven vines where small animals and birds of every kind appear in the most varied shapes and sizes. The whole work, completed by twelve pairs of putti and bunches of flowers painted by Guido Reni, was produced between 1611 and 1612 for Cardinal Scipione Borghese on the southern brow of the Quirinal hill, the site chosen by this powerful prelate, nephew of Pope Paul V (elected on 16 May 1605), to build himself a handsome dwelling surrounded with greenery, erected between 1610 and 1616.

The story of the famous Borghese garden of Montecavallo is already well known.[1] Promoted to extremely high official duties and assured of powerful financial resources by his uncle the pope, by December 1610 Scipione Borghese had already embarked on a frenzied purchase of properties on the side of the hill directly facing the Papal Palace, which had the added charm of containing the ruins of the Baths

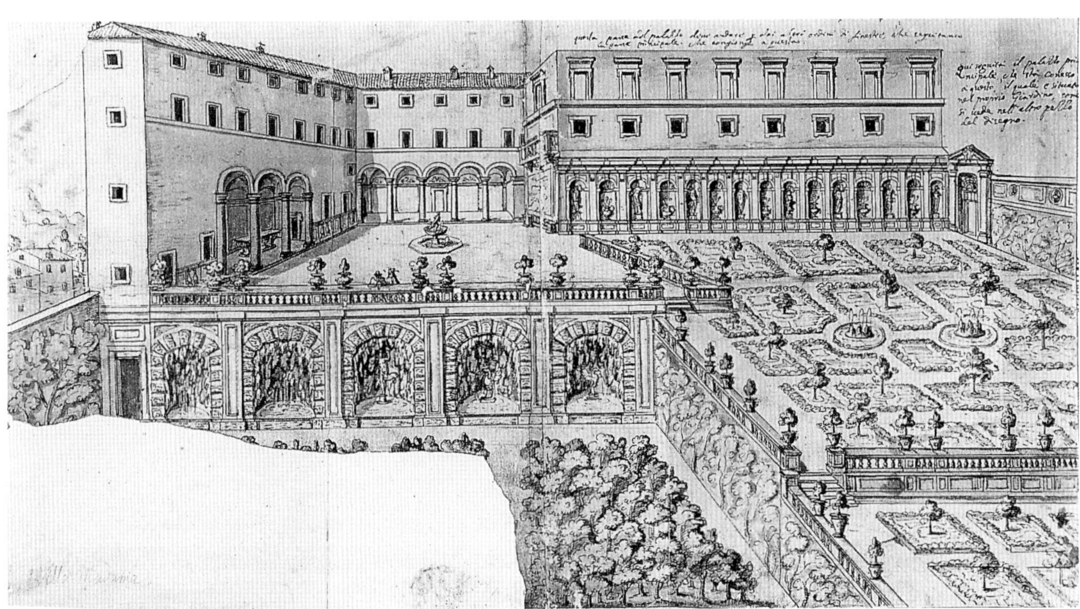

52. Overall view of the ceiling of the Loggia della Pergola.

53. Anonymous, *View of the east side of Palazzo Borghese* (later Altemps-Bentivoglio-Rospigliosi), drawing, c. 1620. In the centre the five arches of the Loggia della Pergola completed according to Scipione Borghese's wishes. Vienna, Graphische Sammlung Albertina, It. Az. Rom. 1255.

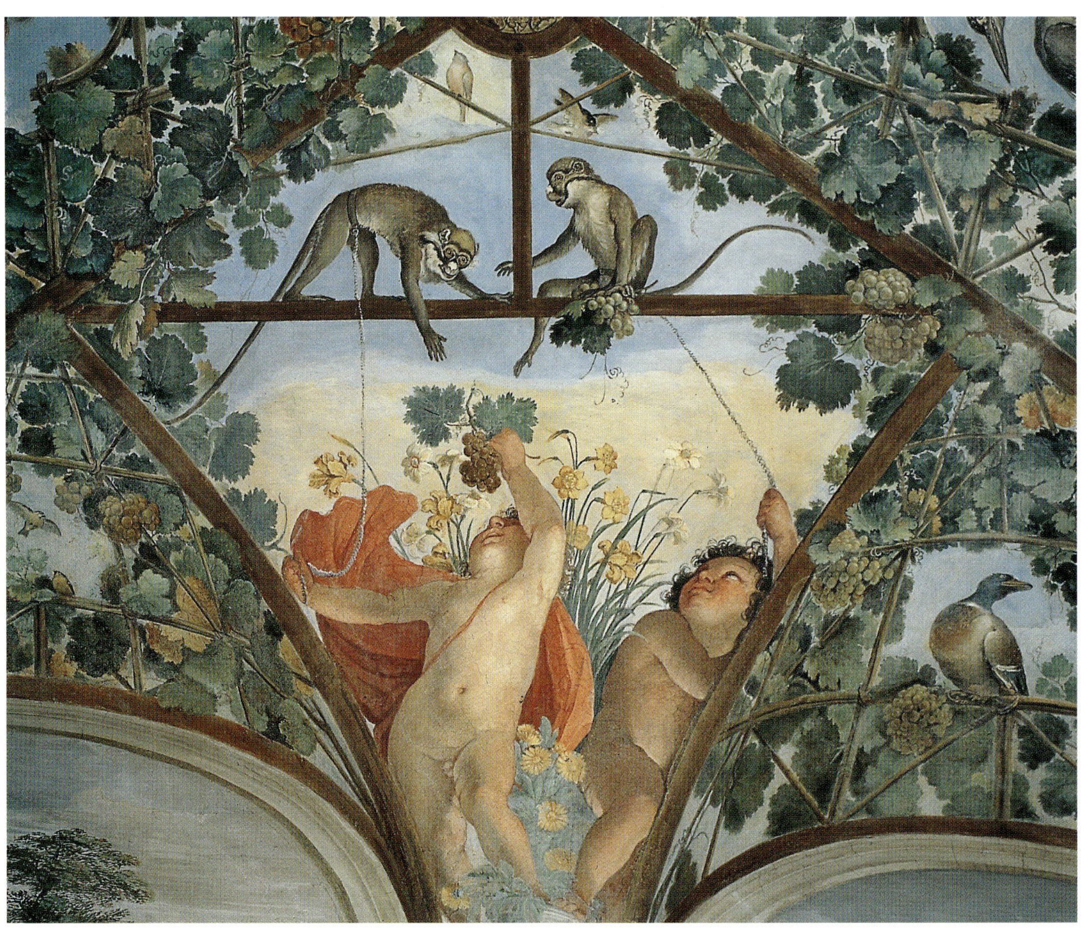

54. Guido Reni, *Putti Holding Two Monkeys*, short wall, north.

of Constantine. His first aim was to create a garden set with four loggias linked by tree-lined paths, where archaeological finds were to be mixed with garden objects, with ancient or contemporary statuary, fountains and flowering shrubs, lending the whole the air of a "place of delight", the pleasing and cultured retreat of a "great prince".[2]

The first of the four loggias to be completed and decorated was the very one containing Paul Bril's pergola. From a structural point of view this simply involved the renovation of a pre-existing building: a construction composed of two wings forming an L-shape, recorded in an anonymous drawing in the Albertina in Vienna, the southern side being the loggia in question (fig. 53) while on the left there extended a wing with a triple arched opening, no longer standing today.[3] This property had been the retreat of Fabio Biondo, the pope's Majordomo and Prefect of the Holy Apostolic Palaces, and was the first to be bought by Scipione Borghese, on 23 December 1610. A small house and garden, recorded by contemporaries as being a place of particular beauty.[4]

In the house, where the loggia with the arches and vaulting that Bril was to paint already existed, alterations and adjustments were under way by 7 June 1611, though periodic payments to Bril began only at the end of the month (28 June) and, as we see from the Borghese documents in the Secret Vatican Archive, he was given overall charge of the decorations. The work must have been completed by 2 August 1612, with the payment of 400 scudi "a M.s Paolo Bricchi [sic] Pittore… per resto di s. 700 p. saldo et intero pagam.to di tutte le Pitture fatte in quindici mesi, loggia et altro".[5] The documents make no reference to the painter's assistants, nor to Guido Reni, who painted the magnificent pairs of cherubs which ornament the endings of the vault and divide the landscapes in the lunettes (fig. 54).[6]

As the documents show, Bril was in charge of the decorations and he is to be ascribed with the design of the pergola as a whole, painting many of the birds and parts of the nine landscapes appearing on the upper section of the walls (fig. 52). After the loggia was restored in 1996 it became possible to identify the painter's hand in six scenes, while the others, three scenes on the short walls (one of which has disappeared but is recorded in an old photograph), are to be ascribed to Pietro Paolo Bonzi, known as the "Gobbo dei Carracci".[7]

Bril was commissioned for the pergola during the latter phase of his Roman career, when he was already the acknowledged master of landscape painting.[8] These were also the years when numerous landscapes by the Flemish artist entered the Borghese collection, including his beautiful *Marine Scene*, still in the Borghese Gallery.[9] This is enough to show that Scipione Borghese had a definite interest in the Flemish painter and explains the personal commission for the loggia.

In those landscaped lunettes which are undoubtedly attributable to Bril, we recognise that gradual distancing from the forced artificiality of Flemish painting mentioned by Mancini, an image bristling with soaring perspectives, still sixteenth-century fancies and meticulous details of script which gradually gave way to a broader more naturalistic image. This is easy to see, if we compare the remaining scenes with the *Deer Hunt* (fig. 55), the first on the right on the back wall of the loggia. This still has its roots in the kind of hunting scene painted in Antonio Tempesta's style and shows a high horizon and swathes of woodland in deep swirling greens and browns. This is still the world of northern fairytales, like the one in Bril's beautiful *Hunt* on copper in the Pitti Palace (1593), and the painting work is carried out in a similar manner too, like an oil painting, an impasto of small overlying brushstrokes which, from the dark tones of the foreground, are gradually and expertly faded into the pale shades of the background, all revolving round a cool silver tone, verging on violet. This is explained by the violet ground which Bril used to prepare the plaster for all his landscapes in the loggia before sketching the outlines of his subject with a brush, using the same brownish violet, and conveying the architectural volumes with shaded lines.

This preparatory technique emerged clearly during the restoration (it was in fact discovered where some parts were missing) and clarified, beyond any doubt, that the painter did not practise indirect engraving or pouncing from a cartoon but transferred the preparatory drawing directly on to the wet, violet-coated plaster, reproducing the drawing in a brown outline which served as a guide for the final painting work.[10]

In Paul Bril's other lunettes, the *Landscape with Two Monks and a Village* (fig. 56), the *View with Boats on a River* (fig. 57) and the great luminous *Marine Scene* (fig.

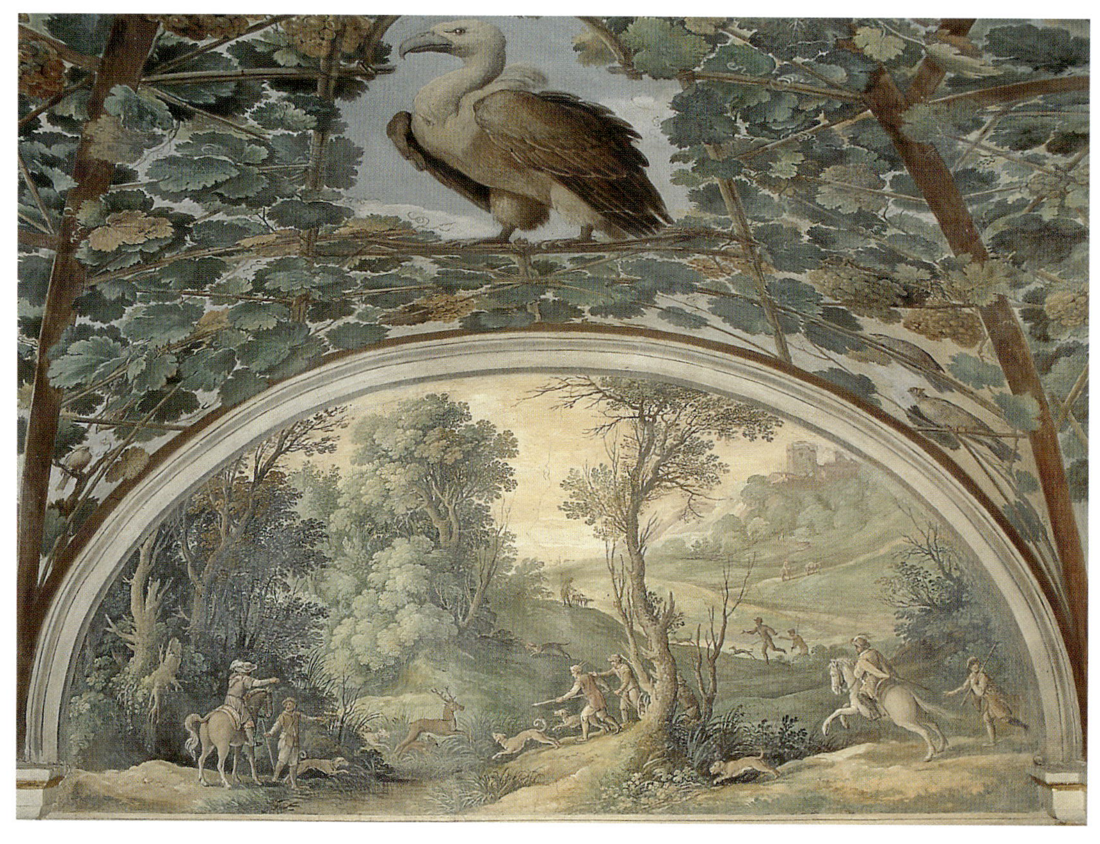

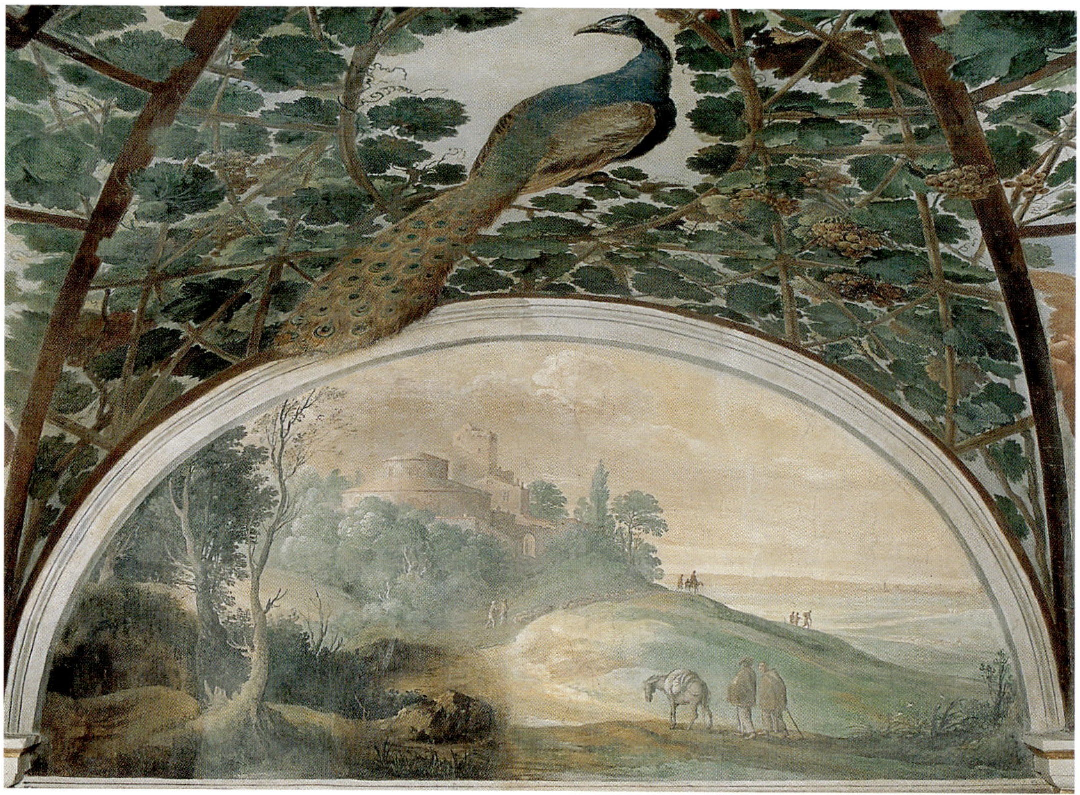

55. Paul Bril, *Deer Hunt*, long wall, west.
56. Paul Bril, *Landscape with Two Monks and a Village*, long wall, west.

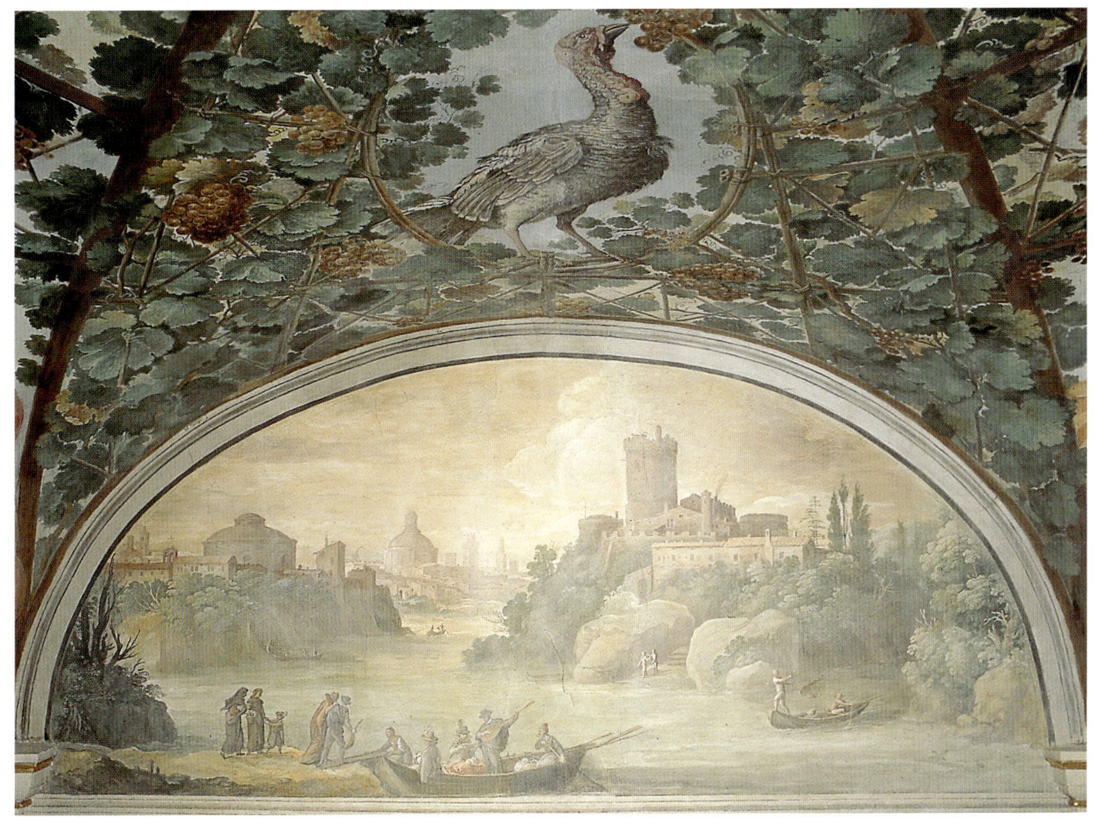

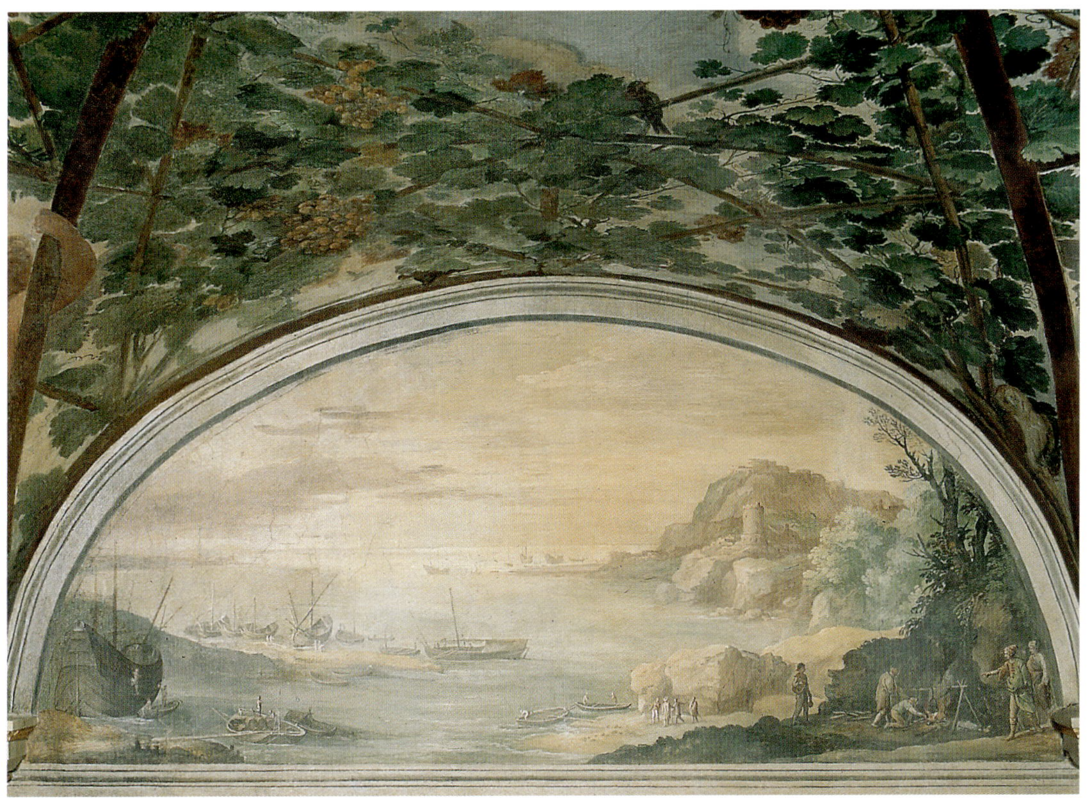

57. Paul Bril, *View with Boats on a River*, long wall, west.
58. Paul Bril, *Marine Scene*, long wall, west.

58), the imagery grows broader and increasingly naturalistic, with larger areas of light and sky. However, the drawing of the figures, boats and buildings in the distance is still very finely done with the point of the brush, the light of the background still chiefly pale and violet, the paint still thick and solid and meticulously applied, with overlying brushstrokes gradually building up the gradations of tone and light. The other two lunettes which are attributed to Pietro Paolo Bonzi are quite different (figs. 59 and 60). They are painted on clear, thin grounds, without any previous colouring of the plaster, and the figures, faces and distribution of the relief are very freely, even roughly executed.

This easy naturalness, the taste for broad scattered woodlands, carelessly and roughly traced (something we find also in Bonzi's drawings), combined with the undeniably Bolognese flavour of the landscape, in the Domenichino-Albani-Grimaldi line, have reinforced the idea of attributing these lunettes to Bonzi, Tuscan by birth but a frequenter of Bolognese circles in Rome. Malvasia describes him as a friend and collaborator of Giovan Battista Viola. Bonzi was also enough of an expert landscape painter to venture to "compete with Brill", as Malvasia records, with two

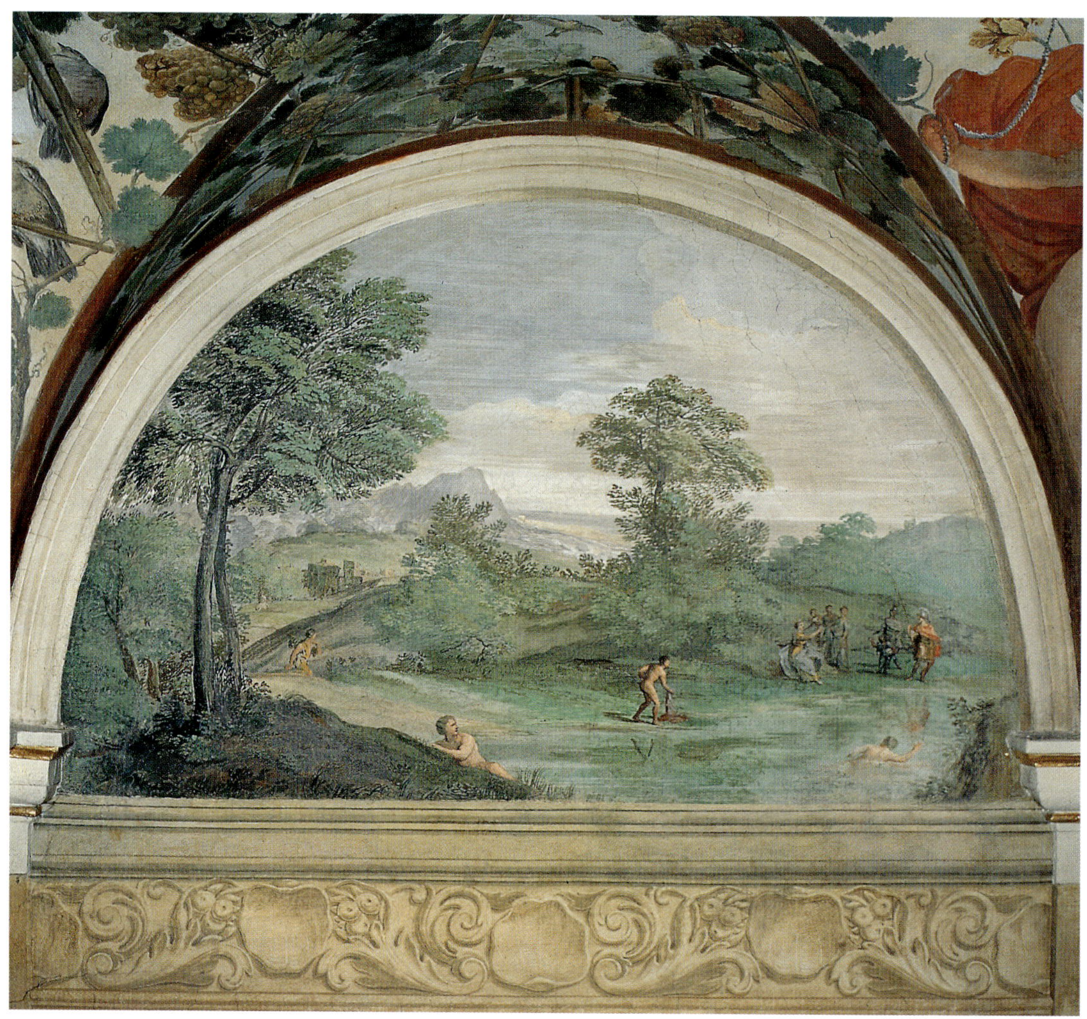

59. Pietro Paolo Bonzi, *Mythological Scene*, short wall, north.

large landscapes frescoed in the gardens of Villa Montalto, now lost.[11]

Bonzi's biographical details are still uncertain, the only firm information being the record of his death which tells us he was sixty years old in 1636. One certain fact, since it is recorded by Baglione, is that in Rome he became installed in the house of the Crescenzi family, in the academy led by Giovan Battista, a painter himself but chiefly a skilled master and promoter of other artists. Giovan Battista Crescenzi, who knew Bril well and was the leading intermediary in all the Borghese family's artistic ventures, may be the person responsible for Pietro Paolo Bonzi's commission for the loggia. It should not be forgotten that Bonzi was chiefly known, according to Baglione, as a still-life painter and "diedesi a depinger frutti al naturale e in quel genio non si poteva far di meglio…".[12]

If Bonzi's stay in Crescenzi's house referred to by Baglione is to be set early in the second decade of the seventeenth century, as Spezzaferro suggests, therefore immediately after the death of Annibale Carracci (1609) and the understandable confusion that ensued among the painters in his entourage, we arrive at the very years when this loggia was painted, 1611-12. It is easy to imagine that Bril, head of oper-

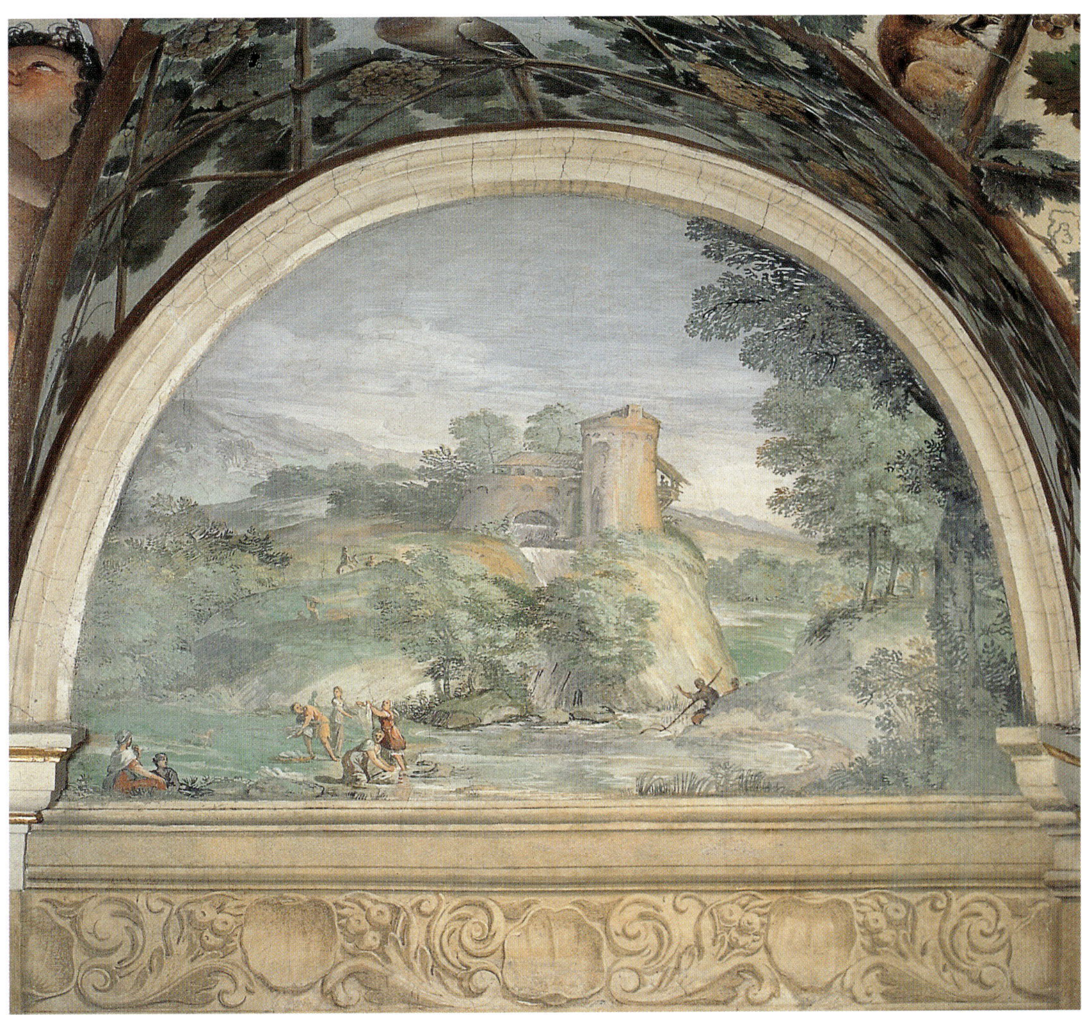

60. Pietro Paolo Bonzi, *Landscape with Two Women at a River*, short wall, north.

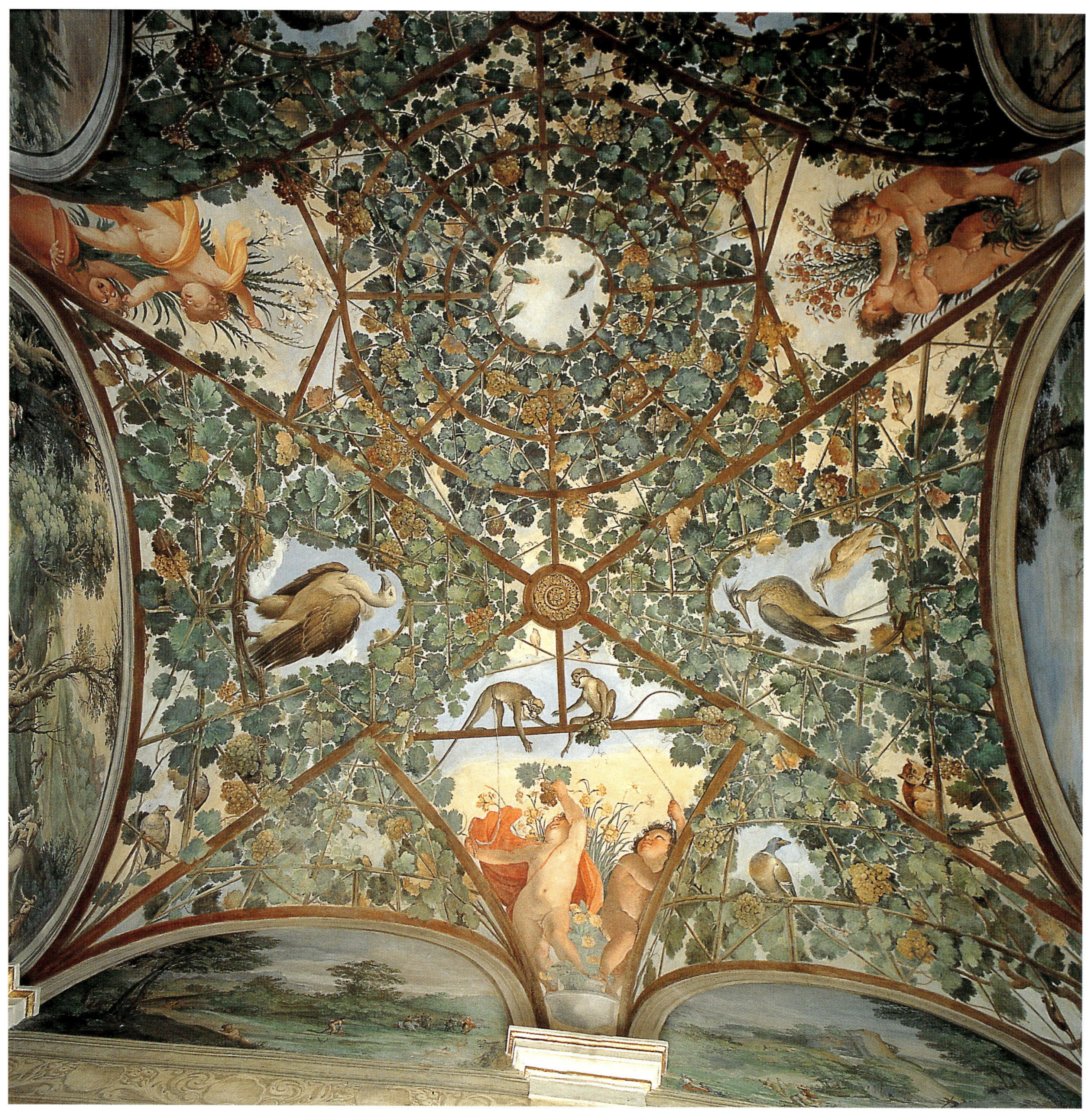

61. First bay of the Loggia.

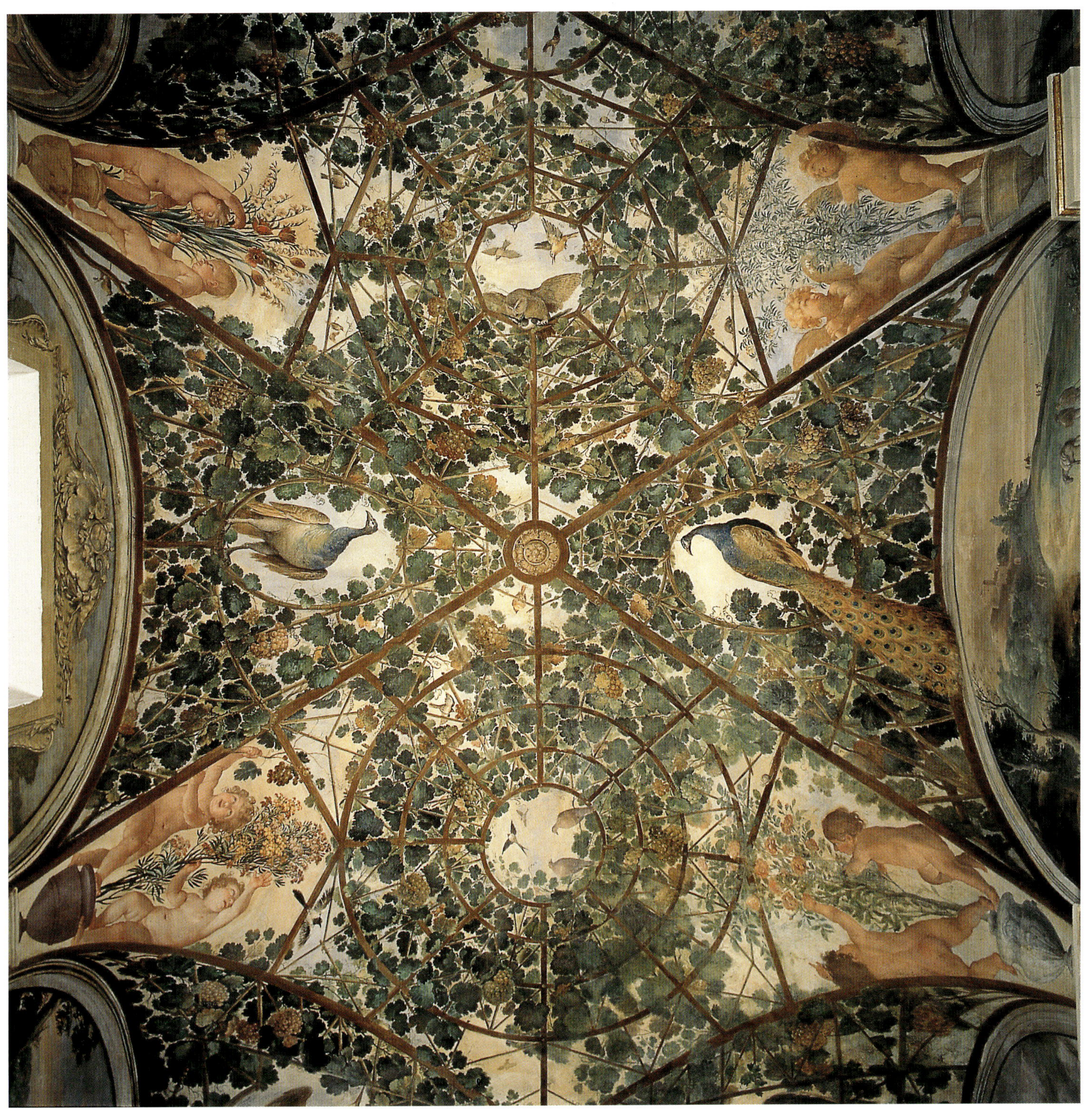

62. Third bay of the Loggia.

ations and designer of the great pergola, sought the assistance of a painter particularly renowned for painting "frutti al naturale", besides being a protégé of Giovan Battista Crescenzi and, through him, close to the Borghese family.

The Borghese pergola is divided into five sections by a painted wooden trellis which spans the vaulting, and rounded 'openings' alternate with the polygonal bars of the trellis which carries a climbing vine and an infinite variety of creatures (figs. 61 and 62). The most striking feature is the naturalistic character of the whole work which makes no attempt to be methodical or instructive but, on the contrary, gives the impression of an actual green microcosm, swarming with the lively creatures which inhabit it and seem to move and sing among its leafy fronds. This living, throbbing tapestry is not even broken by the oculi, open to the sky, where larger birds, always those known to be proud or rapacious, like the peacock, cockerel, eagle, heron and griffin (wonderfully painted with fine brushstrokes) appear in natural and spirited poses, like the turkey pecking a grape or the bittern with its chick (figs. 66 and 67). [13]

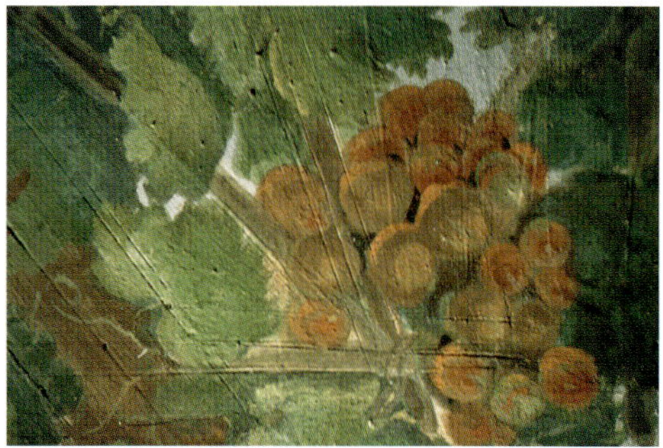 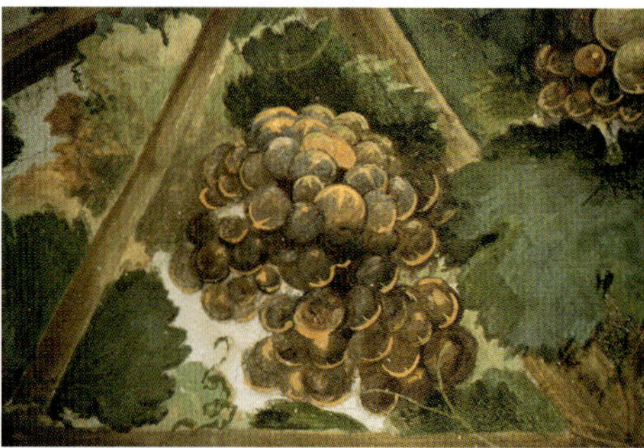 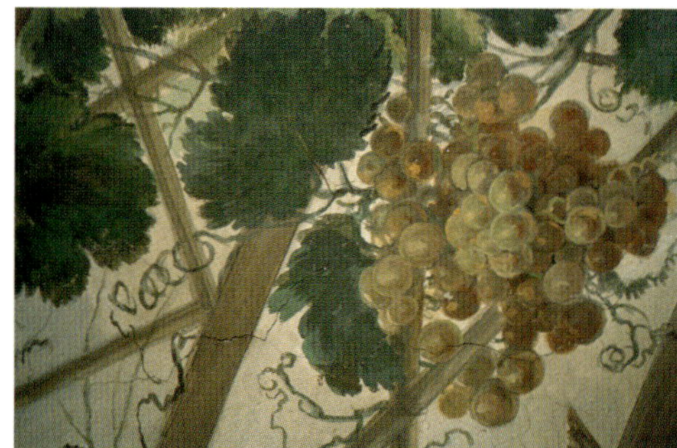

63. Direct engraving, revealed under raking light, carried out to define the structure of the Pergola.

64-65. Details of a bunch of grapes.

Thus, the pergola presents an extraordinary naturalistic spectacle, designed to be in harmony with the surrounding garden, once clearly visible beyond the five previously open arches of the loggia. The light that strikes the grapes and leaves also comes from studying the sources of natural light.

However, this green microcosm, so wonderfully palpitating with life, and still today deeply absorbing to the viewer, was only created after careful planning, as the restoration work carried out in the summer of 1996 by the C.B.C. Cooperative has brought to light. [14] Work would have started from the central span, that is, from the groin above the third lunette (painted in a single day shift, *giornata*) flanked by Reni's putti with jasmine and carnations. Therefore, a first group of six or seven *giornate* must have been carried out in the central part of the loggia, with Bril and Reni working side by side (probably in the summer of 1611) in order to judge the overall effect of the combination of putti and pergola and the manner in which figures and vegetation could be integrated in the decorative scheme. Indeed, the first two of Reni's putti are the only ones to be painted on *giornate* which also include a considerable area of pergola.

The two artists thus worked in close contact during the initial stage of the decoration. Later, Bril and his collaborators continued painting the pergola while leaving

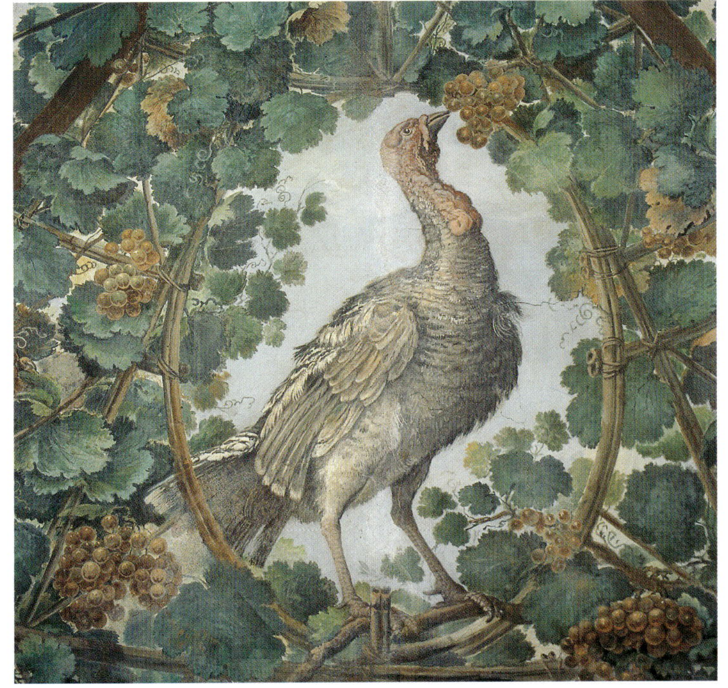

66. Paul Bril, *Turkey*. 67. Paul Bril, *Bittern*.

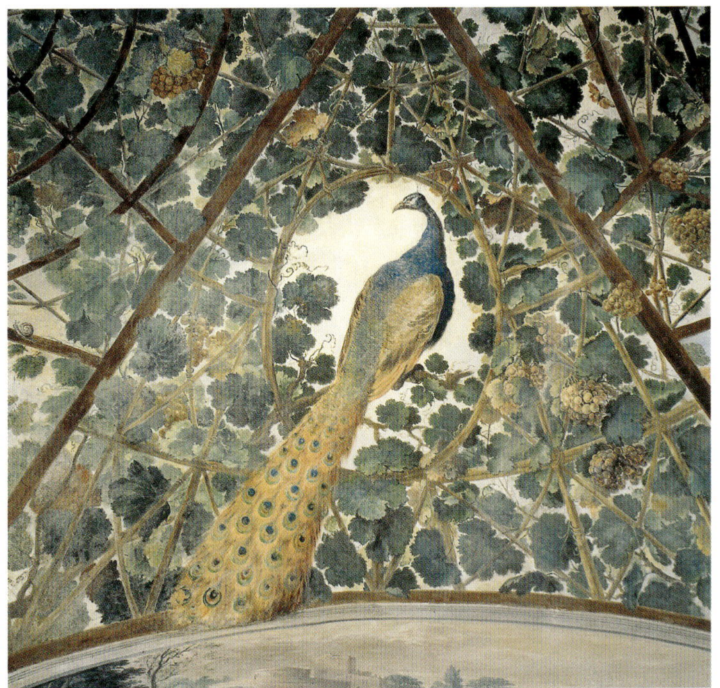

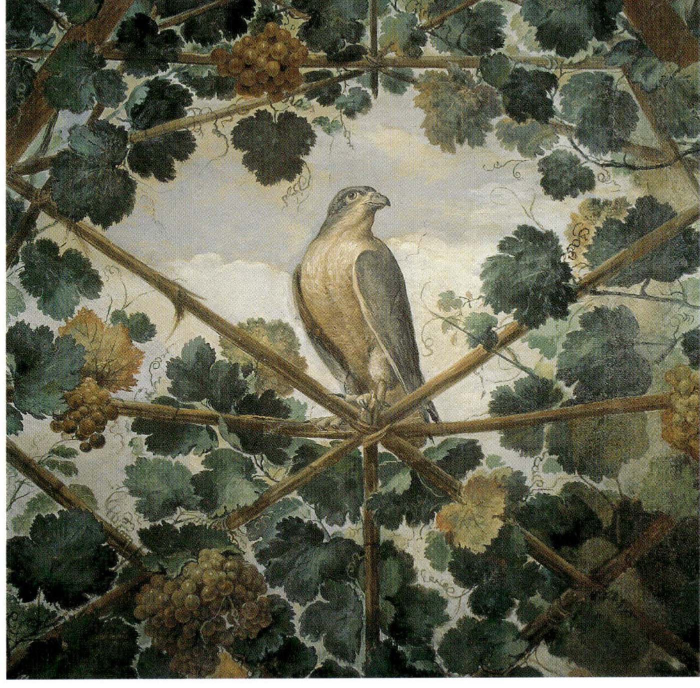

68. Paul Bril, *Peacock*. 69. Paul Bril, workshop, *Peregrine falcon*.

blank the spaces that Reni needed for his figures, thus giving him a certain working autonomy. In fact, the *giornate* on which the figures were painted, after the first two groups of putti, always overlie the plaster of the pergola, previously painted by Bril and his collaborators.

To produce the pergola Bril did not make use of cartoons to transfer the drawing. On close study there are no signs of indirect engraved lines or traces of pouncing, while the painted wooden posts and poles which form the supporting structure of the pergola were produced by engraving directly with a rule and compass (for the circles of the central cupola) and the grooves are easily perceptible (fig. 63). In other instances the line of the wooden poles is drawn in red and it is frequently possible to see the holes made to affix flexible rods to outline the wooden framework correctly before applying the paint.

It is obvious that as far as the painting of the foliage and creatures is concerned Bril, who painted the pergola before the lunettes beneath, made use of his assistants. While we can certainly ascribe him with the larger creatures depicted in the ovals, painted with great finesse and assurance with extremely fine brushstrokes and shading, the same cannot be said of the countless small creatures crowding the vine, more freely and loosely painted: for example, the cat eating a mouse and several small birds in which the restorers discovered obvious signs of *pentimenti* (corrections). But the comparisons to be made in the execution of foliage and clusters of grapes are even more interesting. At least two types of bunches of grapes were brought to light. Some, like those in the area around the peacocks (fig. 68), are painted on a violet ground similar to the one Bril used as a base for his landscapes, and these have muted colours, as do the surrounding leaves. The grapes themselves are round, uniform in shape and defined by outlines in a lighter yellow shade and, painted on the grapes to mark the reflection of light, is a kind of pale semicircular stylised spandrel with a small vertical line in the centre, like a sort of tiny trident (fig. 64). Thus, it would not seem rash to assume that the master himself intervened in this area, with similar tones and materials to those he used in his landscapes.

Elsewhere, as in the central stretch around the falcon (fig. 69) and the parrot and the putti with the tulips, the grapes and the foliage are painted in a quite different style with more strongly contrasting colours on a thin pale ground enriched with touches of rich rusty brown kindled by the golden transparent grapes and yellowing leaves (fig. 65). The whole work is given a truly naturalistic feeling with emphasis laid on brown shadows, projecting volumes and points of light and shade that are not part of a repeated pattern, but freely distributed with quick touches of green, yellow and brown. This is the area that occupies much of the central part of the loggia and is where the idea of the participation of Bonzi, the "Gobbo dei Carracci", seems the most convincing.

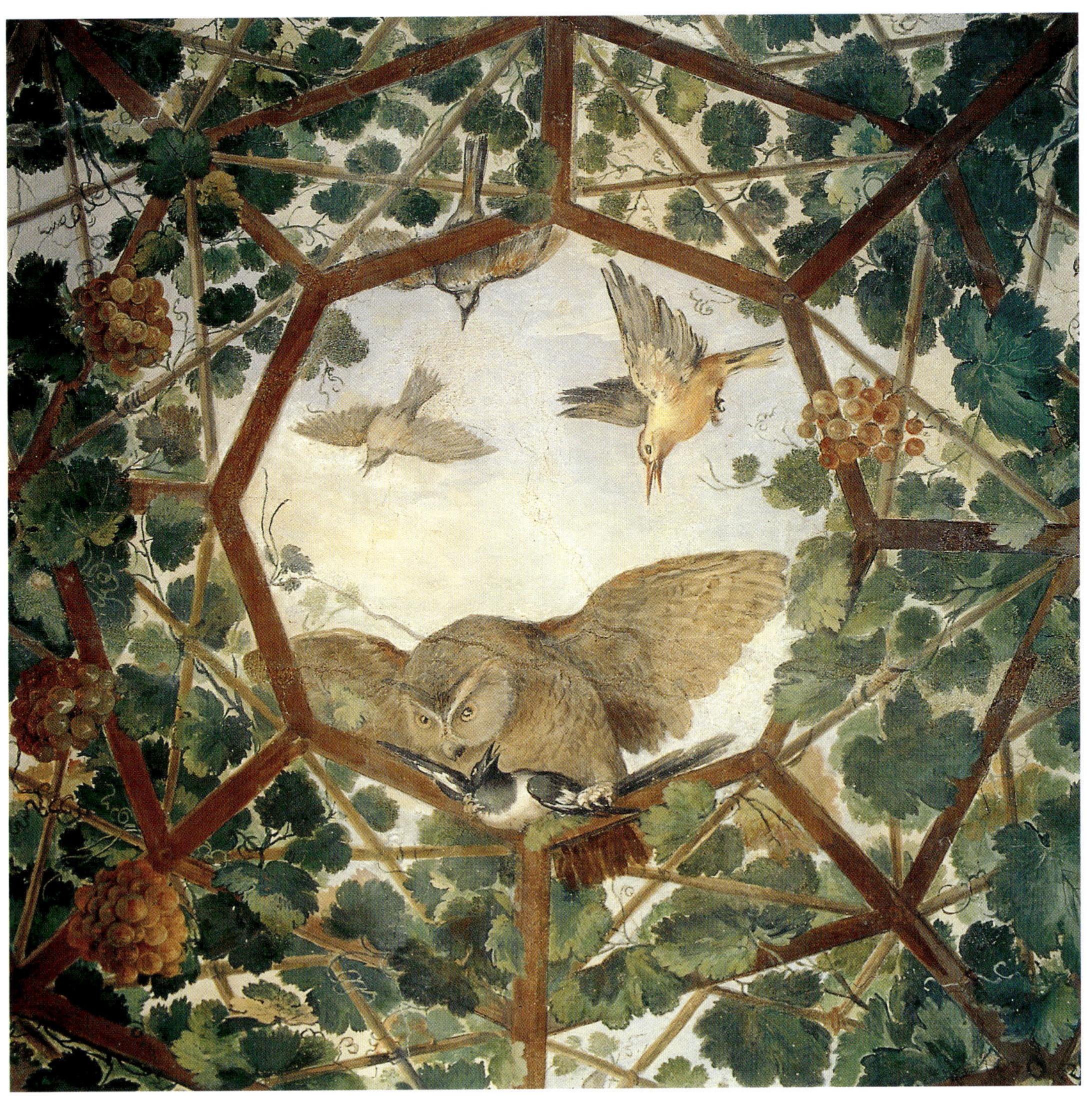

70. Paul Bril, workshop, *Owl Seizing a Magpie*.

1) On the Montecavallo Borghese gardens: Hibbard 1964, pp. 163-192; Hibbard 1971, pp. 192-194; Antinori 1993, pp. 113-151; Negro 1996; Witte 1998, 2, pp. 55-60; Waddy 1999, pp. 204-207; Negro, in course of publication. The text presents a symbolic analysis of the decorations in the various loggias in the garden, totally disagreeing with the hypothesis presented by A. Witte in his critique.

2) Only later, between 1613 and 1615, was a real palace built in the centre of this area. The building was entrusted firstly to Flaminio Ponzio and then to Vasanzio and to Maderno. However, the building, which did not follow the charming playful style of the four highly decorated loggias, was only just completed when Scipione, on 30 May 1616, now completely taken up by his new building venture, the Villa Pinciana (now the Villa Borghese), abandoned his garden on the Quirinal and sold it to Giovan Angelo Altemps. The palace and the garden then went through other changes of ownership, and though the arches leading outside have been closed the loggia painted by Bril still remains almost intact in a wing of the present Palazzo Pallavicini Rospigliosi, the ground and third floors now the property of the Confederazione Nazionale Coltivatori Diretti.

3) Vienna, Graphische Sammlung Albertina, It. Az. Rom. 1255. I have dated the drawing to the time of the building of Scipione's palace, between 1613 and 1614, while Waddy shifts it to 1621, the time when the complex was remodelled by the Bentivoglio family, the new proprietors (Waddy 1999, p. 218 and p. 255 note 83). However, the drawing is a perfect reproduction of the loggia and facing garden, with the appearance conferred by Scipione Borghese.

4) Felini 1610, p. 215.

5) Archivio Segreto Vaticano, Borghese, 23, *Rincontro di Banco 1607-1614*, c. 134r.

6) This information would suggest that the decoration's execution is to be set between the summer of 1611 and late spring of 1612, a period when Reni had a close and continuing professional relationship with Scipione Borghese, begun in 1608 with the decoration of the Oratory of Santa Silvia in San Gregorio al Celio, and culminating in the decoration of the Pauline Chapel in Santa Maria Maggiore, completed in April 1612. During these years the contact between painter and patron (who, from January 1608 also paid for his lodgings) was so close and so packed with commissions that a small undertaking like painting the putti on the pergola probably failed to involve a specific, separate payment.

7) The attribution to the "Gobbo [hunchback] dei Carracci" is based on an idea of Sir Denis Mahon, taken up by me (1996); about the "Gobbo dei Carracci": Battisti 1954, pp. 290-302; Hess 1954, pp. 303-315; Emiliani 1962, pp. 321ff.; Volpe 1964, p. 31; Borroni 1970, pp. 485-487; Chiarini 1973, pp. 23-24; Pugliatti 1975, pp. 15-23; Salerno 1977-1978, vol. I, pp. 12-29, pp. 100ff.; Salerno 1984, pp. 92-97; Spezzaferro 1985, pp. 50-73; Howard 1988, pp. 227-249; Cottino 1989, vol. II, pp. 698ff.; Cottino 1995, pp. 125-136.

8) On this matter, Mancini says: "Vive hoggi anch'orchè di progress'età Paul Bril, qual di molti anni in simil sorte di pittura par che abbia tenuto il primo luogo et invero meritatamente poiché con la lunghezza dello star in Italia, vedendo le cose dei Carracci et del Cavalier Giuseppe ha nelle figure fatto assai passaggio, e nel paesaggio lasciato quello stento fiammingo accostandosi più al vero, né facendo l'horizzonte così alto com'usano i fiamminghi, che per il loro paesaggi son più tosto una maestà scenica che prospetto di paese" (Mancini 1956, vol. 1, p. 260).

9) The work was produced between 1611 and 1612 and on the flag appear the eagle and dragon of the Borghese coat of arms. Della Pergola firmly attributes to the painter another seven paintings in the collection, while in a further four she identifies the hands of assistants (Della Pergola 1955-1959, pp. 148-155).

10) On this see Martellotti, in Negro 1996, p. 137. On the drawings in the Louvre Museum, sketches for two of the landscapes in the pergola, see in this volume Wood Ruby, *Before the Frescoes...*

11) Malvasia 1844, vol. II, p. 91.

12) Baglione 1649, reprinted, and edited by C. Gradara, Velletri 1924, see p. 343.

13) I described this bird as *Corvus Sylvaticus* but it was later identified as a bittern by Carlo Violani of the Department of Animal Biology at the University of Pavia (written communication of 6 October 1998). I thank Dr Violani for this helpful correction.

14) On this see the observations of the restorer, Giovanna Martellotti in Negro 1996, pp. 135-136.

Repertory of the Frescoes

With the exception of the landscapes
in Monterotondo all the frescoes are
in Rome and the Vatican. They are
listed alphabetically according
to location.
Other artists involved in the projects
are also mentioned.
For literature concerning the single
projects, see the notes to chapter
The Frescoes.
Measurements, when known, are given,
width preceding height.
*= The work has not been viewed from
sufficiently close by to study the technique.

a.

Matthijs Bril assisted by Paul Bril

Eight landscapes (in a frieze on the four walls, c. 2 x 1 m each scene), fresco and secco Commissioned by Giordano (?) Orsini

Datable 1581

1. *Landscape with Ruins and Bridge*

2. *Coastal Landscape*

3. *Winter Landscape with Ruins*

4. *Landscape with Ruins and Obelisk*

5. *River Landscape with Herdsman and Animals*

6. *Landscape with Roman Ruins and a Fountain*

7. *Coastal Landscape with Herdsman and Animals*

8. *Landscape with Ruins, Horseman and Servant*

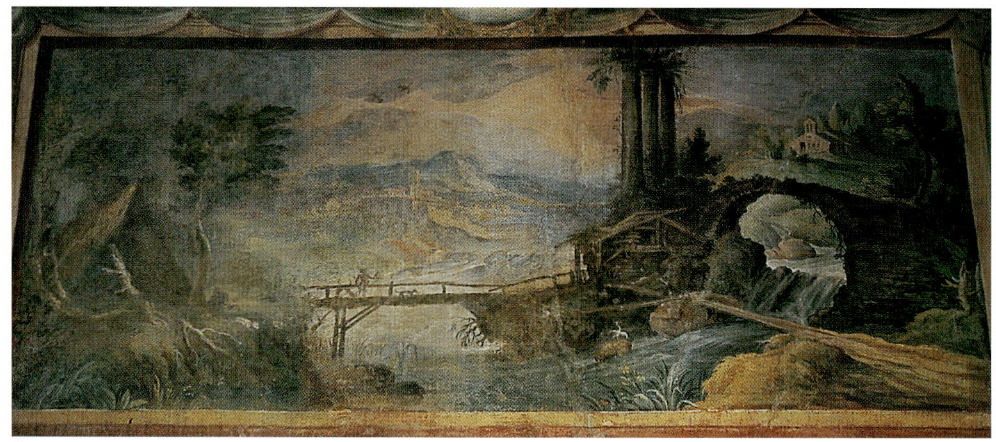

1

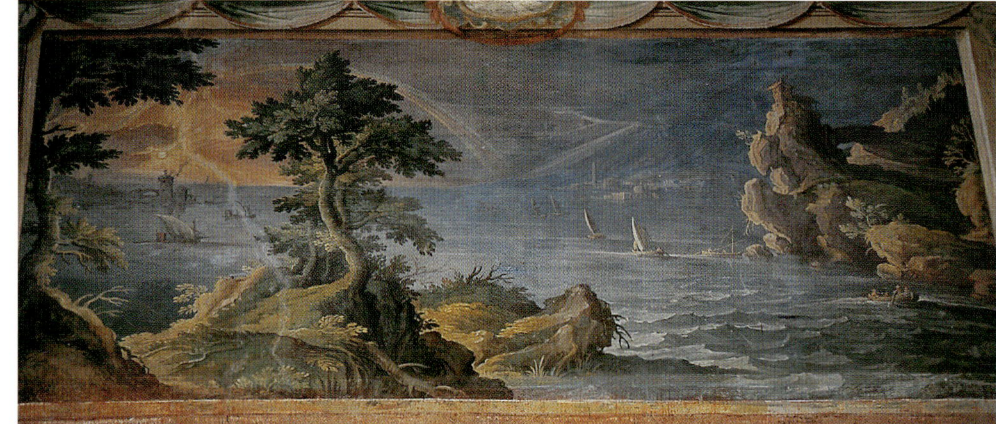

2

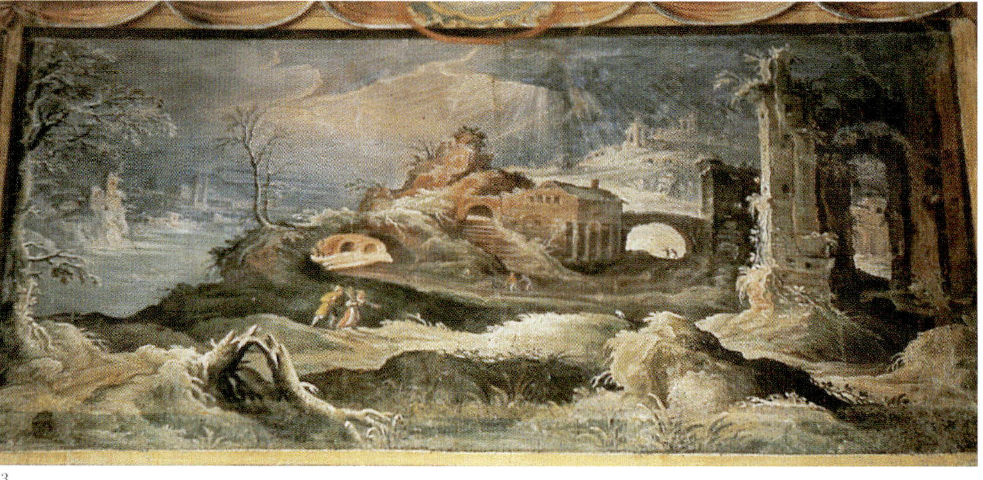

3

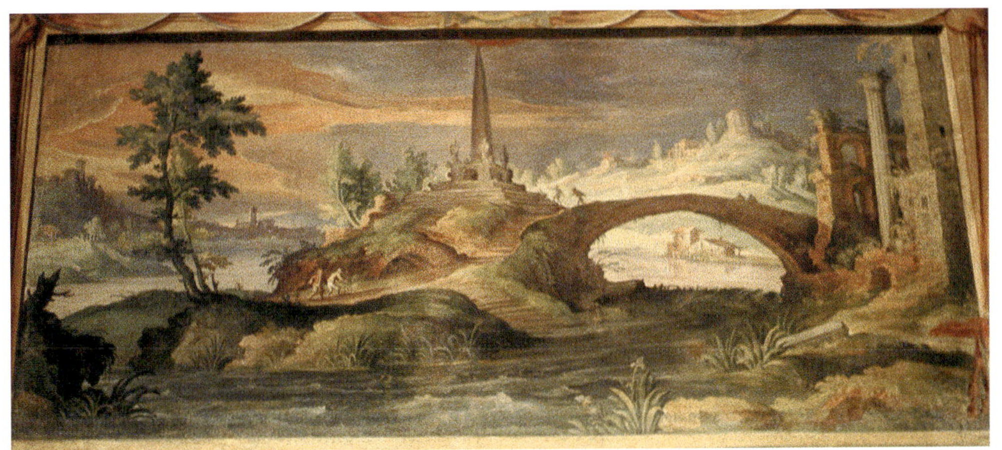

4

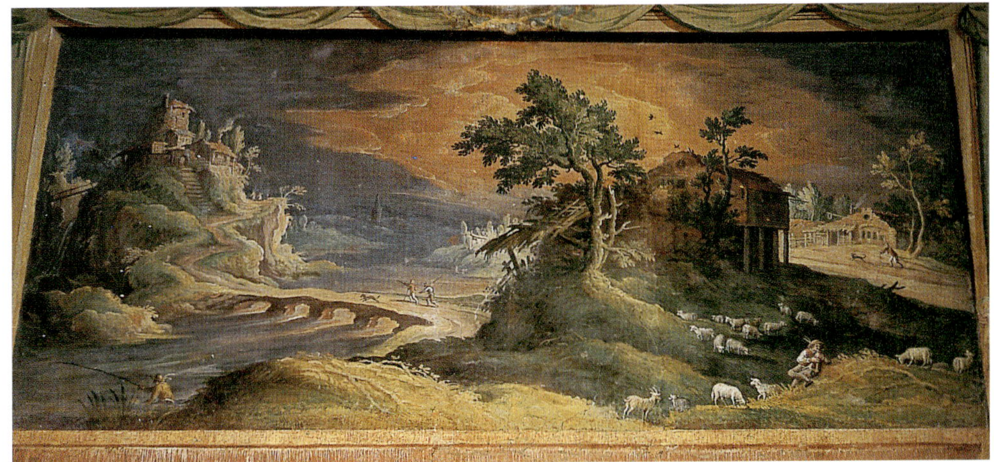

5

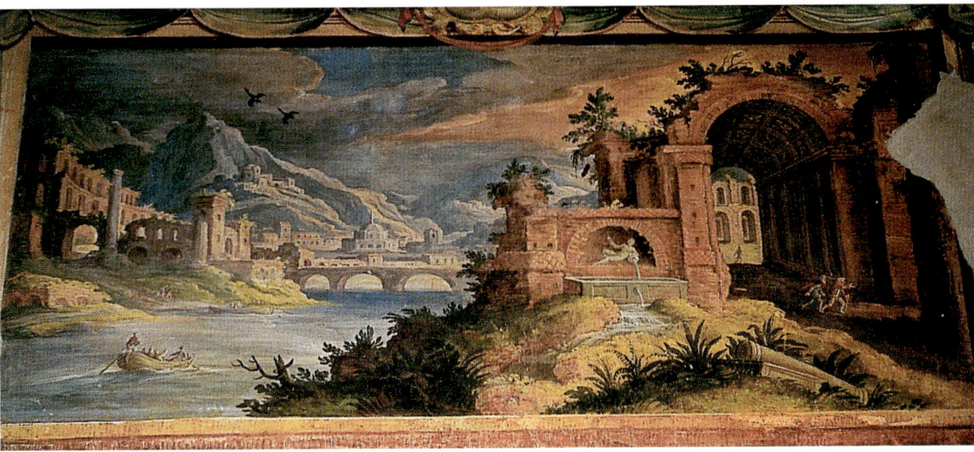

6

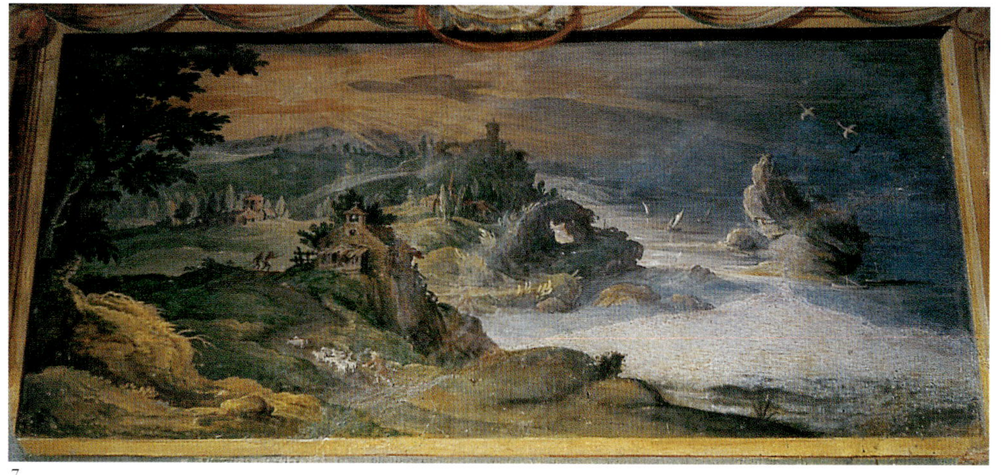

7

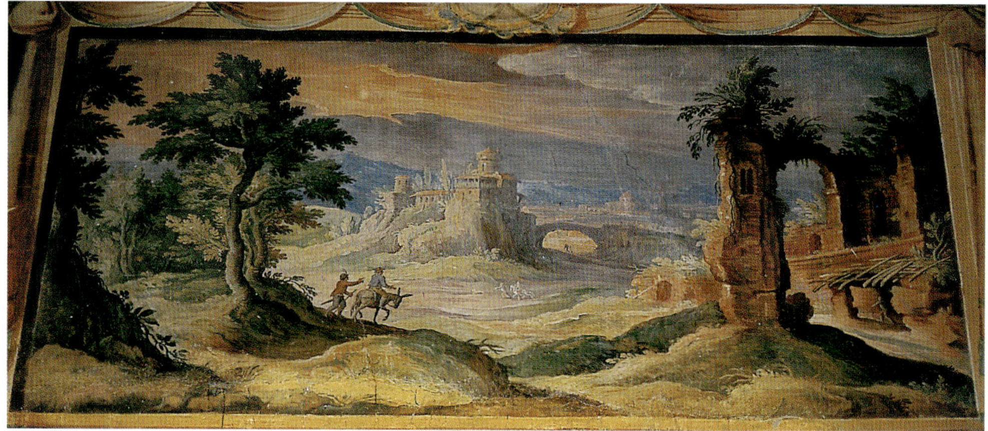

8

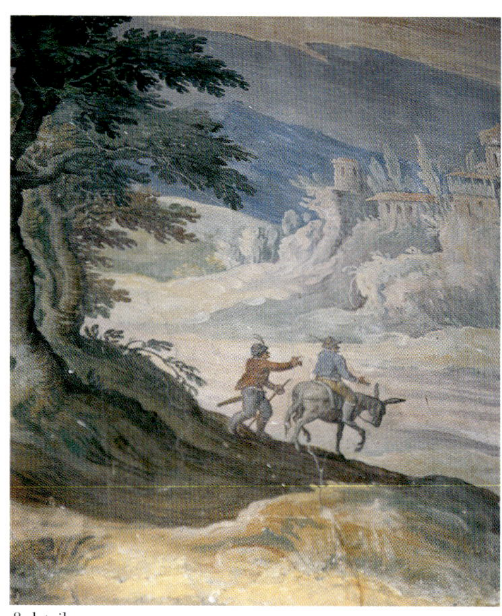

8 detail

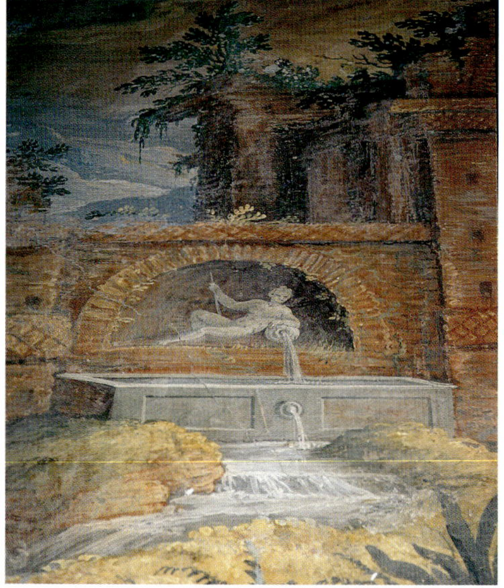

6 detail

b.

Matthijs Bril assisted by Paul Bril

Hunting scenes near Monterotondo
(in a frieze on the four walls,
c. 22 x 1 m), fresco
Commissioned by Giordano (?)
Orsini

Dated 1581

Signed with a pince-nez on the painted
frame under the view of Monterotondo
and dated 1581 under the stone bridge
on the opposite wall.

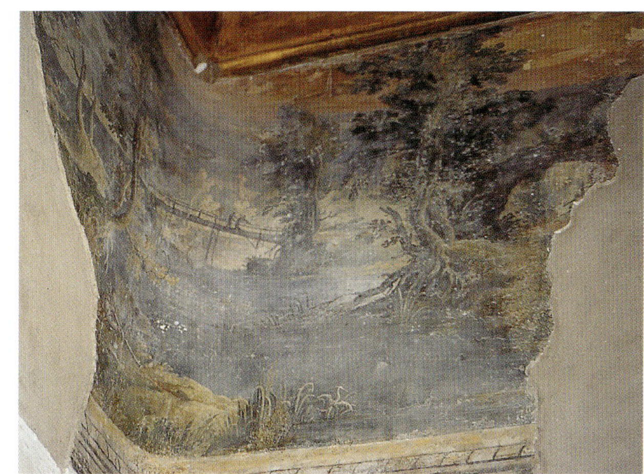

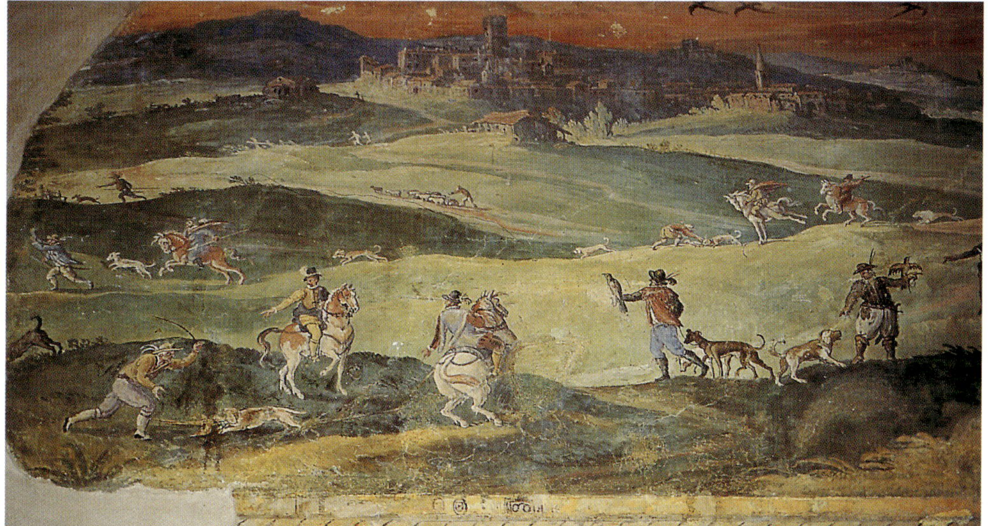

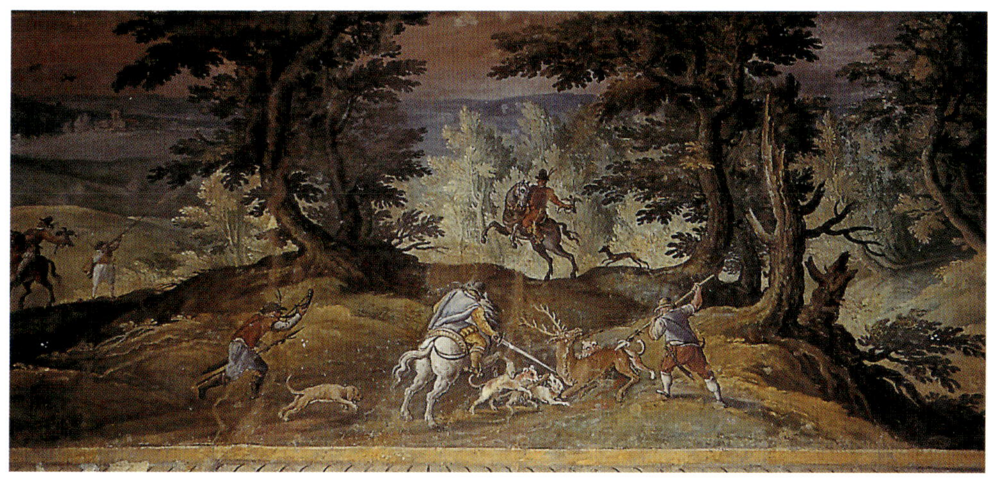

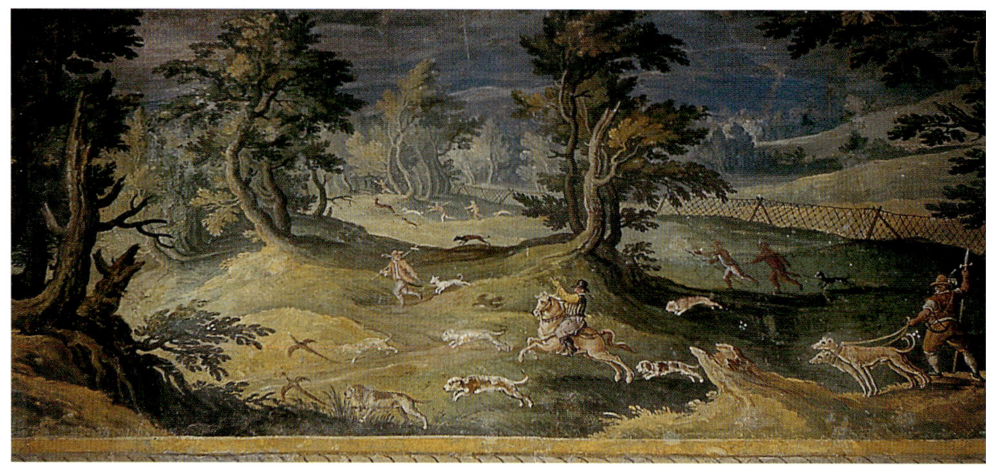

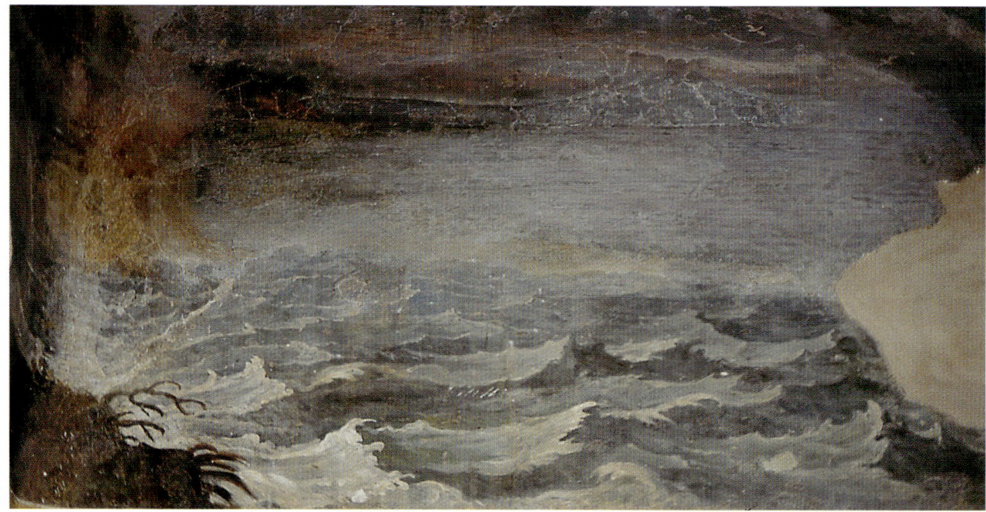

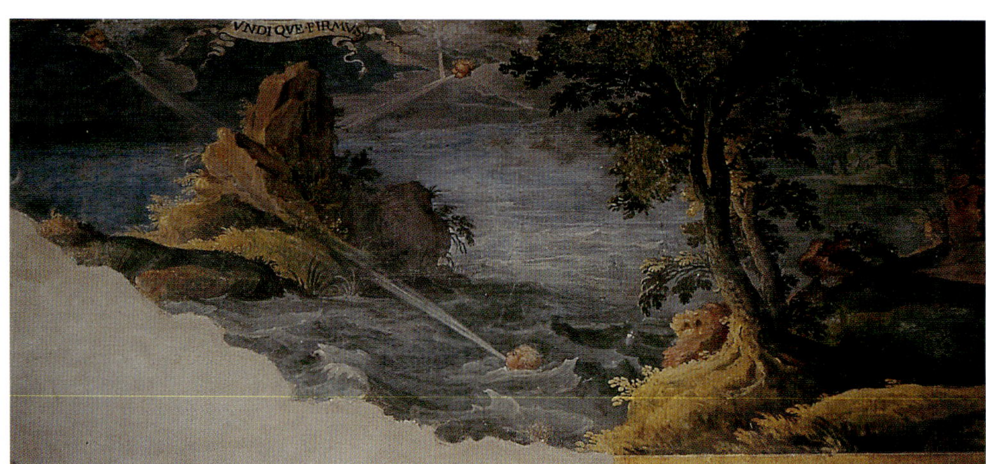
VNDIQVE·FIRMVS

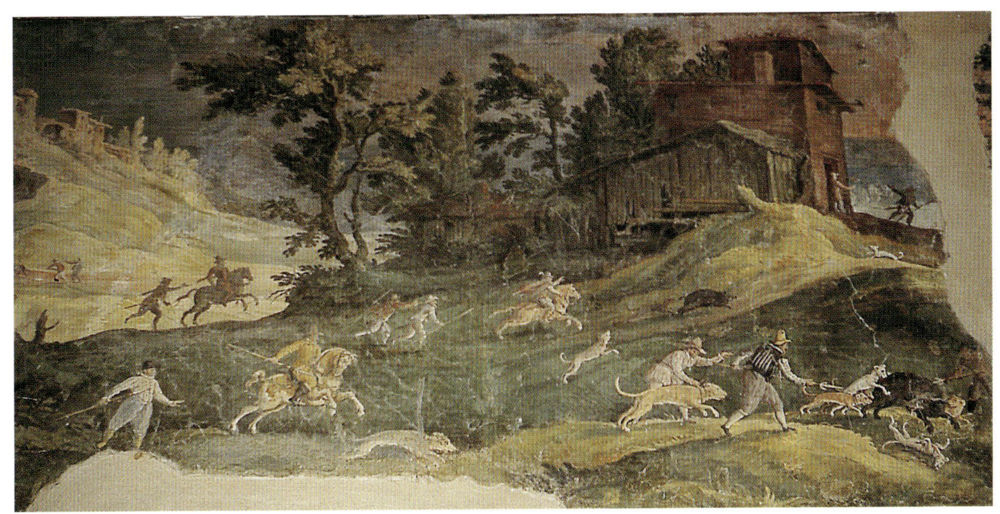

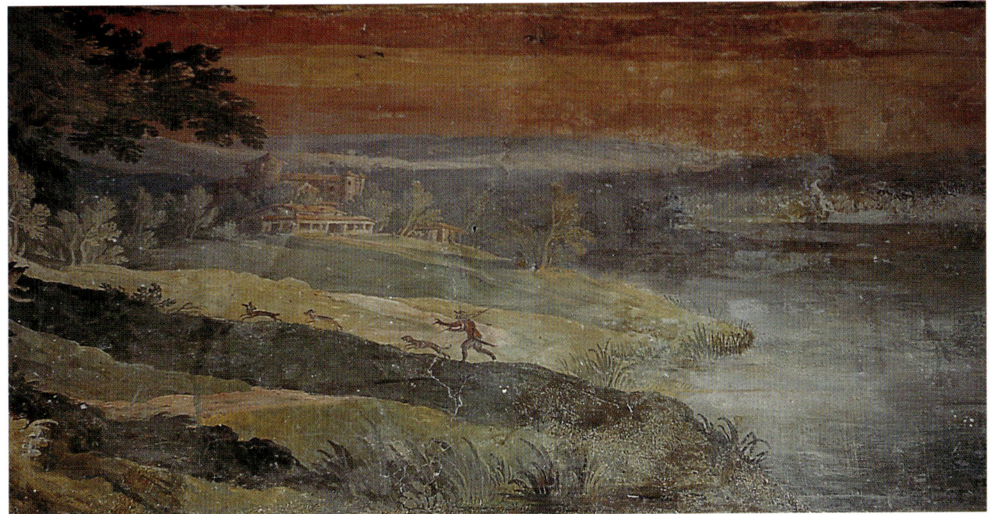

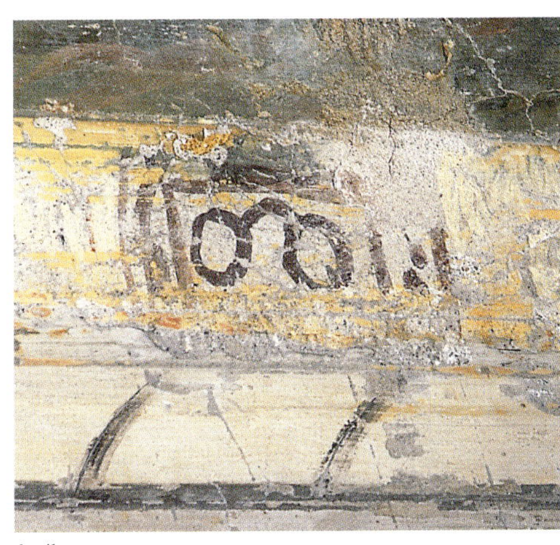

detail

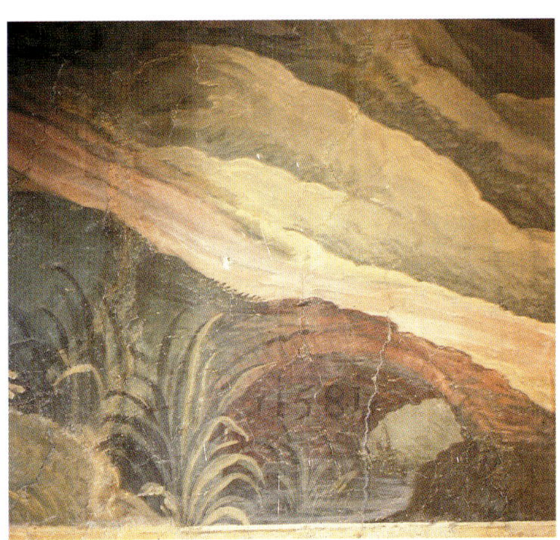

detail

Paul Bril
(other frescoes, one landscape each:
Giovan Francesco Barbieri called
Guercino, Domenico Zampieri called
Domenichino and Giovanni Battista
Viola)

*Rocky Landscape with a Bridge and
Figures Walking* (1.50 m x 1.50 m),
vault, fresco*
Commissioned by Cardinal Ludovico
Ludovisi

Datable 1621-23

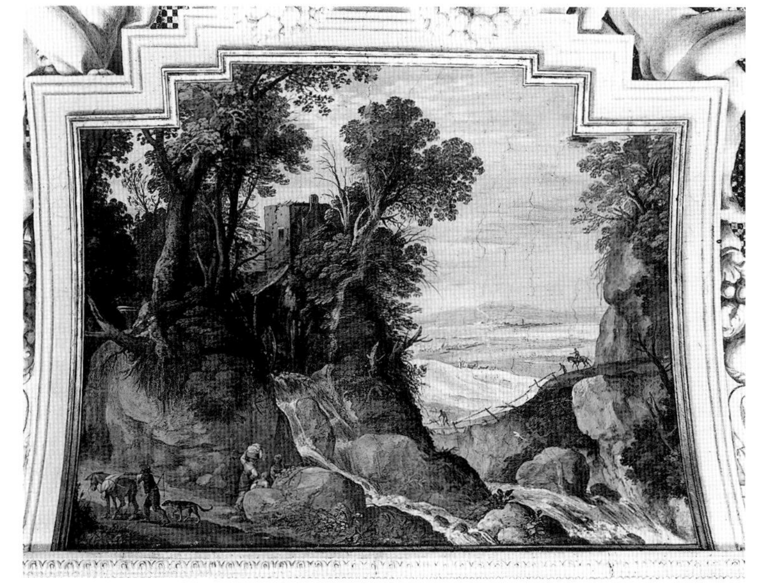

III. Chiesa Nuova (Santa Maria in Vallicella)
Capella Cesi

Paul Bril
(figures: Paris Nogari)

*Landscapes with the Creation
of Adam and Eve and the Last
Judgment*
Commissioned by Cardinal Pier
Donato Cesi
Destroyed

Datable 1593-94

IV. Collegio della Compagnia di Gesù (Collegio Romano)
Sala

Paul Bril
(other frescoes: Cristoforo Roncalli
called Pomarancio)

Two landscapes
Commissioned by Pope Gregory XIII
Destroyed

Documented 1584

a.

Paul Bril and assistant(s)
(other frescoes in the vault: Cesare
Nebbia and Giovanni Guerra)

One seascape, three landscapes,
vault (in the corners), fresco*
Commissioned by Pope Sixtus V

Datable 1586

1. *Seascape with Galleys, Rock
and Trees*
2. *Woodland with River, Bridge
and Vista*
3. *Landscape with Harvesting Peasant*
(with assistant)
4. *Woodland* (with assistant)

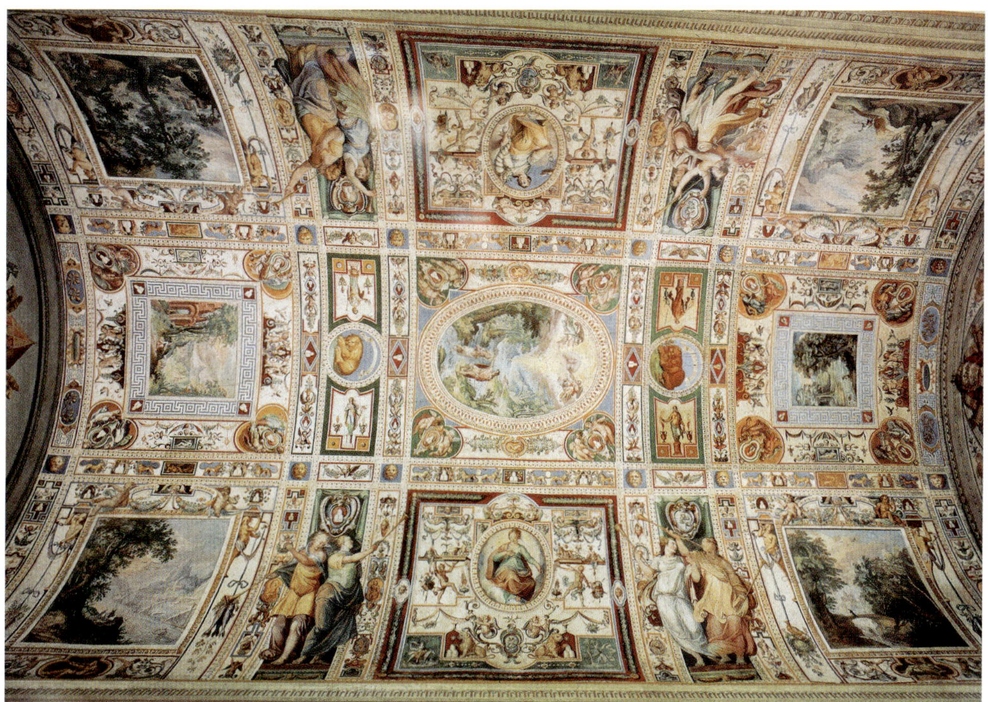

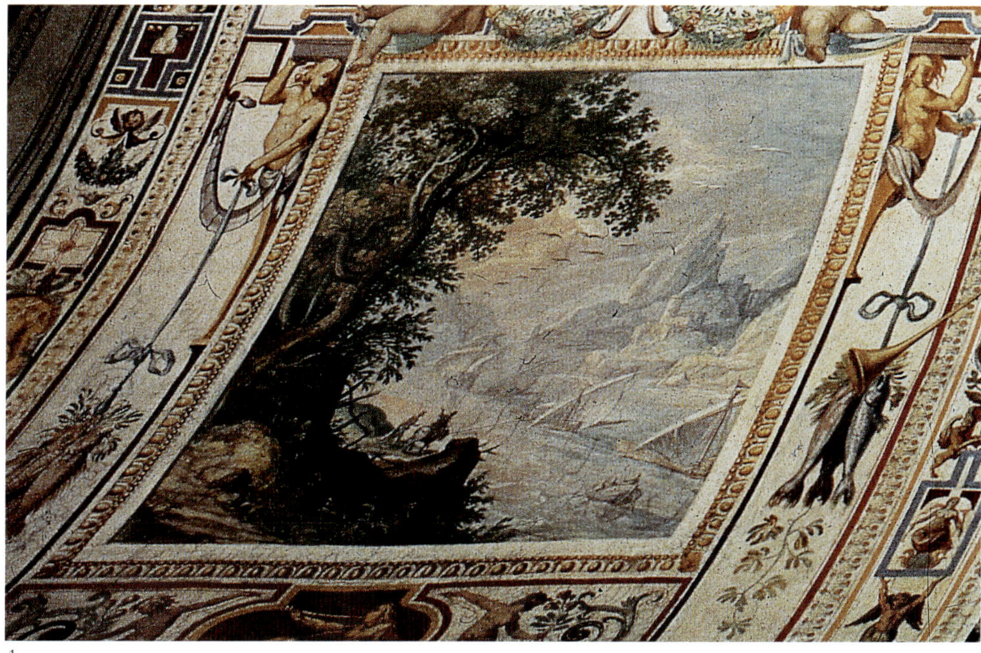

1

b.

Paul Bril and assistant(s)
(other frescoes in the vaults: Cesare
Nebbia and Giovanni Guerra)

Sixteen landscapes, lunettes, fresco*
Commissioned by Pope Sixtus V

Datable 1588-89

south loggia:

1. (X) *Landscape with Ruins, River
with Bridge and Horseman*

2. (XI) *Landscape with Buildings,
Herdsmen and Animals*

3. (XII) *Landscape with River and Ruins*

4. (XIII) *Landscape with Farmhouse*

5. (XIV) *Landscape with Hills, Waterfall
and Herdsmen*

6. (XV) *River with a Town in the Distance*

7. (XVI) *Landscape with River
and Bridge*

west loggia:

8. (XVII) *Woodland with Houses
and a Bridge*

9. (XVIII) *Landscape with River
and Rapids* (with assistant A)

10. (XIX) *Landscape with a Man
on Horseback and Rocky Landscape
in the Distance*

11. (XX) *Landscape with Bridges
and Figures, a Town in the Distance*
(with assistant B)

12. (XXI) *Landscape with Ruins
and Figures Walking* (with assistant B)

13. (XXII) *Coastal Landscape
with a Man on Horseback, Hounds,
a Cross, Herdsmen and Fishermen
with a Town on a Bay*

14. (XXIII) *Rocky Landscape* painted
around a window (with assistant A)

15. (XXIV) *Landscape with Vista
and Figures Walking* painted around
a window (with assistant A)

16. (XXV) *Landscape with Herdsmen
and Town with Tower and Windmill
in the Distance* (with assistant A)

Note: Paul Bril made an engraving dated
1590 of landscape no. 13 (see fig. 8,
p. 24). The Latin numbers were
originally under the landscapes.

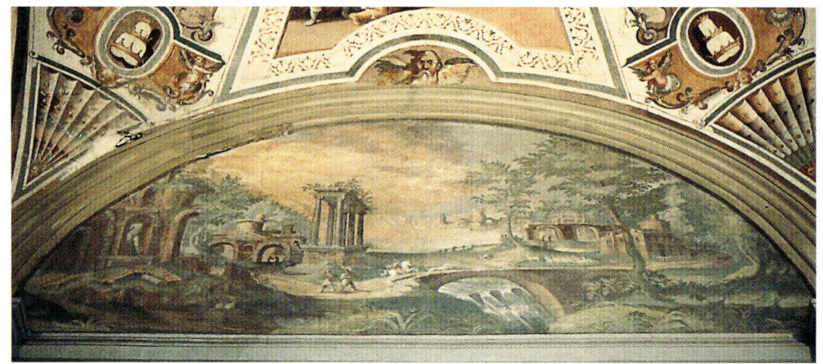

1

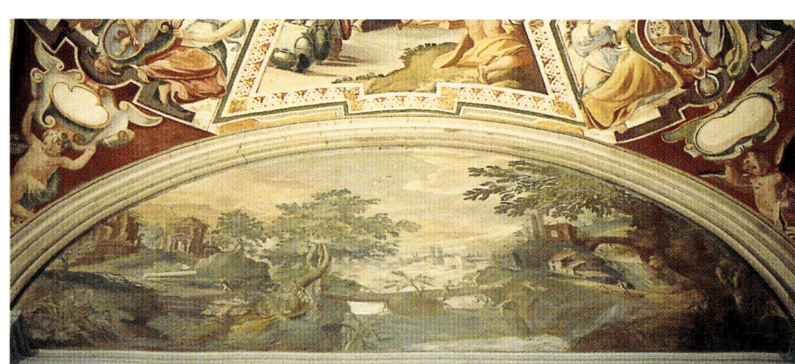

3

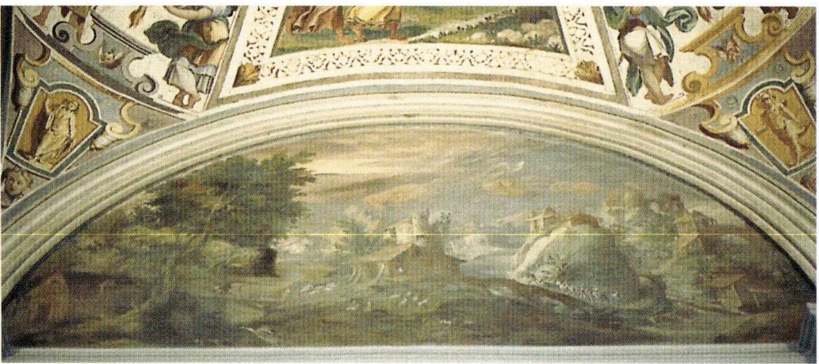

2

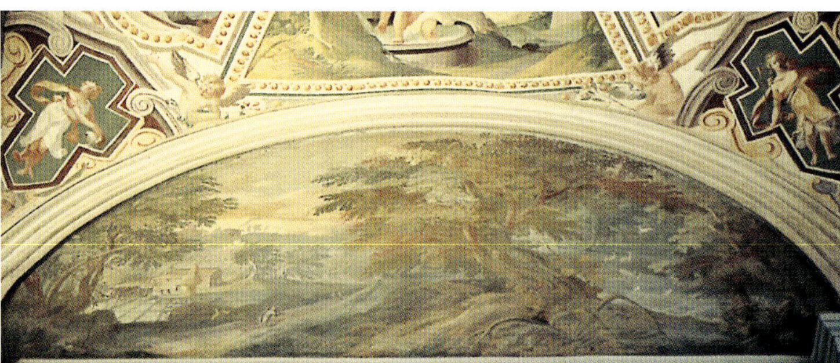

4

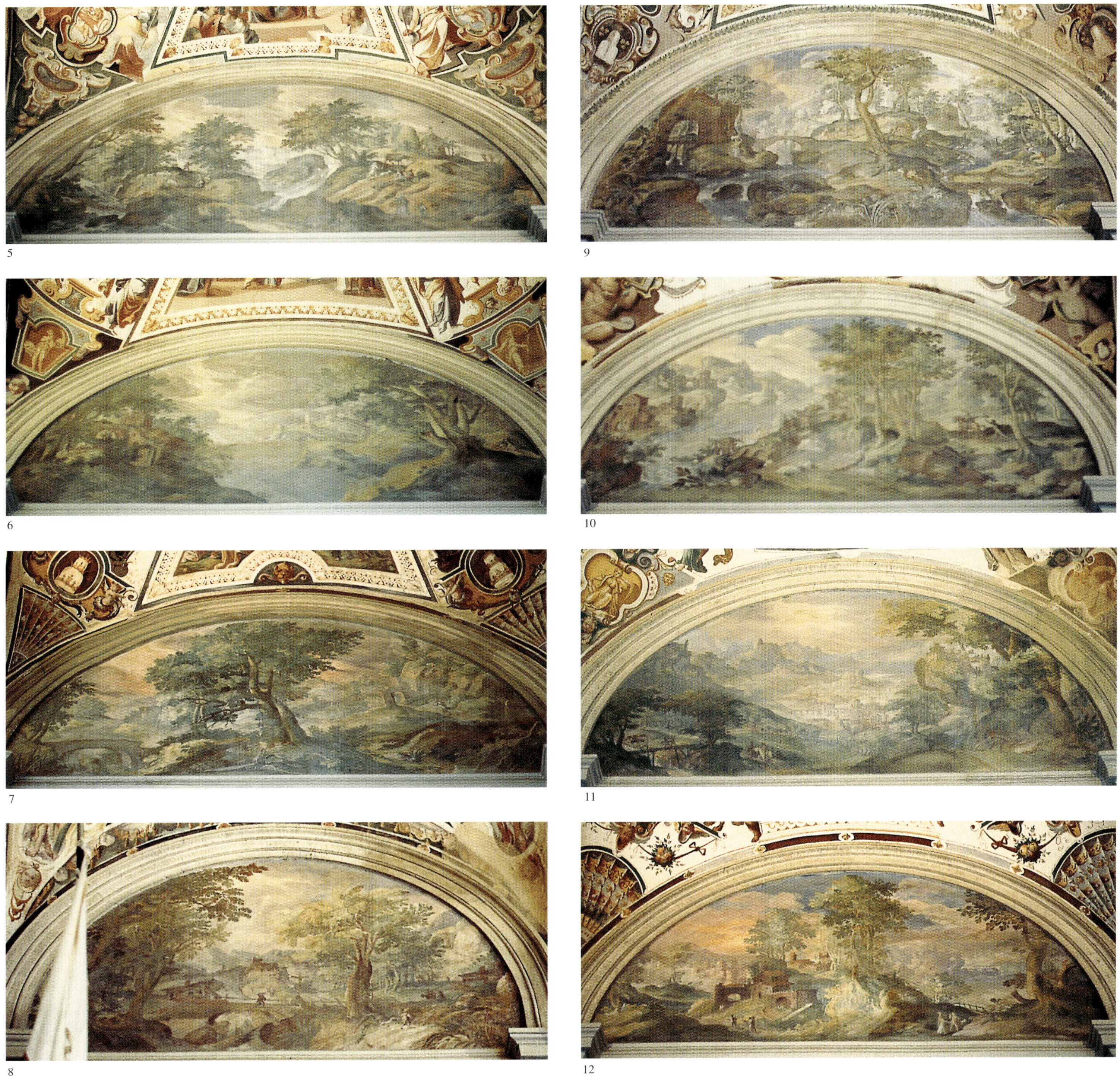

5

9

6

10

7

11

8

12

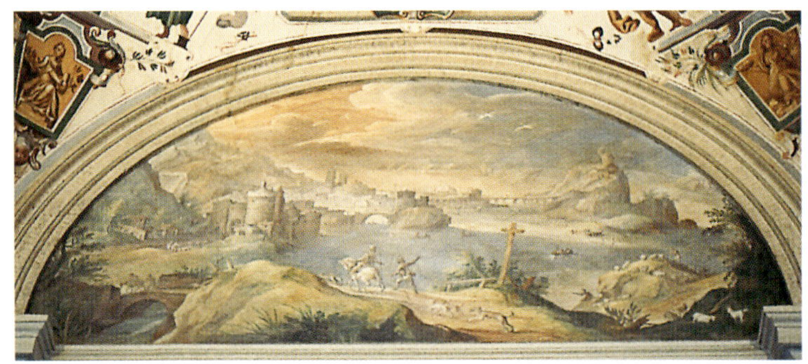

13

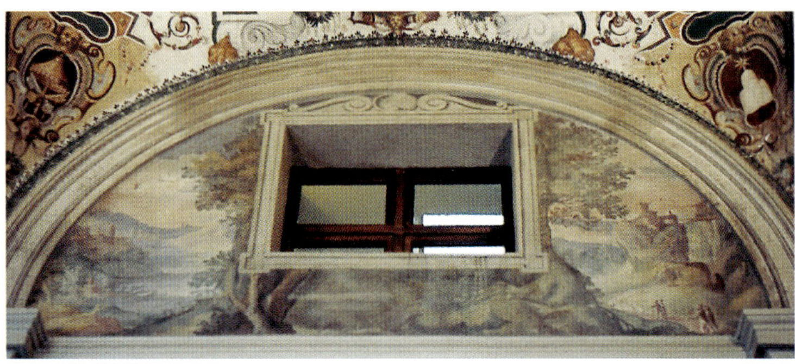

15

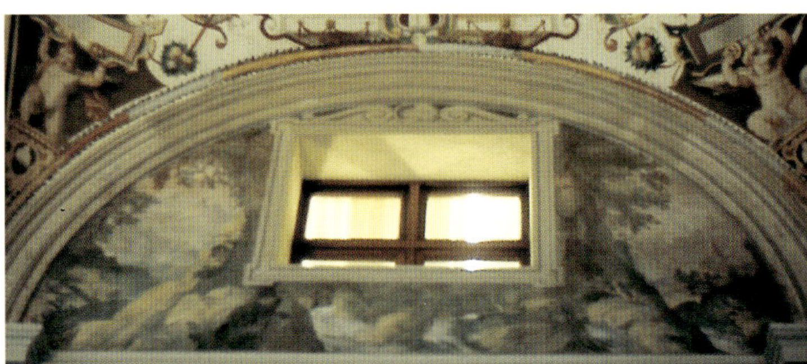

14

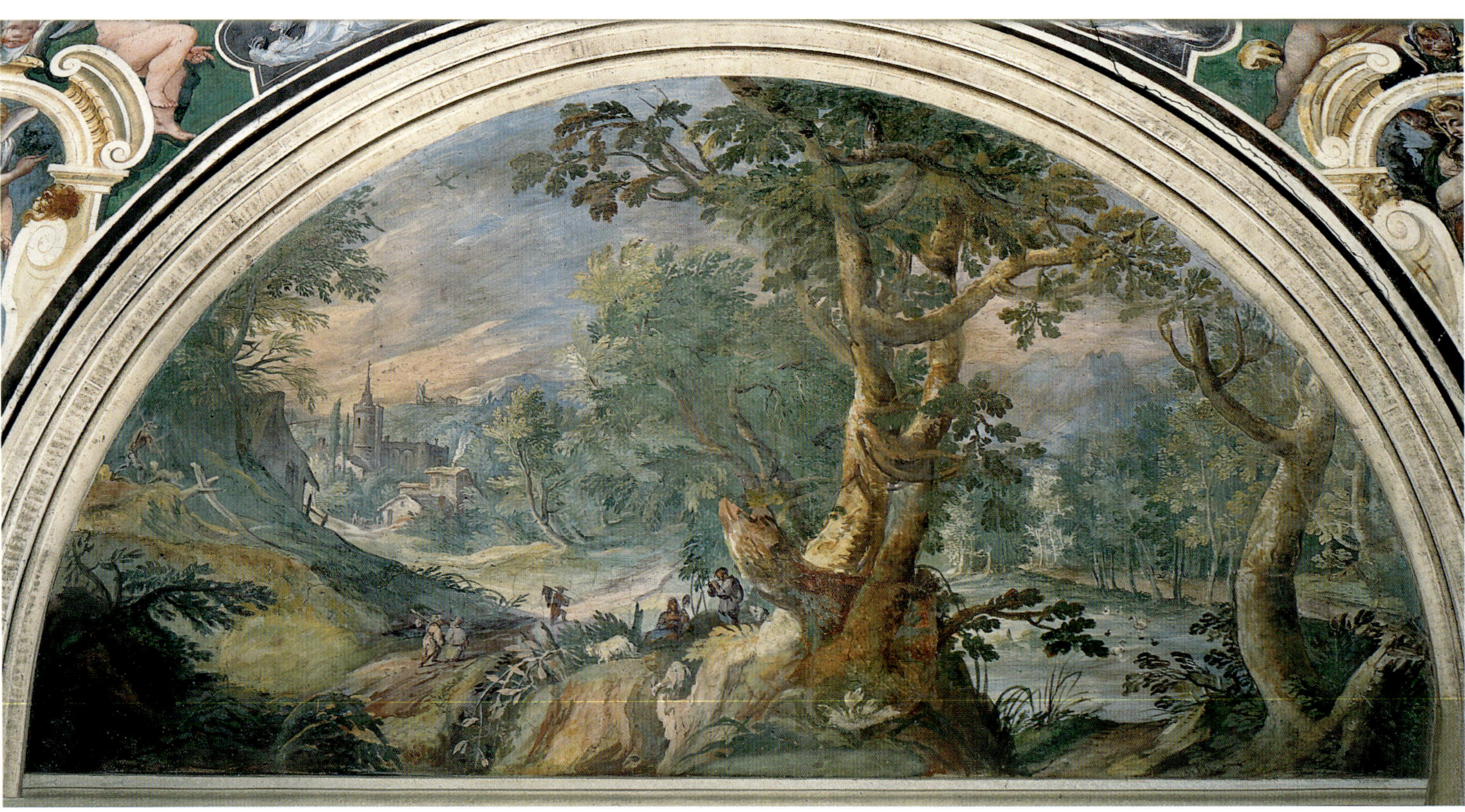

16

c.

Paul Bril and assistant(s)
(other frescoes: Cesare Nebbia
and Giovanni Guerra)

*Three landscapes, one seascape,
fresco**
Commissioned by Pope Sixtus V

Datable 1588-89

1. *Woodland with Fowler*

2. *Rocky Landscape with a Man
on Horseback*

3. *Seascape with Papal Galleys and Fort
and a Town in the Distance*

4. *Woodland with River and Waterfall
and a Town in the Distance*
(with assistant A)

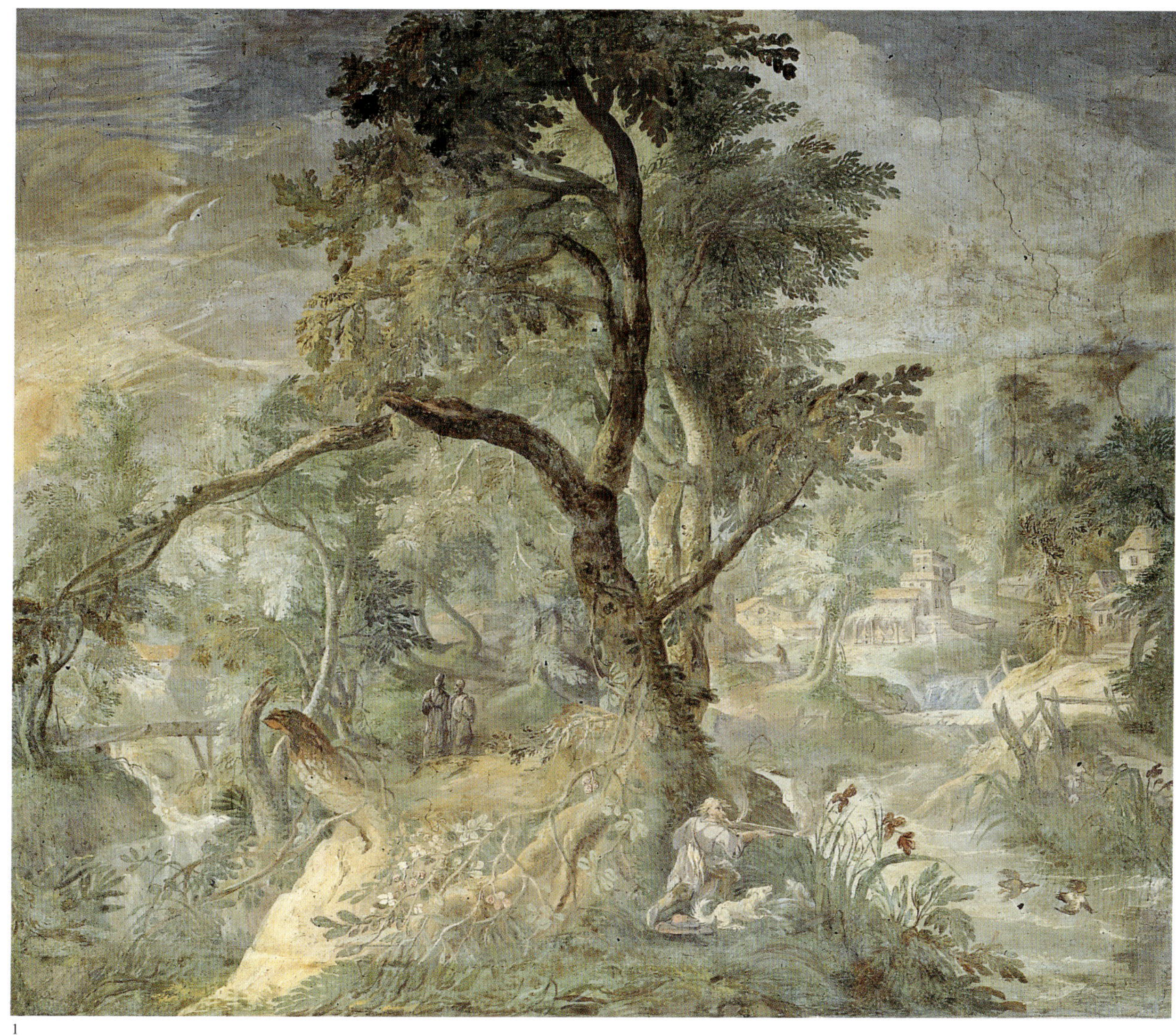

1

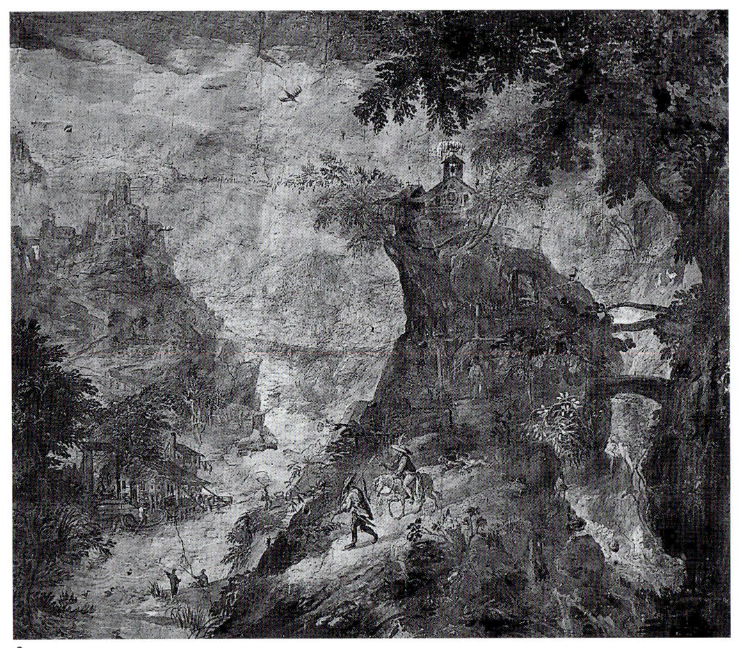

2

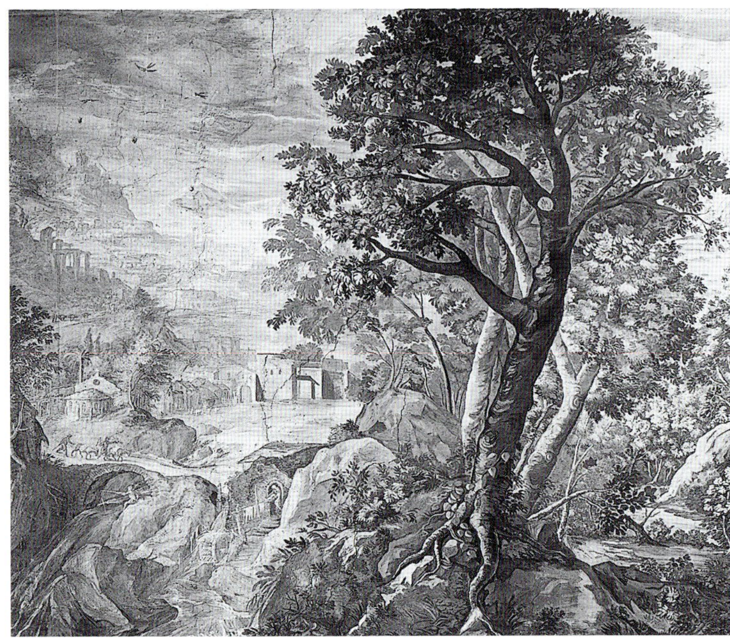

4

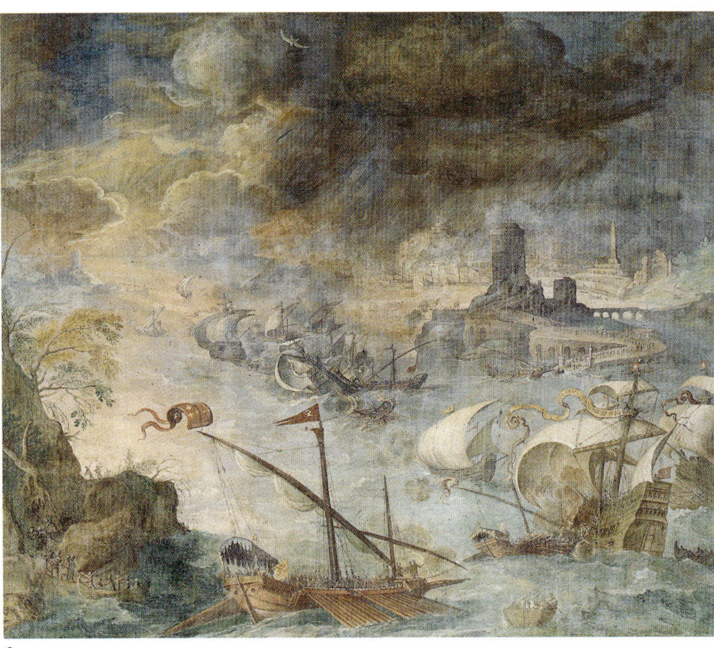

3

a.

Matthijs Bril
(three other landscapes: Cesare
D'Arbasia)

Nocturnal Landscape with Elephant
(in a frieze), fresco*
Commissioned by Pope Gregory XIII

Datable 1575

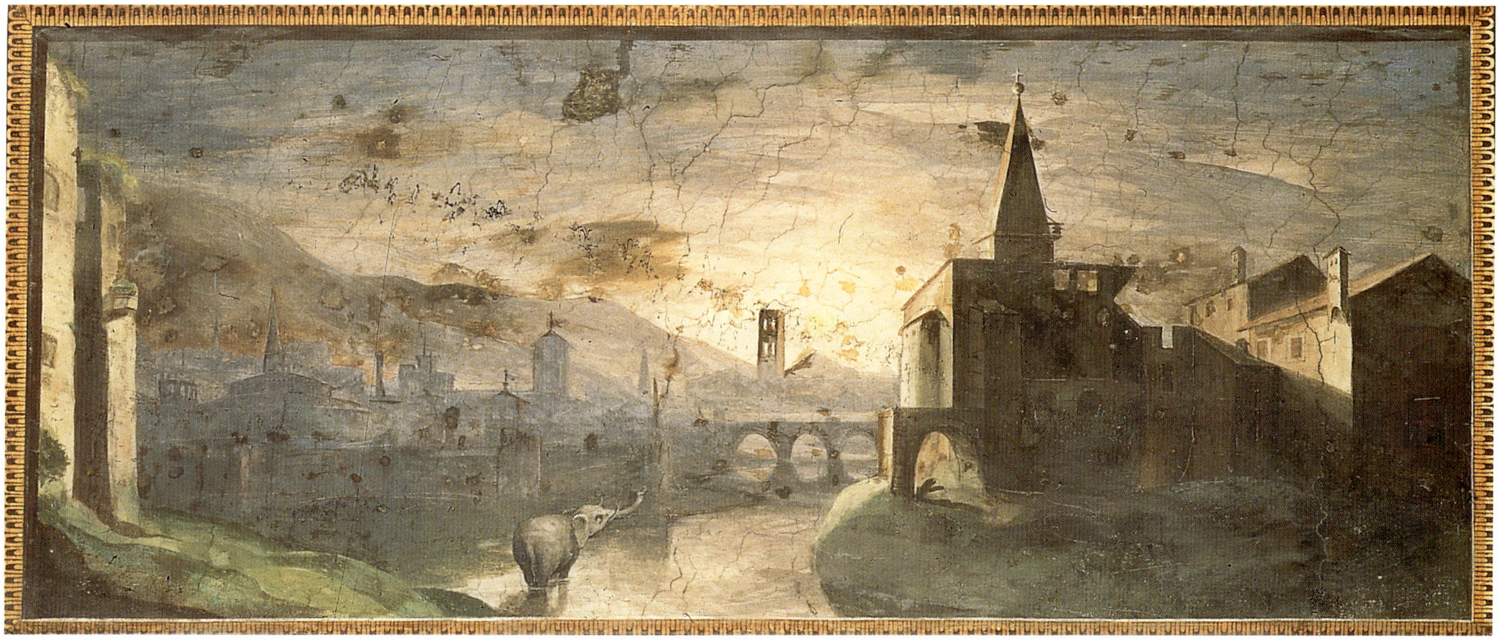

b.

Matthijs Bril
(quadratura: Ottaviano Mascarino;
supervisor: Lorenzo Sabbatini)

Three pergolas with animals, fourth
(below), fifth and sixth vaults, fresco*
Commissioned by Pope Gregory XIII

Datable 1575

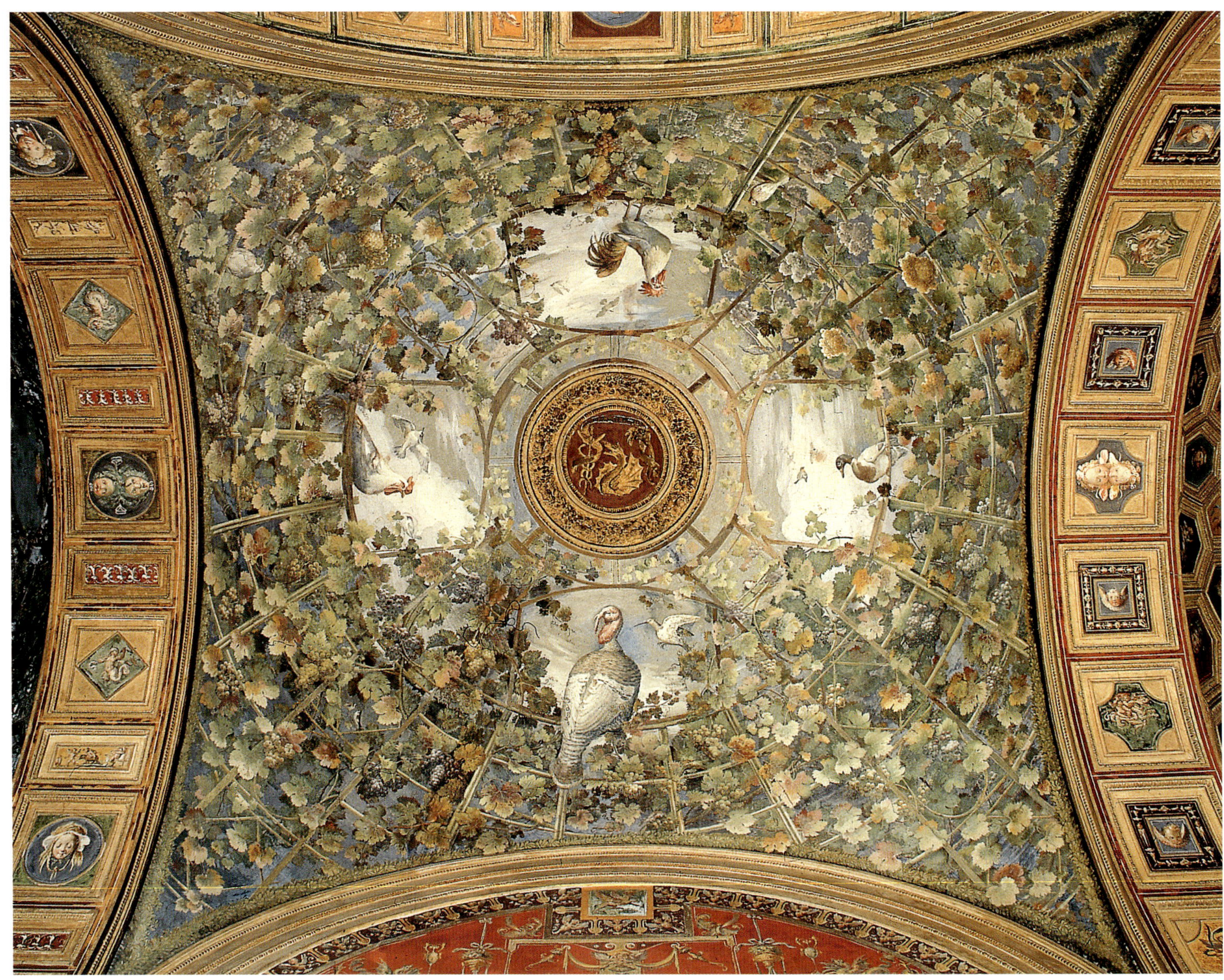

c.

Matthijs Bril

Four landscapes (in a frieze), fresco*
Commissioned by Pope Gregory XIII

Datable c. 1578

1. *River View*
2. *River View*
3. *Rocky Landscape*
4. *River View*

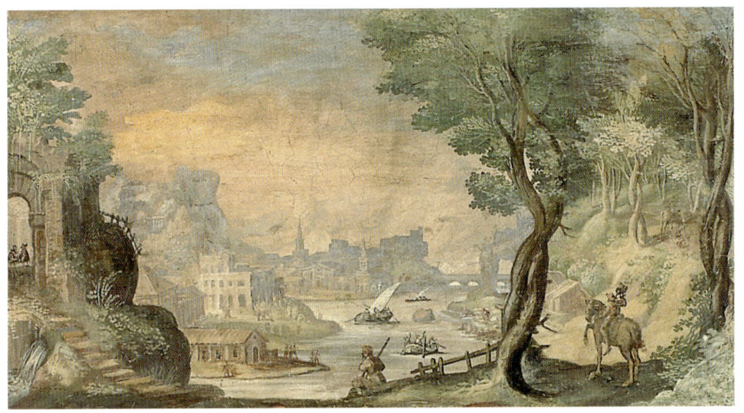

1

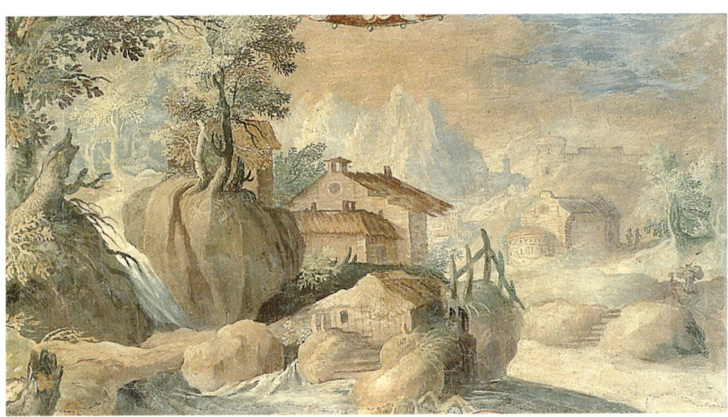

3

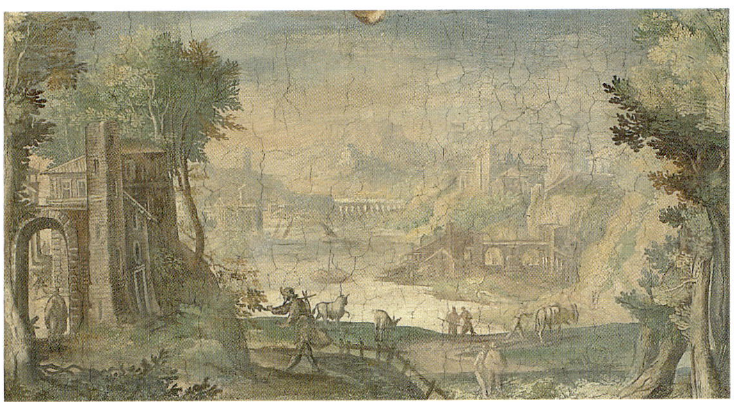

2

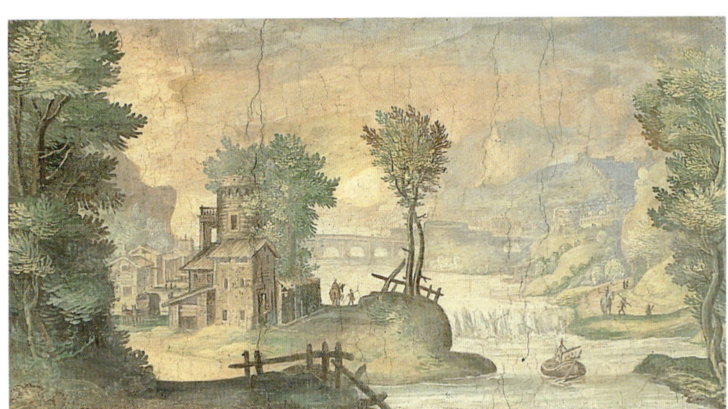

4

d.

Matthijs Bril
(figures: Antonio Tempesta)

*Ten Views of Rome
with the Procession with Pope
Gregory XIII Transferring the Relics
of St Gregory of Nazianzus* (frieze),
fresco*
Commissioned by Pope Gregory XIII

Datable 1580

1. *The Procession in front of Santa Maria
in Campo Marzio*

2. *'La Scrofa' Inn with Façade
of San Luigi dei Francesi*

3. *The Procession in the Square in front
of Sant'Apollinario*

4. *The Procession Passes Santa Maria
dell'Anima*

5. *The Procession at the Statue
of Pasquino*

6. *The Procession Passes through
the Streets around Chiesa Nuova*

7. *The Procession Arrives
at the Sant'Angelo Bridge*

8. *The Procession on the Bridge
by Castel Sant'Angelo*

9. *The Procession in Scossa Cavalli
Square*

10. *The Procession in St Peter's Square*

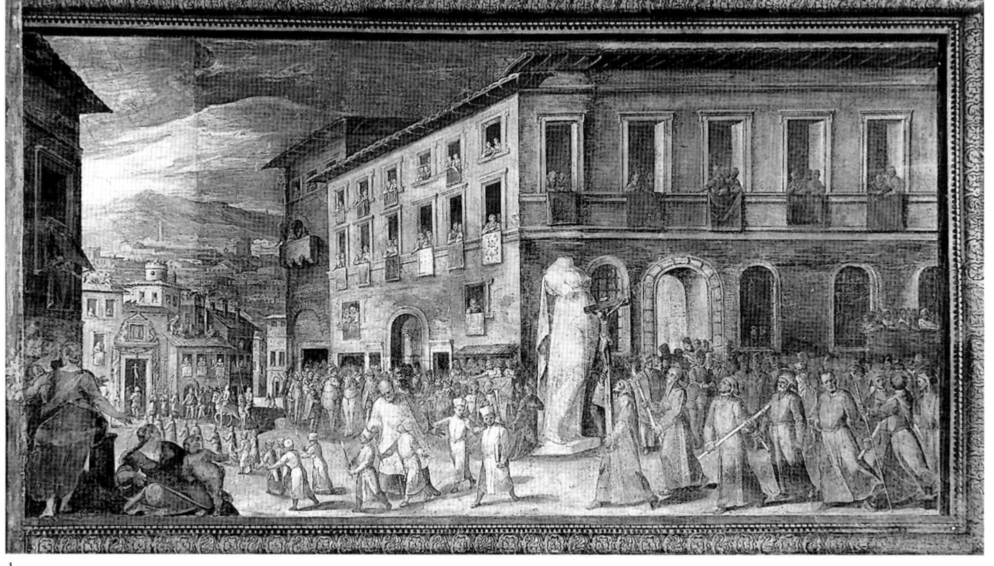

1

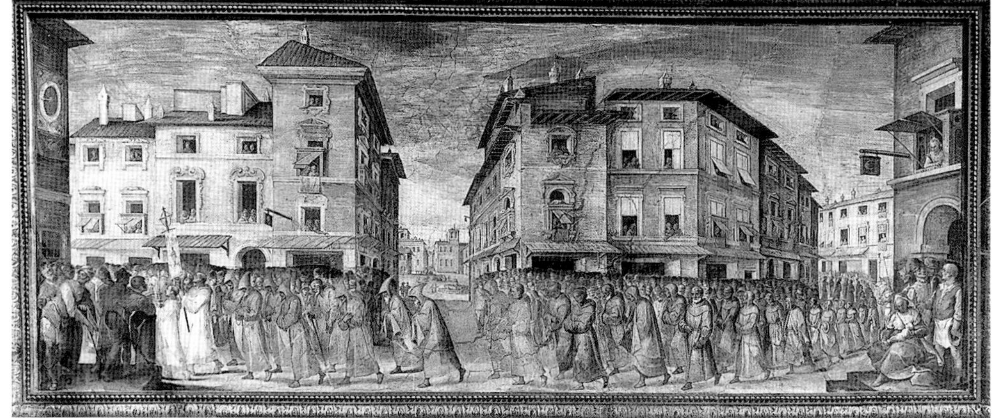

3

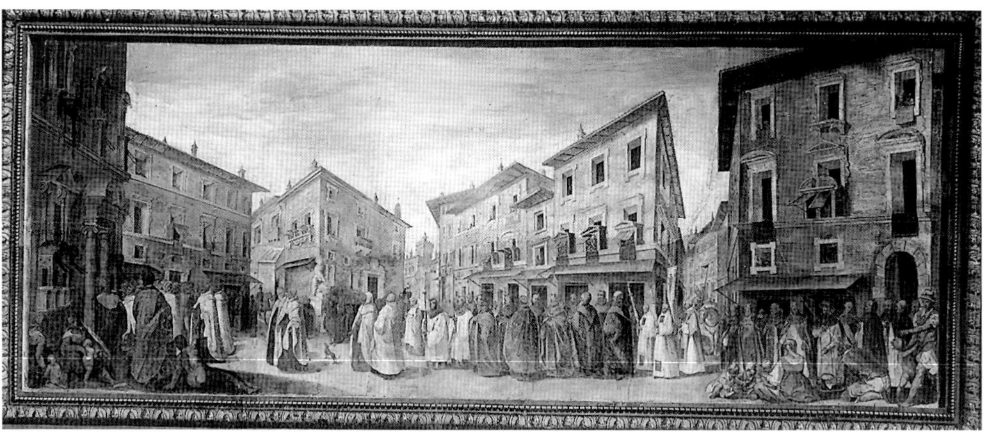

5

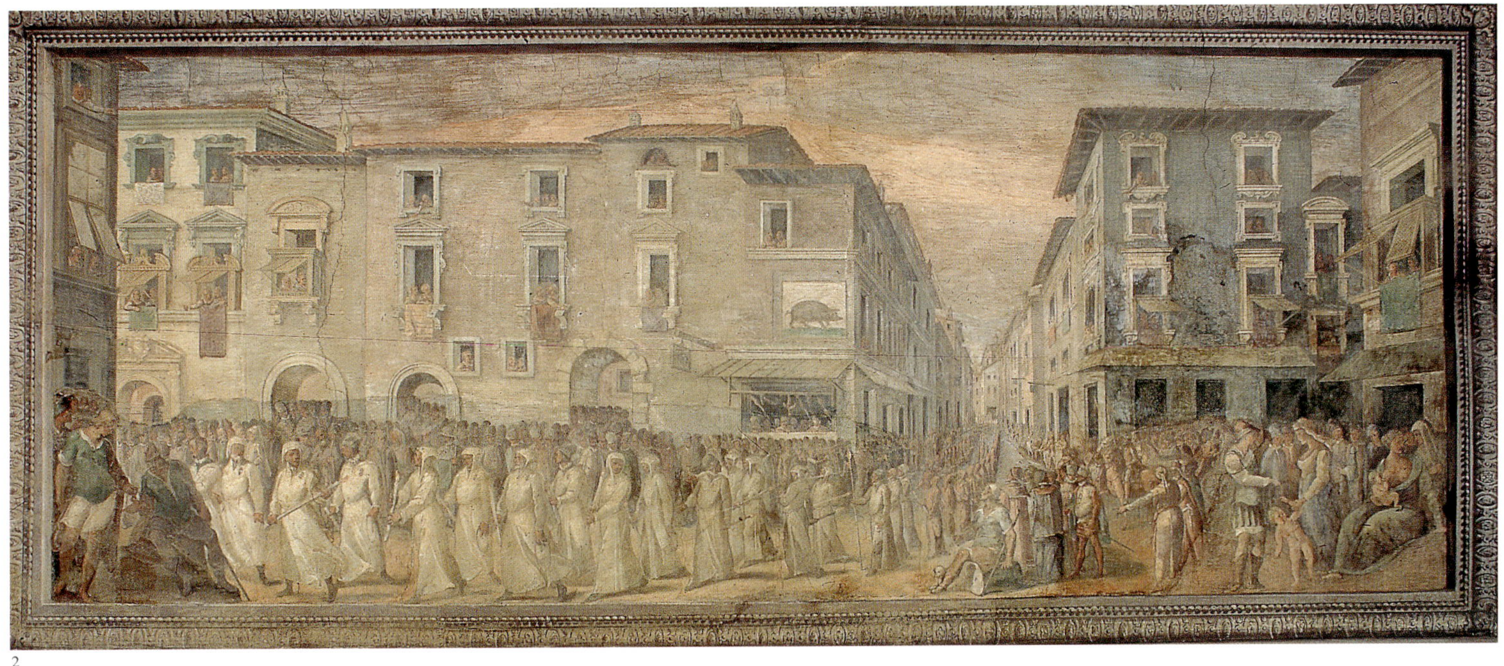

2

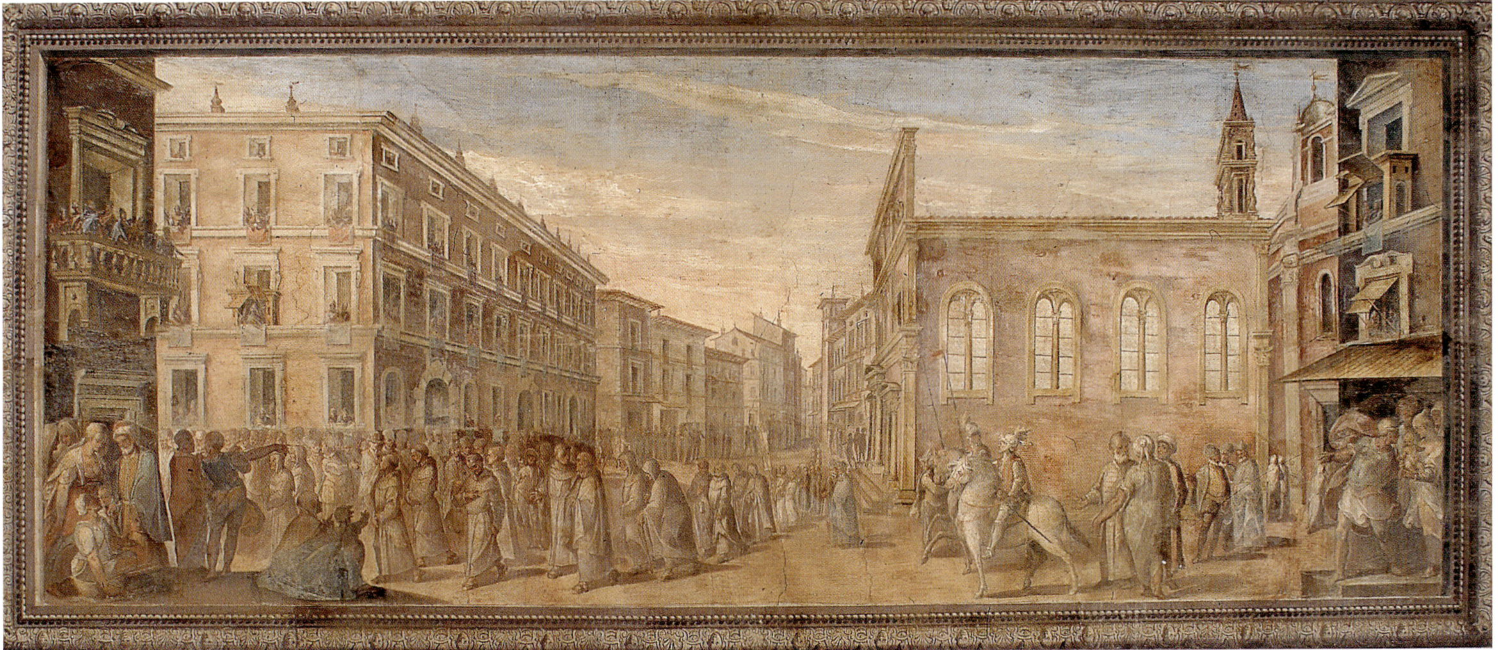

4

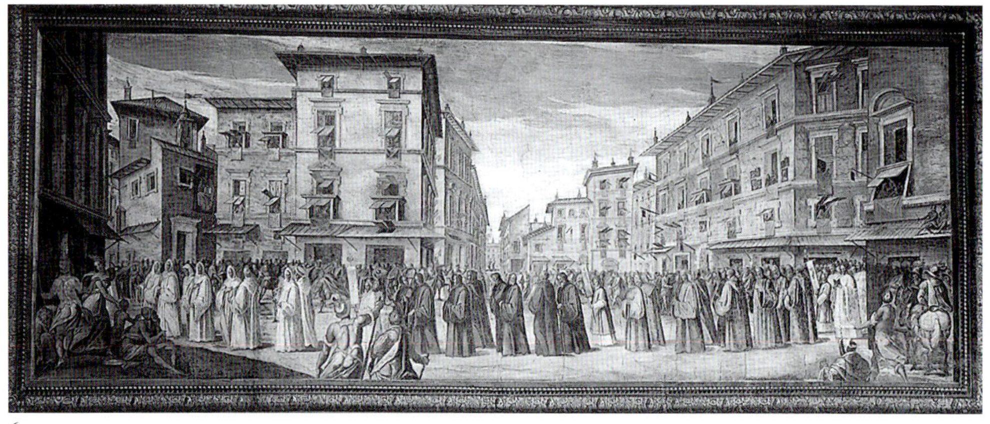

6

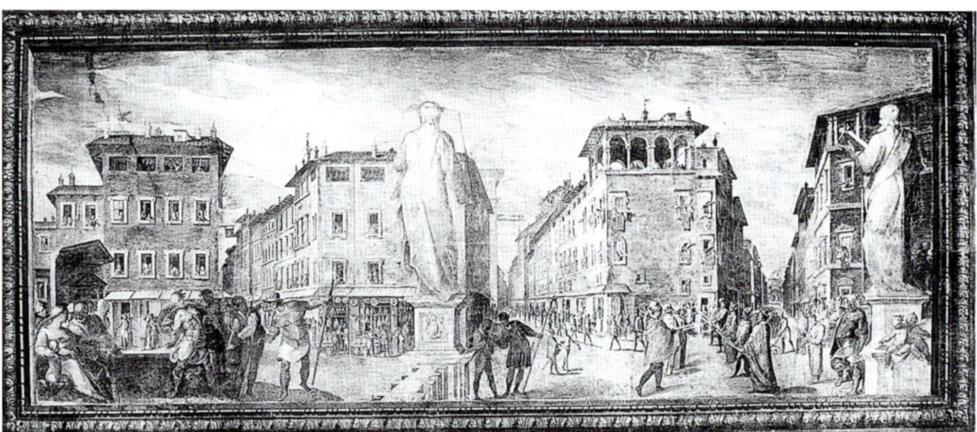

7

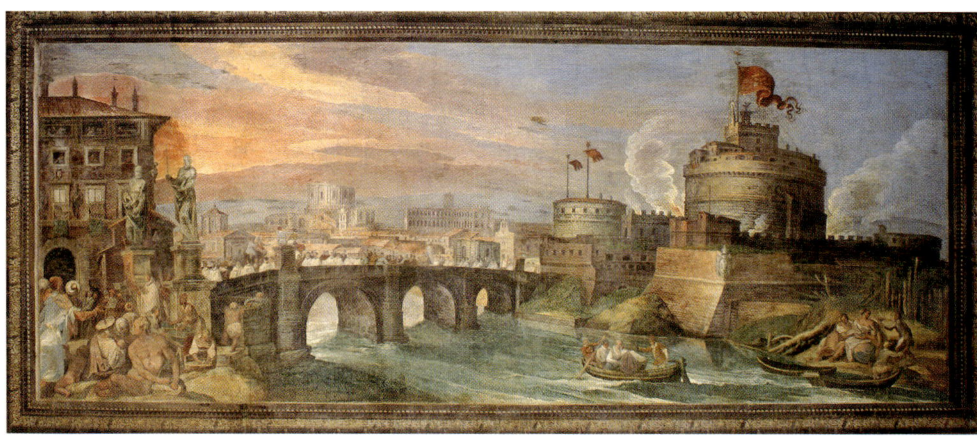

8

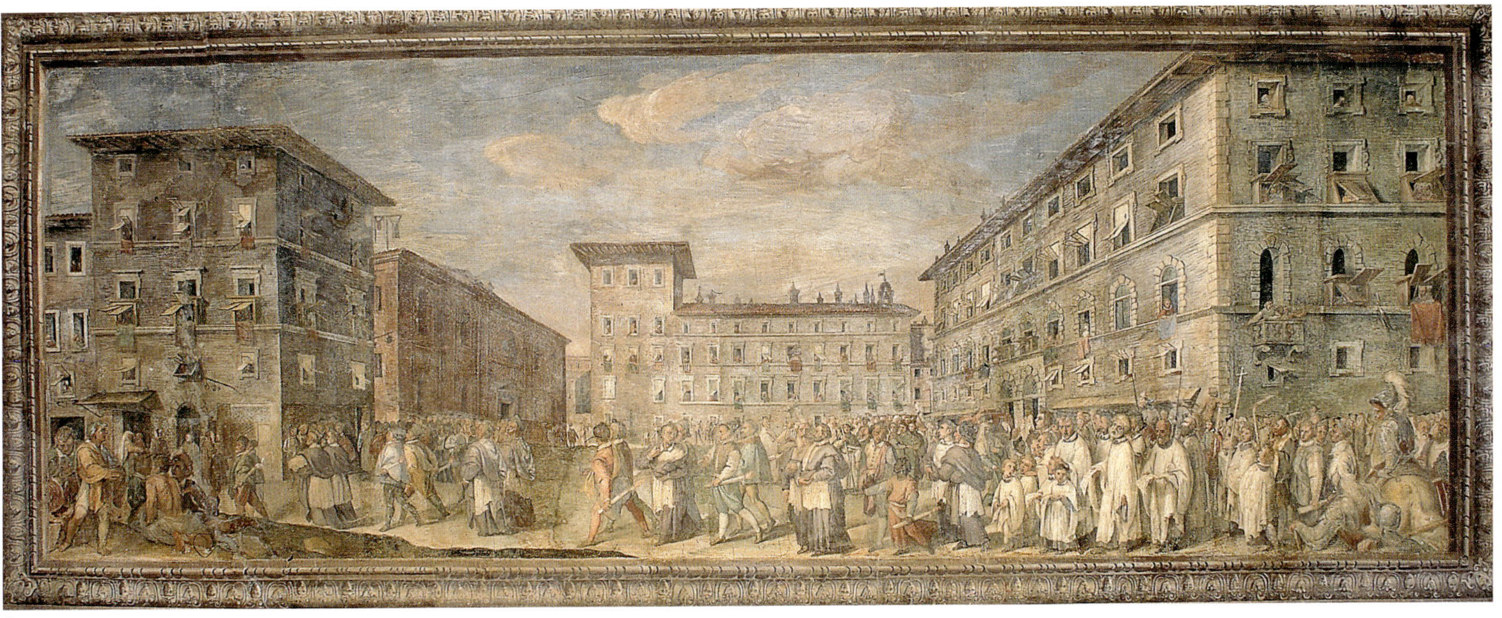

9

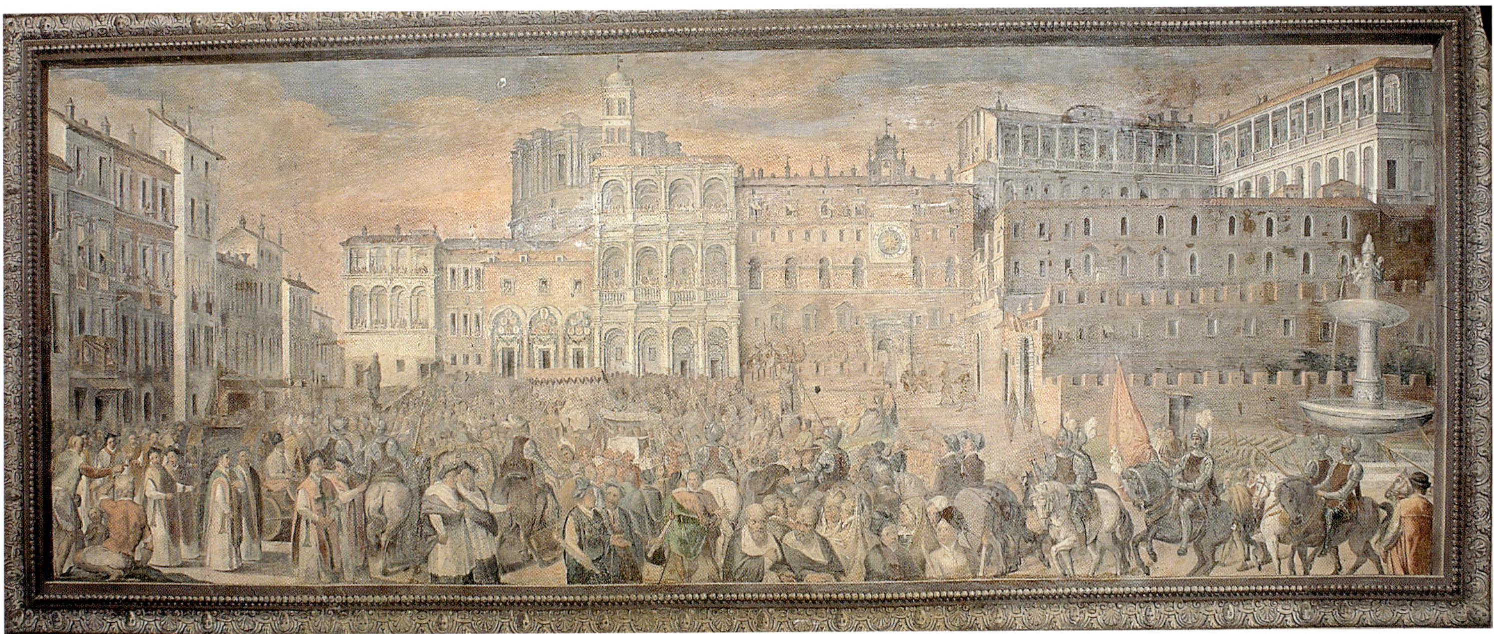

10

e.

Matthijs Bril
(figures and ships: Niccolò Circignani
called Pomarancio)

Two seascapes, two landscapes, fresco
Commissioned by Pope Gregory XIII

Datable 1580-82

1. *Christ Calms the Storm*
2. *Paul Shipwrecked on Malta*
3. *The Angels of the Apocalypse hold back
the Winds; an Angel Delivers the 114,000
Redeemed from Israel with the Sign
of the Cross*
4. *The North Wind*

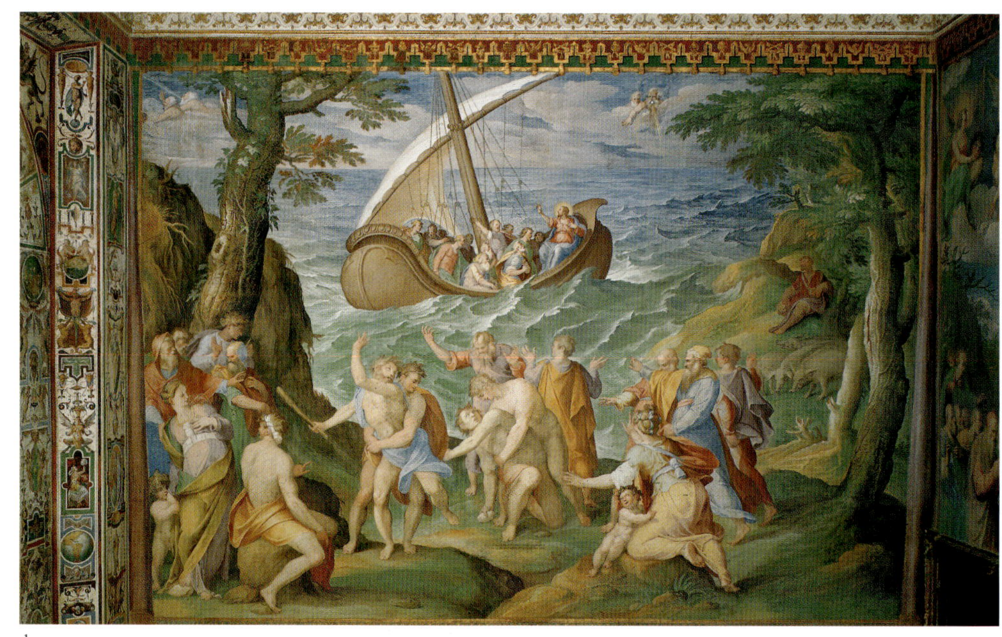

1

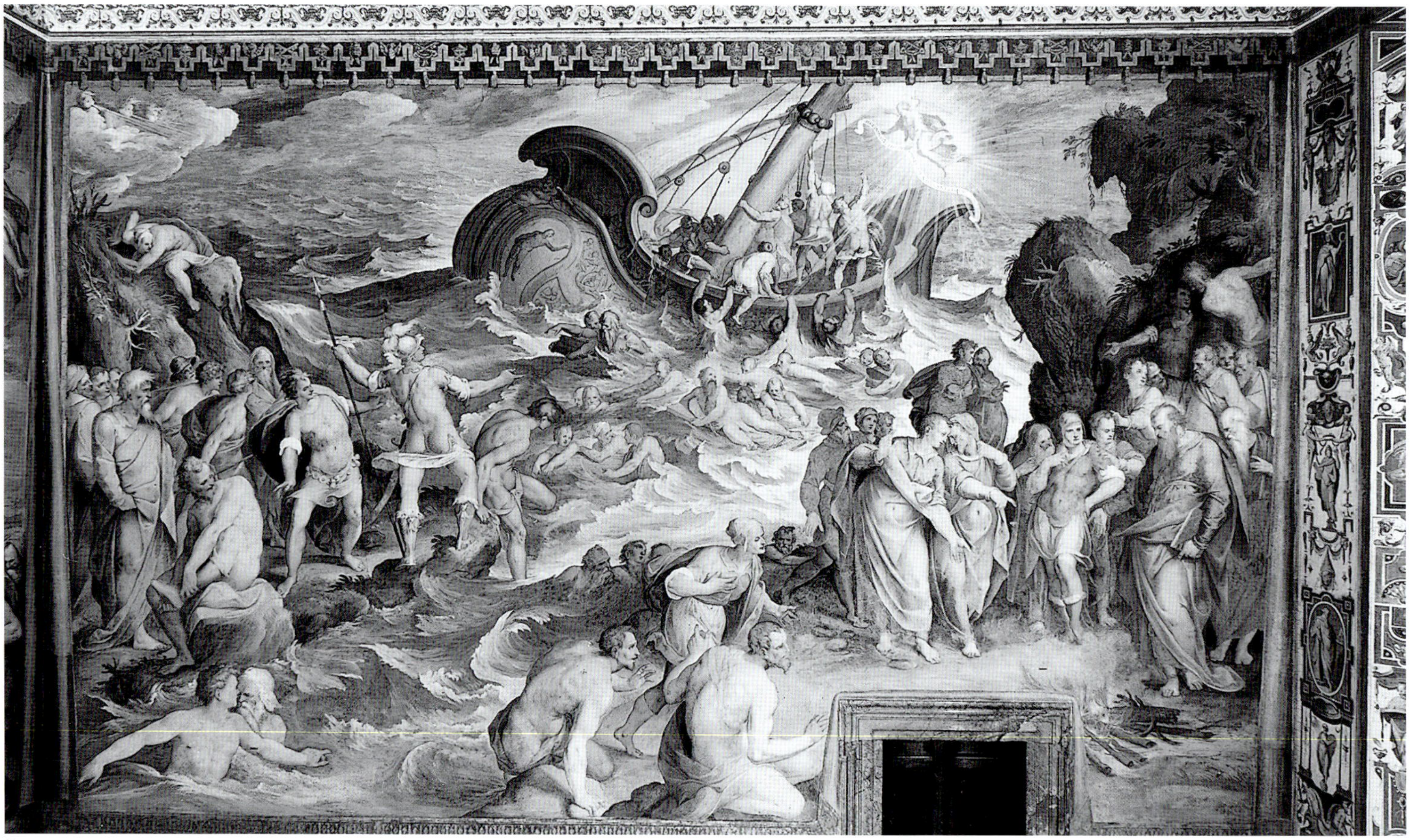

2

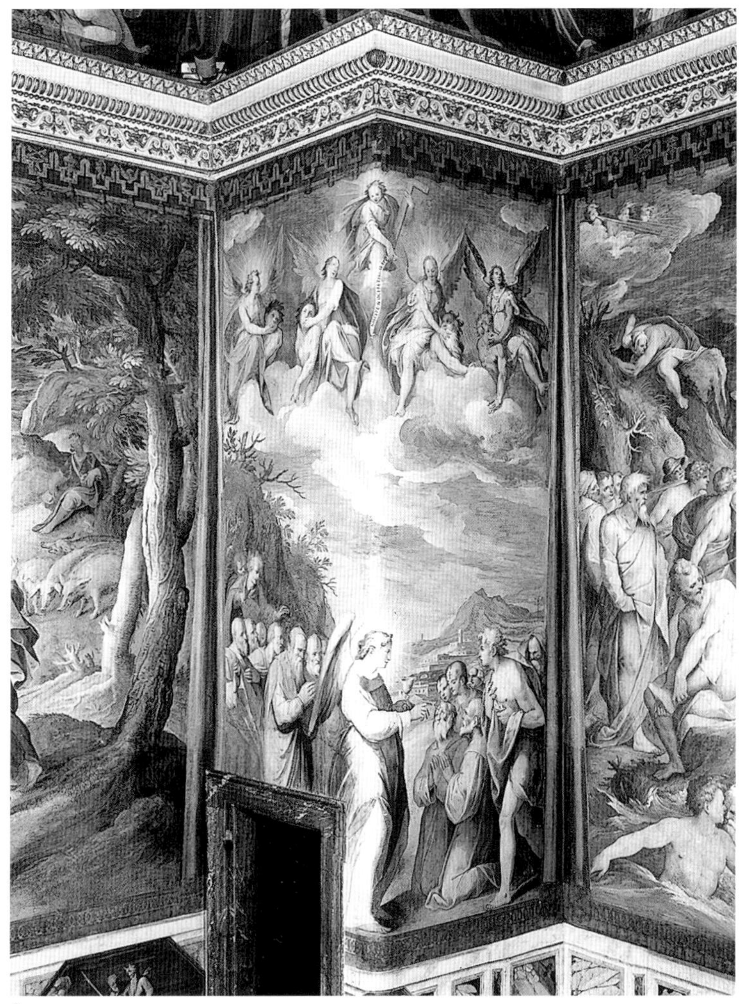

3

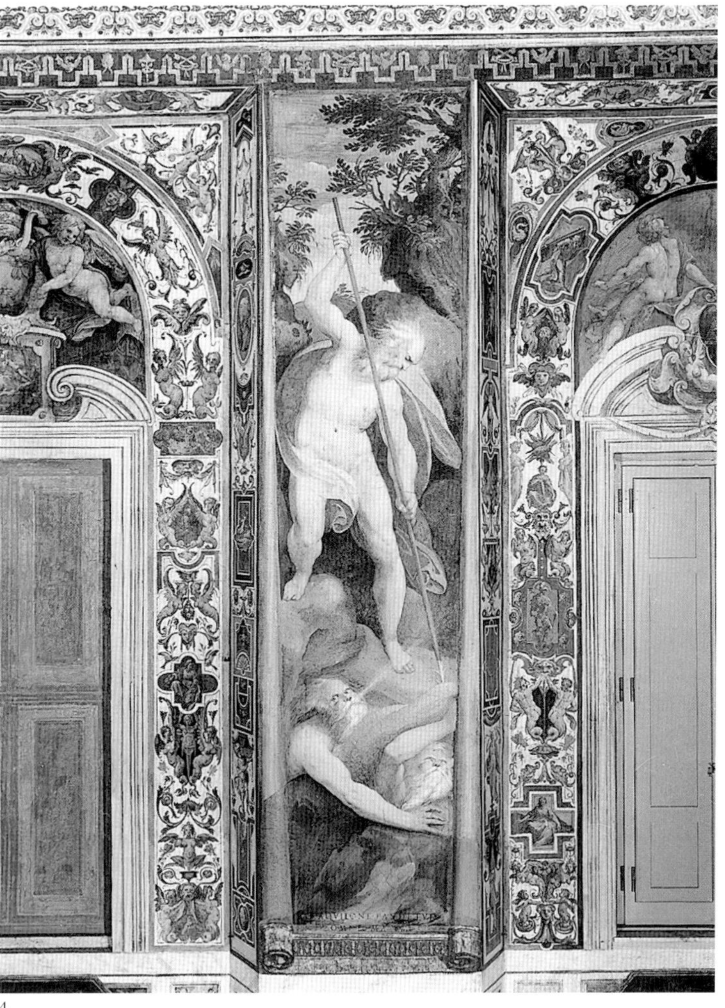

4

f.

Matthijs Bril
(allegorical figures and putti
surrounding the scenes: Niccolò
Circignani called Pomarancio)

*Twelve landscapes with biblical
scenes* (in a frieze), fresco
Commissioned by Pope Gregory XIII

Datable 1580-82

1. *God Appears to Abraham*

2. *Abraham Welcomes Three Strangers
(Yahweh and Two Angels)*

3. *Abraham Banishes Hagar and Ishmael
to the Desert*

4. *Hagar and Ishmael in the Desert
with the Angel*

5. *The Sacrifice of Isaac*

6. *Rebecca and Eliezer at the Well*

7. *Esau Gives Jacob his Birthright*

8. *Jacob's Dream*

9. *Jacob and Rachel at the Well*

10. *Jacob Wrestles with the Angel*

11. *The Reconciliation of Jacob and Esau*

12. *The Birth of Benjamin and the Death
of Rachel*

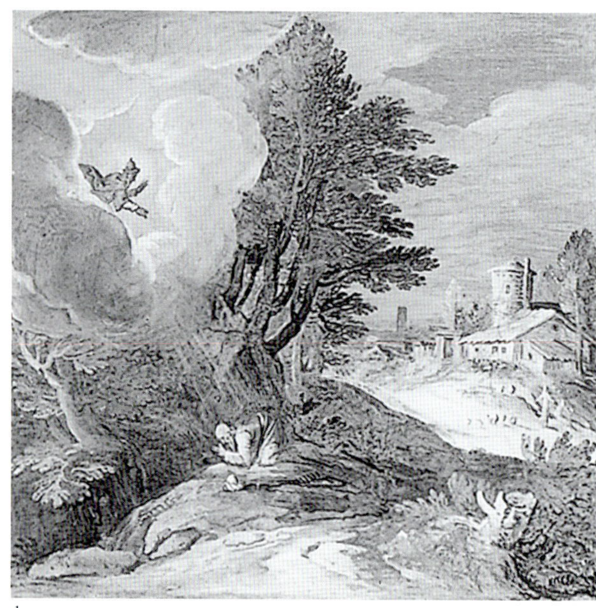

1

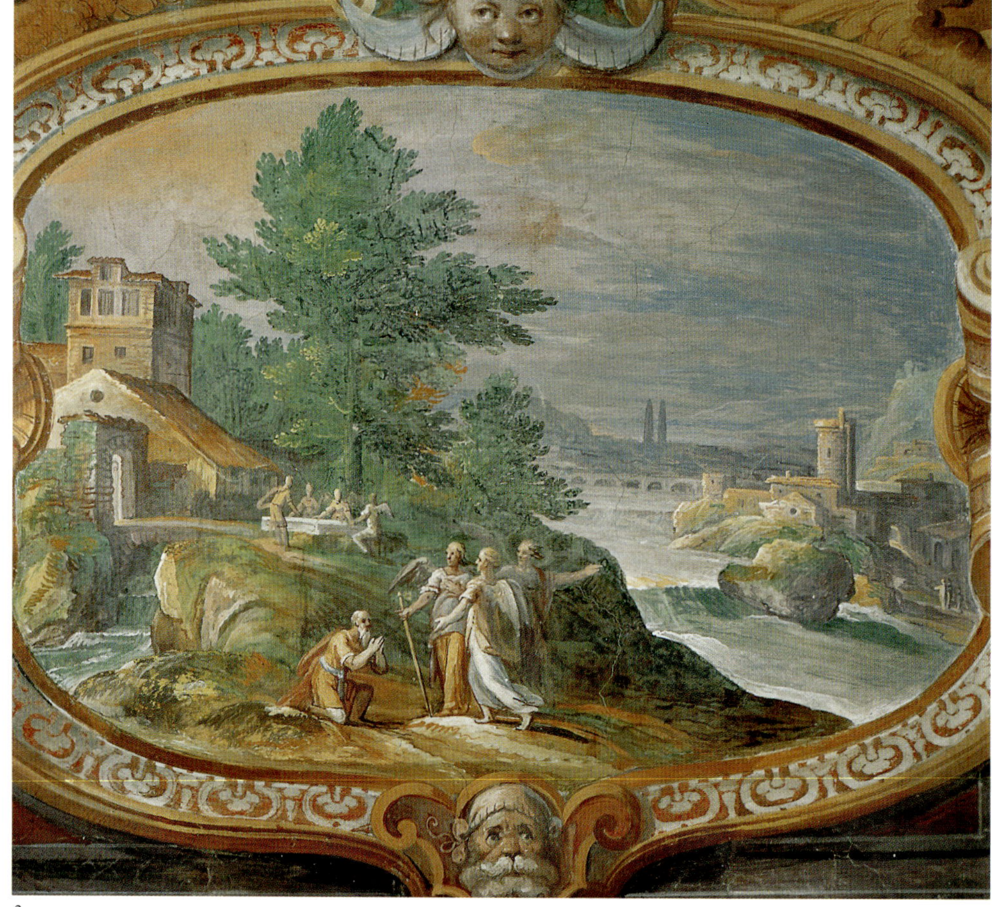

2

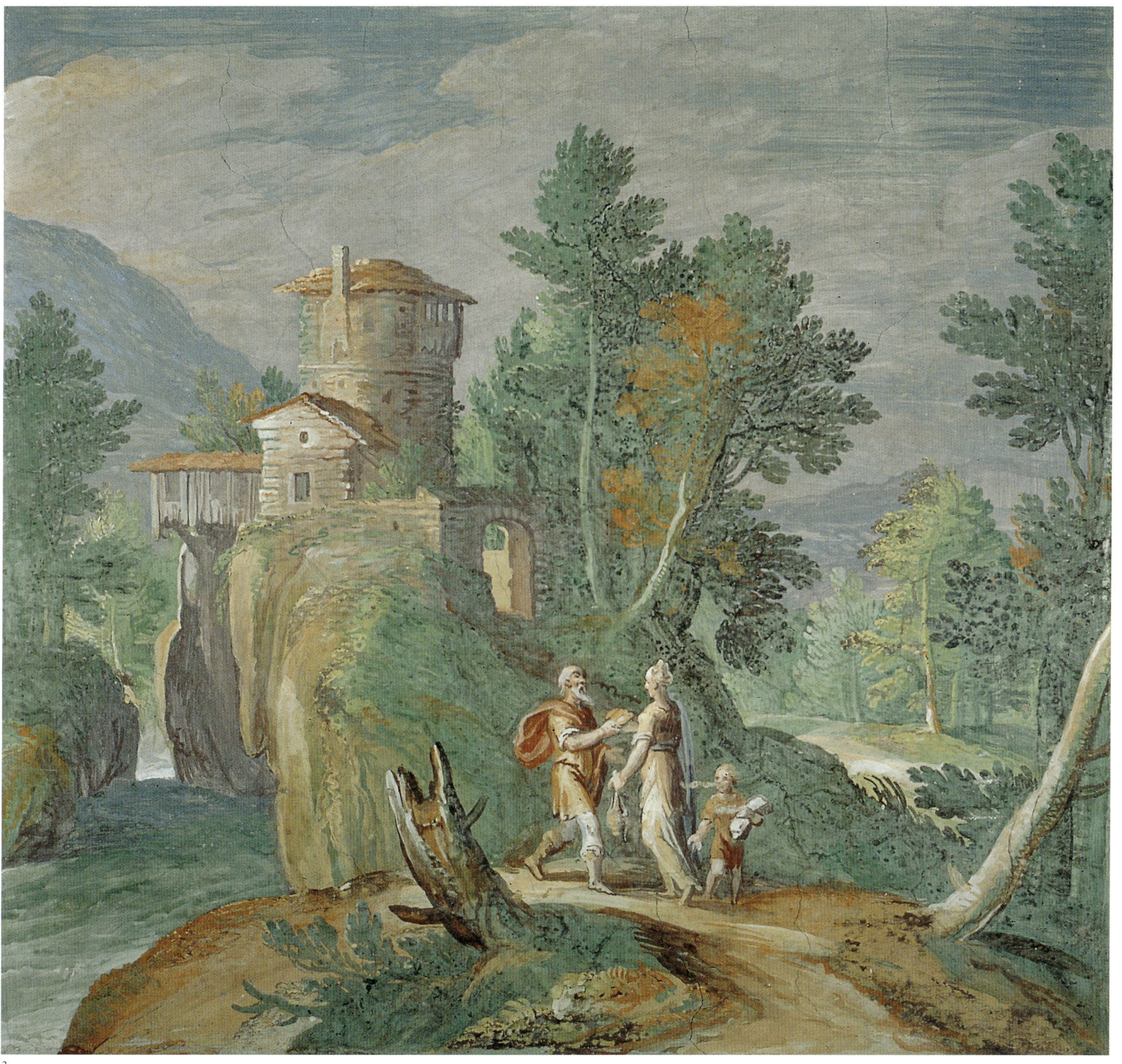

3

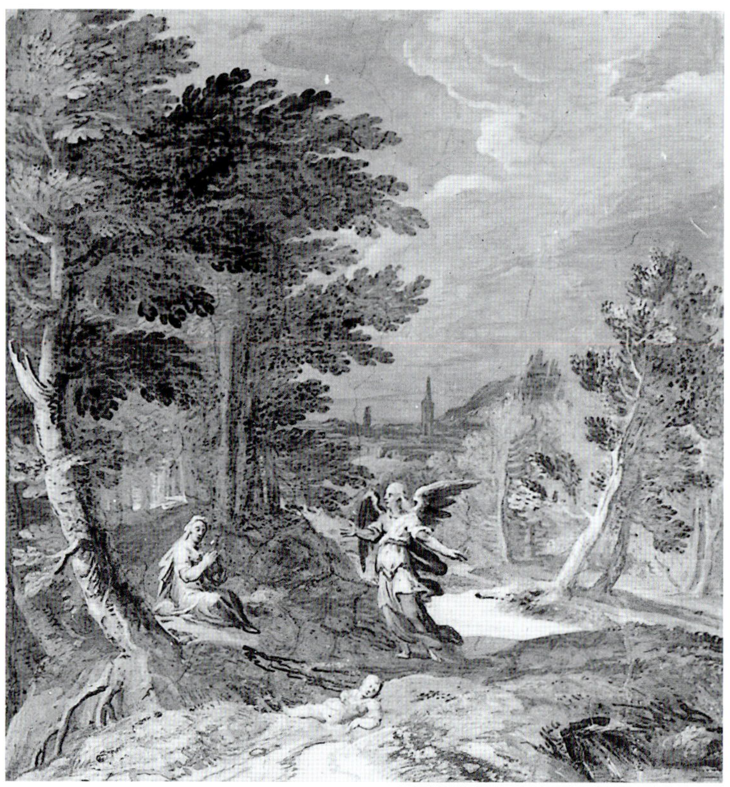

4

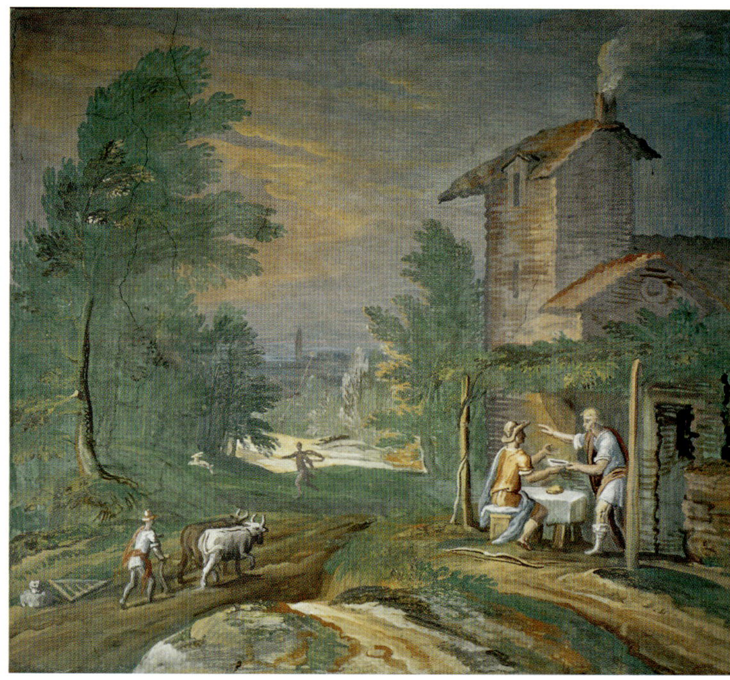

7

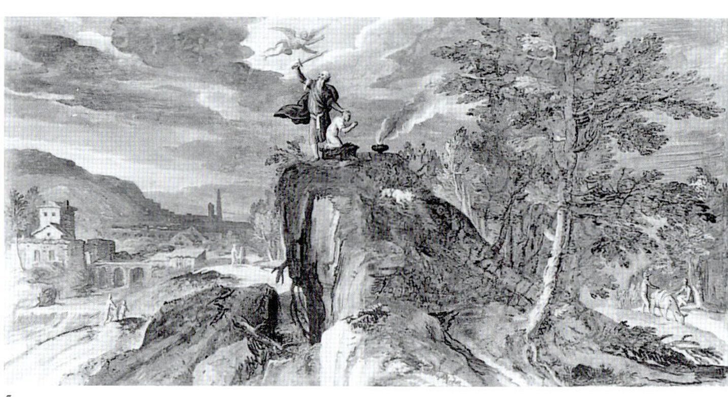

5

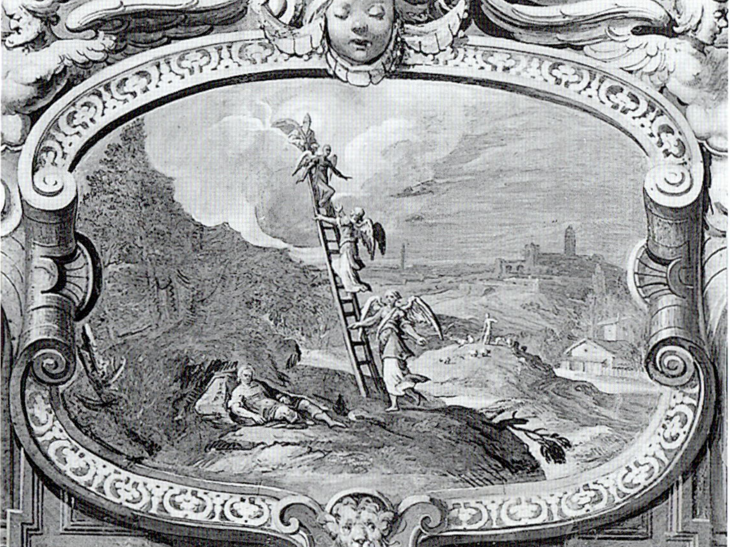

8

Torre dei Venti, Room of the Old Testament Patriarchs (first floor)

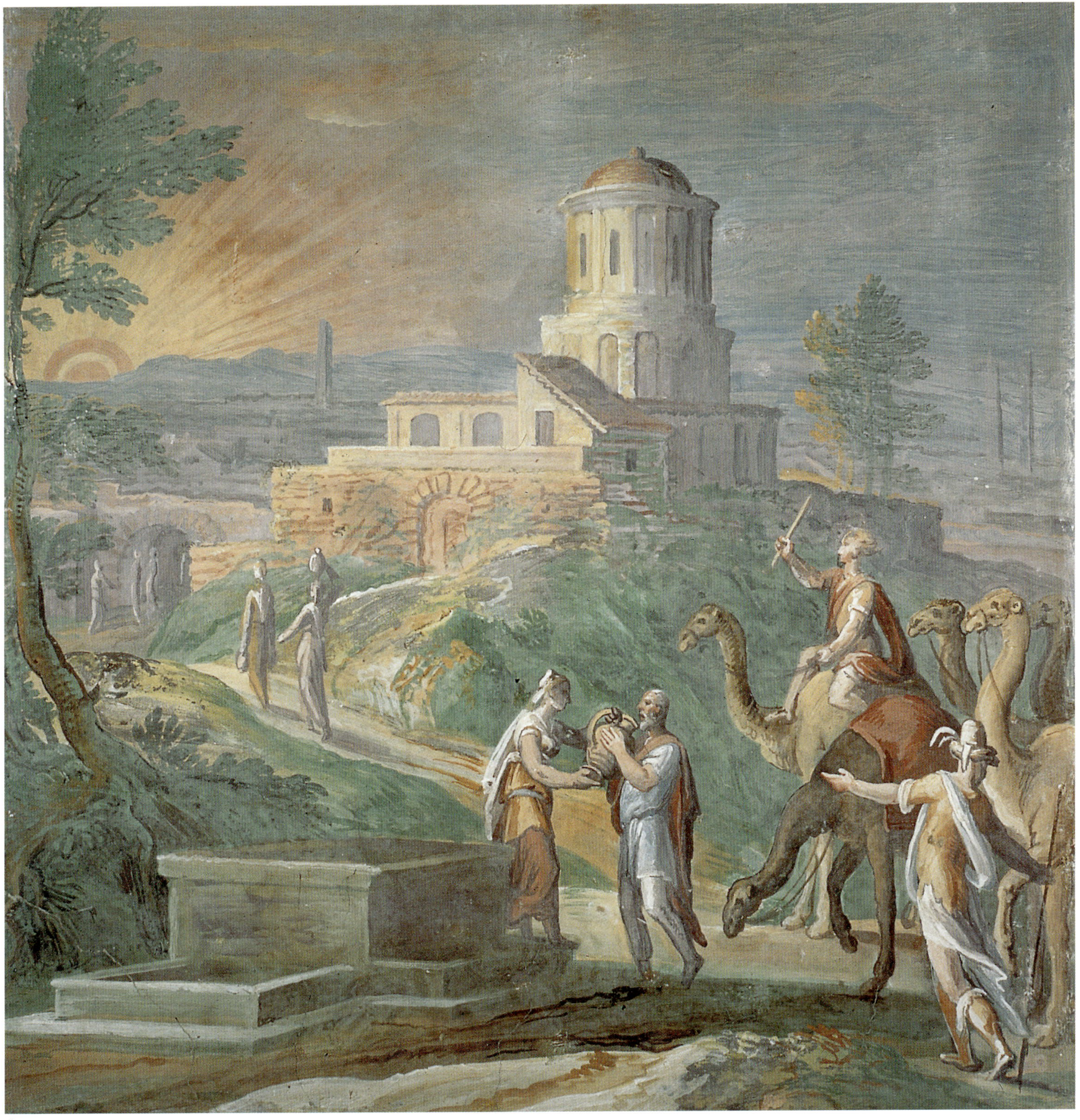

6

Torre dei Venti, Room of the Old Testament Patriarchs (first floor)

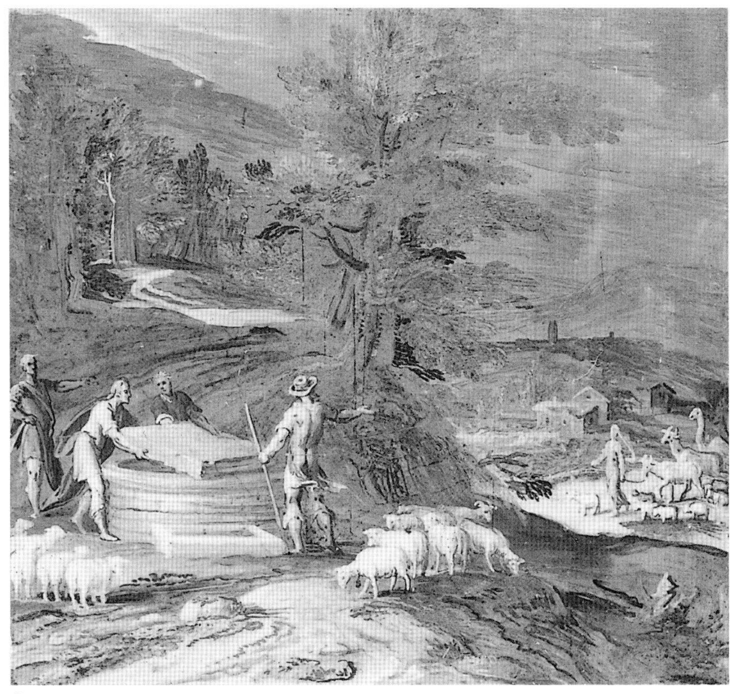

9

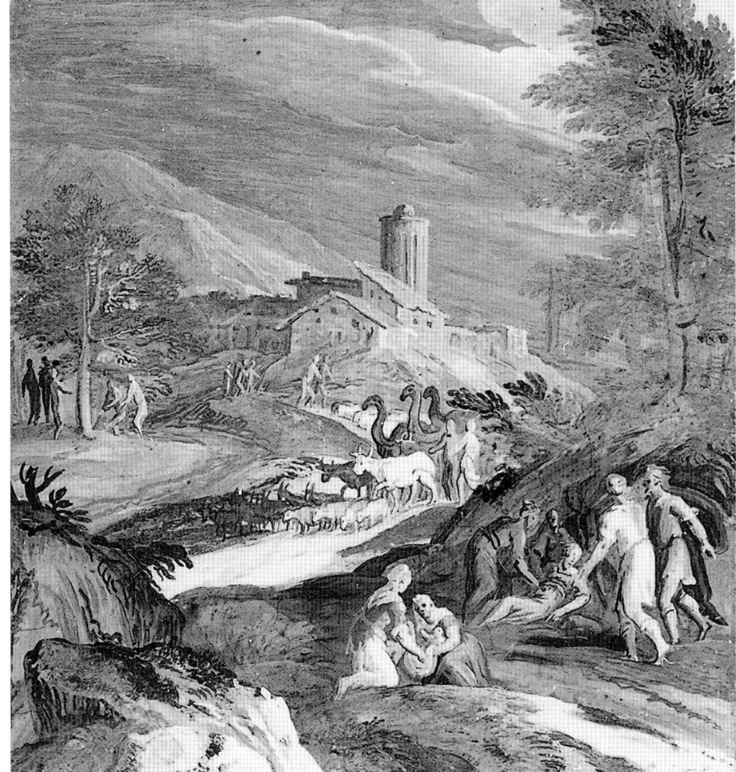

12

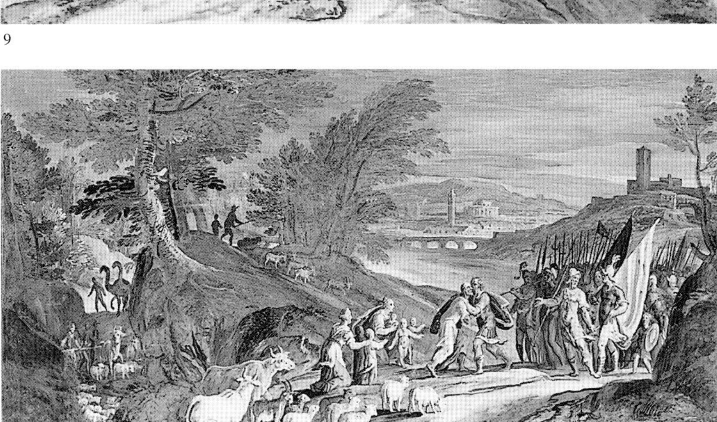

11

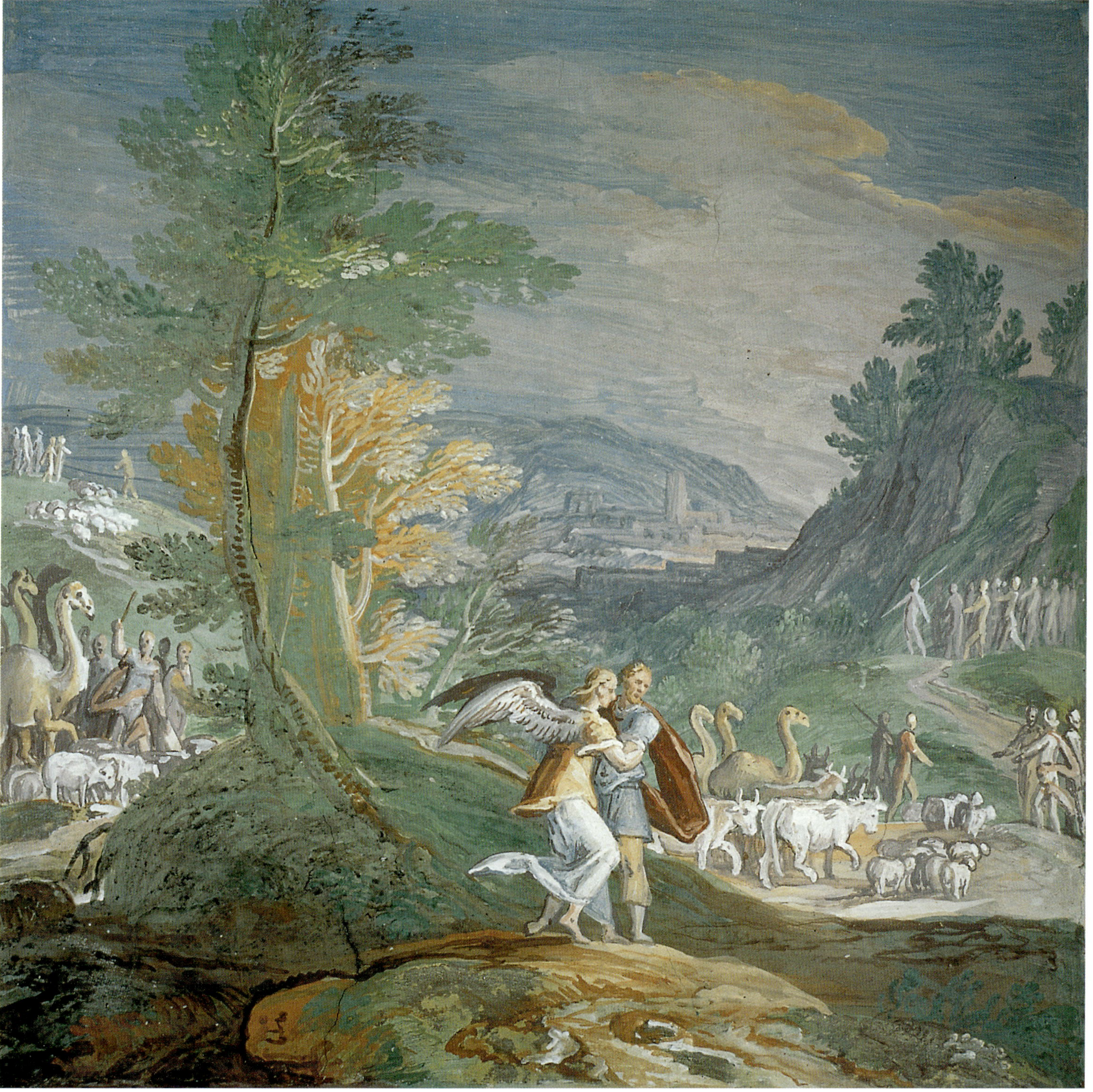

10

g.

Matthijs Bril
(putti: Niccolò Circignani called
Pomarancio)

*Twenty-four biblical scenes
in landscapes* (in a frieze
on the four walls), fresco
Commissioned by Pope Gregory XIII

Datable 1580-82

1. *The Fall of Simon Magus*
2. *Domine Quo Vadis?*
3. *The Fall of Eutychus*
4. *Paul Restores the Boy to Life*
5. *Paul's Vision in Troas*
6. *Andrew Raises the Body of Philopator*
7. *The Angel Leads Andrew to Deliver
Matthew from Prison*
8. *James the Greater Orders Philetus
to Free Hermogenes*
9. *James the Greater Gives his Staff
to Hermogenes*
10. *John the Evangelist Raises Drusiana
from the Dead*
11. *John's Vision on Patmos*
12. *Thomas Destroys an Idol*
13. *Thomas and the Death of the Major
Domo at the Wedding of King
Gundafero's Daughter*

14. *Philip Institutes Two Tribunals*
15. *Philip Rescued by a Dragon
at the Altar of Mars*
16. *Bartholomew Heals the Sick
in the Heathen Temple*
17. *Bartholomew Exorcises King Polymus'
Lunatic Daughter*
18. *Matthew Baptises the King of Ethiopia*
19. *Matthew Commends the Dragons*

of the Magicians Zaroes and Arphaxat
20. *Simon Makes the Sign of the Cross
on the Forehead of an Orator*
21. *Simon and the Army of Xerxes*
22. *Judas Thaddeus Heals a Blind King*
23. *Judas Heals King Abgar*
24. *An Apostle Heals (James the Lesser?)*
25. *An Apostle (James the Lesser?)*

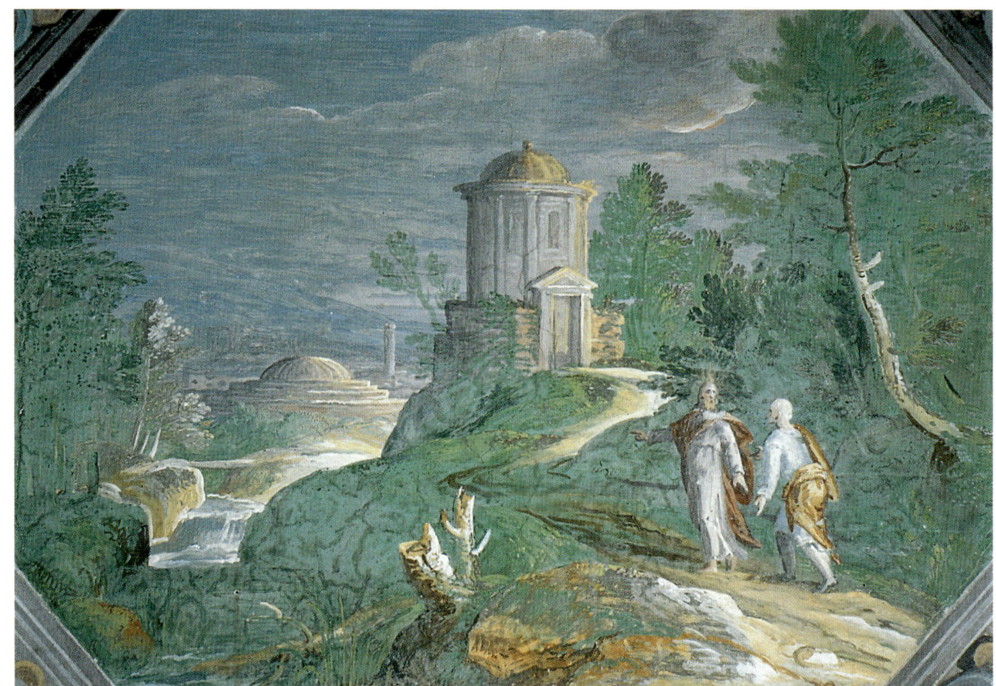

2

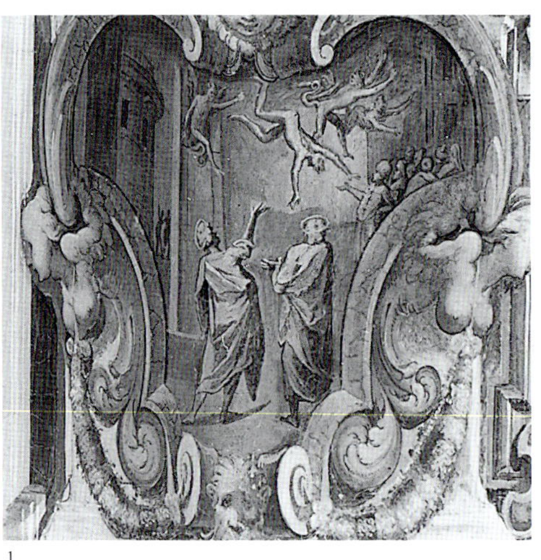

1

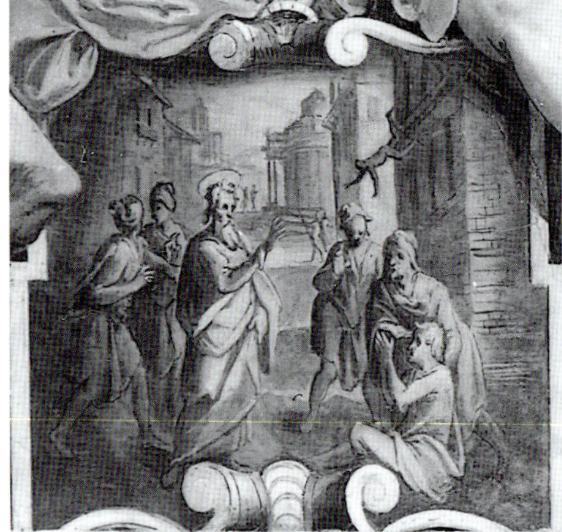

3

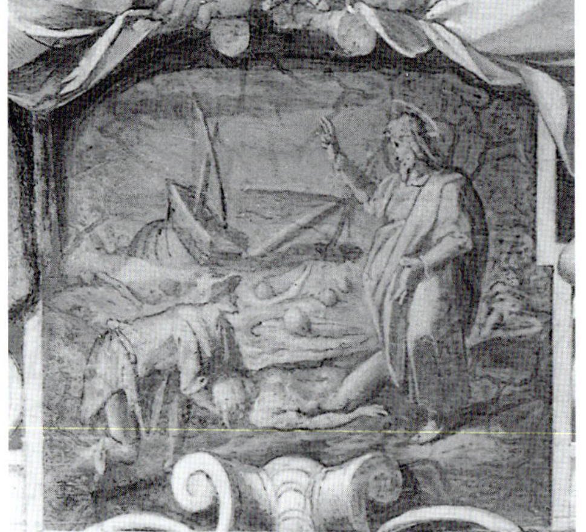

6

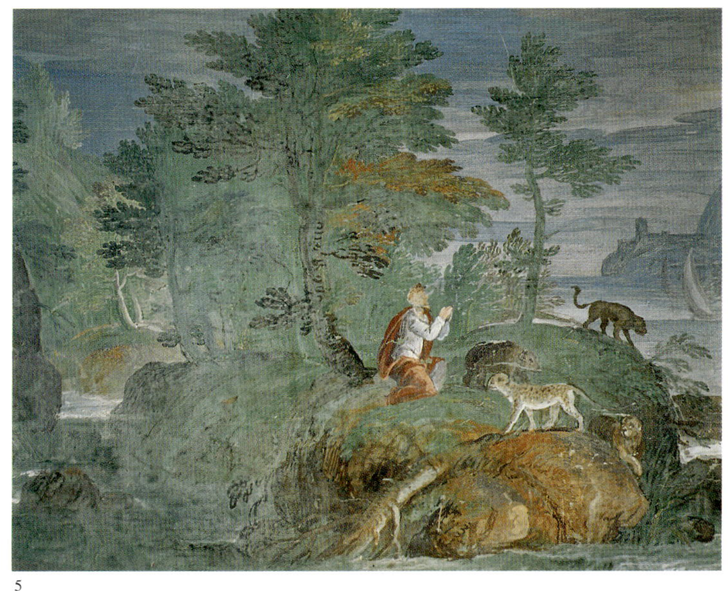

5

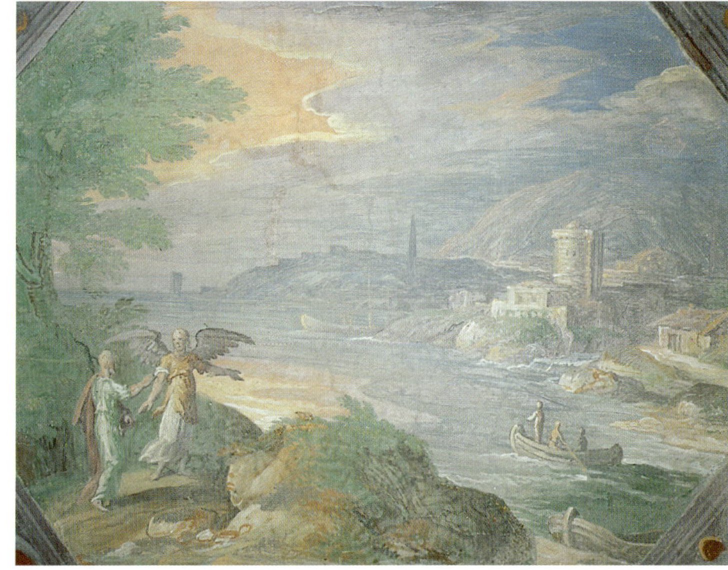

7

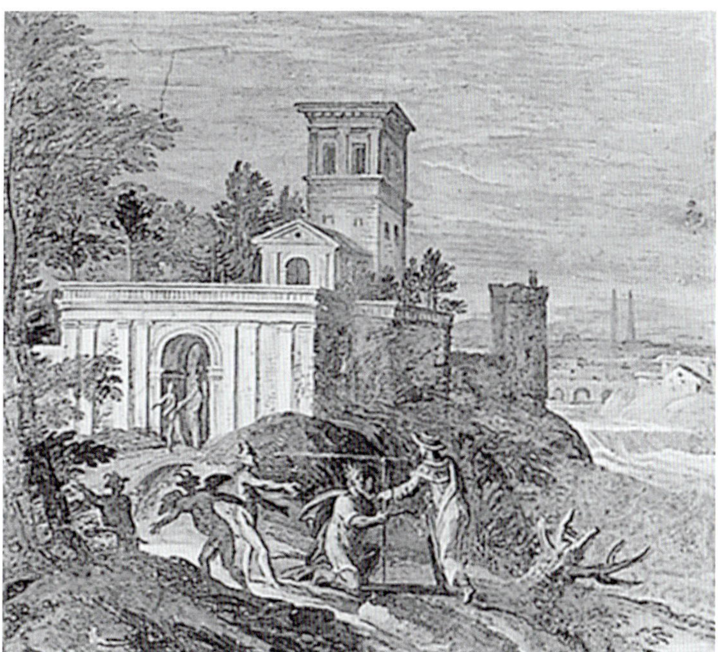

8

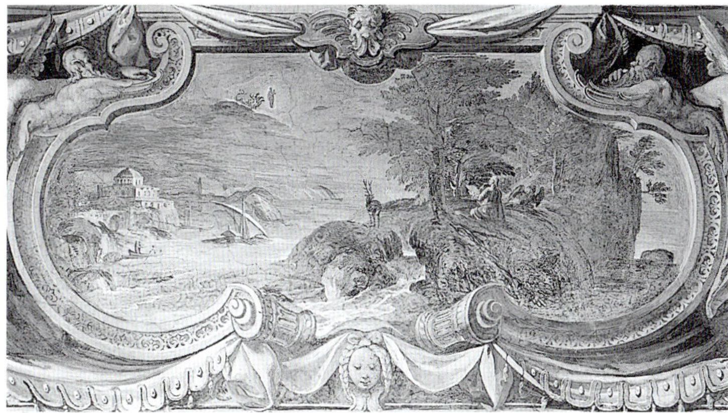

11

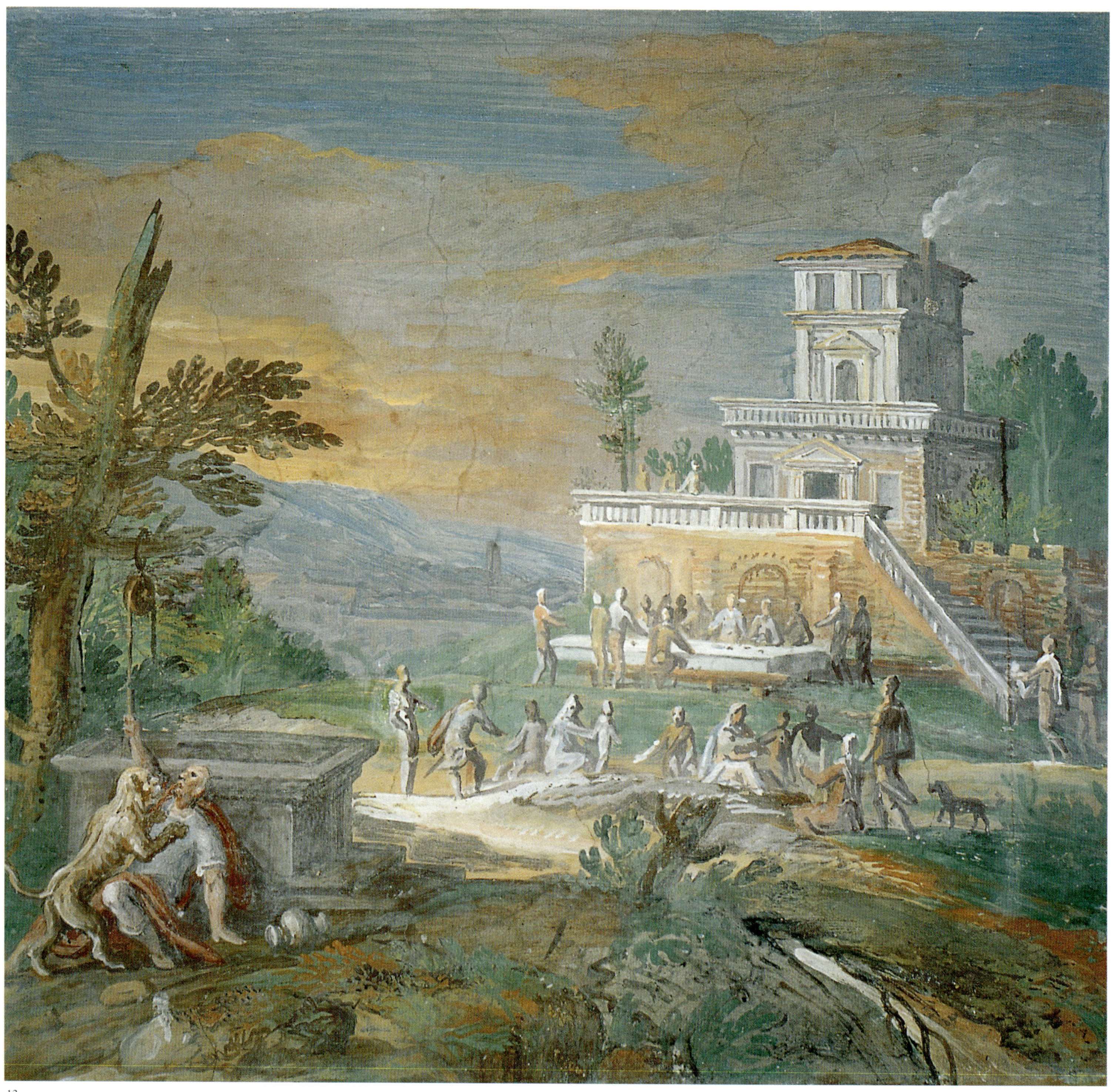

13

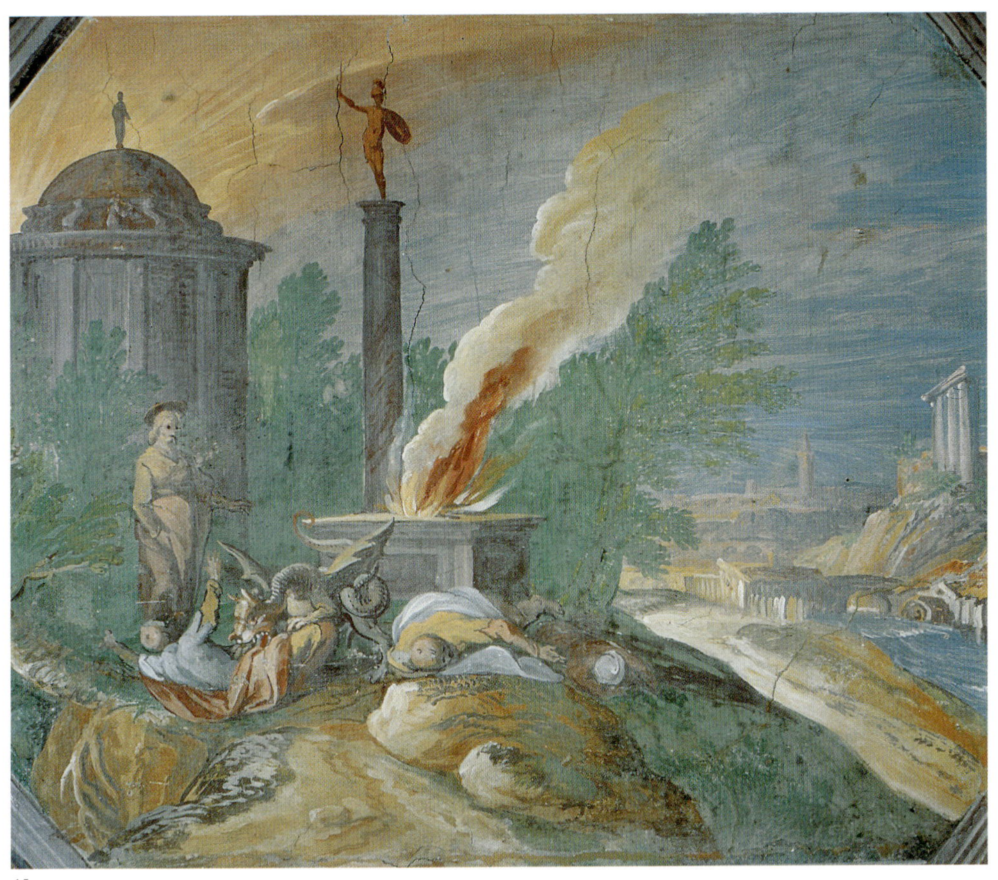

15

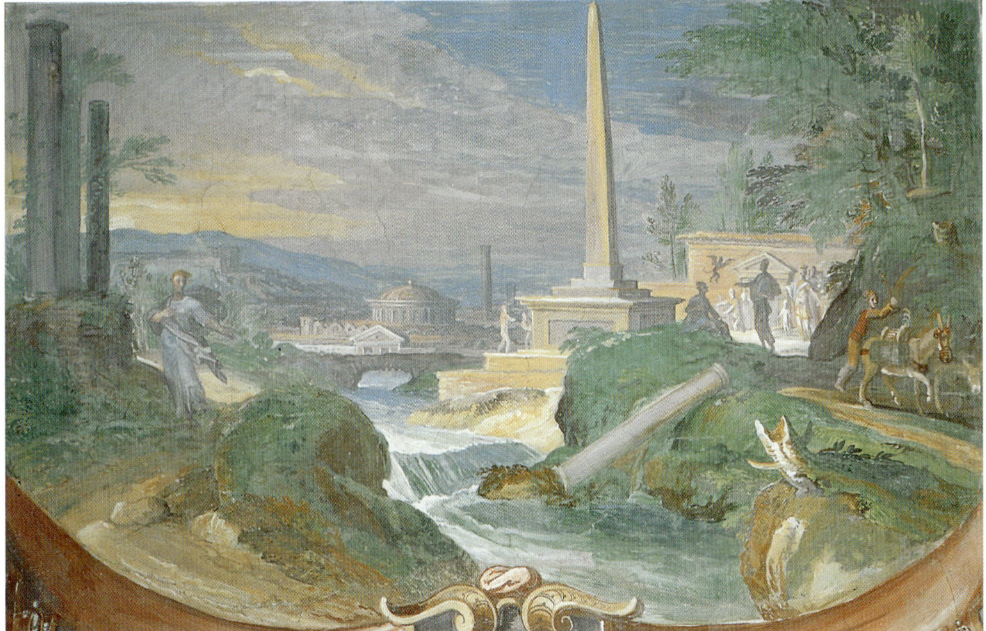

17

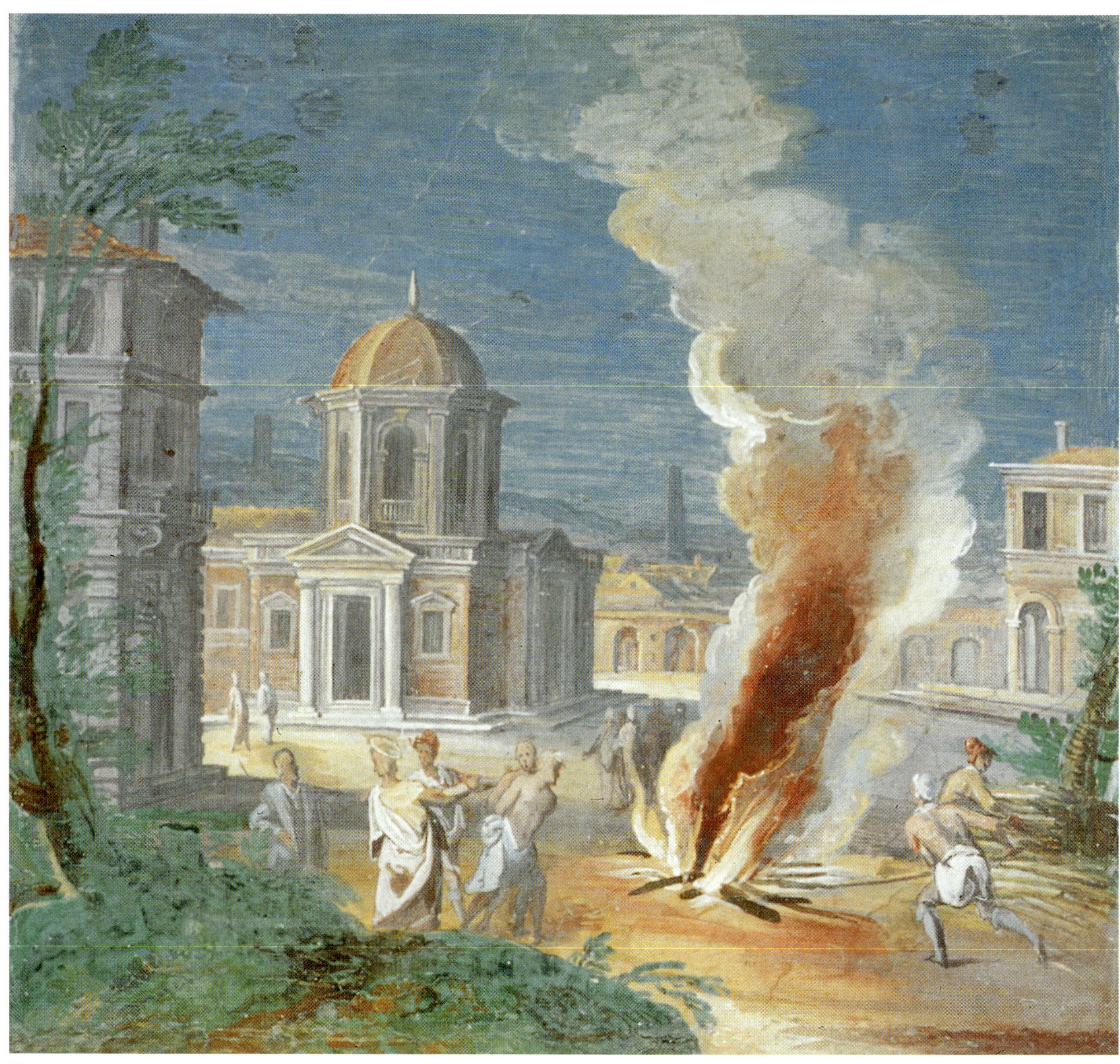

21

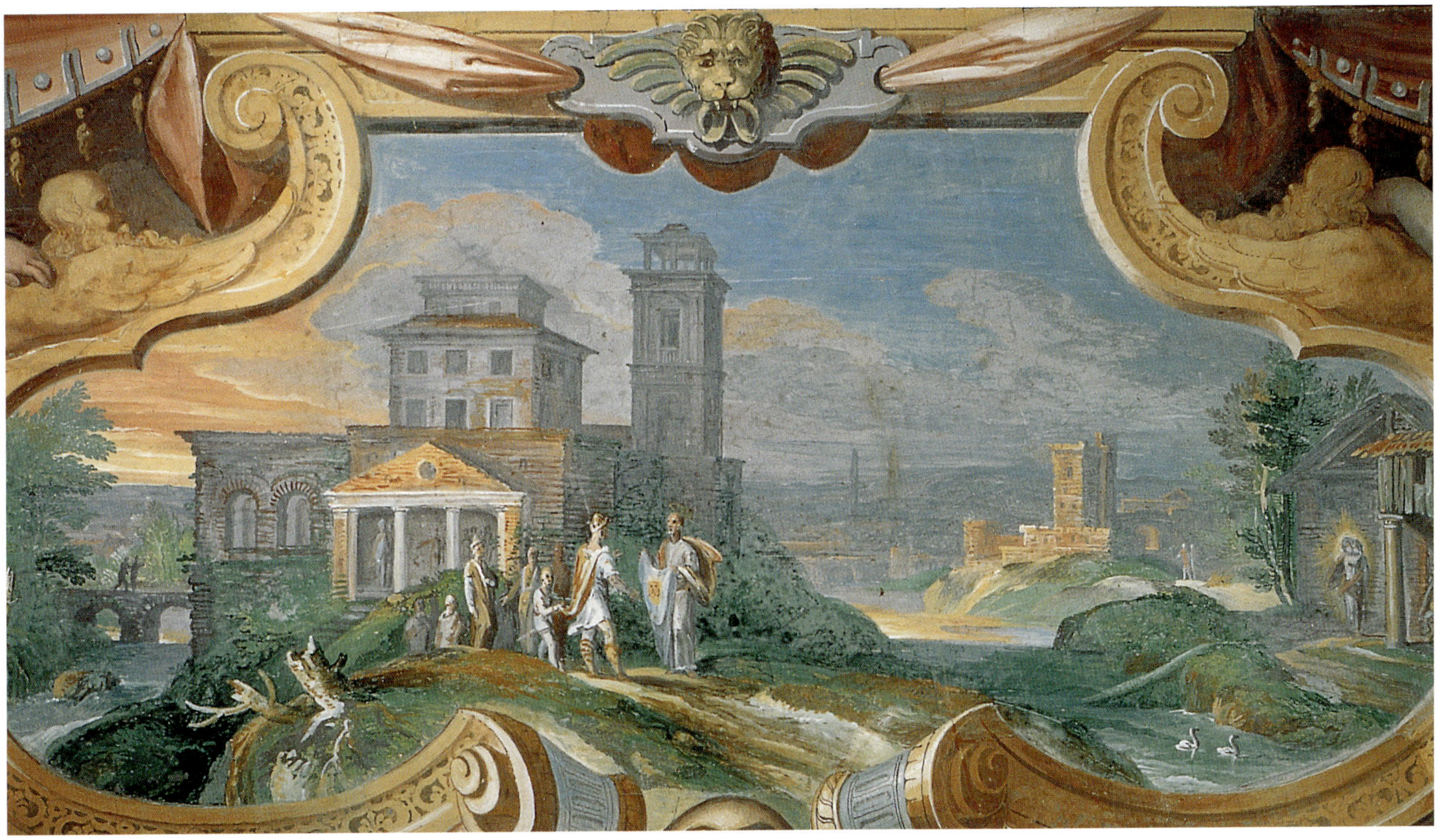

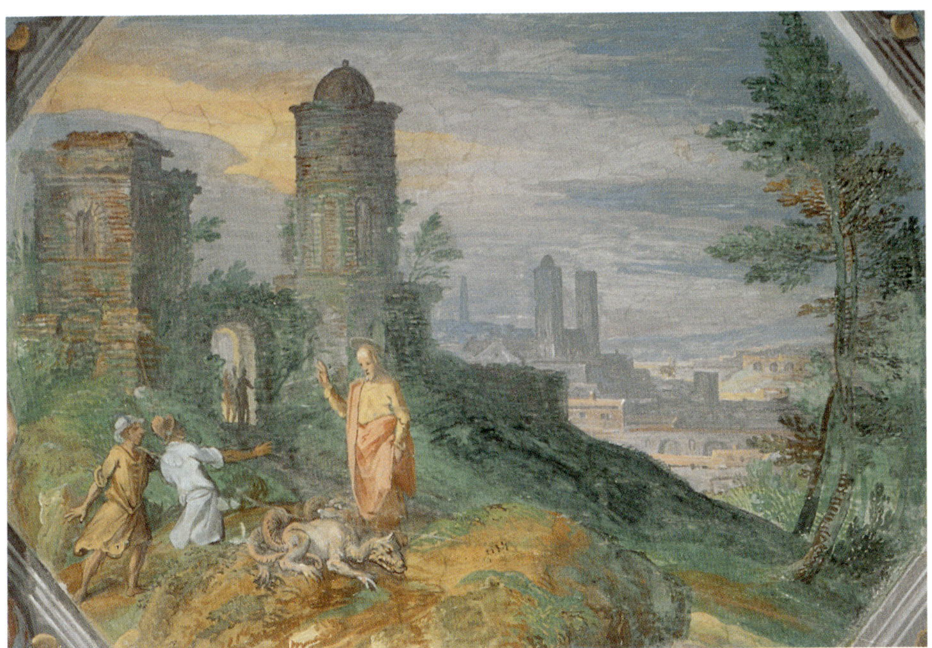

23

19

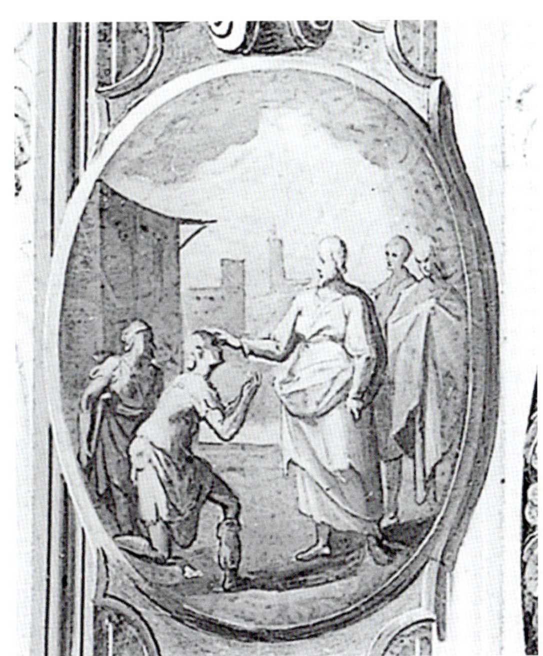

24

h.

Matthijs Bril assisted by Paul Bril
(caryatids framing the scenes: Niccolò
Circignani called Pomarancio)

Four landscapes (on the four walls,
framed as an illusionistic open
loggia), fresco and secco
Commissioned by Pope Gregory XIII

Datable 1580-83 (?)

1. *View From the Viminale*
2. *Imaginary Landscape*
3a. *View from the Gianicolo*
3b. *Imaginary Landscape*
(with a Roman Monument)
4. *Imaginary Landscape*
(with a Fortress above a Harbour)

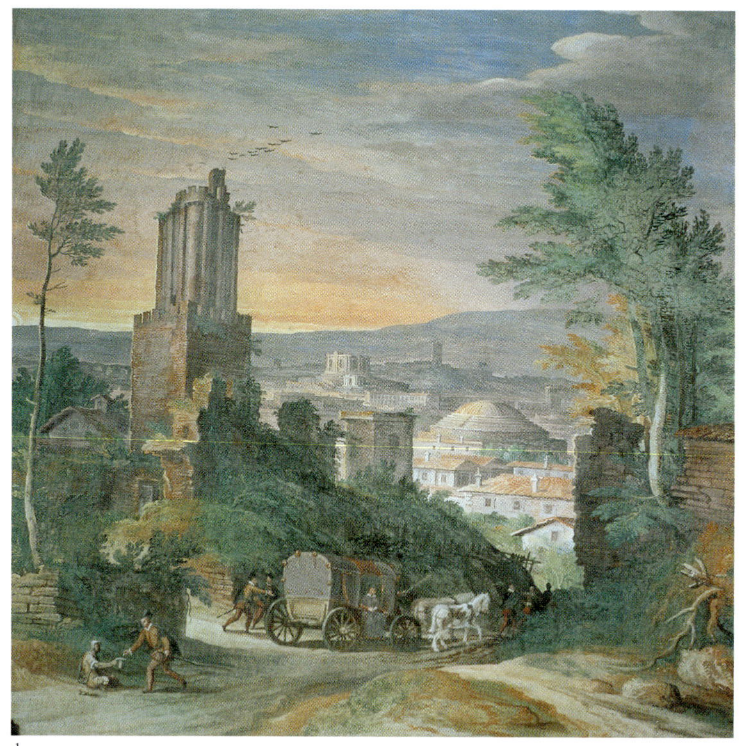

1

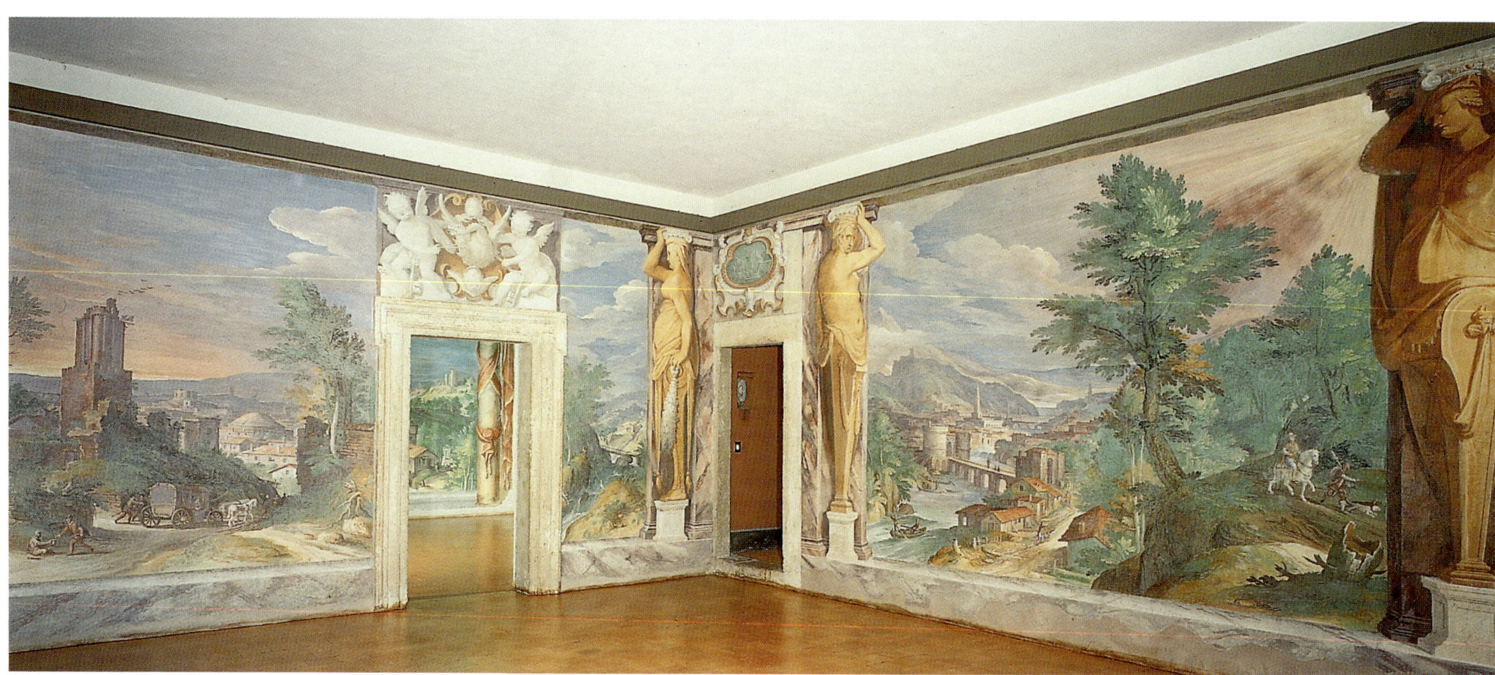

1, 2

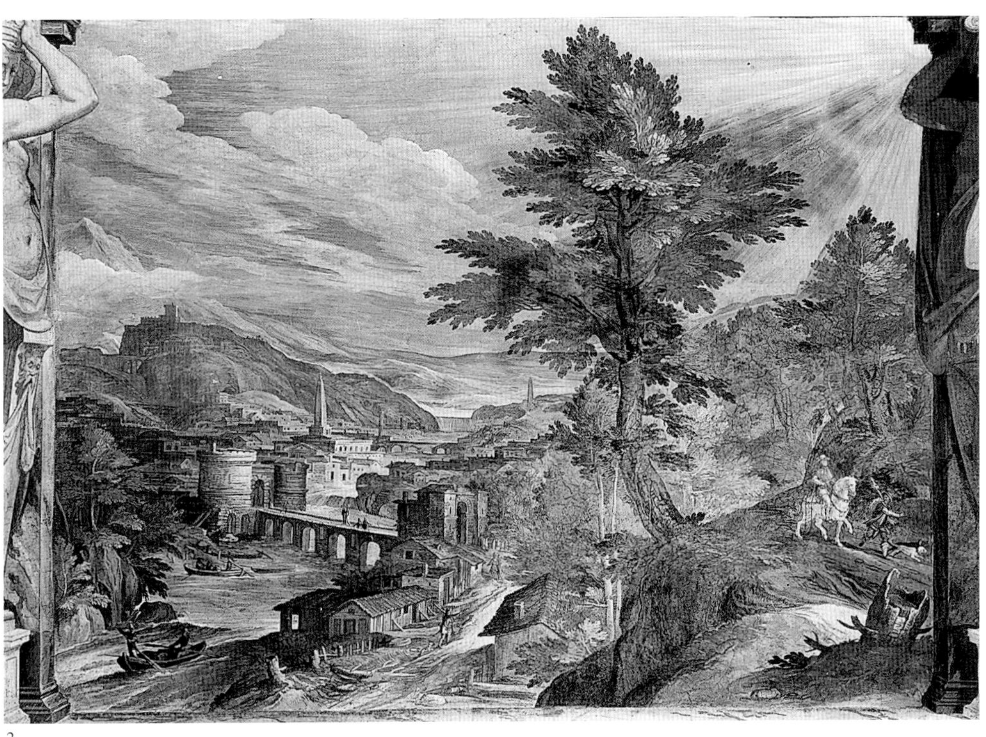

2

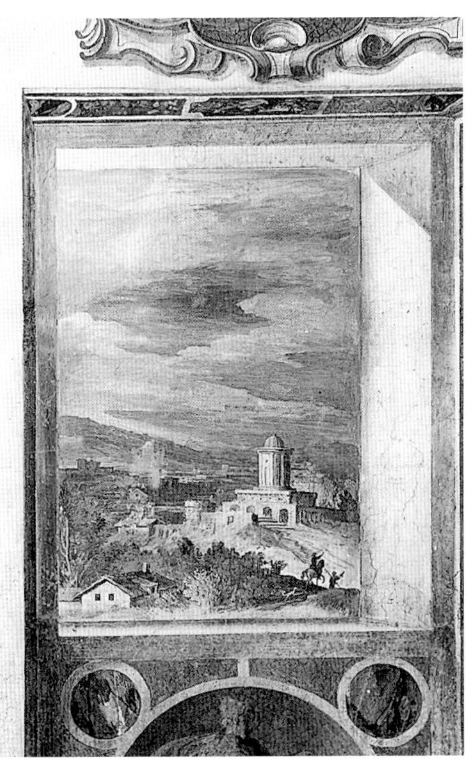

3b

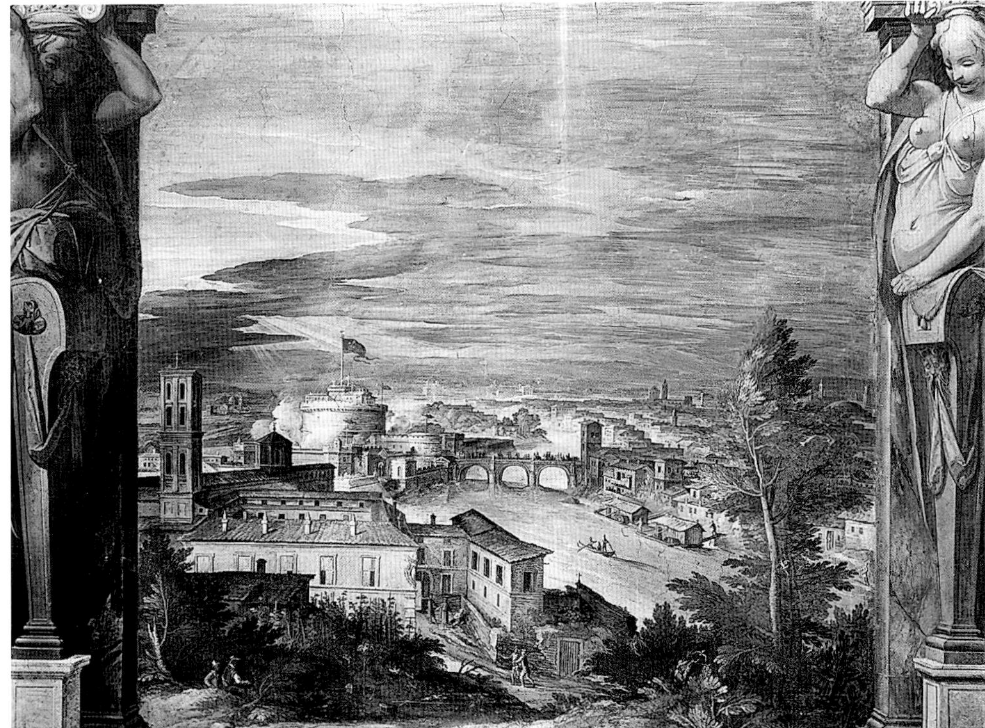

3a

i.

Matthijs Bril assisted by Paul Bril
(putti and other decoration
surrounding the scenes: Niccolò
Circignani (?) called Pomarancio)

Four imaginary landscapes
(framed by illusionistic architecture
with columns and drapery
on the four walls), fresco and secco
Commissioned by Pope Gregory XIII

Datable 1580-83 (?)

1. *Landscape with River and Roman
Ruins*

2. *River View*

3. *View of a Coastal Landscape
with Galleys*

4. *View of a Fort on a River
with Pastoral Scenes*

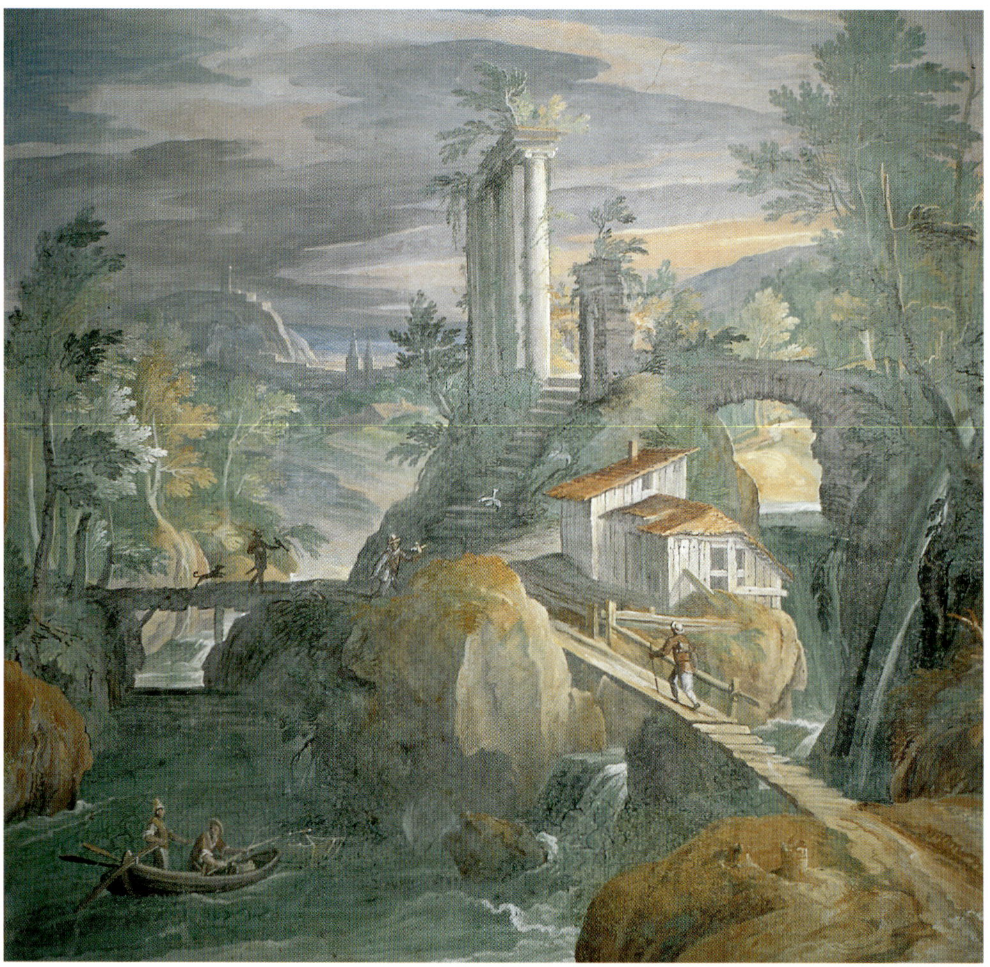

1

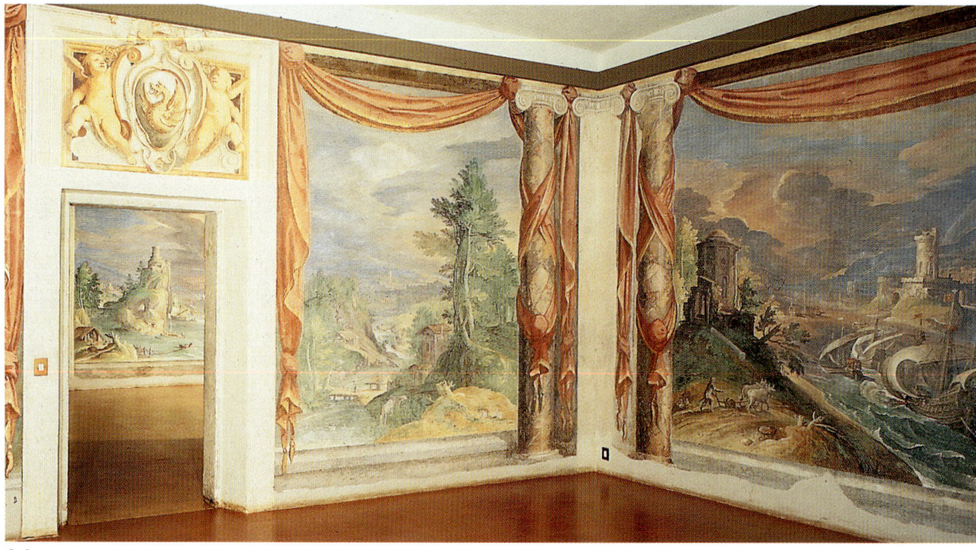

2, 3

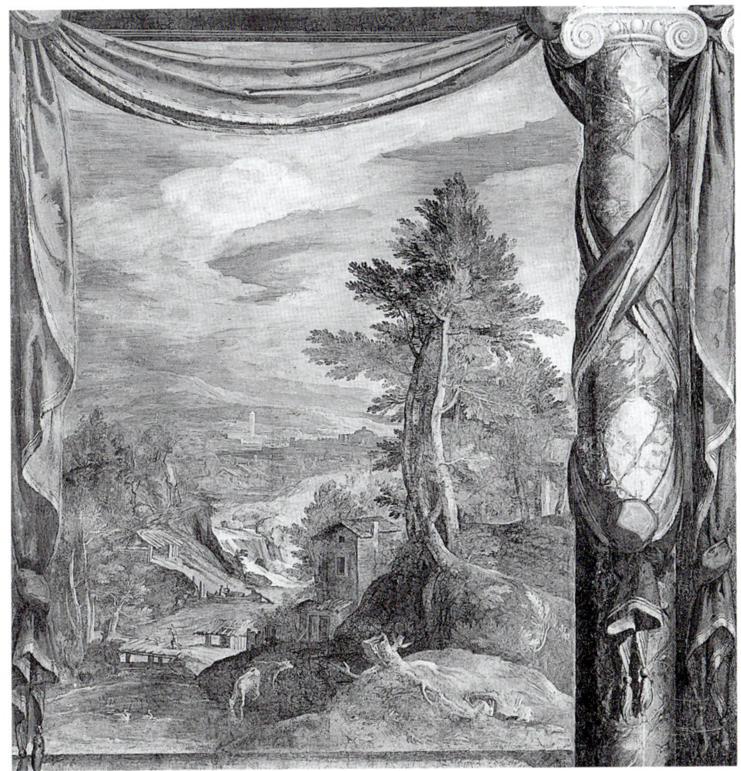

2

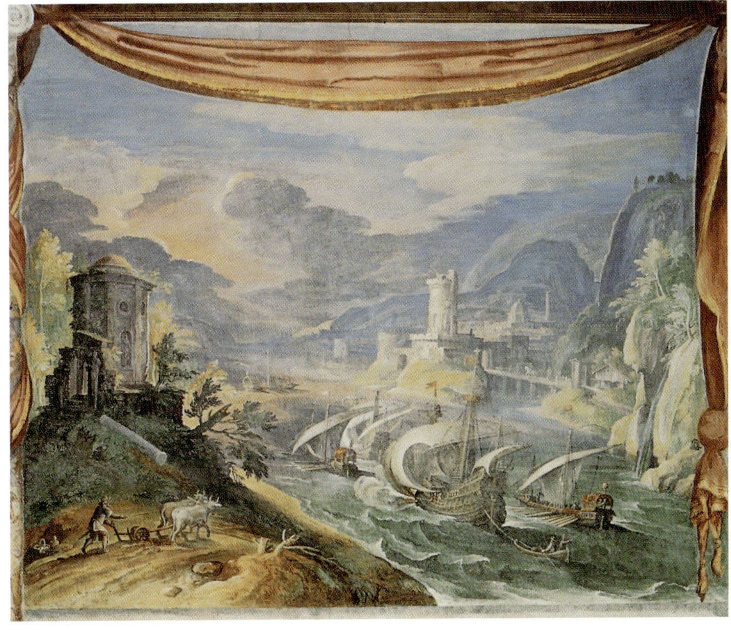

3

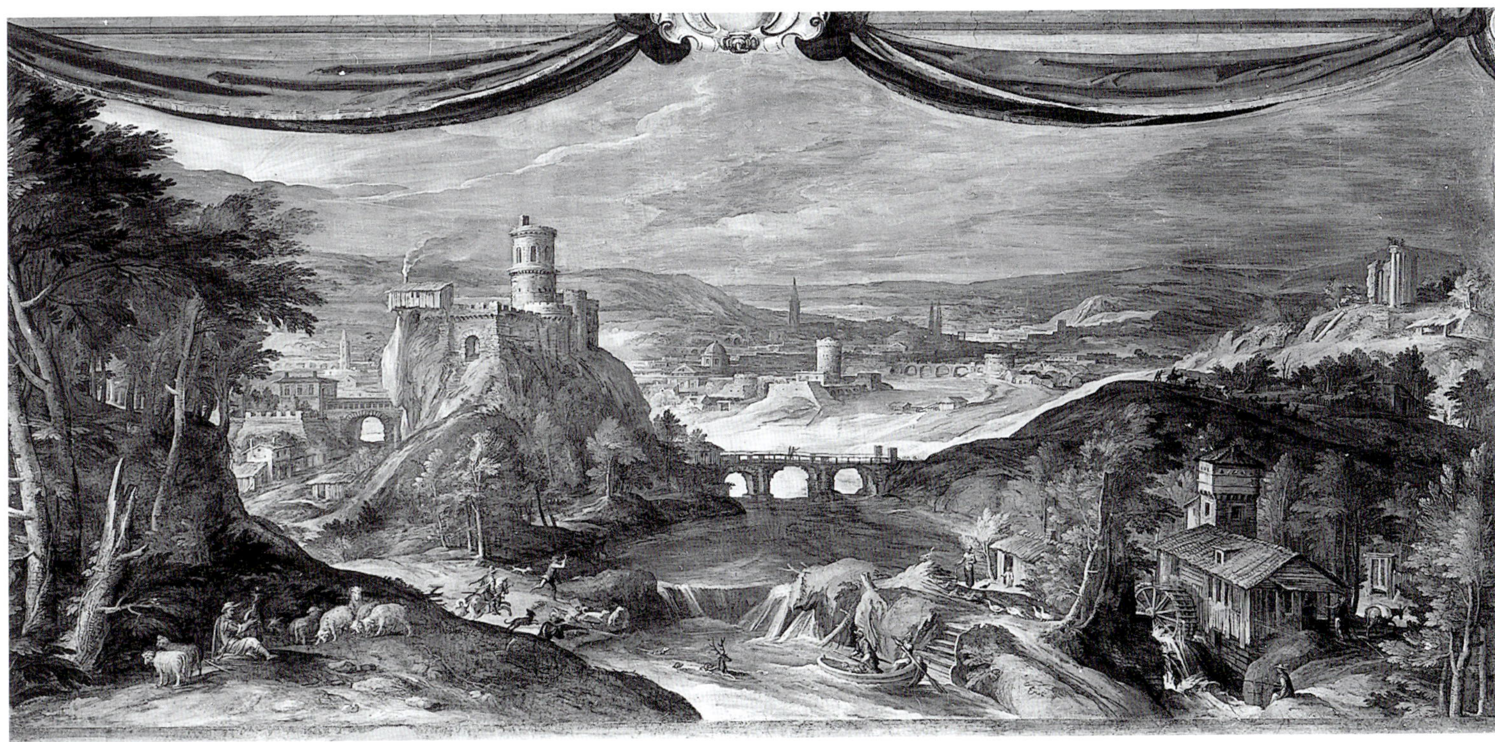

4

Torre dei Venti, Room of the Old Testament Women (second floor)

j.

Matthijs Bril
(allegorical figures surrounding
the scenes: Niccolò Circignani (?)
called Pomarancio)

Twelve biblical scenes in landscapes;
four landscapes in the corners
(in a frieze on the four walls), fresco
Commissioned by Pope Gregory XIII

Datable 1580-82

1. *Nabal Refuses to Let the Soldiers*
Bring Food to David

2. *Abigail Meets David and his Soldiers*

3. *Abigail Kneels before David*

4. *Judith Kneels before Holofernes*

5. *Judith Puts Holofernes' Head*
in a Sack

6. *Holofernes' Head on the Bulwark*

7. *Deborah Urges Barak to take up Arms*
against Sisera

8. *Deborah Prays for Barak's Victory*
over Sisera

9. *Jael Slays Sisera*

10. *Orpa Leaves Naomi and Ruth*

11. *Ruth Gleans Corn in the Fields*
of Boaz

12. *Ruth Sleeps at Boaz's Feet*

(in the corners):

13. *Landscape with a Classical Fountain*

14. *Landscape with a Cottage*
and a Ruin

15. *Landscape with a Mill*
and a Waterwheel

16. *Landscape with a Tower*
and a Herdsman

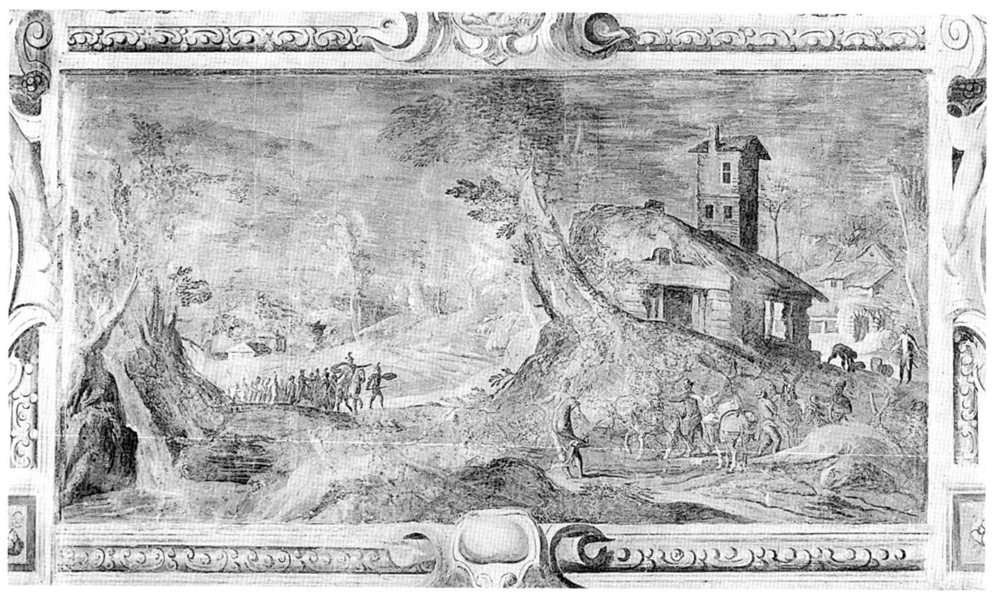

2

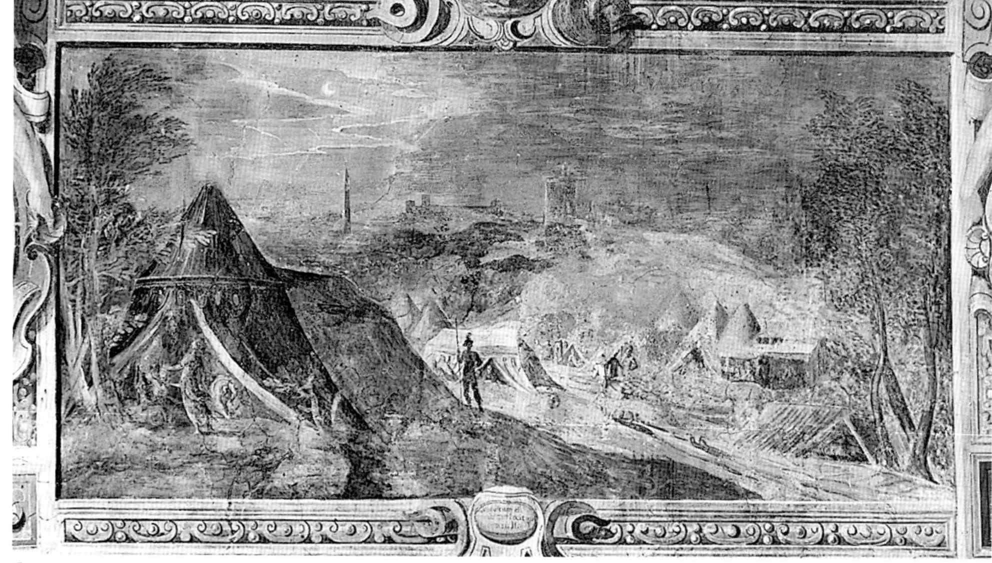

5

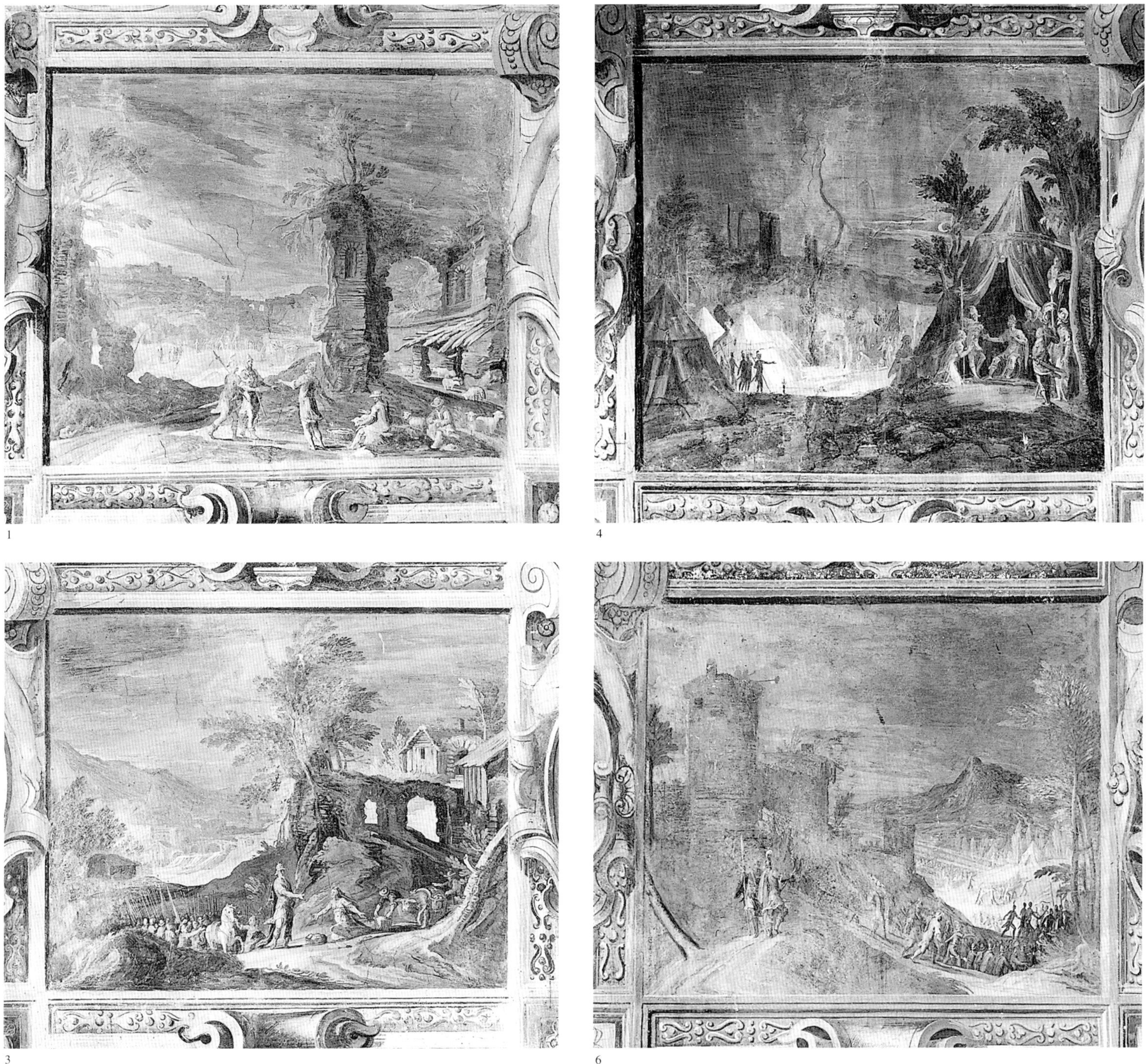

1

4

3

6

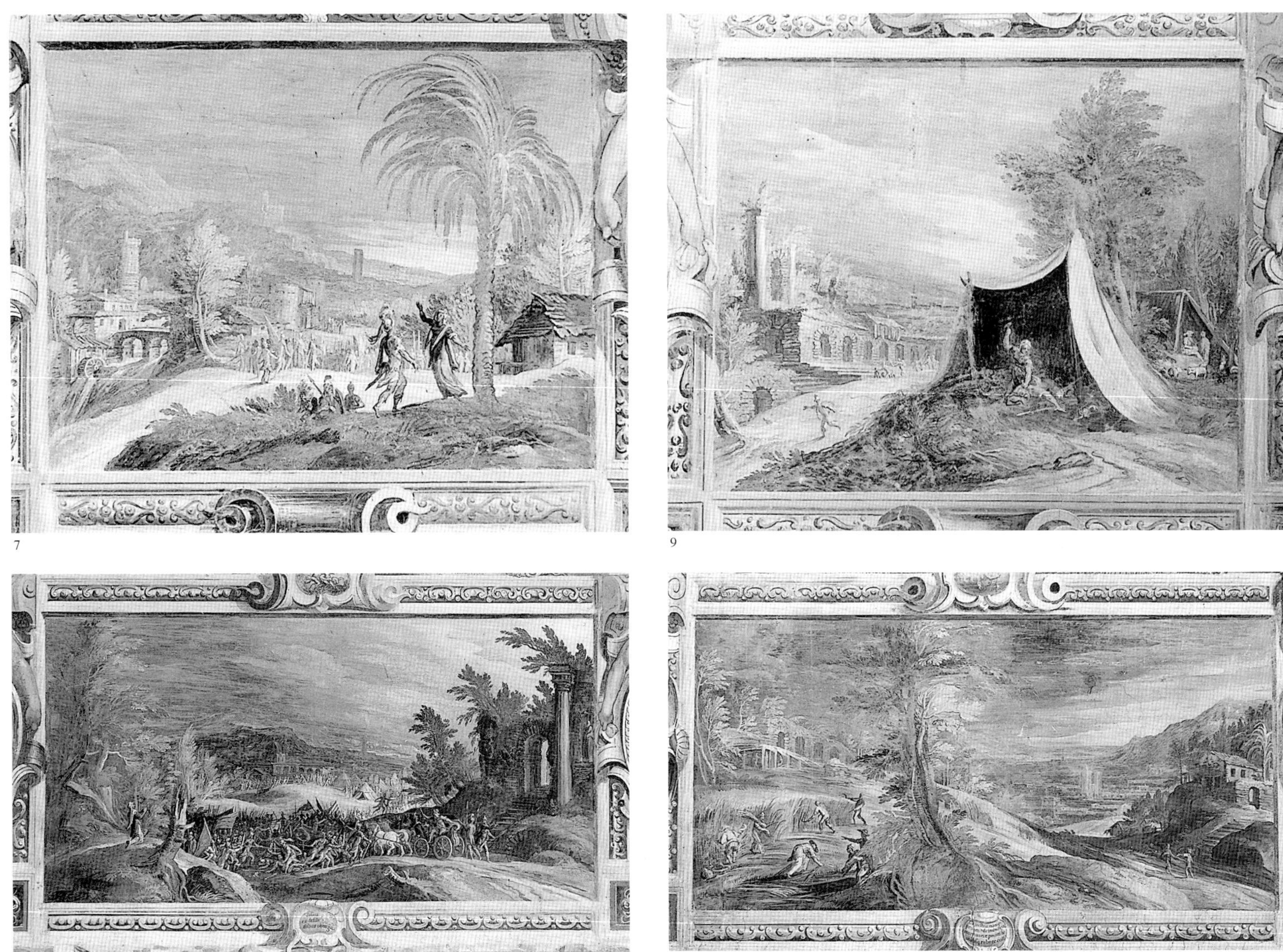

7

9

8

11

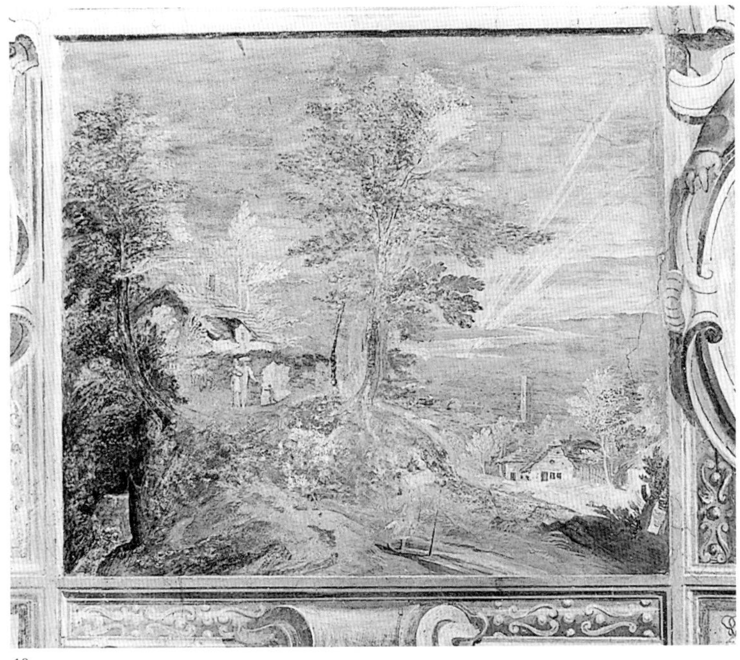

10

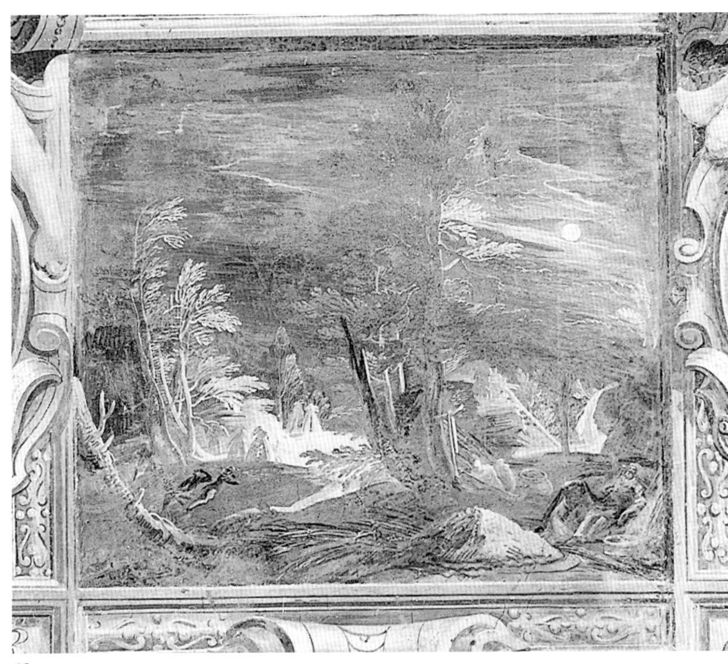

12

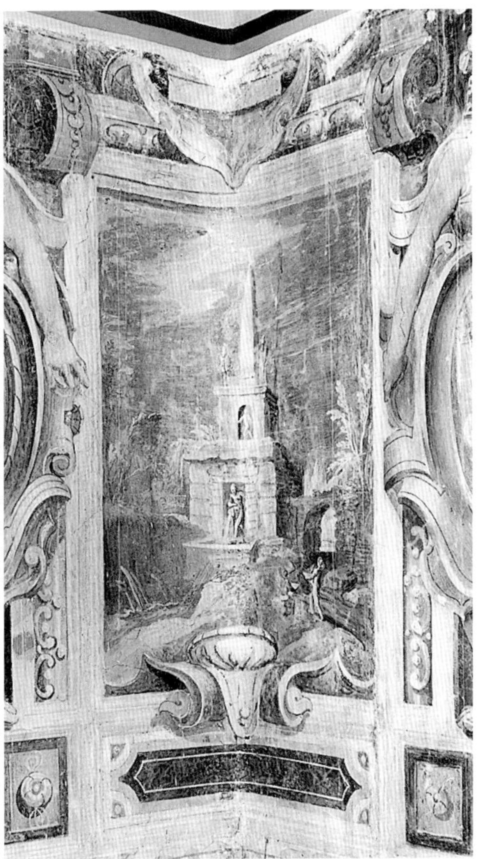

13

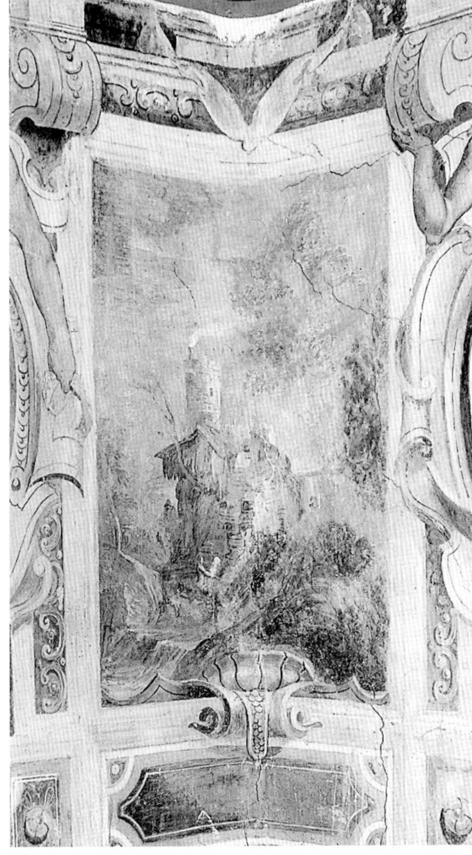

14

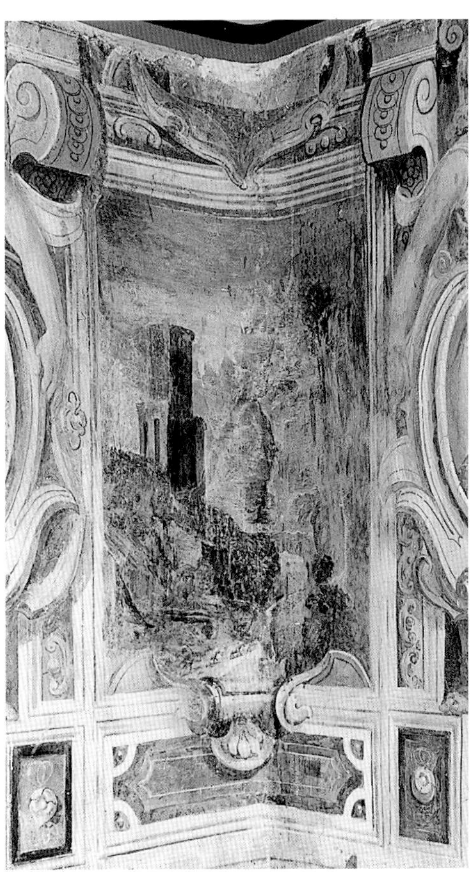

16

k.

Matthijs Bril

*Twelve biblical scenes in landscapes
(in a frieze on the four walls), fresco*
Commissioned by Pope Gregory XIII

Datable 1580-82

1. *Tobit Leaves the Feast Table*

2. *Tobit Buries the Dead Jew and Turns
Blind*

3. *The Departure of Tobias and Raphael*

4. *Tobias Catches the Fish*

5. *Tobias is Greeted by Raguel*

6. *Raphael on his Journey to Claim
Tobit's Money from Gabael*

7. *Tobias Greets Raphael on his Return*

8. *The Marriage of Tobias and Sarah;
Raphael ties up the Devil*

9. *Tobias, Sarah and Raphael on their
Return Journey*

10. *Anna Awaits Tobias's Return*

11. *Tobias Restores his Father's Sight*

12. *The Departure of Raphael*

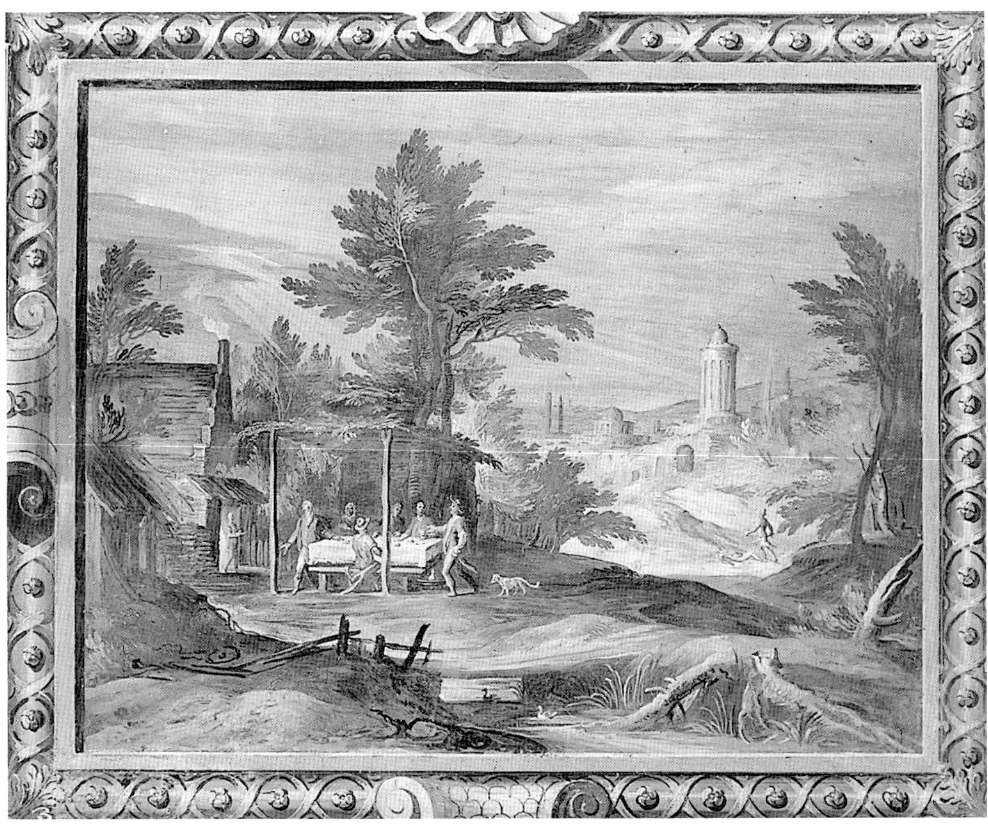

1

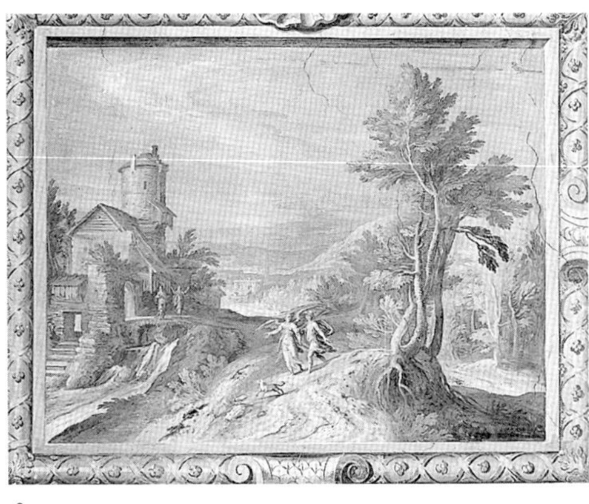

3

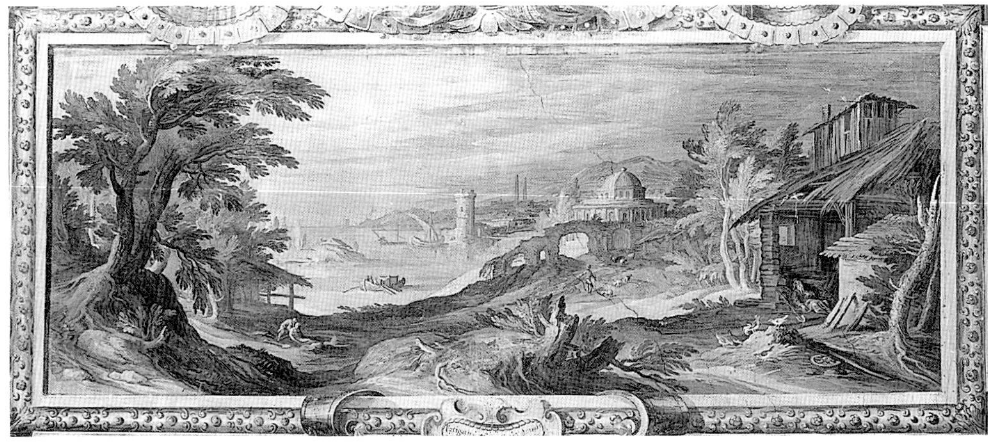

2

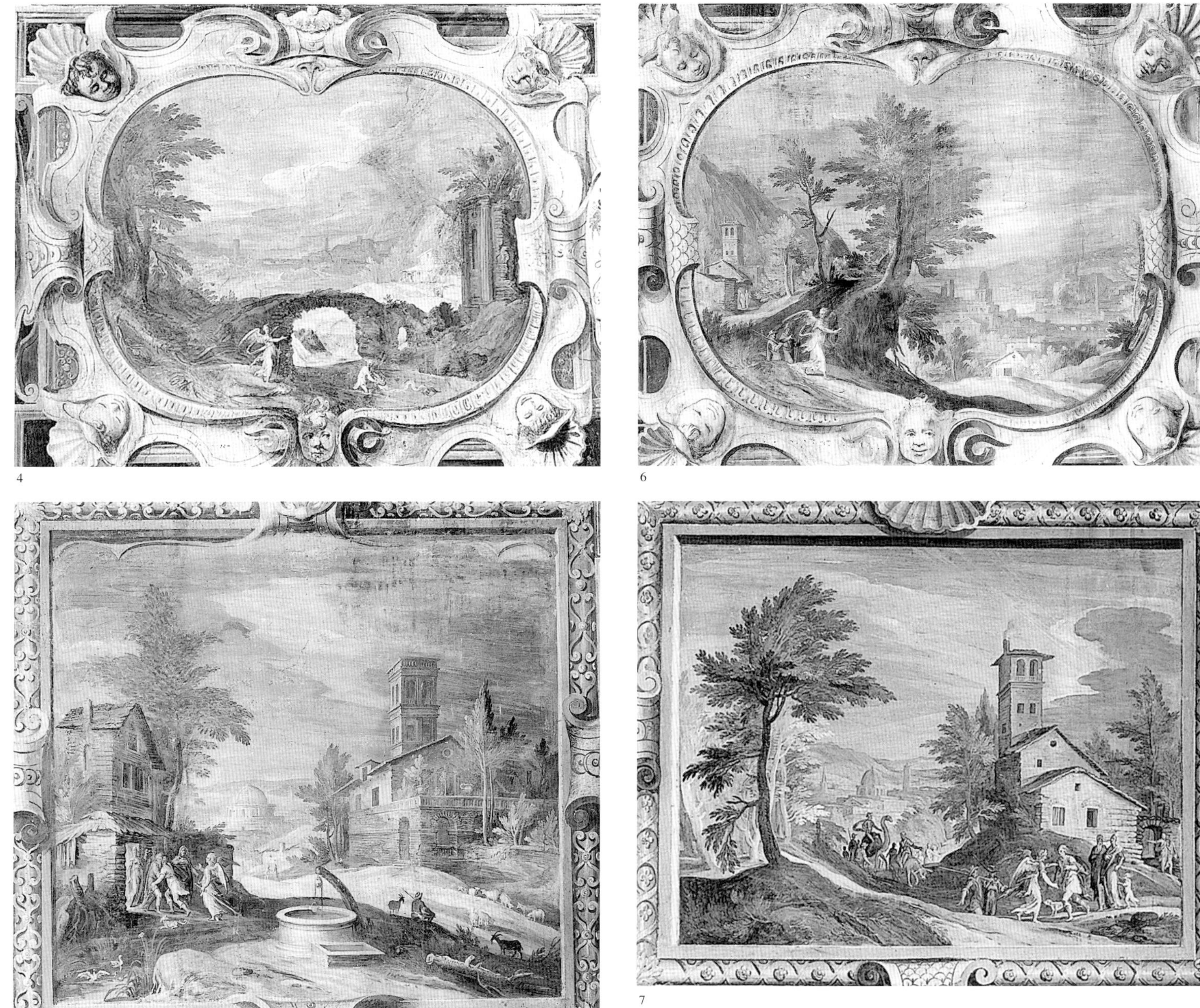

4

6

5

7

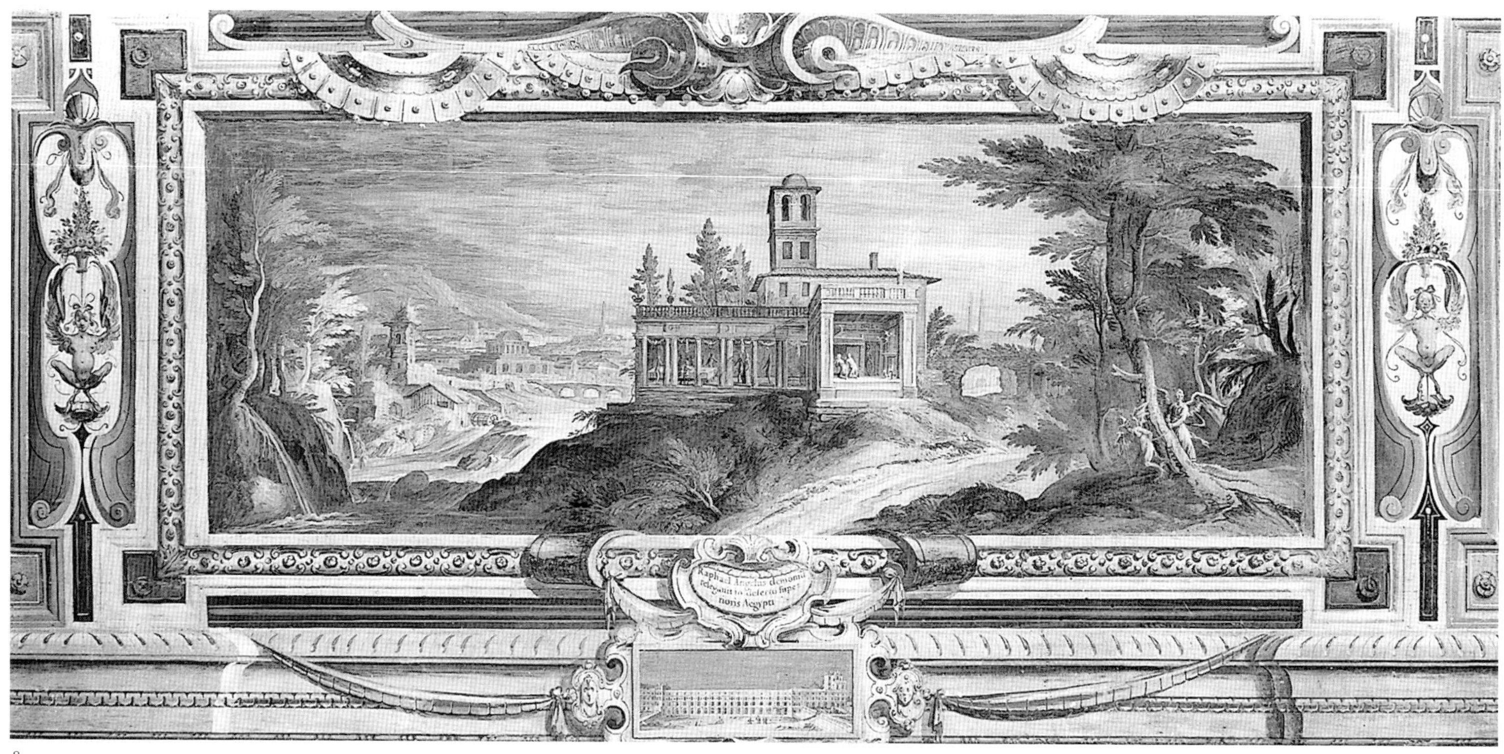

8

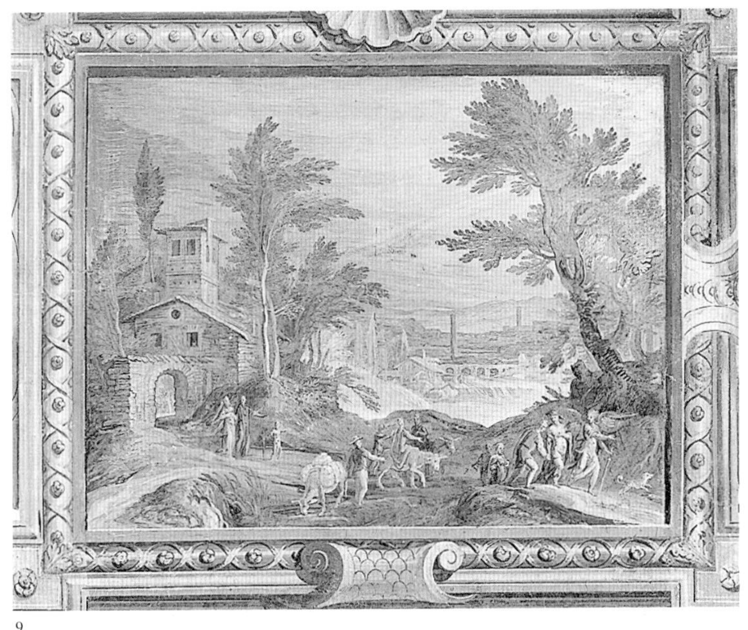

9

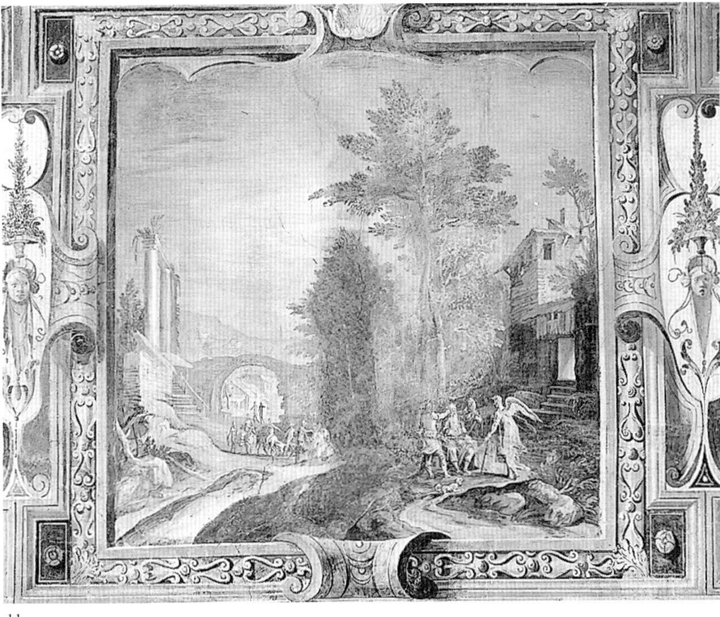

11

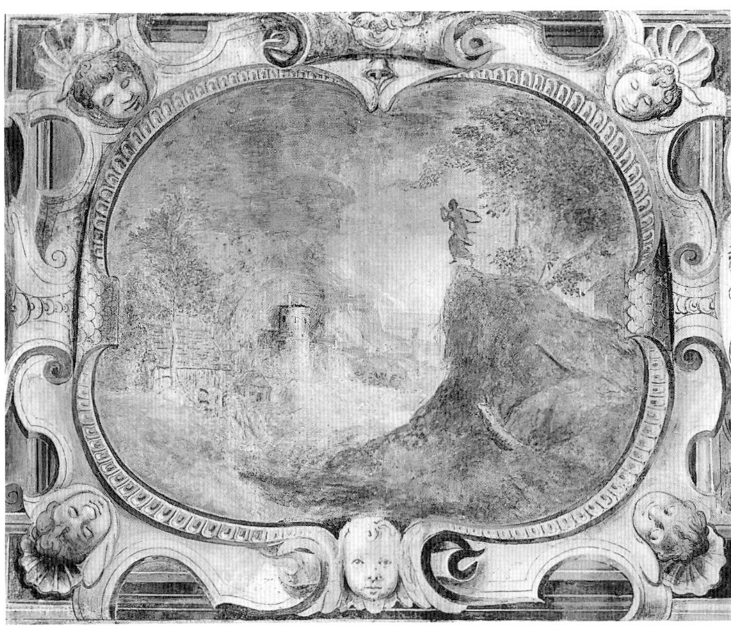

10

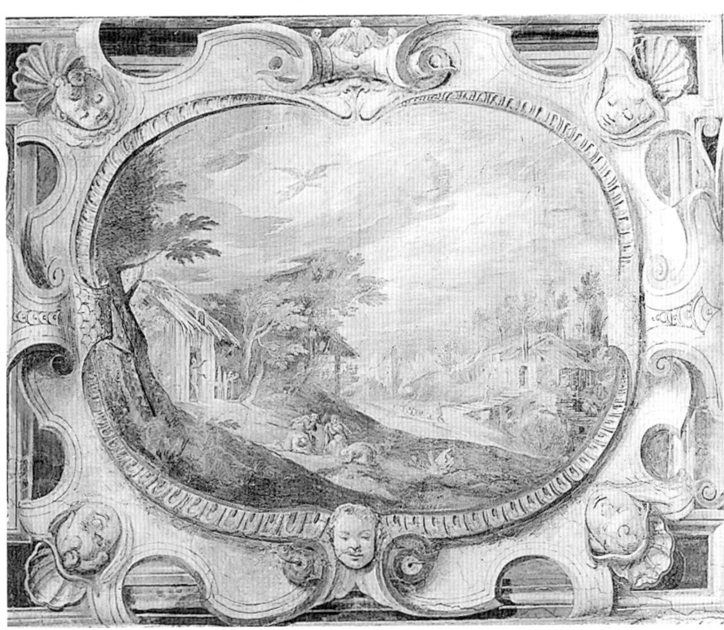

12

I.

Matthijs Bril assisted by Paul Bril
(maps: Egnazio Danti; supervision:
Girolamo Muziano and Cesare
Nebbia)

Twenty-five small landscapes
in the lower section of the maps,
fresco and secco
Commissioned by Pope Gregory XIII

Datable 1580-81 (inscription "anno
VIIII" in the vault on the north wall)

right wall from south to north:

1. LIGVRIA: *Landscape with Two Monks,
River with a Bridge, a Fisherman
and Hunters*, Matthijs and Paul Bril

2. PERVSINVS AC TIFERNAS: *Trees
and Rocks*, lower left and right,
Matthijs and Paul Bril

3. PATRIMONIVM S. PETRI: *Tree*,
lower right, Matthijs or Paul Bril

4. VMBRIA: *Trees*, lower left and right,
Paul Bril

5. CAMPANIA: *Hunter and Hound, Trees*,
Matthijs Bril

6. PRINCIPATVS SALERNI: *Trees*, left
and centre, Matthijs Bril

7. LVCANIA: *Hares and Cattle*,
lower right, *Two Goatherds with a Flock*,
Matthijs and Paul Bril

8. CALABRIA CITERIOR: *Trees*,
lower right, Paul Bril

9. CALABRIA VLTERIOR: *Trees*,
lower right, Paul Bril

10. AVENIONEN(SIS) DITIO
ET VENAISINVS COMITATVS: *Trees*,
lower left and centre, Paul Bril

left wall from south to north:

11. PEDEMONTIVM ET MONSFERRATVS:
Trees, lower left, Paul Bril

12. MEDIOLANENSIS DVCATVS: *Trees*,
lower right, Paul Bril (?)

13. TRANSPADANA VENETORVM DITIO:
Trees, Matthijs and Paul Bril

14. PLACENTIAE ET PARMAE DVCATVS:
Trees and Rocks with Waterfall, left,
Trees, centre and right, Matthijs Bril

15. MANTVAE DVCATVS: *Trees*,
centre and lower right, Matthijs Bril

16. FERRARIAE DVCATVS: *Cluster
of Trees*, lower right, Paul Bril (?)

17. BONONIENSIS DITIO: *Trees*,
Matthijs Bril

18. FLAMINIA: *Trees*, lower left and right,
Matthijs or Paul Bril

20. URBINI DVCATVS: *Trees*, Matthijs Bril

21. PICENVM: *Trees with Waterfall
and Woman with Dog, Deer and Rabbits*,
Matthijs and Paul Bril

22. ACONITANUS AGER: *Trees*, Paul Bril

23. APRVTIVM: *Trees*, lower left
and right, Paul Bril

24. APVLIA: *Trees and a River*, lower left
and right, Matthijs and Paul Bril

25. SALLENTINA HYDRVNTI TERRA:
Trees, left and right of cartouche,
Matthijs Bril

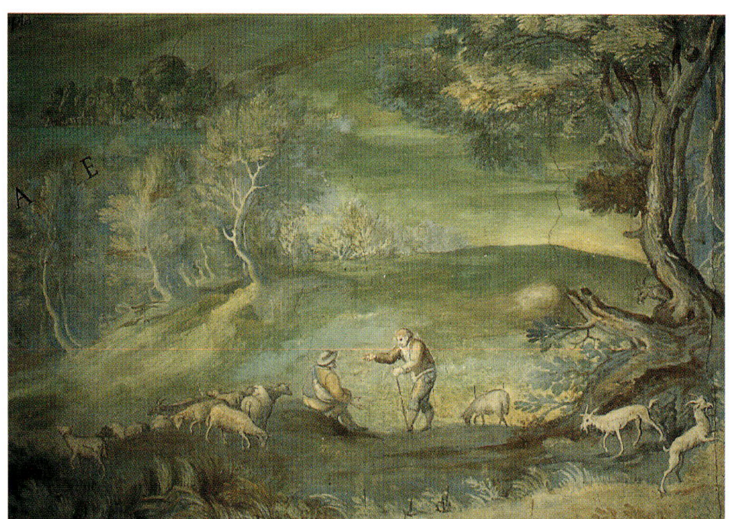

7 detail

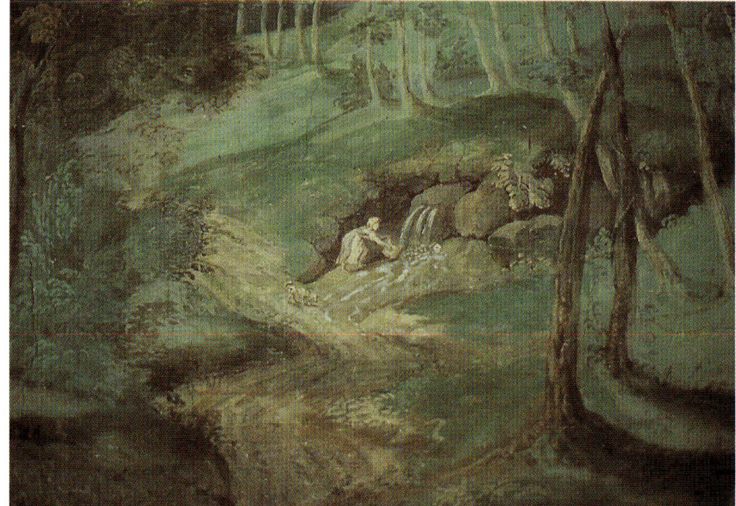

21 detail

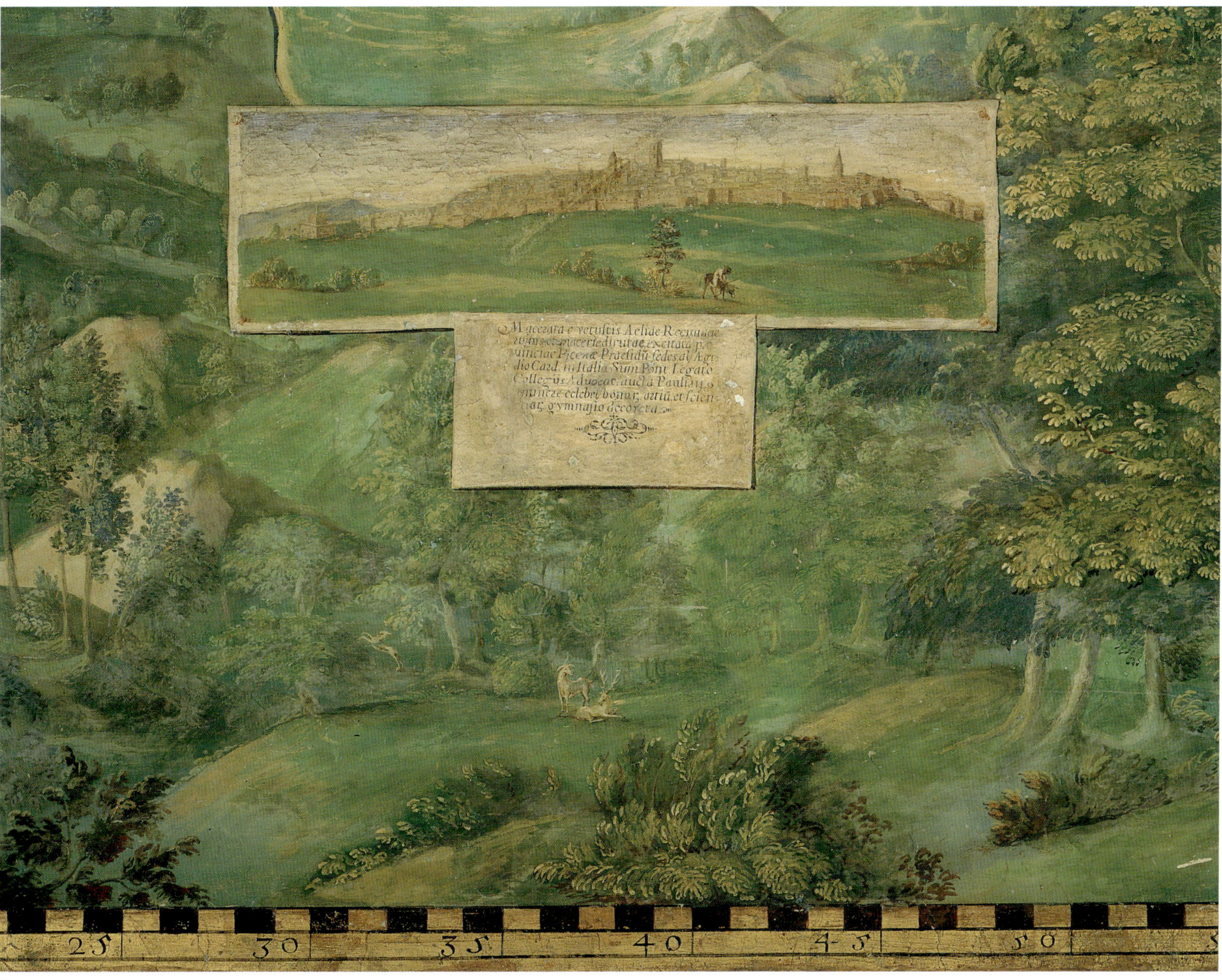

21

m.

Matthijs Bril assisted by Paul Bril
(supervision: Girolamo Muziano;
iconographic programme: Egnazio
Danti; design of figures
and landscapes: Cesare Nebbia)

*Twenty landscapes in religious
scenes*, vault, fresco*
Commissioned by Pope Gregory XIII

Documented 1580-81 (inscription
"anno VIIII" in the vault on the
north wall)

from south to north:

1. *St Romuald Founds Camaldoli*, large
scene in the central section, Matthijs Bril

2. *St Ambrose Banishes the Heretics
to Milan*, small scene, Matthijs Bril

3. *St Francis Receives the Stigmata*,
small scene, Matthijs and Paul Bril

4. *Mathilda of Canossa Donates her
Possessions to the Church*, large scene
in the central section, Matthijs Bril

5. *Pope St Leo the Great Holds back
Atilla*, large scene in the central section,
Matthijs and Paul Bril

6. *The Encounter between Christ
and Peter at the Gates of Rome (Domine
Quo Vadis)*, large scene in the central
section, Matthijs Bril

7. *The Fall of Simon Magus*, large scene
in the central section, Matthijs and Paul
Bril

8. *St Geminian Delivers Modena
from Atilla*, small scene, Matthijs Bril

9. *St Benedict Unmasks King Totila*,
large scene in the central section,
Matthijs Bril

10. *St Petronius Raises a Builder
from the dead*, small scene, Matthijs Bril

11. *Angels Deliver Bread to St Dominic
and his Fellow Brothers*, small scene,
Matthijs Bril

12. *Ranulphus, Duke of Puglia,
Triumphs despite St Bernard's
Intervention*, large scene in the central
section, Paul Bril (?)

13. *St Peter Damiani Writes the Charter
of his Congregation*, large scene
in the central section, Paul Bril (?)

14. *St Francis of Paola Emerges
Unharmed from a Fiery Oven*,
Matthijs Bril

15. *The People of Corsica Recognise
the Sovereignty of Pope Gregory VII*,
large scene in the central section,
Matthijs Bril

16. *The Hermit St Peter of Murano
Receives Tidings of the Pope's Election*,
large scene in the central section,
Matthijs and Paul Bril

17. *The Appearance of the Archangel
at Gargano*, large scene in the central
section, Matthijs and Paul Bril

18. *Pope Simmaco Sends Clothing
and Goods to the Bishops Banished
to Sardinia*, small scene, Paul Bril

19. *St Bernard Orders the Burning
of Books and Playing Cards*, small scene,
Matthijs Bril

20. *Paul Healing on Malta*, large scene
in the central section, Matthijs Bril

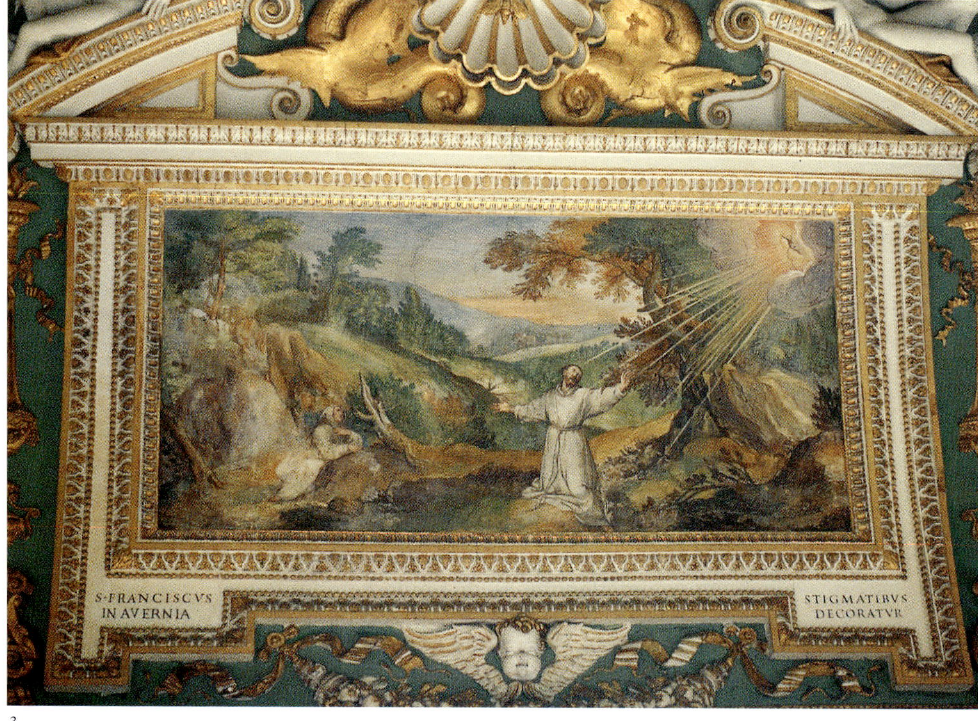

3

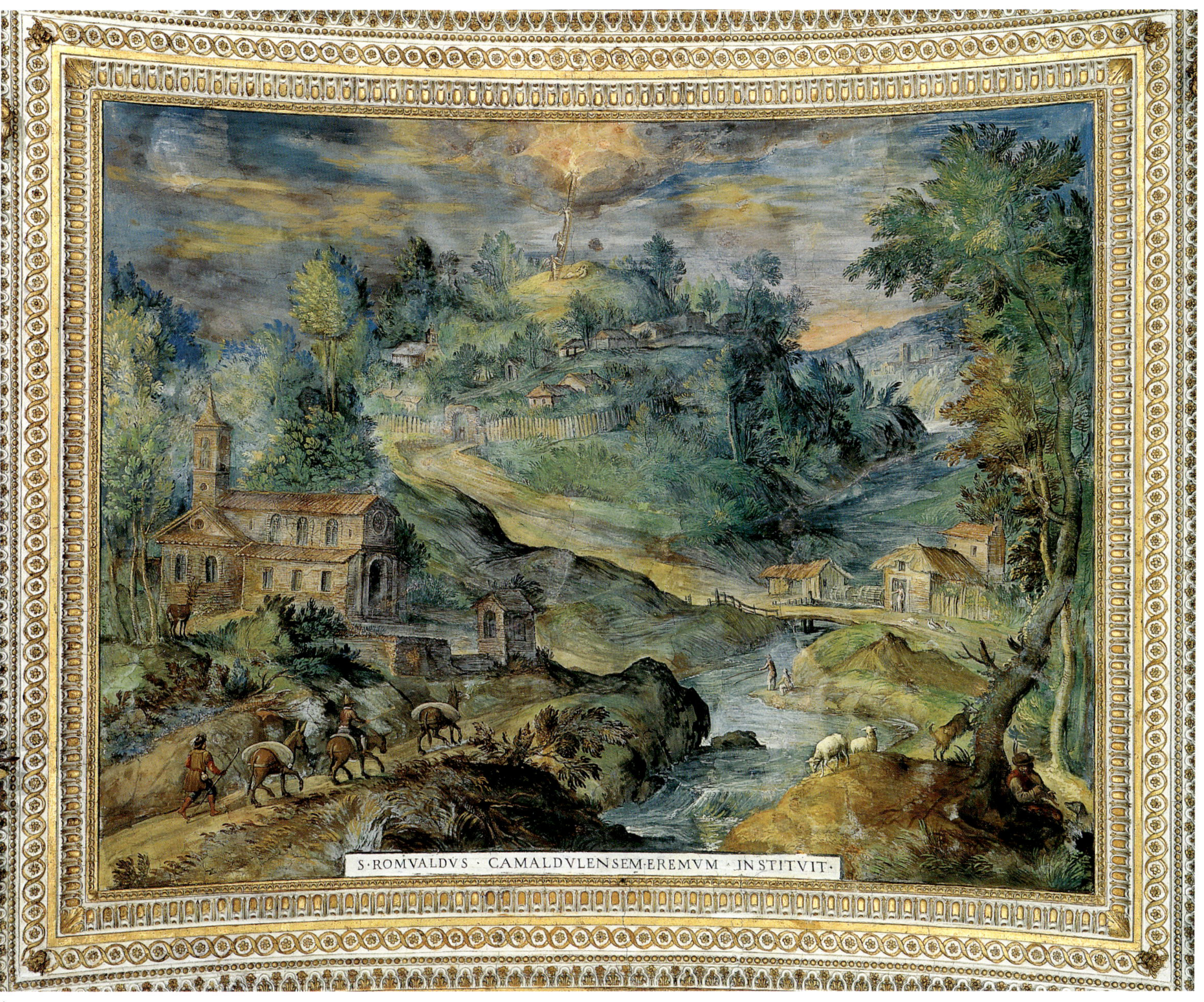

1

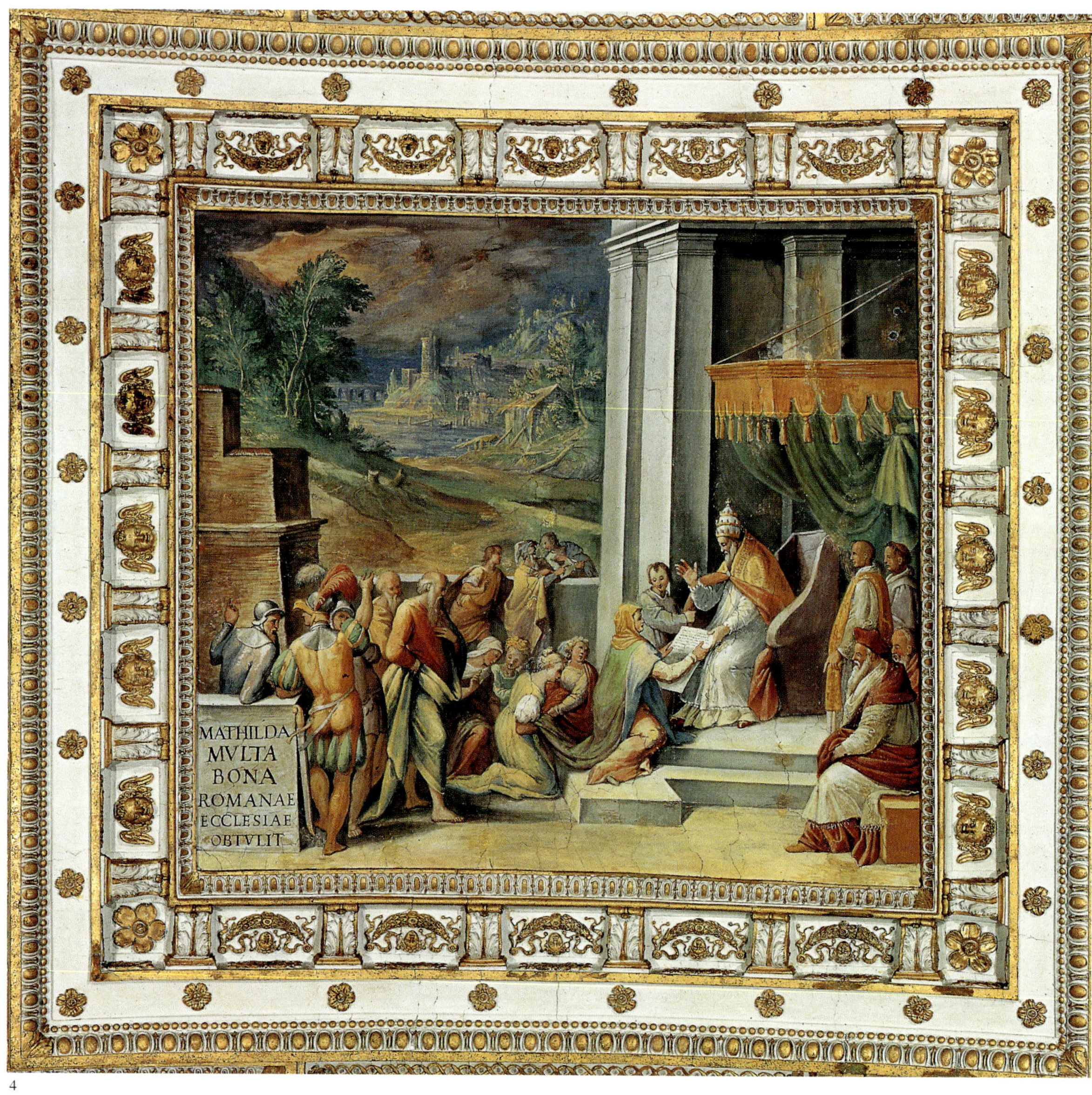

4

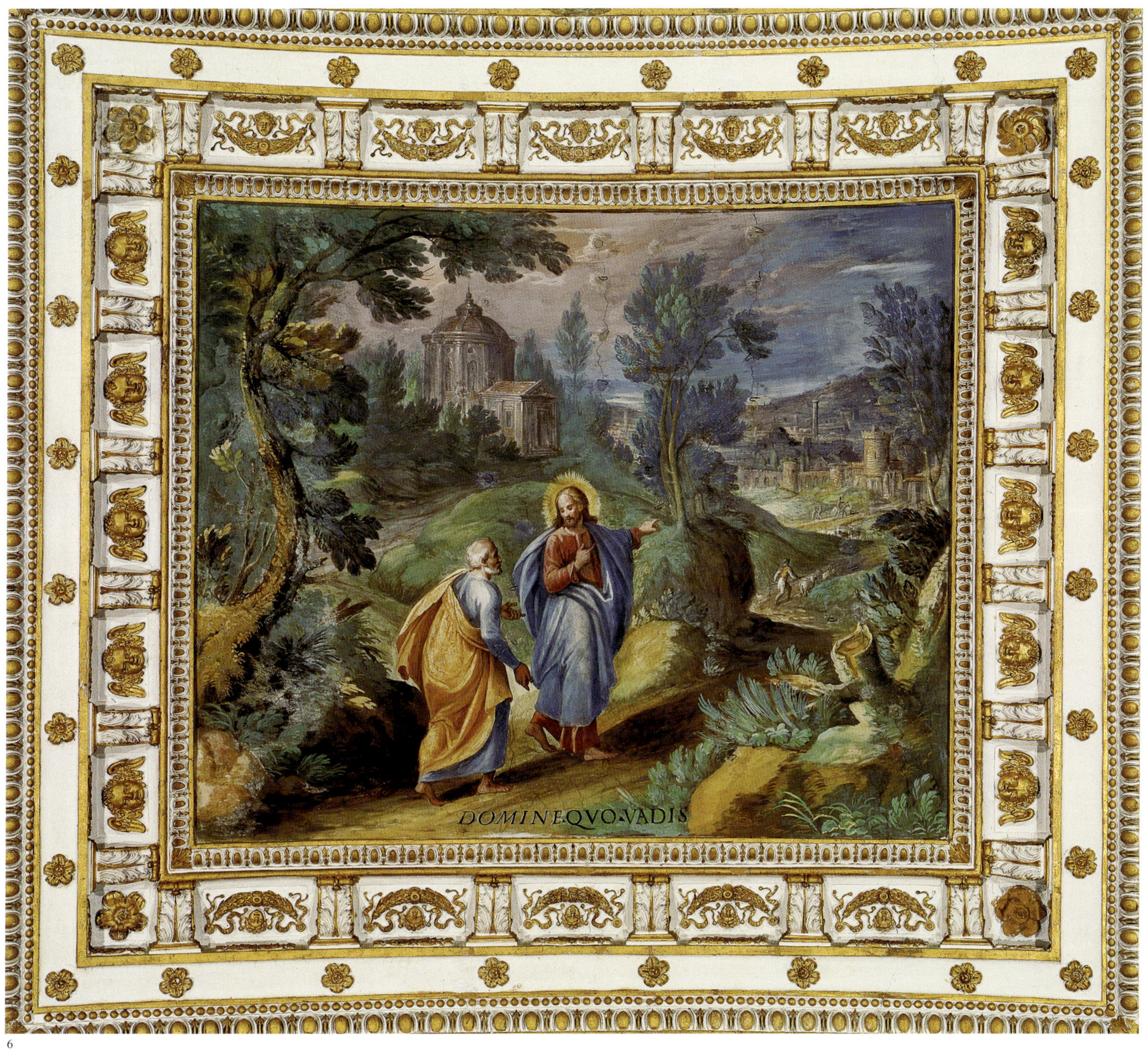

6

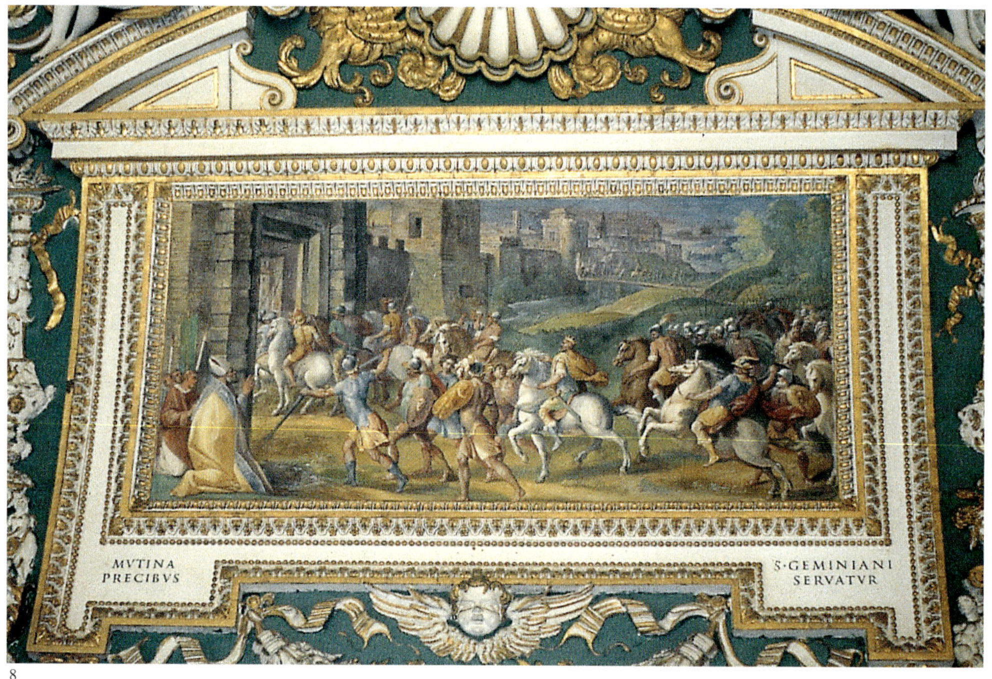
MVTINA
PRECIBVS
S·GEMINIANI
SERVATVR

8

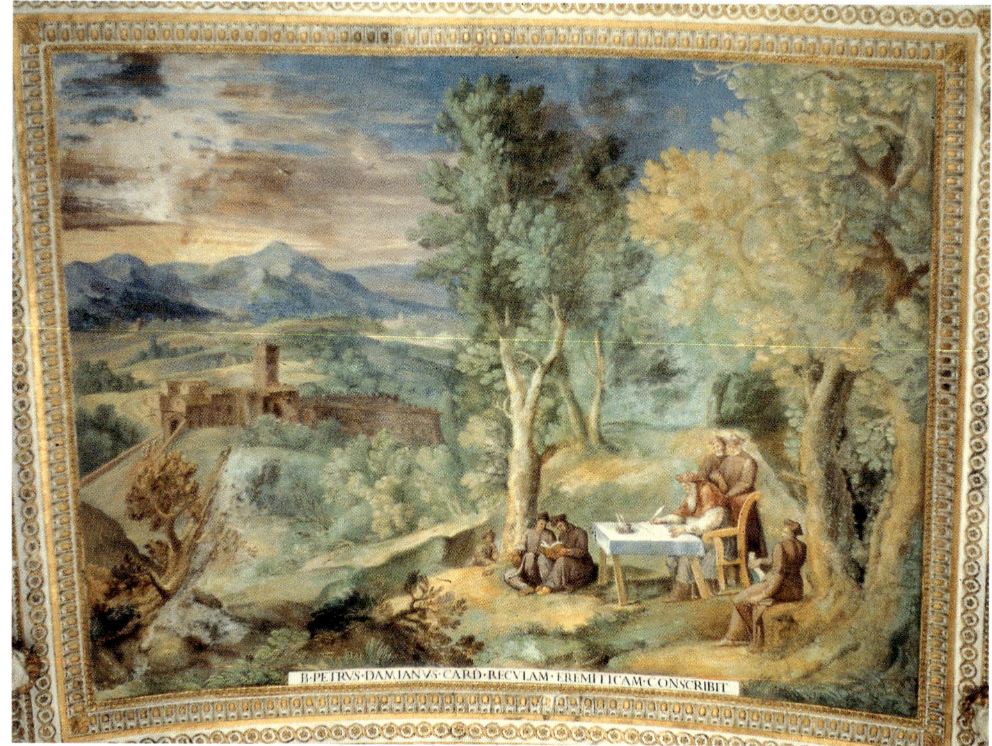
B·PETRVS·DAMIANVS·CARD·REGVLAM·EREMITICAM·CONSCRIBIT

13

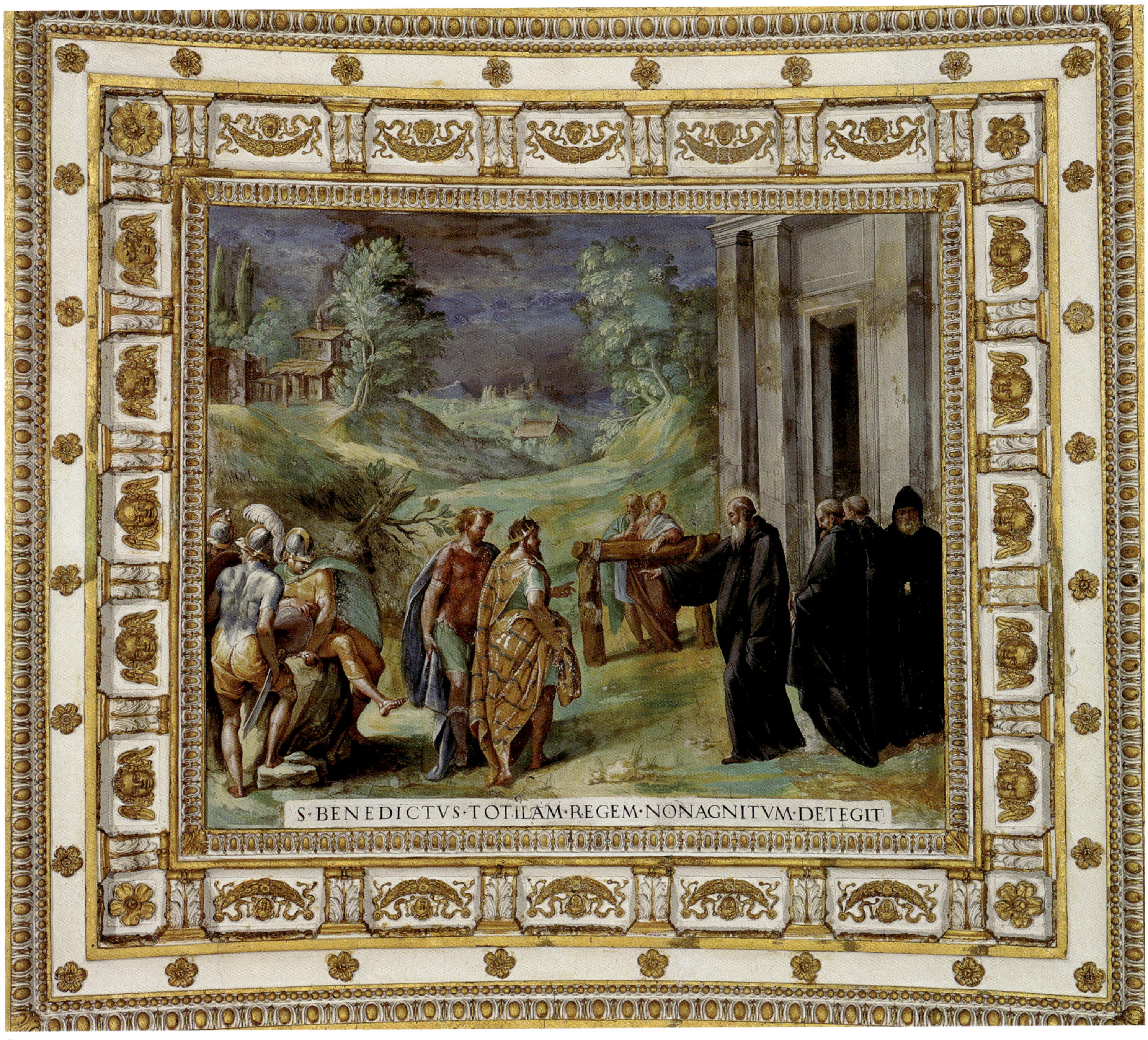

9

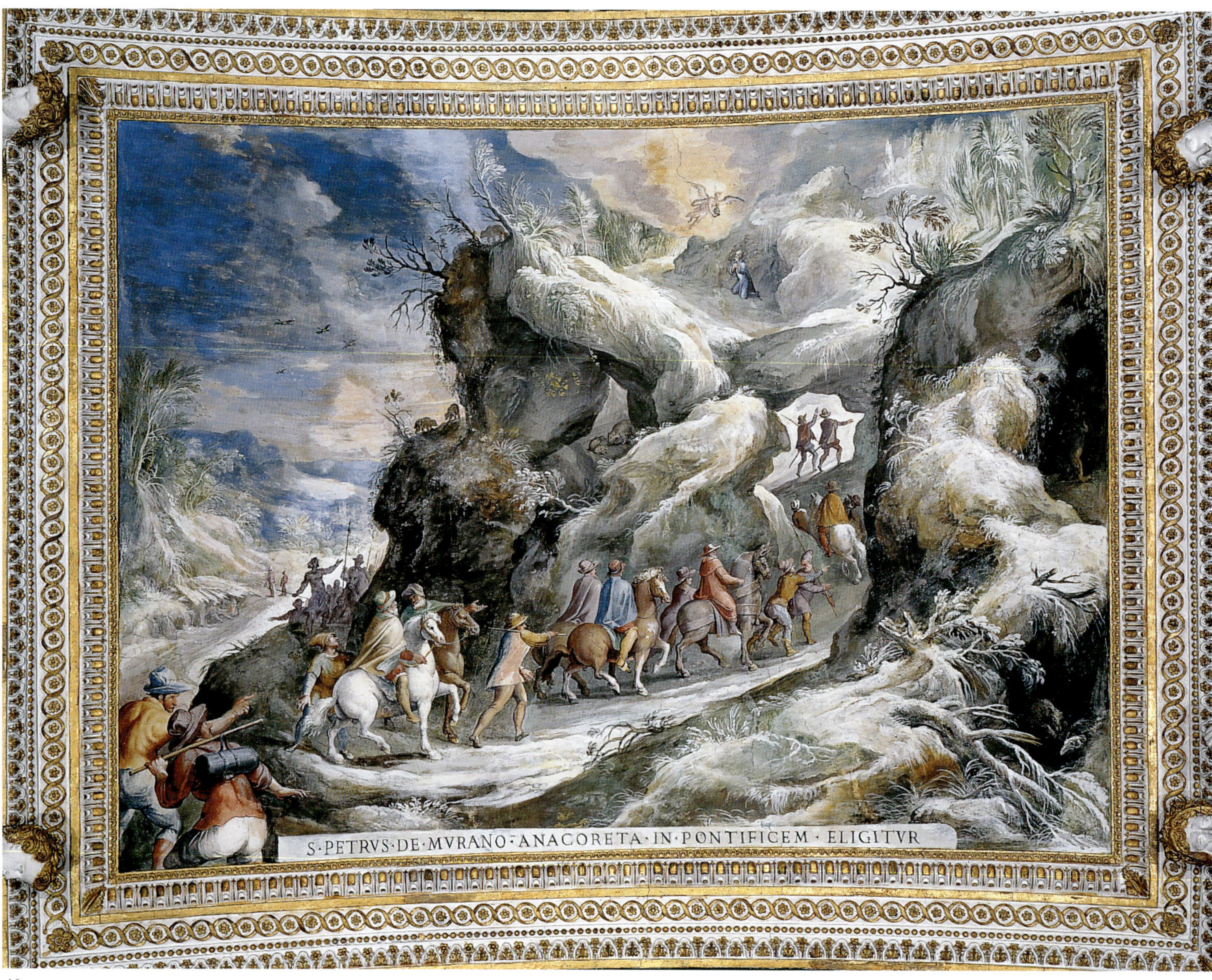

16

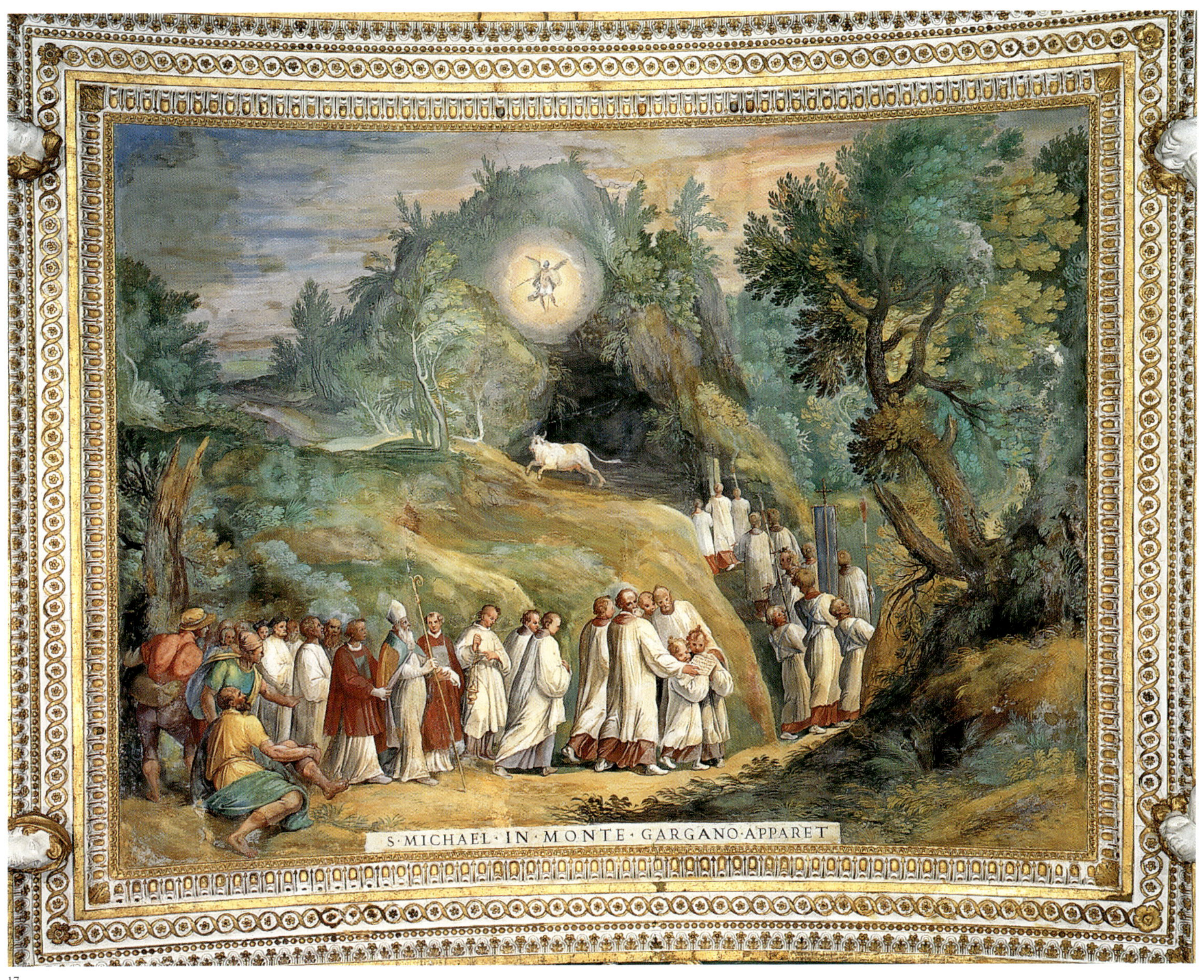

17

n.

Paul Bril
(scenes: Baldassare Croce, Ventura
Salimbeni, Francesco Morelli (?),
Giovanni Baglione, Ferraù Fenzoni,
Pietro Facchetti, Giacomo Stella (?);
supervision: Cesare Nebbia
and Giovanni Guerra)

*Six landscapes in the background
of library scenes*, south wall;
Seascape, vault, fresco*
Commissioned by Pope Sixtus V

Datable 1588-89

1. BIBLIOTHECA CAESARIENSIS
(Baldassare Croce): *Window with a View
of a Harbour*

2. BIBLIOTECA HIEROSOLIMITANA
(Ventura Salimbeni): *Landscape
with Ruins*

3. BIBLIOTHECA ROMANORUM
(Francesco Morelli (?) and Giovanni
Baglione): left and right (with *a Town
in the Distance and Bridges*)

4. BIBLIOTHECA ATHENIENSIS (Ferraù
Fenzoni): left, *Window with a View
of Ruins* and right, *Landscape
with a Port in the Distance*

5. BIBLIOTHECA BABYLONICA (Francesco
Morelli (?) and Giovanni Baglione):
*Landscape with the Tower of Babel,
Obelisks and Ruins*

6. BIBLIOTHECA HEBREAE, (Pietro
Facchetti and Giacomo Stella ?): *Town
with Mountain Landscape*

vault, northern part:

7. *Fleet of Sixtus V*

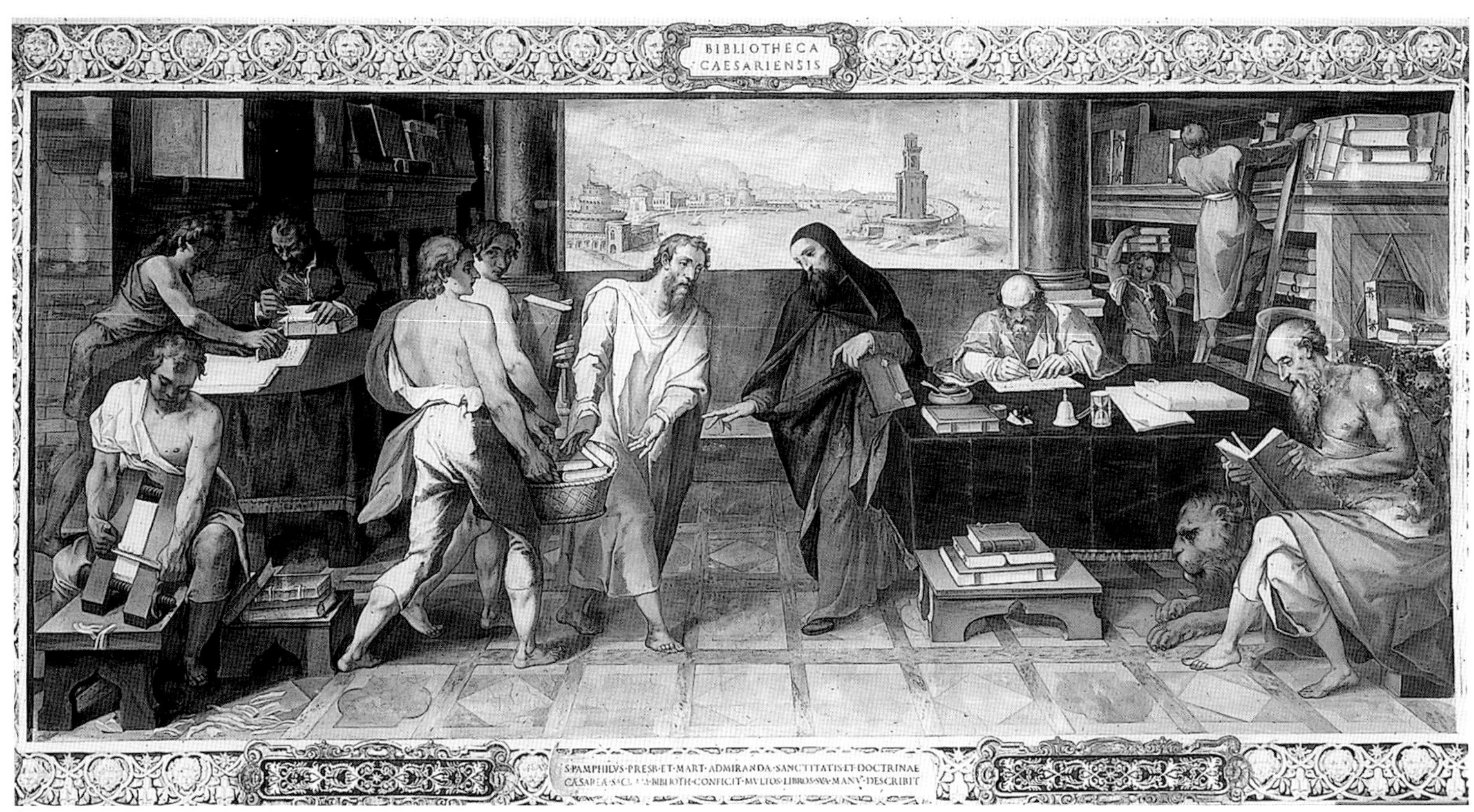

1

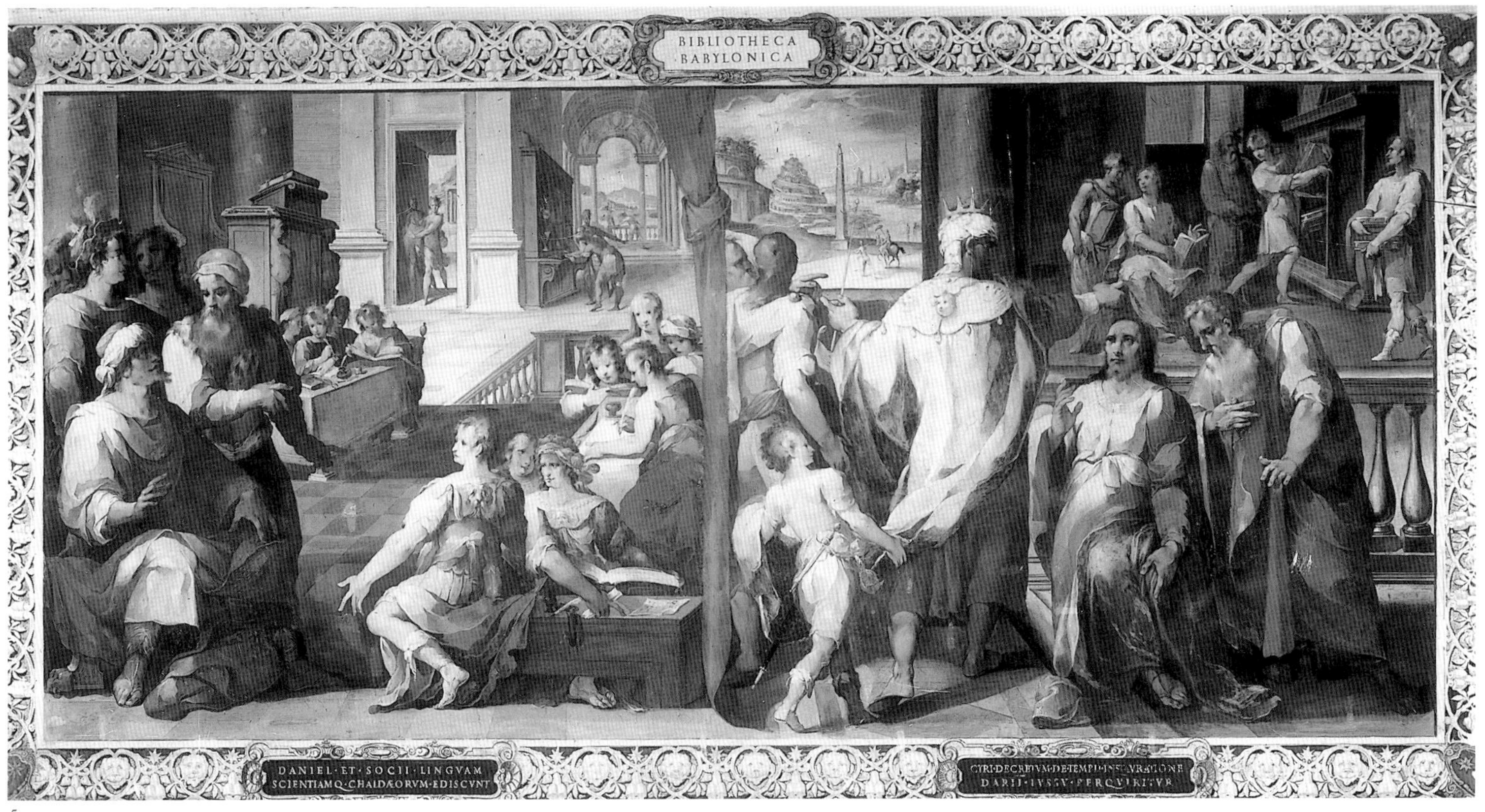
BIBLIOTHECA
BABYLONICA

DANIEL · ET · SOCII · LINGVAM
SCIENTIAMQ · CHALDÆORVM · EDISCVNT

CYRI · DECRETVM · DE · TEMPLI · INSTAVRATIONE
DARII · IVSSV · PERQVIRITVR

5

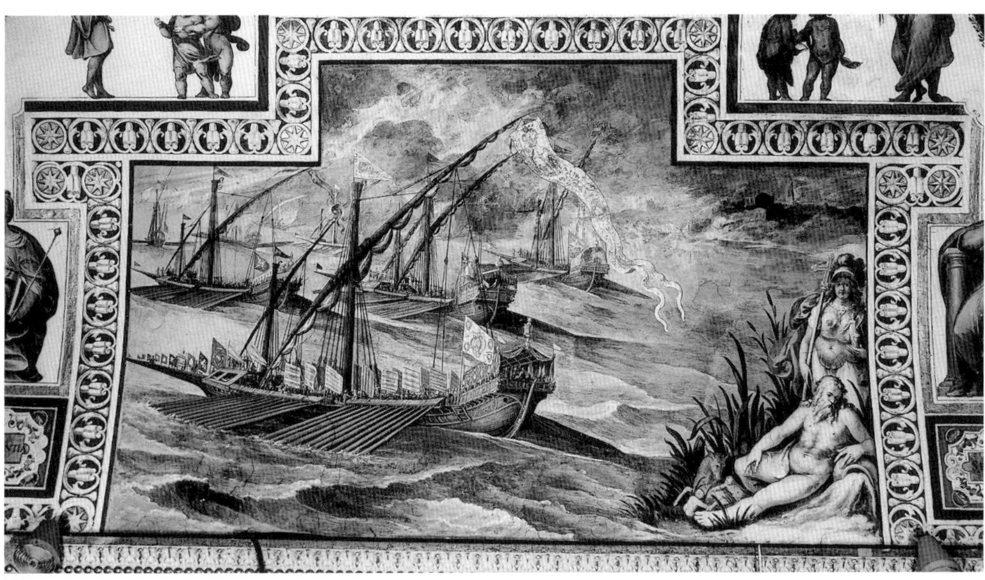

7

0.

Paul Bril
(supervision: Cesare Nebbia
and Giovanni Guerra)

Four landscapes, lunettes above
the doors, fresco
Commissioned by Pope Sixtus V

Datable 1586-87 (inscription "anno II")

bottom of staircase:

1. *Landscape with the Ruins of a Tower
and a Figure Walking*

2. *Landscape with Figures Walking
and a Town in the Distance*

top of staircase:

3. *Landscape with Herdsman
and Figures Walking*

4. *Landscape with Cottages
and a Figure Walking*

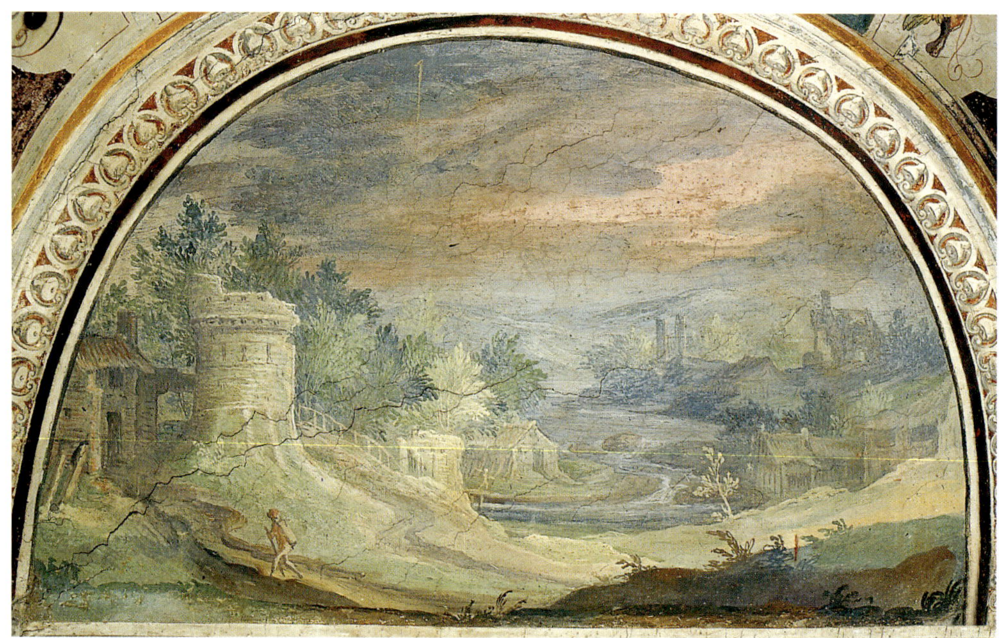

1

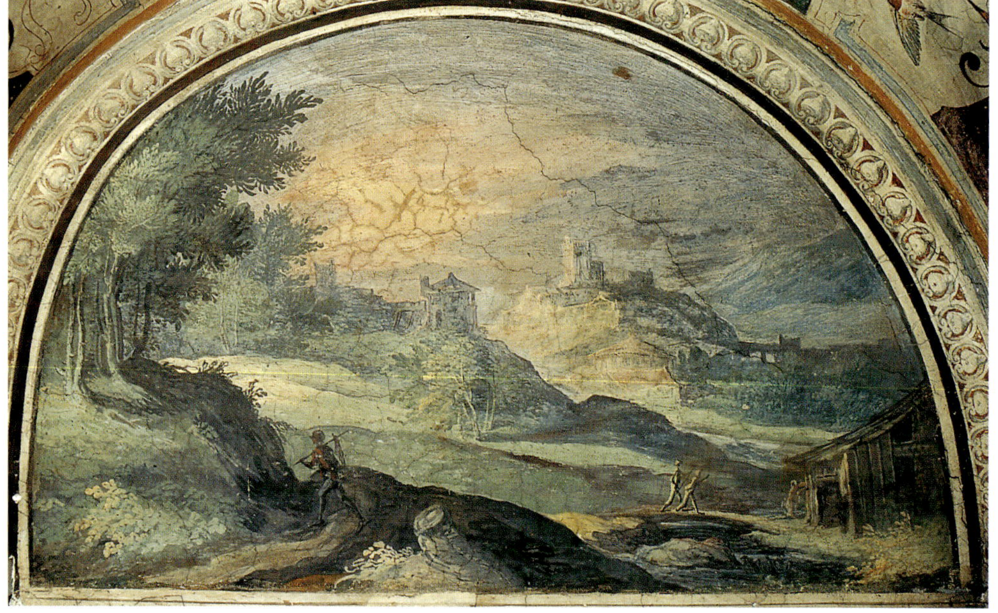

2

P.
Paul Bril
(figures in the scene: Cherubino
Alberti and Giovanni Alberti)

*Seascape with the Martyrdom
of St Clement*, fresco*
Commissioned by Pope Clement VIII

Documented 1599-1601

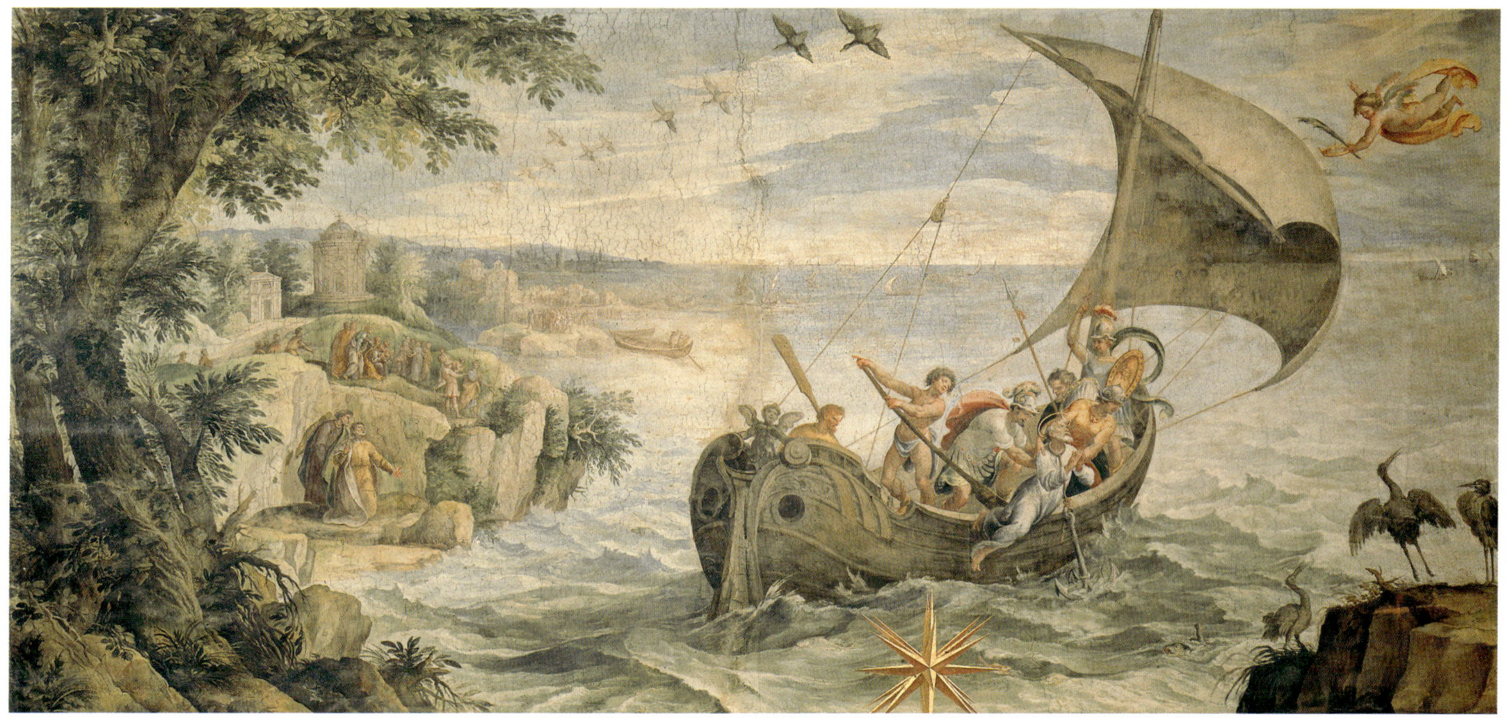

q.
Paul Bril
(decoration surrounding the scenes:
Cherubino Alberti)

Seven landscapes with monasteries
*(frieze), fresco**
Commissioned by Pope Clement VIII

Documented 1602

1. *Landscape with the Monastery*
of Montecassino

2. *Landscape with the Monastery*
of Camaldoli

3. *Landscape with the Monastery*
of La Verna

4. *Landscape with the Monastery*
of Monteoliveto Maggiore

5. *Landscape with the Monastery*
of Santa Scolastica, Subiaco

6. *Landscape with the Monastery*
of Monte Vergine

7. *Landscape with the Monastery*
of Vallombrosa

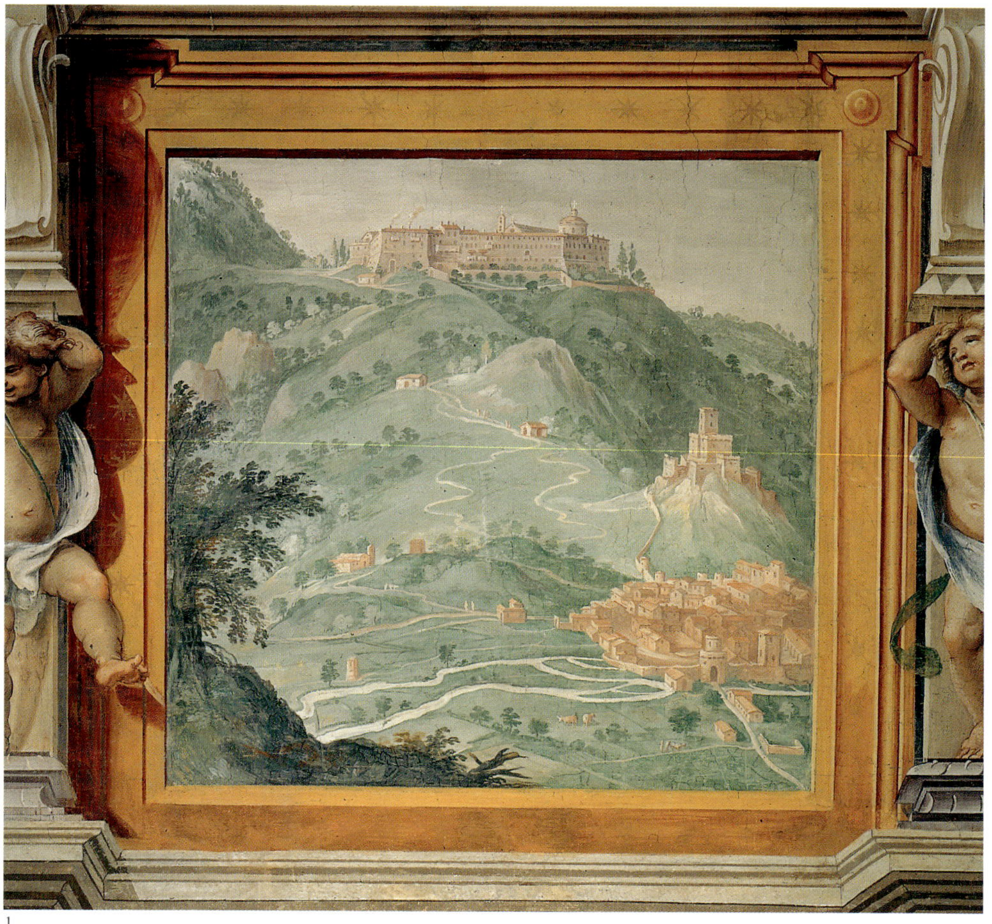

1

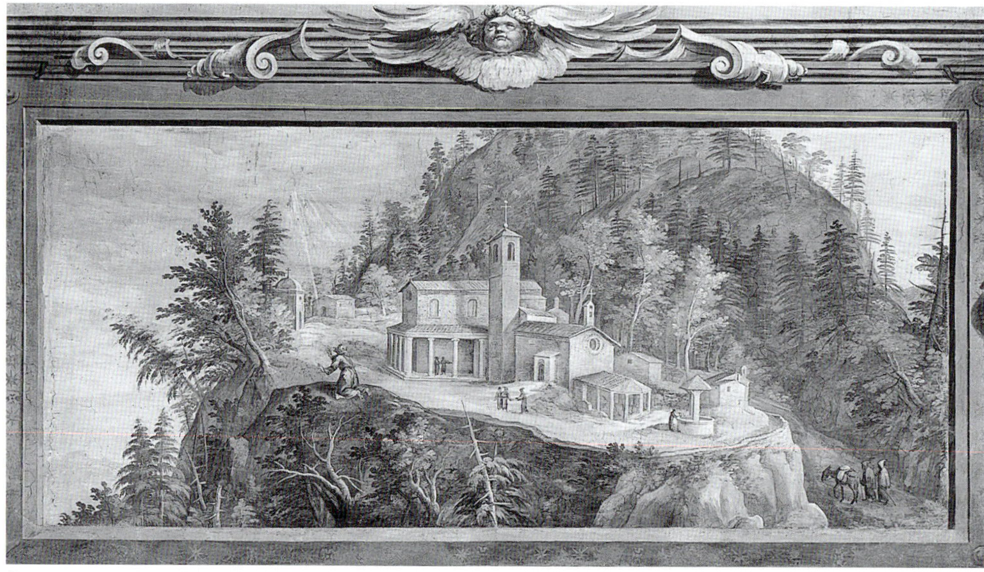

3

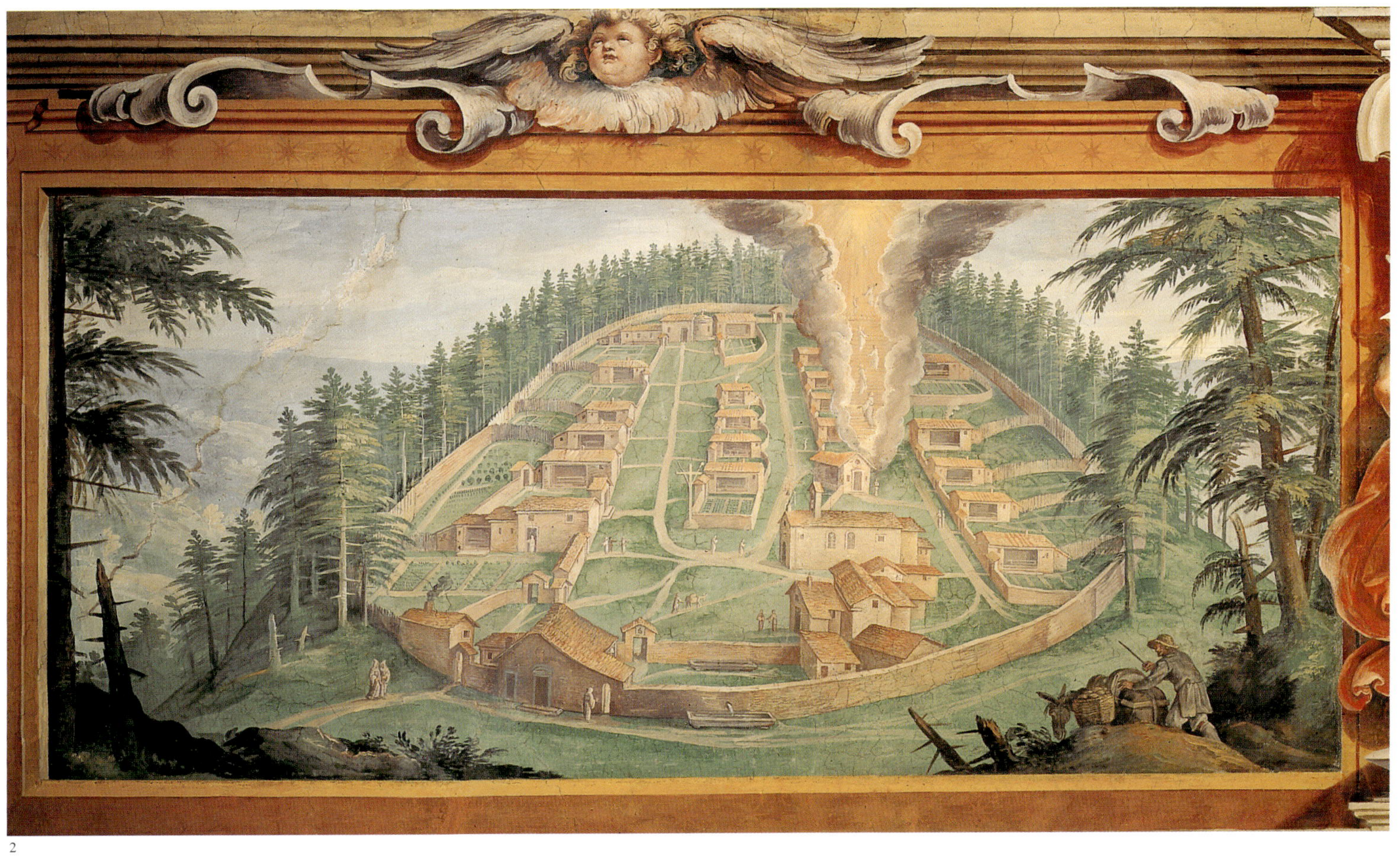

2

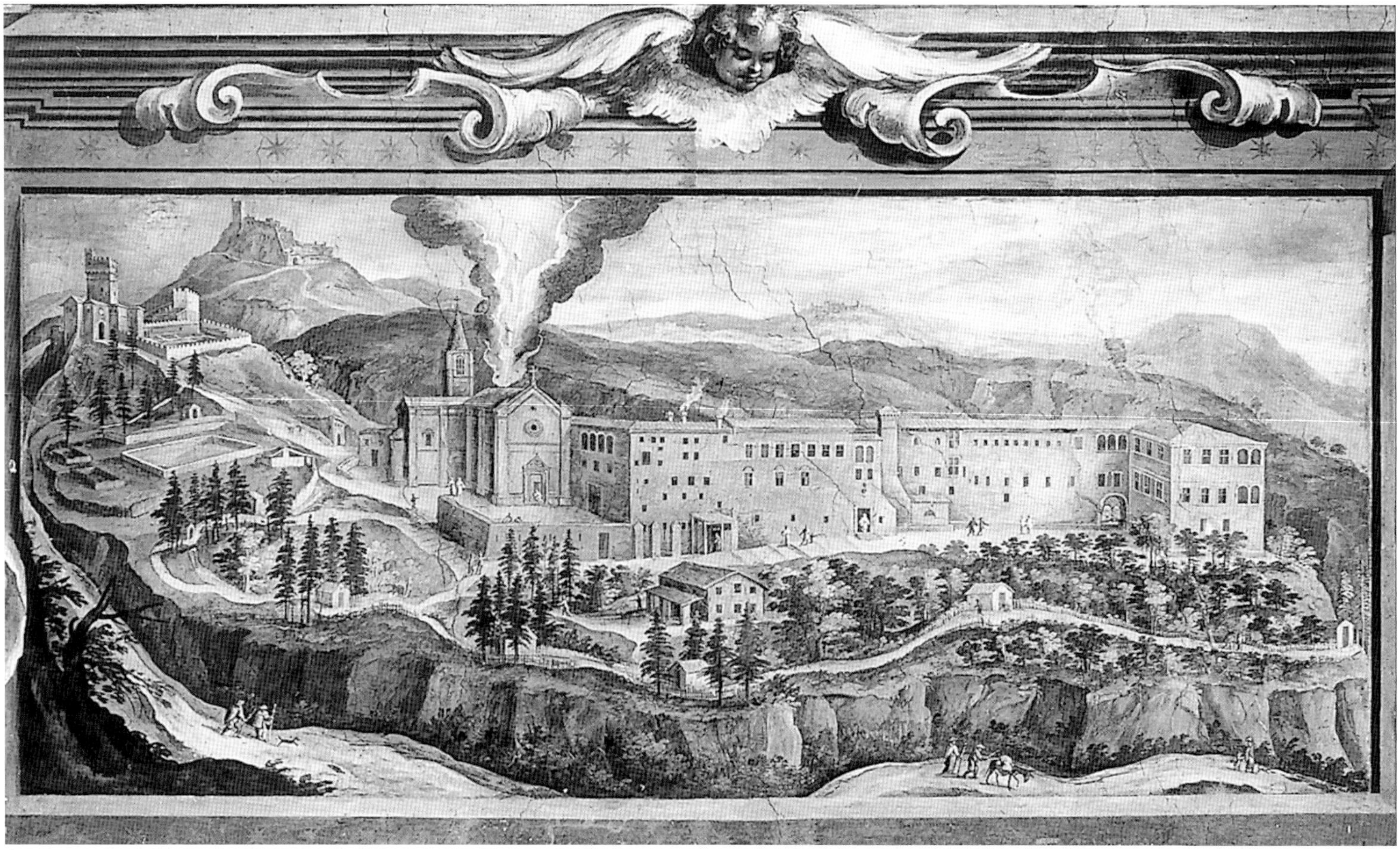

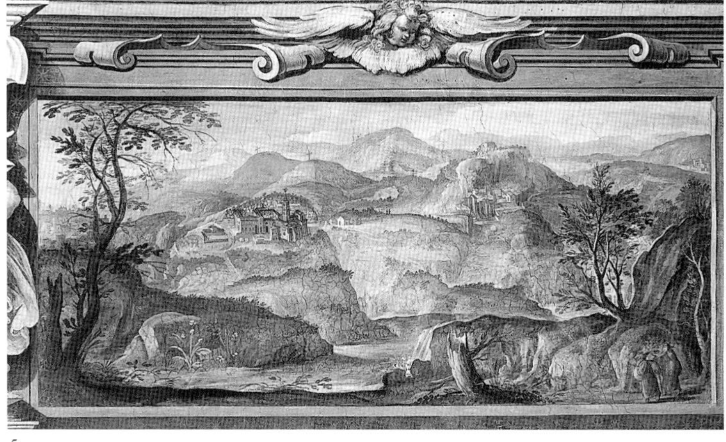

5

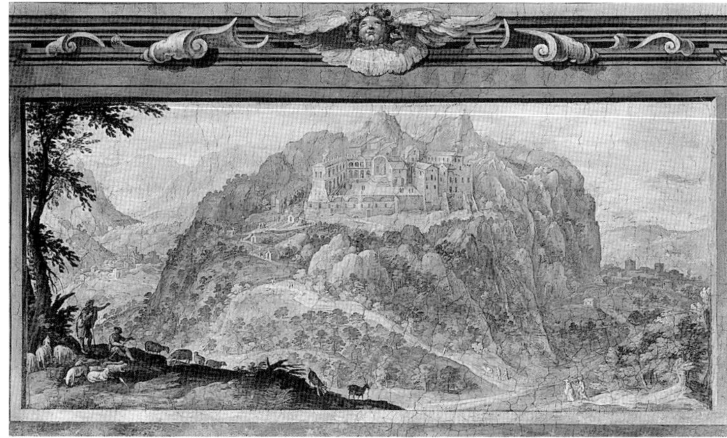

6

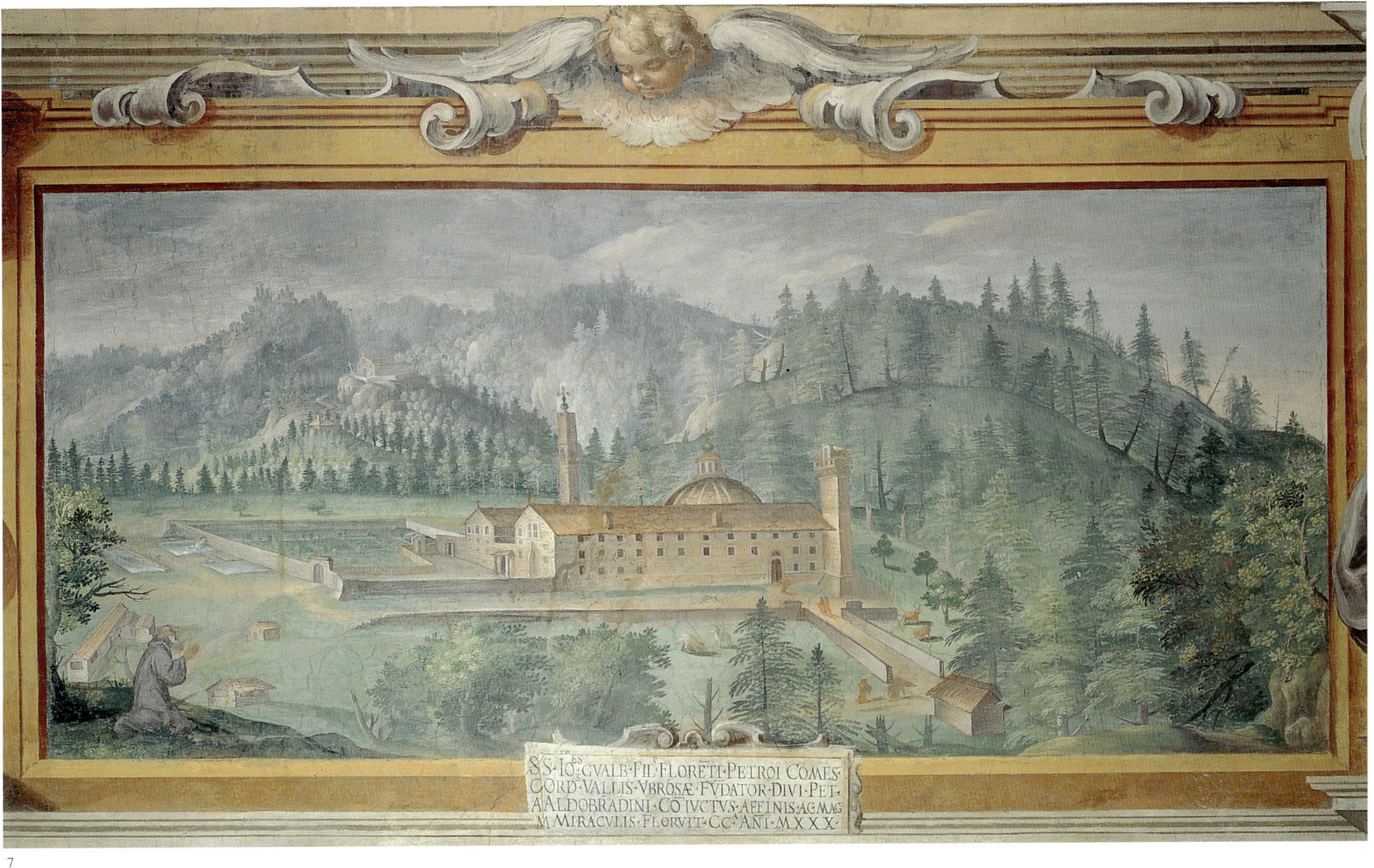
S·S· IO· GVALB· FIL· FLORETI· PETROI· COMES·
CORD· VALLIS· VBROSÆ· FVDATOR· DIVI· PET·
A· ALDOBRADINI· CÕ IVCTVS· AFFINIS· AC· MAG
M· MIRACVLIS· FLORVIT· CCᴬ ANI· M·XXX·

7

r.

Paul Bril and assistant (Balthasar Lauwers?)

*Eight landscapes with hermits (in a frieze), fresco**
Commissioned by Pope Paulus V

Datable c. 1605-07

1. *Winter Landscape*

2. *River Landscape with a Hermit and Roman Ruins*

3. *Woodland with a Hermit at a River*

4. *Landscape with a Hermit, Walkers and Roman Ruins*

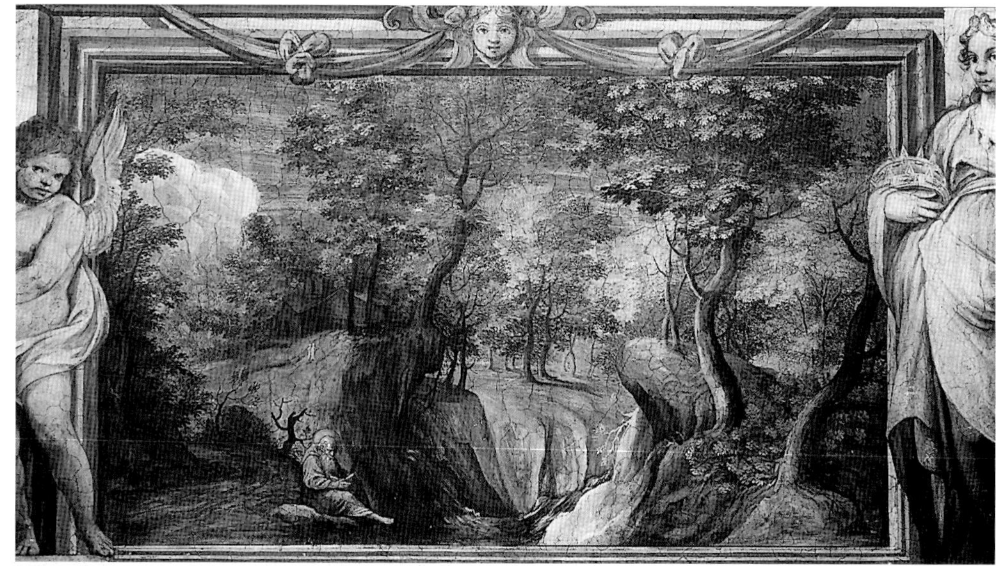

3

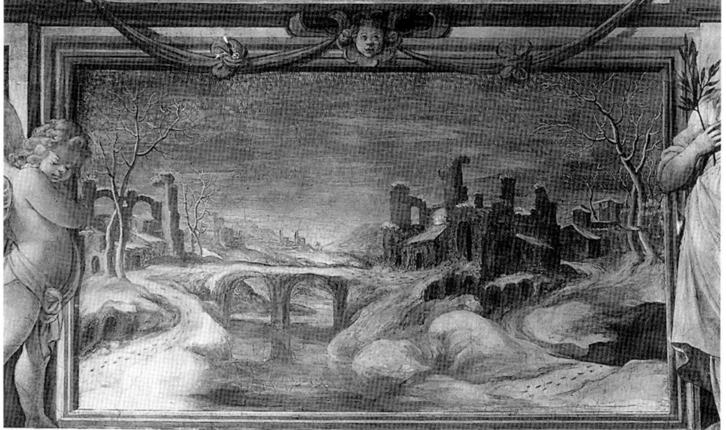

1

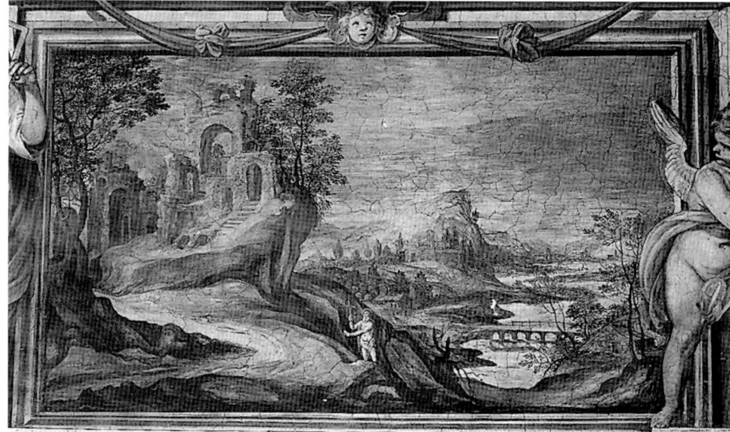

2

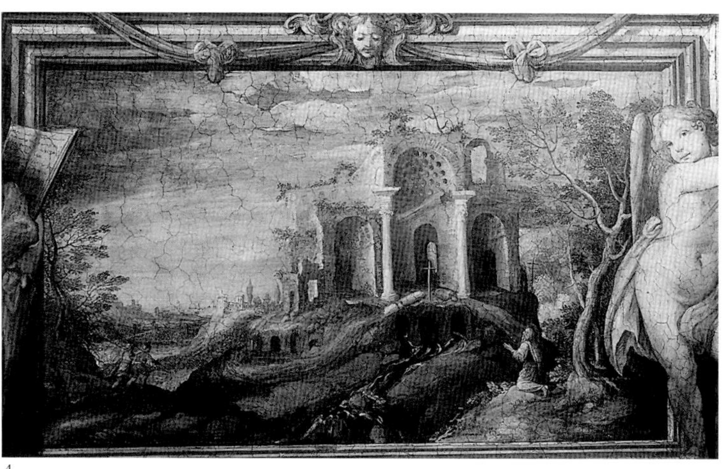

4

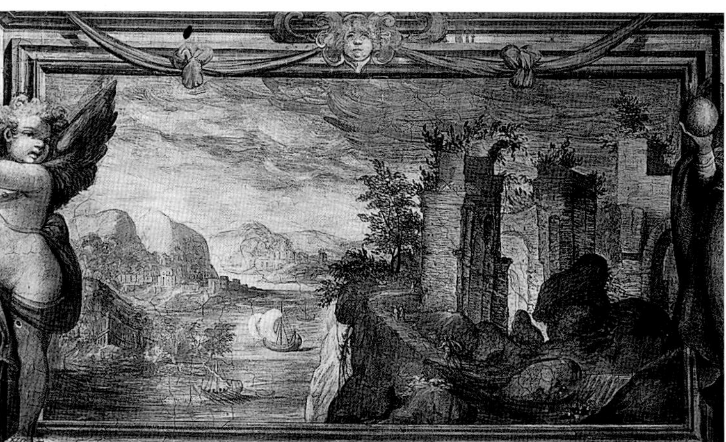

5

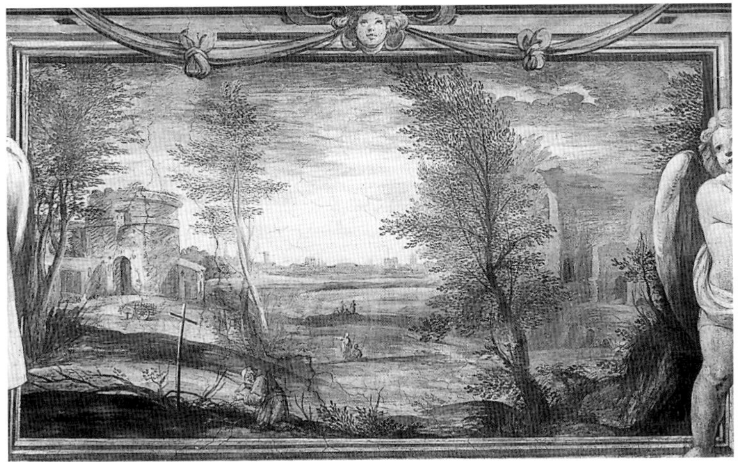

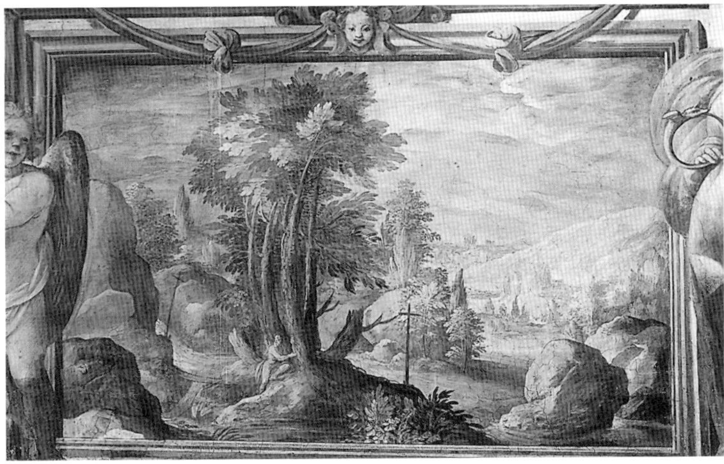

6

7

5. *River Landscape with Roman Ruins*
(assistant)

6. *Landscape with a Hermit
and Buildings* (assistant)

7. *Rocky Landscape with a Hermit
and a Cross* (assistant)

8. *Landscape by Night with a Burning
Town on a River*

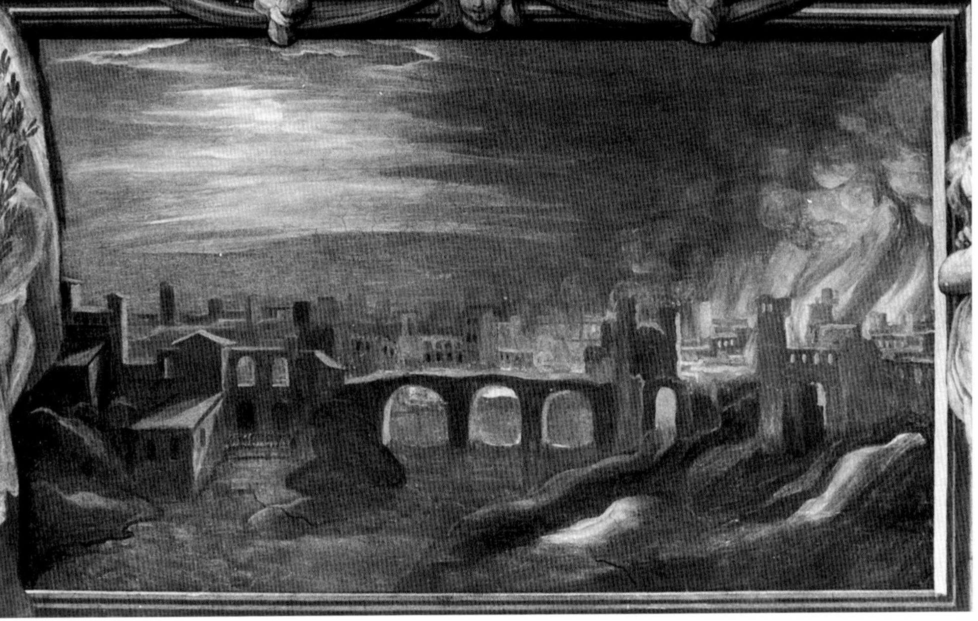

8

s.

Paul Bril

Four landscapes (in a frieze), fresco*
Commissioned by Pope Paul V

Datable c. 1605-07

1. *River View with Two Walkers Resting*
2. *Coastal Landscape with Boats
and the Ruins of a Tower*
3. *Landscape with Roman Ruins
and Figures Walking*
4. *Landscape with a Resting Herdsman
and his Animals*

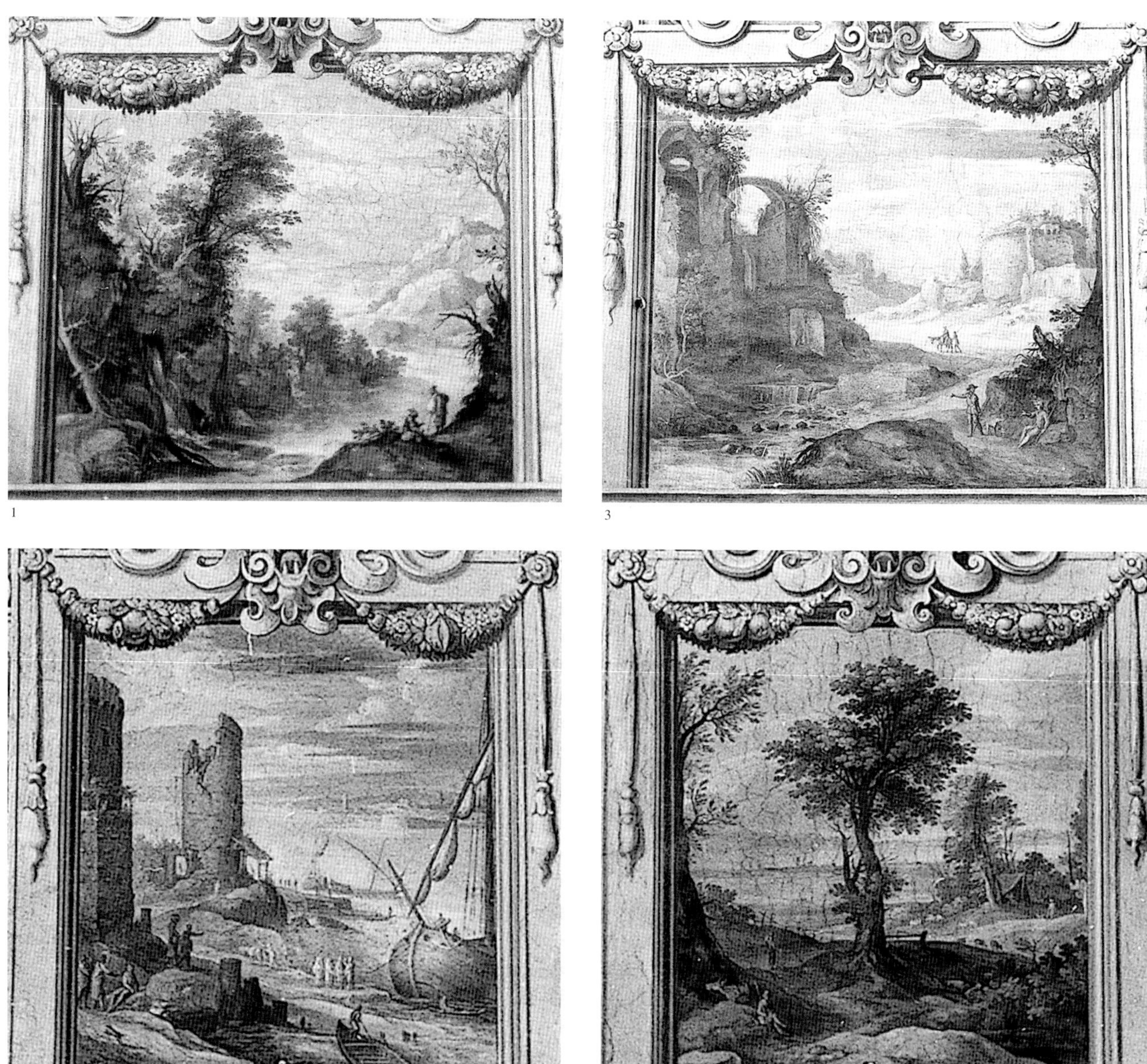

t.

Paul Bril

*Six landscapes with hermits
(in a frieze), fresco**
Commissioned by Pope Paul V

Datable c. 1605-07

1. *Landscape with a Hermit Kneeling
before a Cross*
2. *Landscape with a Hermit Kneeling
before a Cross*
3. *Rocky Landscape with a Waterfall
and Hermit Seated before a Cross*
4. *Rocky Landscape with a Hermit
and Cross*
5. *Landscape with a Hermit and Cross
and Two Figures on a Bridge*
6. *Landscape with a River and a Town
on a Bay*

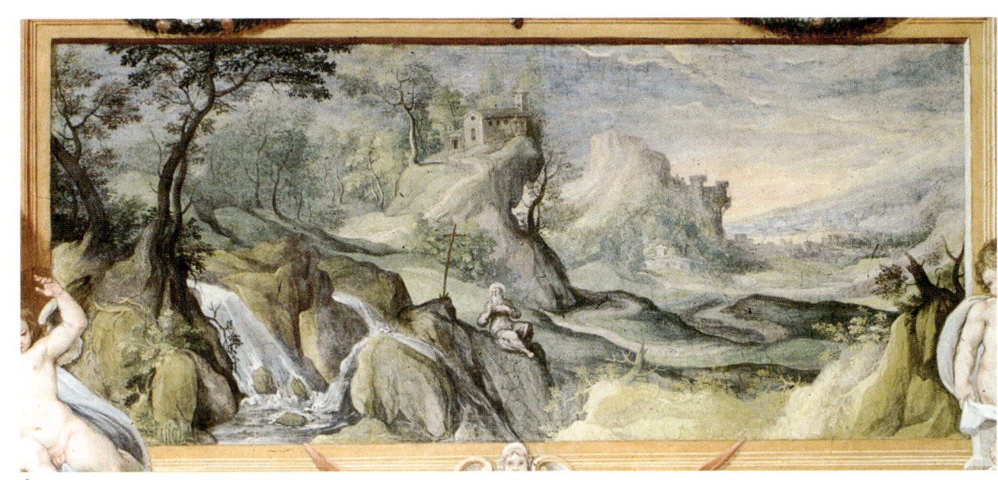

3

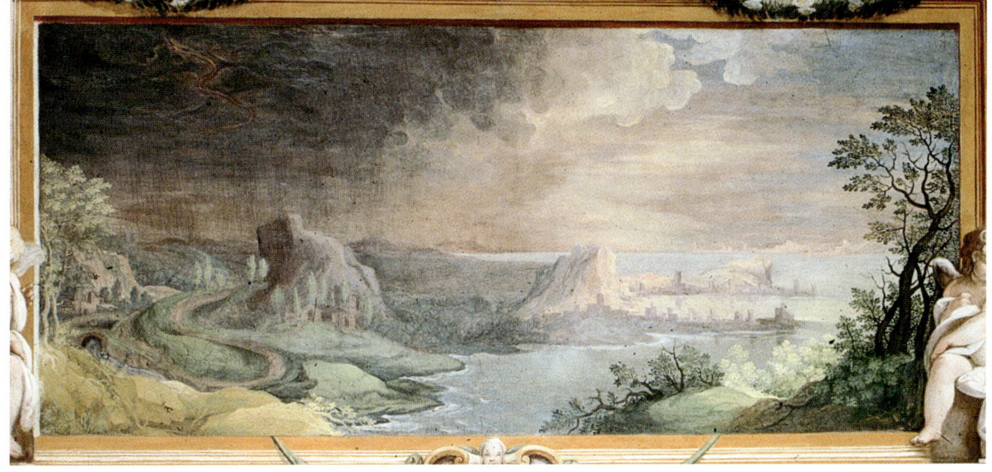

6

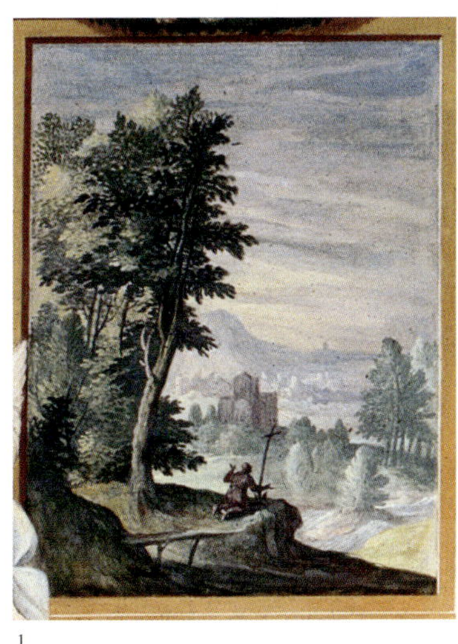

1

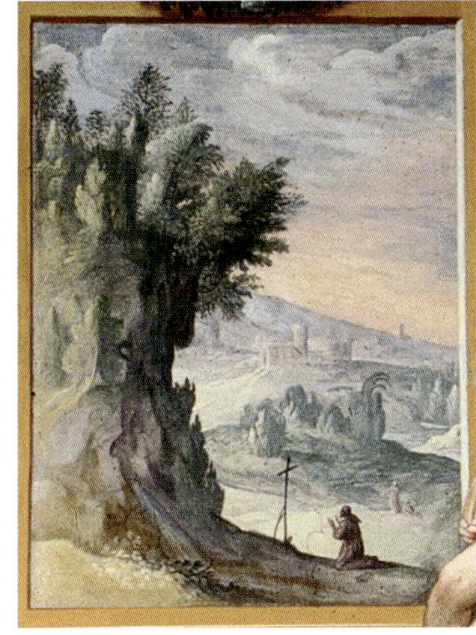

2

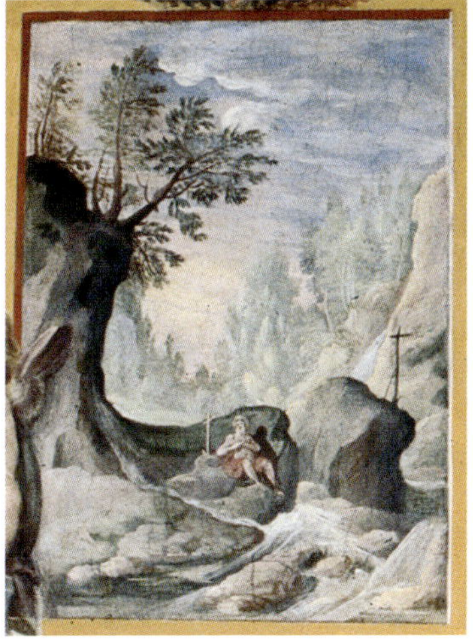

4

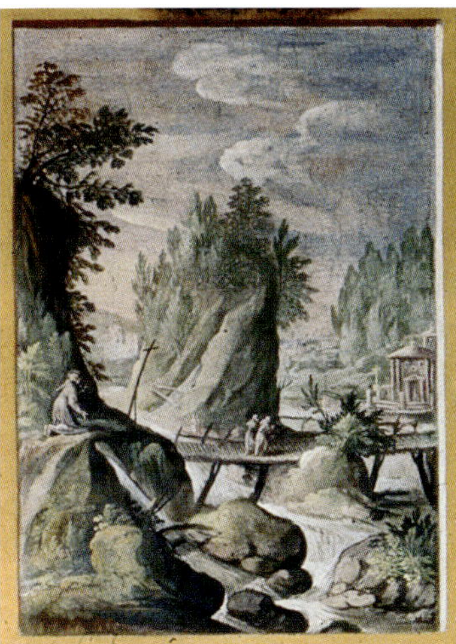

5

Salone

a.

Paul Bril
(allegorical figures and putti
surrounding the scenes: Cristoforo
Roncalli (?) called Pomarancio)

Nine landscapes (in a frieze), fresco*
Commissioned by Cardinal Girolamo
Mattei

Documented 1599

south, west and north walls:

1. *River Landscape with Waterwheel*

2. *Landscape with Hunting Scenes*

3. *River Landscape with Fishermen*

4. *Storm at Sea with Ships*

5. *View of a Port with Tower*

6. *Landscape with a Church on a Hill
and Monks*

7. *Woodland with Hunters*

8. *Woodland with a Herdsman
and Fishermen*

9. *Landscape with a Herdsman
and his Animals*

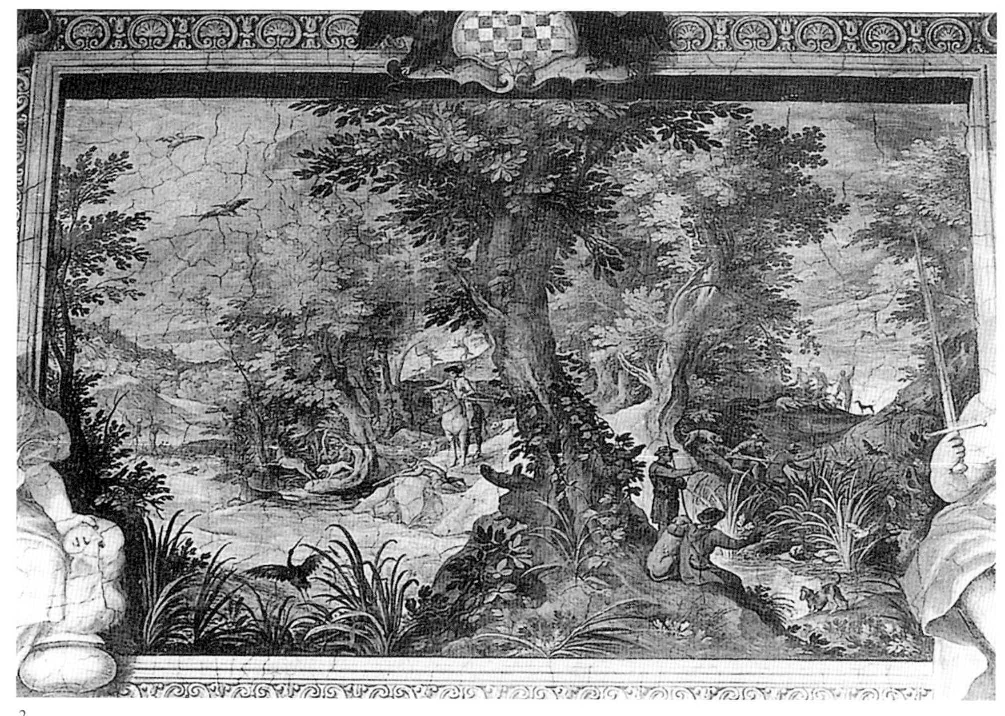

2

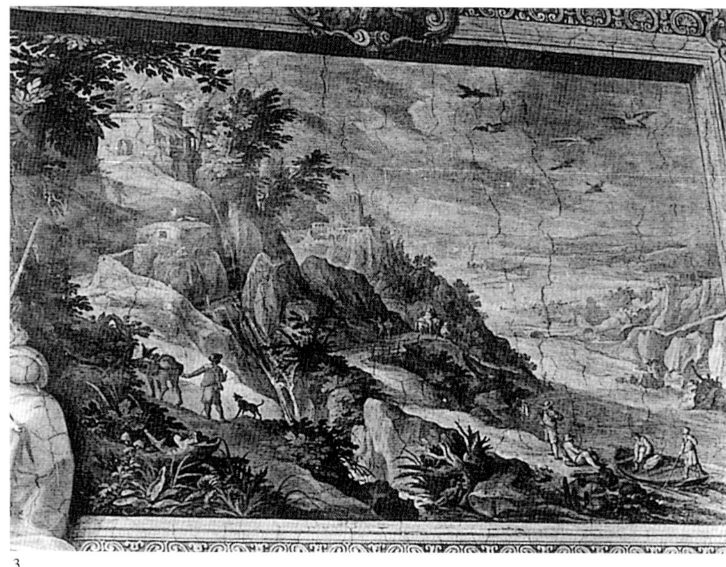

3

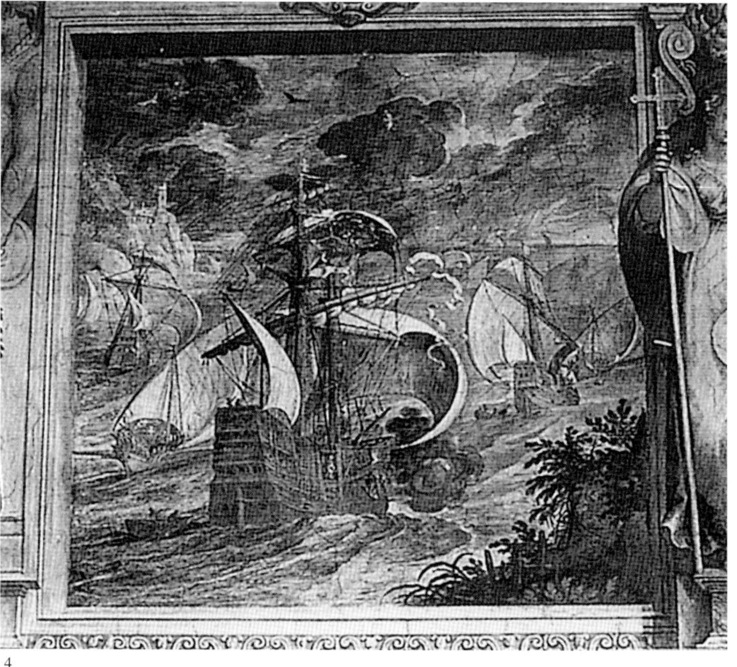

4

b.

Paul Bril
(decoration surrounding the scenes:
Bril's assistant)

Ten small landscapes, fresco*
Commissioned by Cardinal Girolamo
Mattei

Documented 1599

north and east walls (on either side
of the windows):

1a. *Landscape with a Tree, Hunters
and a River*, left

1b. *Landscape with a Man and a Woman
on a Donkey crossing a Bridge*, right

2a. *Landscape with a Herdsman
and Animals*, left

2b. *Landscape with Resting Travellers,
a Donkey and Ruins*, right

3a. *Landscape with a Round Temple
on a Hill and Ruins*, left

3b. *Landscape with Women Washing
at a River*, right

4a. *Landscape with Ruins of a Temple,
Figures and Chickens*, left

4b. *Landscape with a River, Women
Washing and Ruins*, right

5a. *Landscape with a Man
on Horseback, a Servant and Dogs*, left

5b. *Landscape with a Waterfall
and a Castle in the Distance*, right

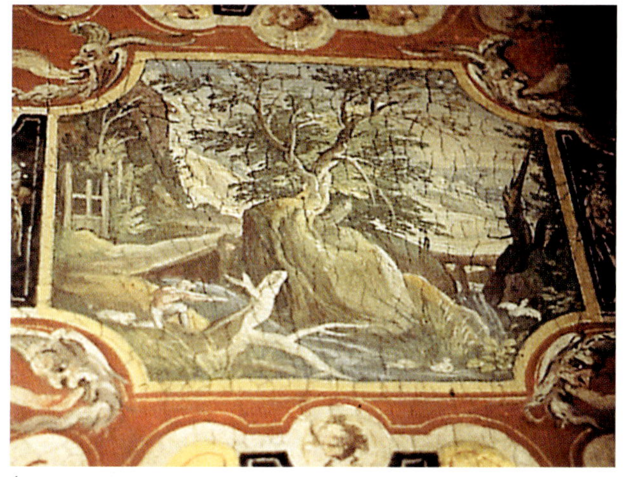

1a

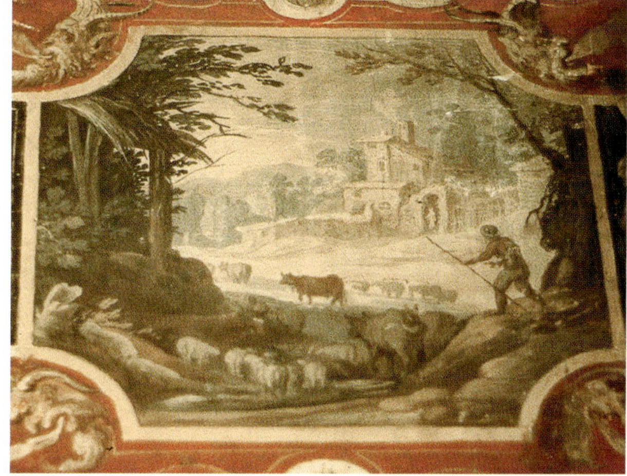

2a

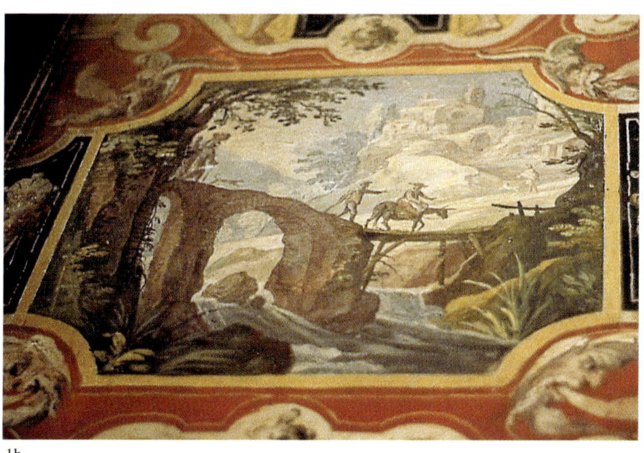

1b

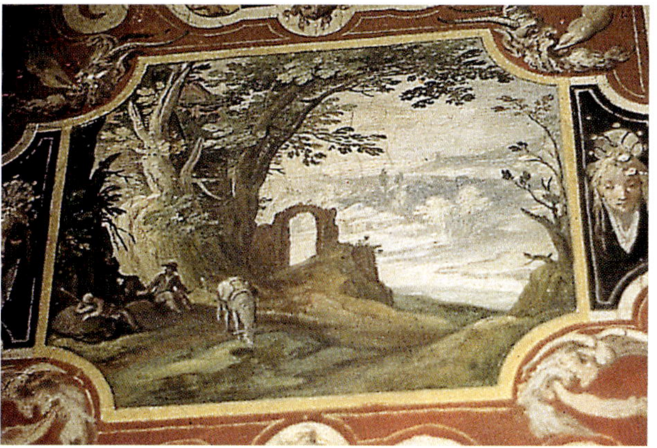

2b

Salone

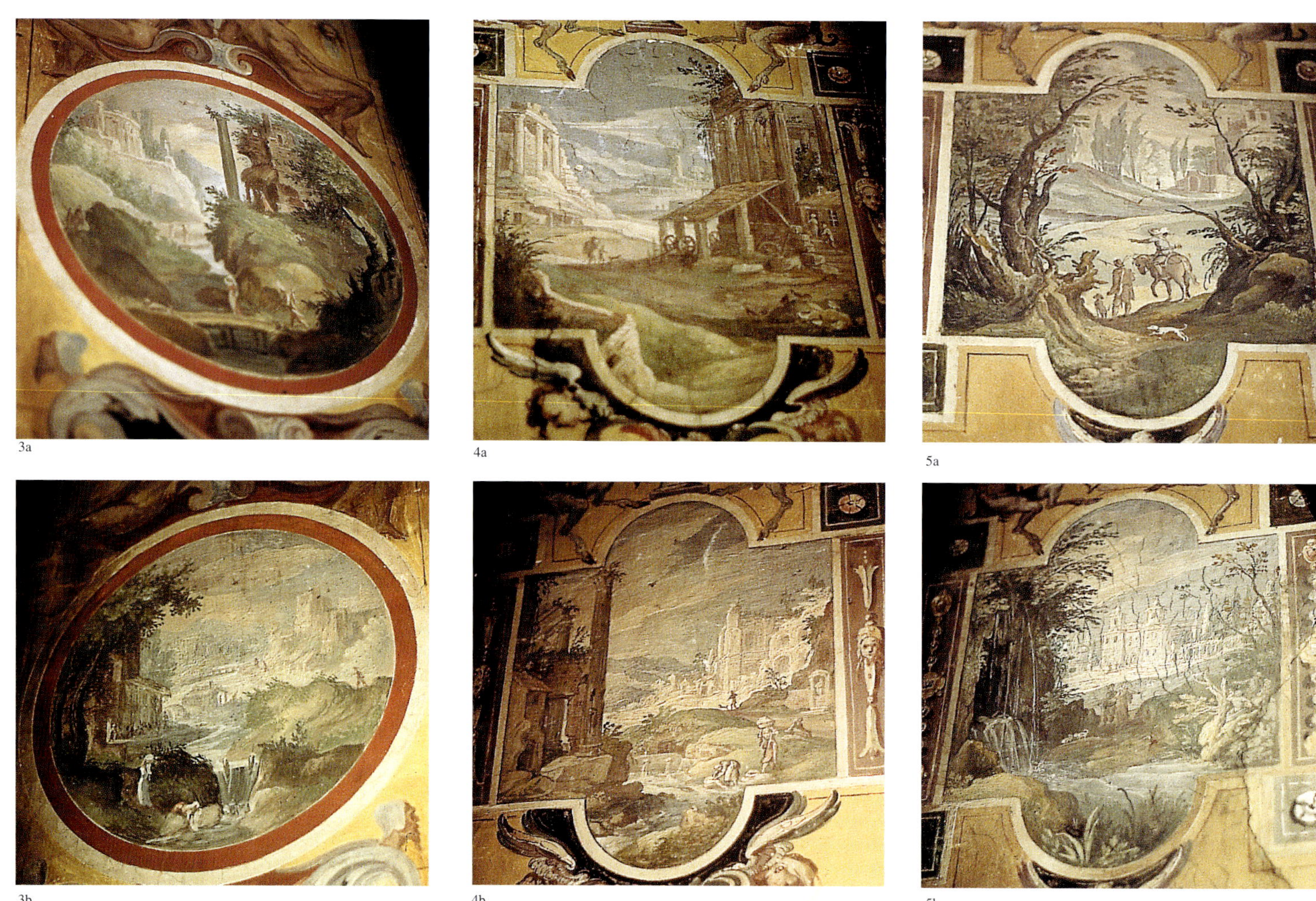

3a

4a

5a

3b

4b

5b

a.

Paul Bril
(part of pergola and grapes,
two landscapes, a third destroyed:
Pietro Paolo Bonzi called Gobbo
dei Carracci; putti: Guido Reni)

Six landscapes, lunettes under
the vault with painted *Pergola,*
fresco
Commissioned by Cardinal Scipione
Borghese

Documented 1611-12

1. *Deer Hunt*

2. *View with Boats on a River*

3. *Marine Scene*

4. *Landscape with Two Monks
and a Village*

5. *Landscape with a Woman
on a Donkey and a Herdsman
with his Animals*

6. *Landscape with Heron Hunt*

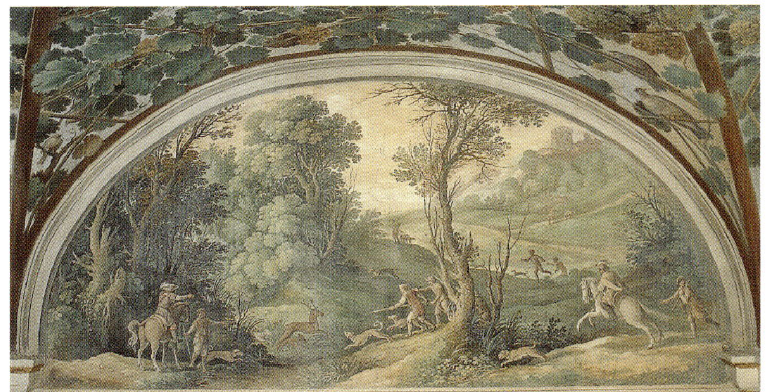

1

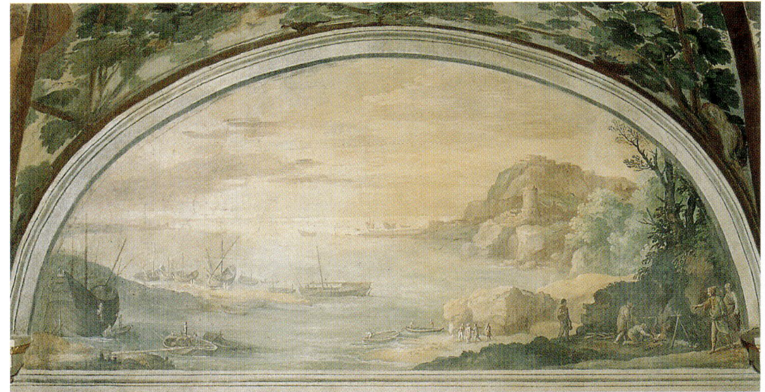

3

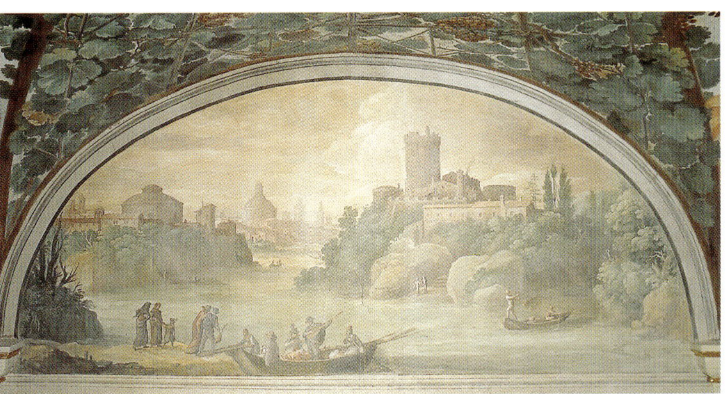

2

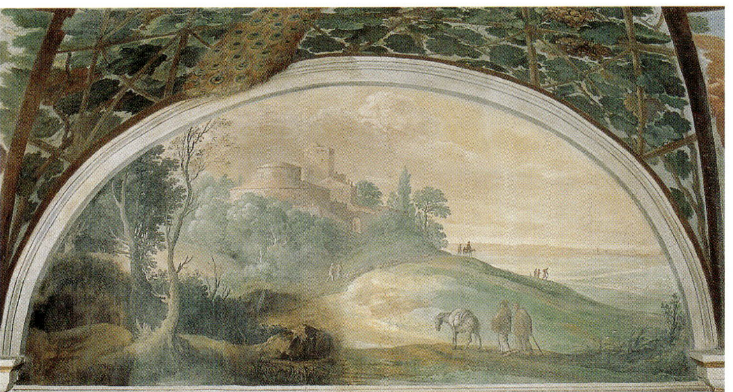

4

b.

Paul Bril
(two friezes: Antonio Tempesta;
Aurora: Guido Reni)

The Four Seasons (1.70 x 1 m each),
fresco*
Commissioned by Cardinal Scipione
Borghese

Documented 1613-16

1. *Spring*
2. *Summer*
3. *Autumn*
4. *Winter*

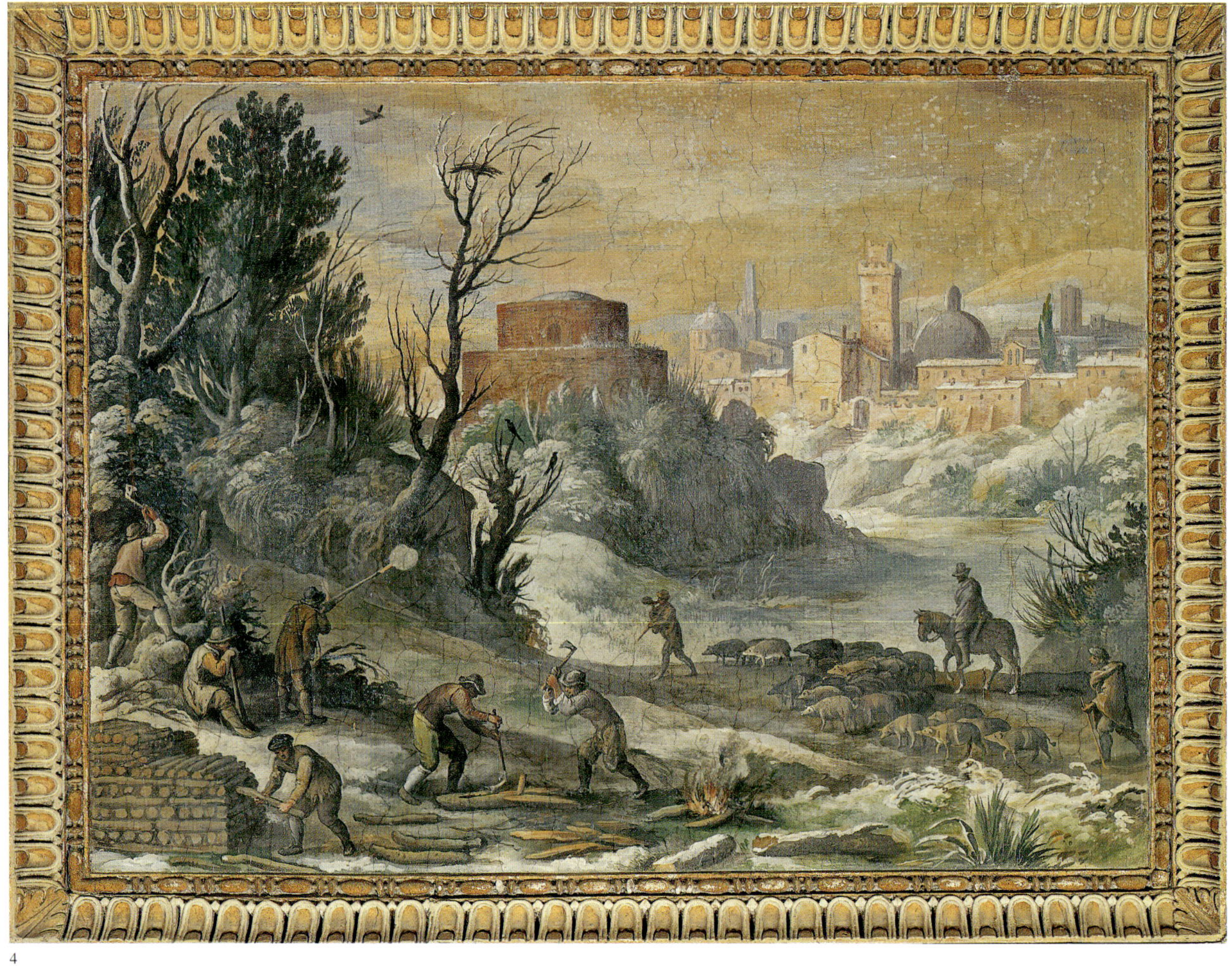

4

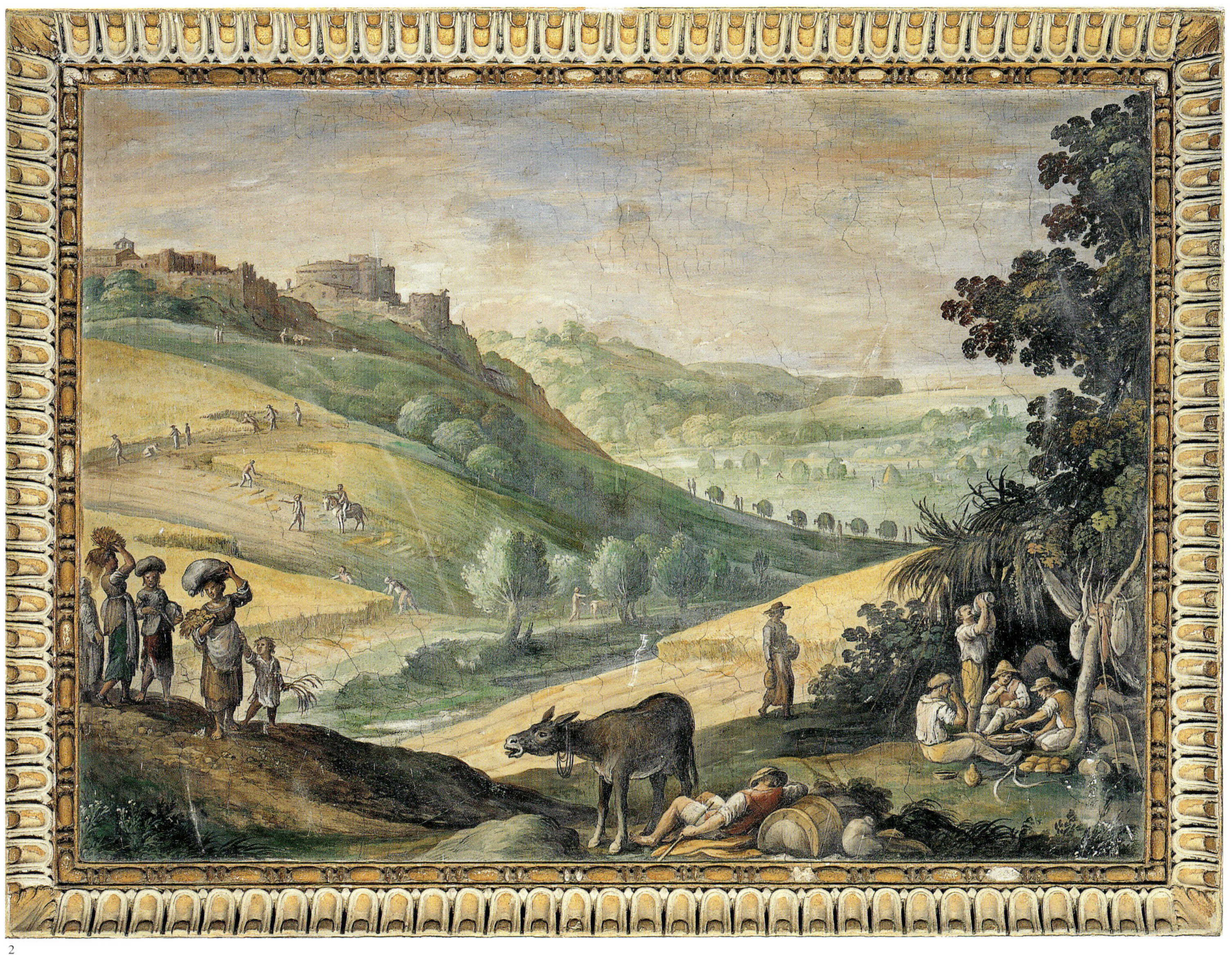

2

Paul Bril and assistant
(decoration surrounding the scenes:
Cristoforo Roncalli called
Pomarancio)

Thirteen landscapes with saints,
walls and vaults, fresco and secco
Commissioned by Cardinal Paolo
Sfondrati

Datable 1599-1600

right wall:

1. *Mary Egyptiaca and Zozimos*
(2 x 1.50 m), Paul Bril

2. *Mary Magdalen and a Female Saint*
(2.10 x 1.50 m), Paul Bril

3. *Silvia* (0.81 x 1.50 m), Paul Bril

left wall:

4. *St Francis in a Rocky Landscape*
(0.72 x 1.50 m), Paul Bril

5. *Female Saint at the Edge of a Forest
with a Stream and a Vista* (2 x 1.50 m),
Paul Bril

6. *Saint under a Thatched Roof near
a Stream* (0.73 x 1.50 m), Paul Bril

lunettes:

7. *St Eulogius* (2.40 x 1 m), assistant
after a design by Bril

8. *St Hilary* (2.40 x 1 m), assistant
after a design by Bril

vault:

9. *St Spiridonis* (0.80 x 0.60 m),
Paul Bril

10. *St Antony* (0.80 x 0.60 m),
Paul Bril and assistant

11. *St Honofrius* (0.80 x 0.80 m),
Paul Bril

12. *St Jerome* (0.80 x 0.80 m),
Paul Bril and assistant

13. *St Paul* (0.80 x 0.60 m),
Paul Bril and assistant

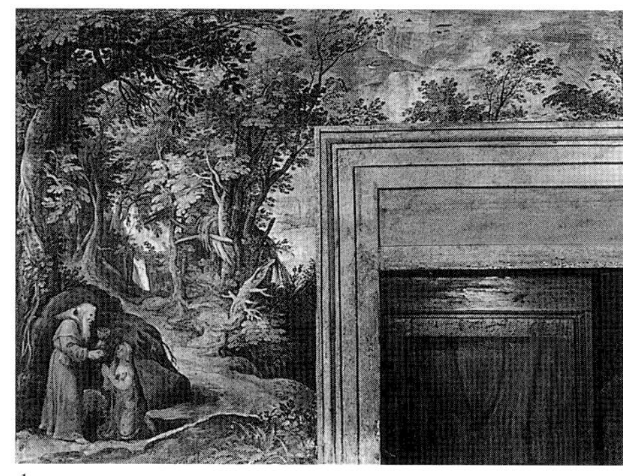

1

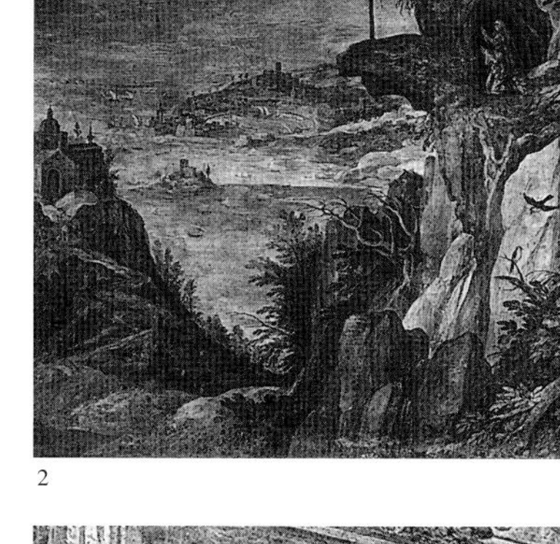

2

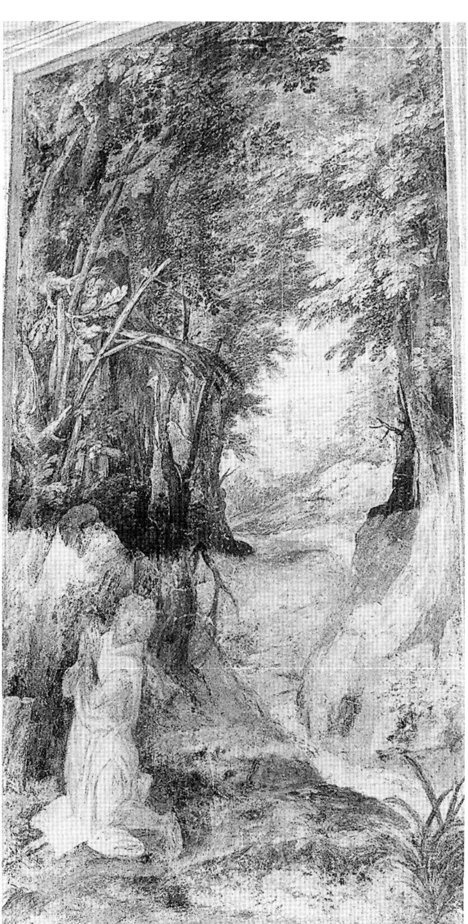

3

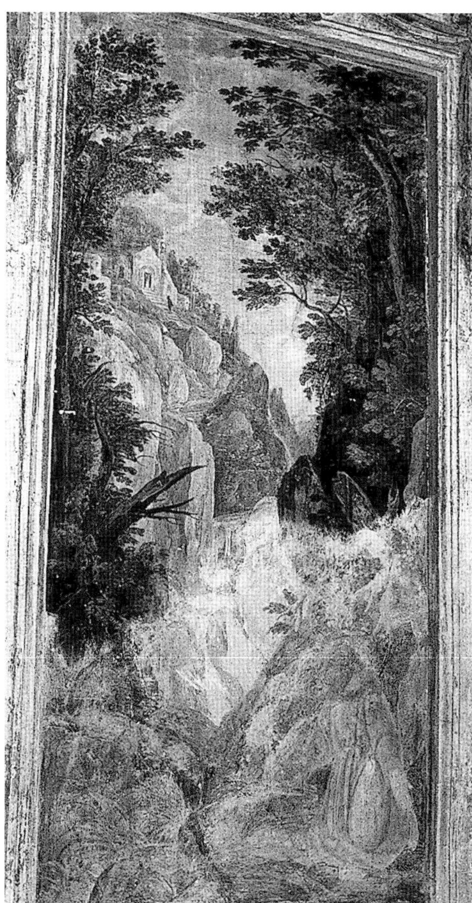

4

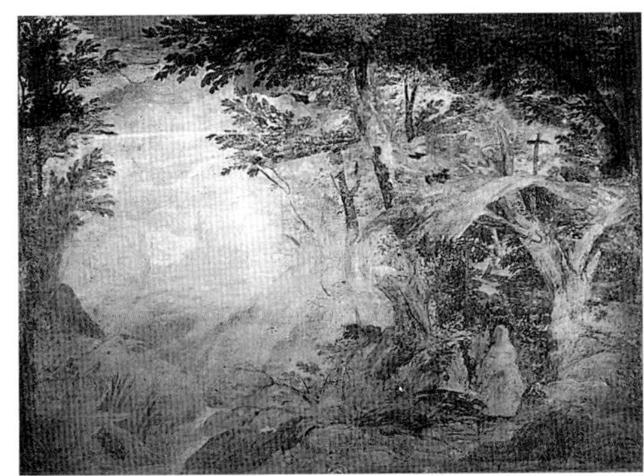

5

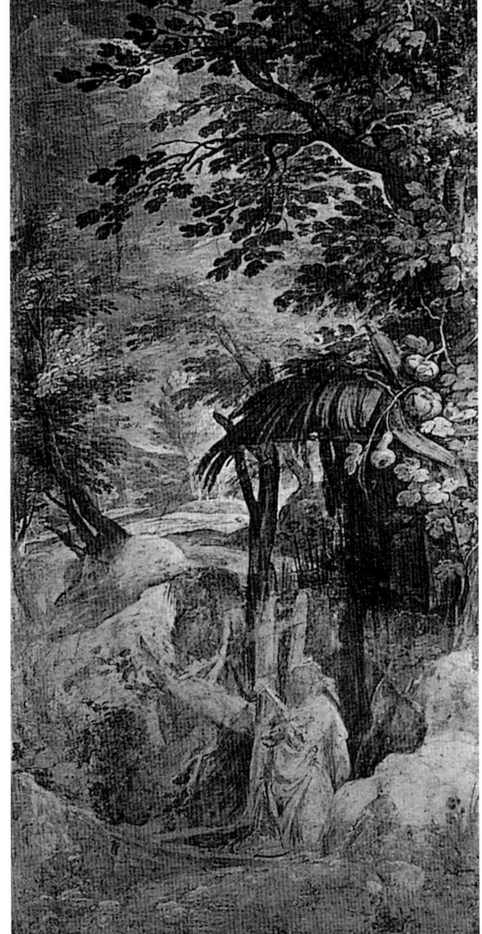

6

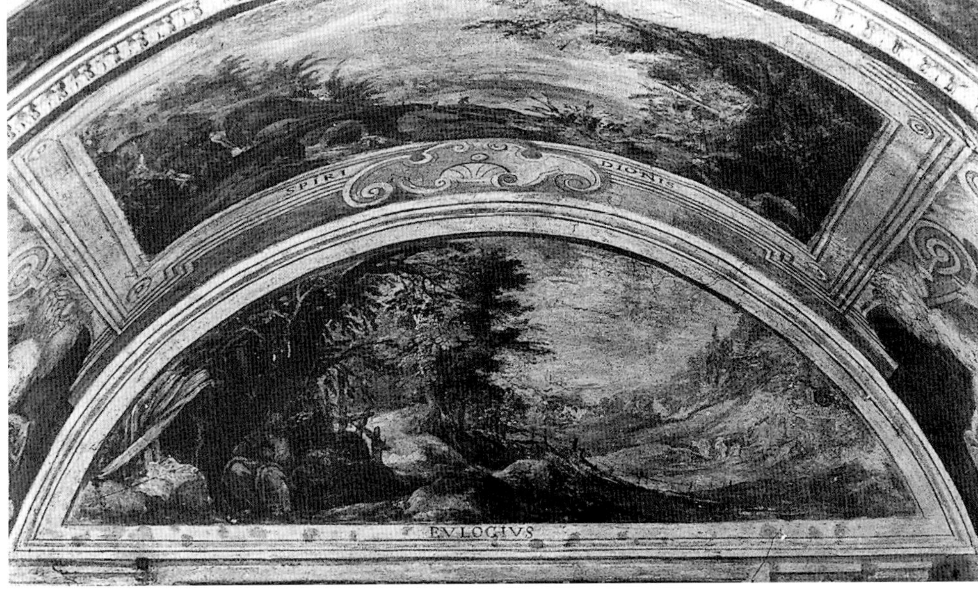

7

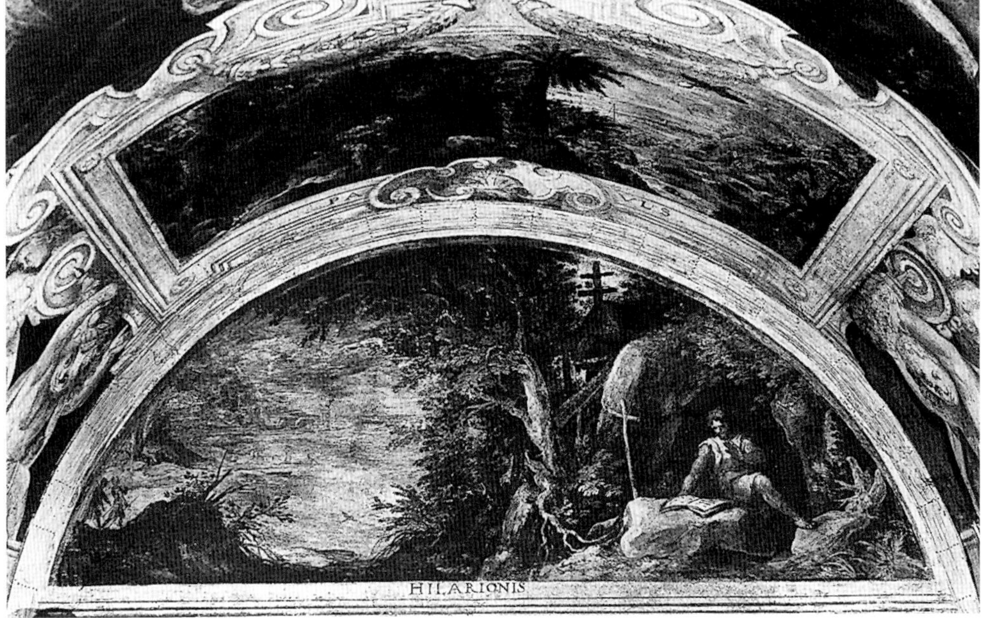

8

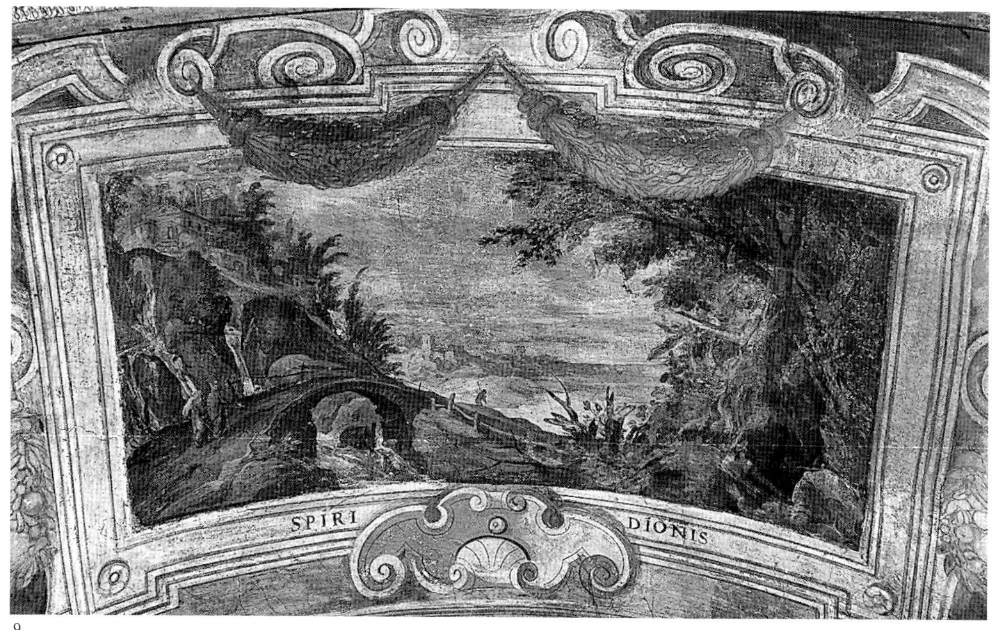

9

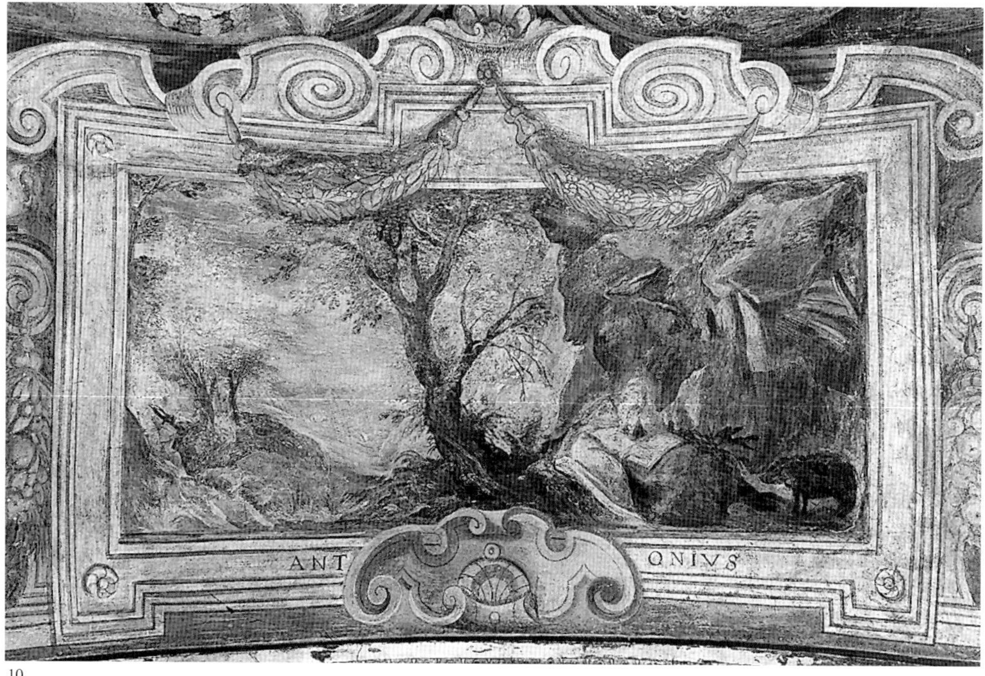

10

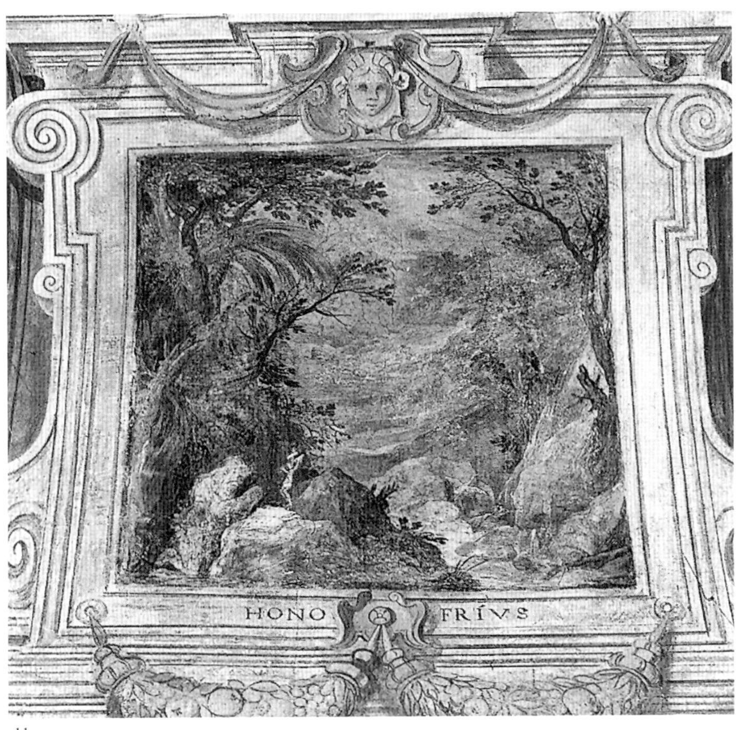

11

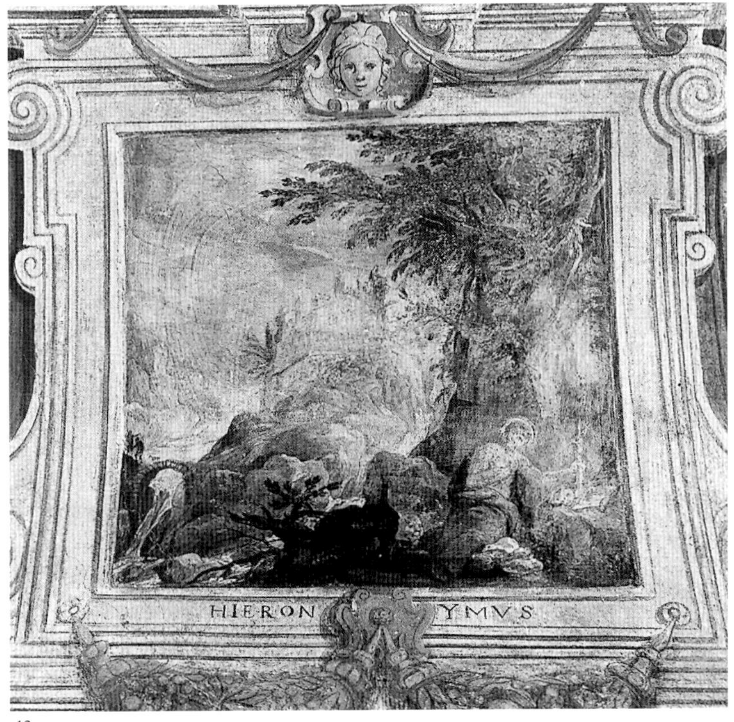

12

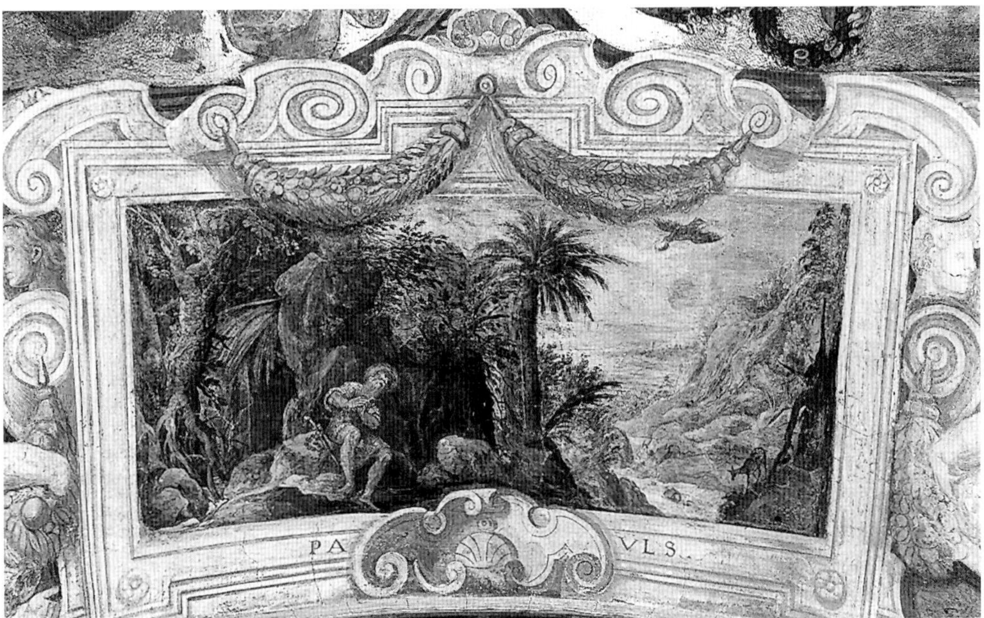

13

Paul Bril
(figures: Giovanni Baglione, Giovan
Battista Ricci, Paris Nogari;
supervision: Cavalier d'Arpino)

Four landscapes in the Constantine
cycle (c. 5 x 2 m), fresco*
Commissioned by Pope Clement VIII

Documented 1599-1601

left transept, left wall:

1. *Landscape* in the background
of the *Triumphal Entry of Constantine*

1a. *Landscape* (painted on another strip
near the triumphal arch)

left transept, right wall:

2. *Landscape* in the background
of *Constantine Presenting a Gift
to the Basilica*

right transept, right wall:

3. *Landscape* in *St Sylvester on Mount
Soracte*

3a. *Landscape* (narrow strip to the right
of the previous scene extending
to the triumphal arch)

right transept, left wall:

4. *Landscape* in the background
of the *Laying of the First Stone
of the Lateran Basilica*

4a. *Landscape* (far right)

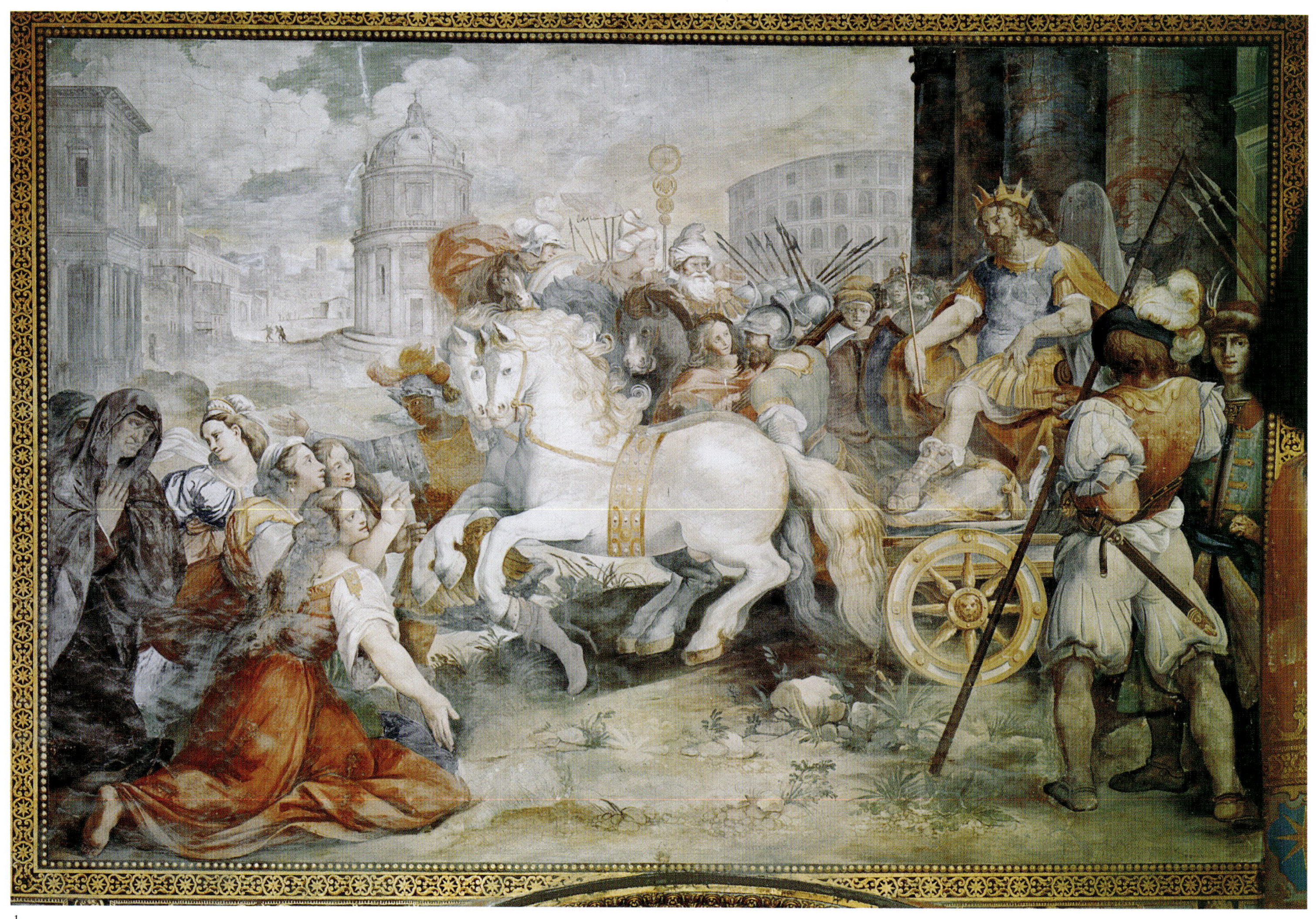

1

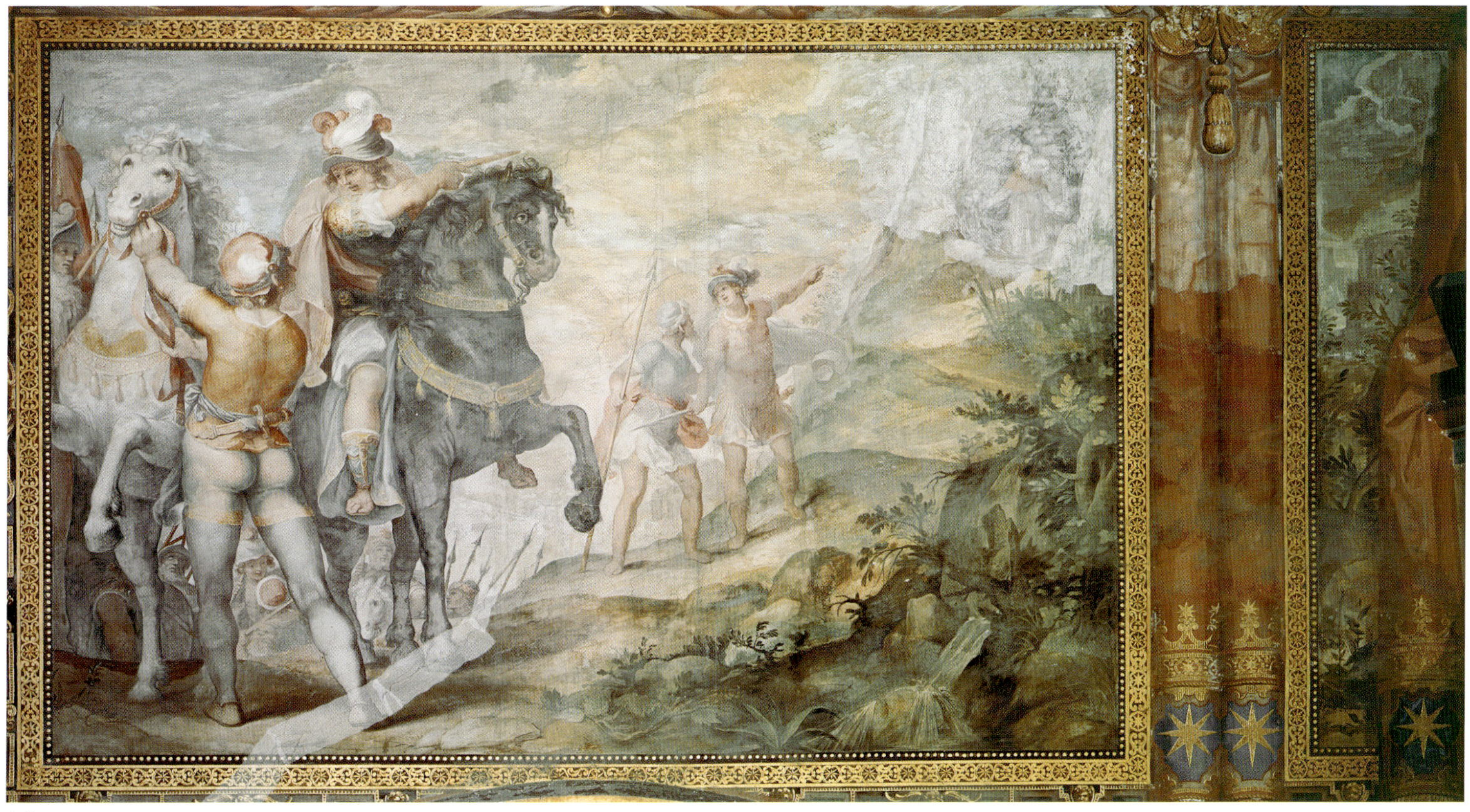

3, 3a

Paul Bril and Cesare Nebbia
(other decoration in the vault:
Giovanni Guerra)

Six landscapes (c. 1.70 x 0.80 m),
lunettes, fresco
Commissioned by Pope Sixtus V

Datable 1587

1. *Woodland with a Crevice and a Bridge*

2. *Rocky Landscape with Mules
and Towers in the Distance*

3. *Seascape with Galleys and a Town
in the Distance*

4. *River View with Herdsman
and Animals*

5. *Rocky Landscape with a River*

6. *River View with a Waterfall*

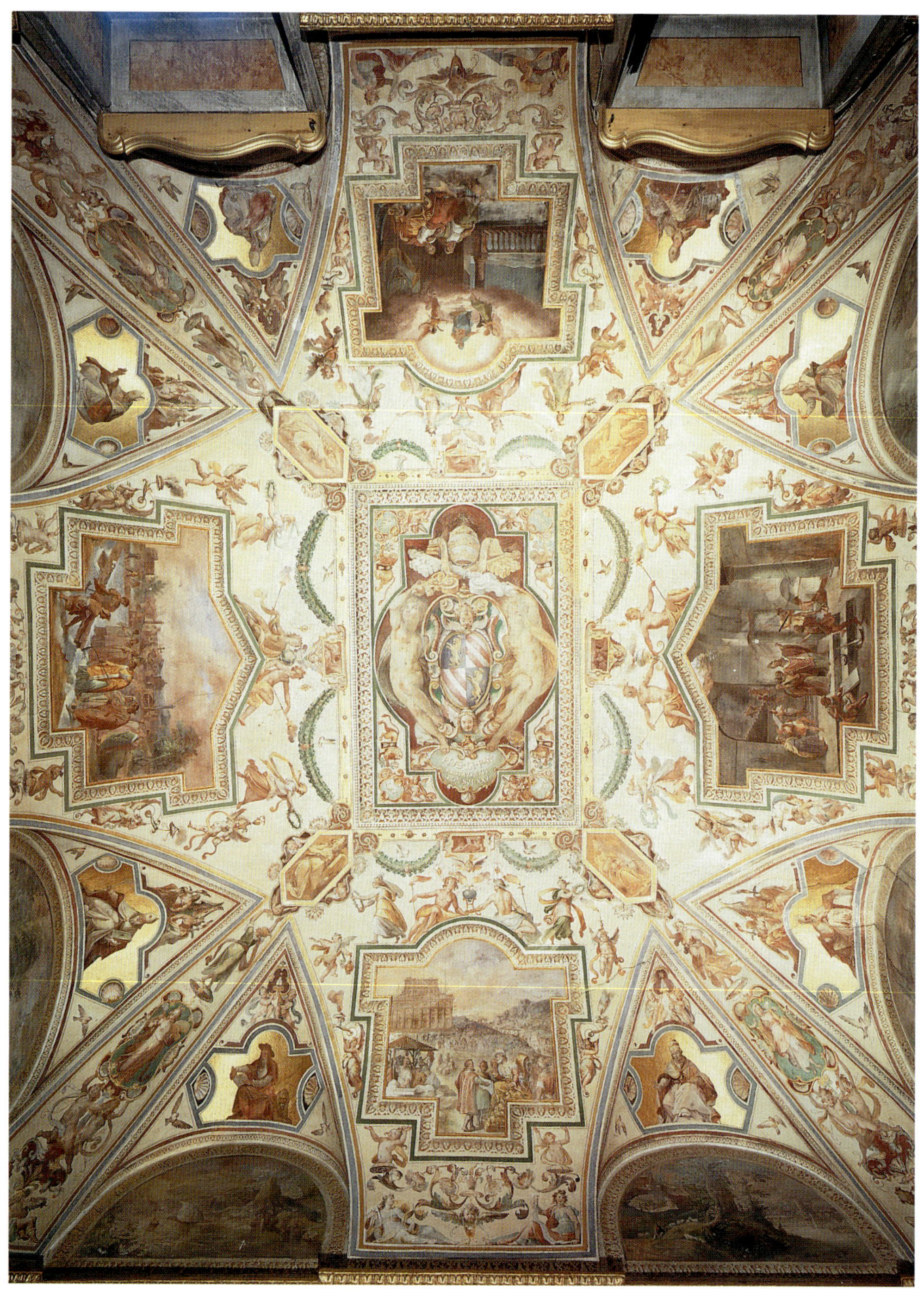

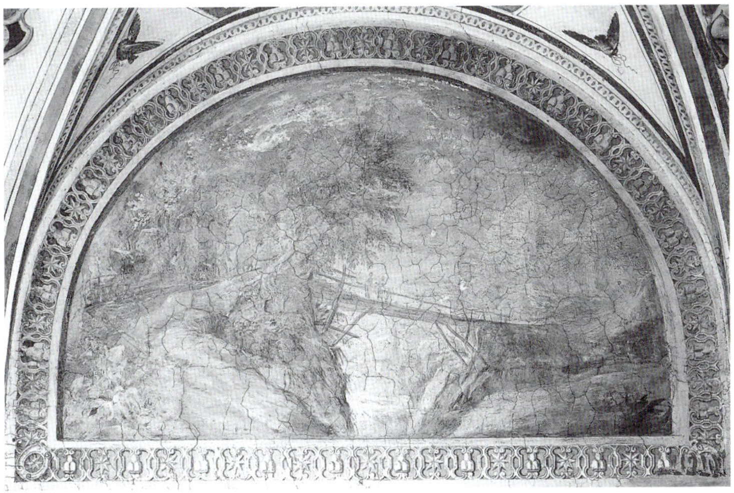

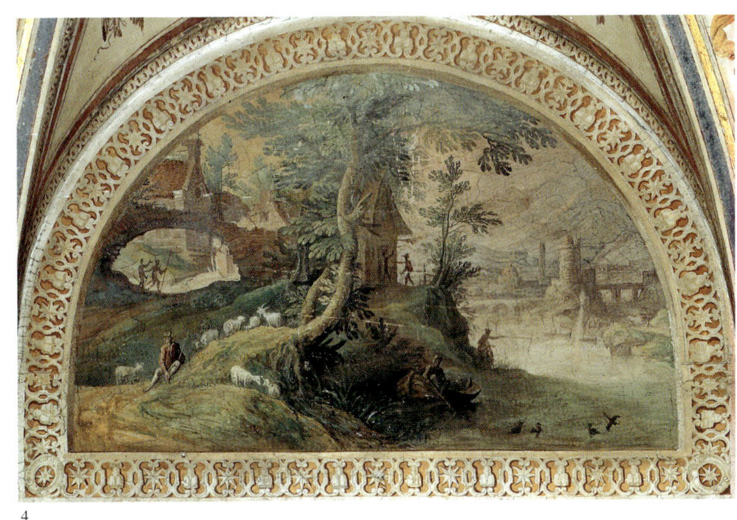

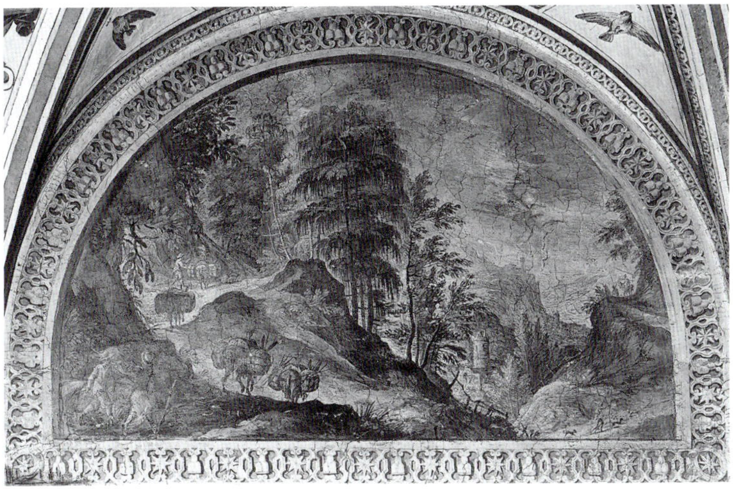

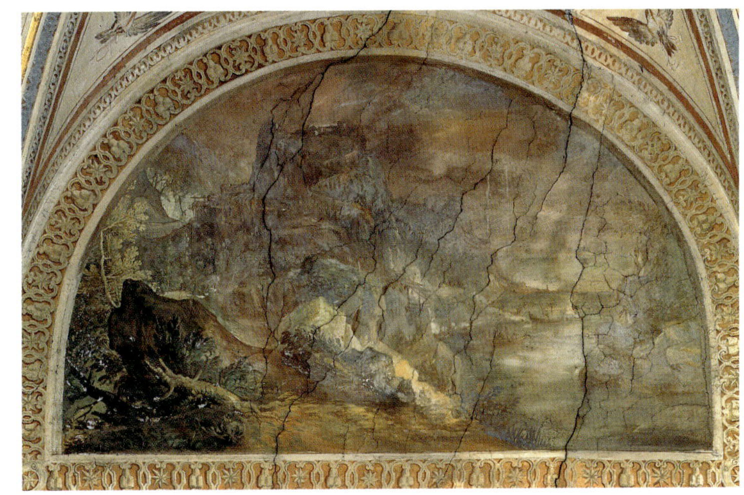

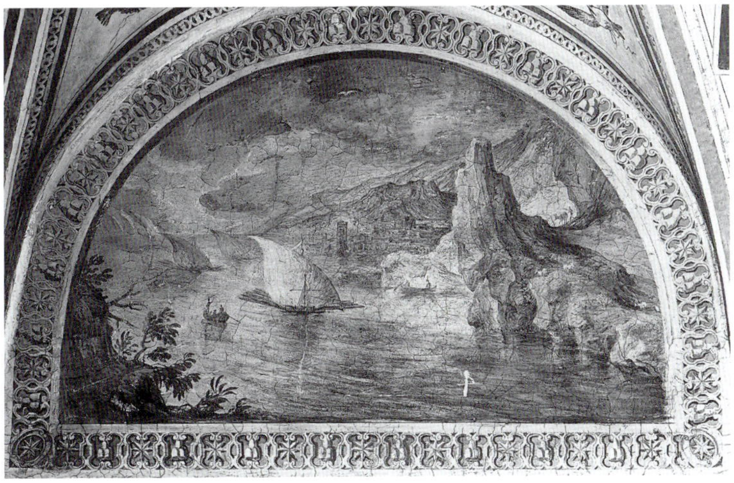

a.

Paul Bril
(figures: Giacomo Stella, Paris
Nogari, Giovan Battista Ricci, Antonio
Viviani, Ferraù Fenzoni, Cesare
Nebbia, Andrea Lilio; supervision:
Cesare Nebbia and Giovanni Guerra)

*Twenty-eight landscapes in biblical
scenes*, walls and vaults, fresco*
and secco
Commissioned by Pope Sixtus V

Datable 1587-88

Scala Santa (central staircase, from
the bottom up):

1. *Christ and the Apostles in the Garden
of Gethsemane*, vault, right

2. *Christ Reveals Peter's Betrayal*, vault,
left

3. *Christ on the Mount of Olives*, left wall
(Paris Nogari)

4. *Christ on the Mount of Olives
with Peter, Jacob and John*, right wall
(Paris Nogari)

5. *Christ and an Angel*, vault, right
(Paris Nogari)

6. *Christ Indicates Judas, who is Siding
with the Roman Soldiers*, vault, left
(Andrea Lilio)

7. *The Kiss of Judas*, left wall

8. *Christ and the Soldiers*, right wall

9. *Peter Amputates the Ear*, vault, right
(Giovanni Baglione)

10. *Christ Taken Prisoner*, vault, left
(Cesare Nebbia)

11. *The Crucifixion*, front wall at the top
of the staircase

left staircase (from the top down):

12. *The Creation of Eve*, left wall at
the top of the staircase (Giacomo Stella)

13. *The Earthly Paradise (Tree of Life)*,
right wall (Paul Bril)

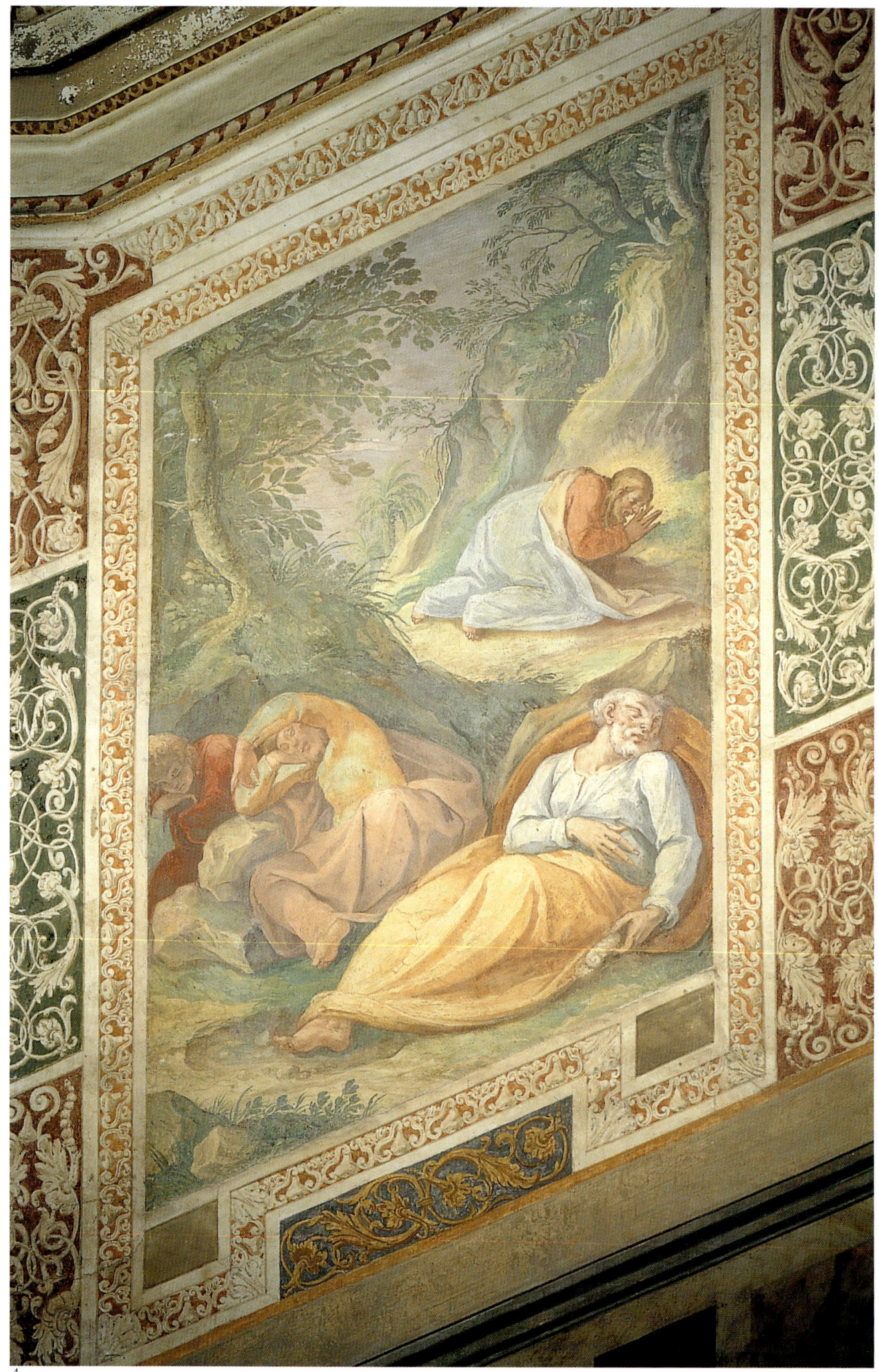

4

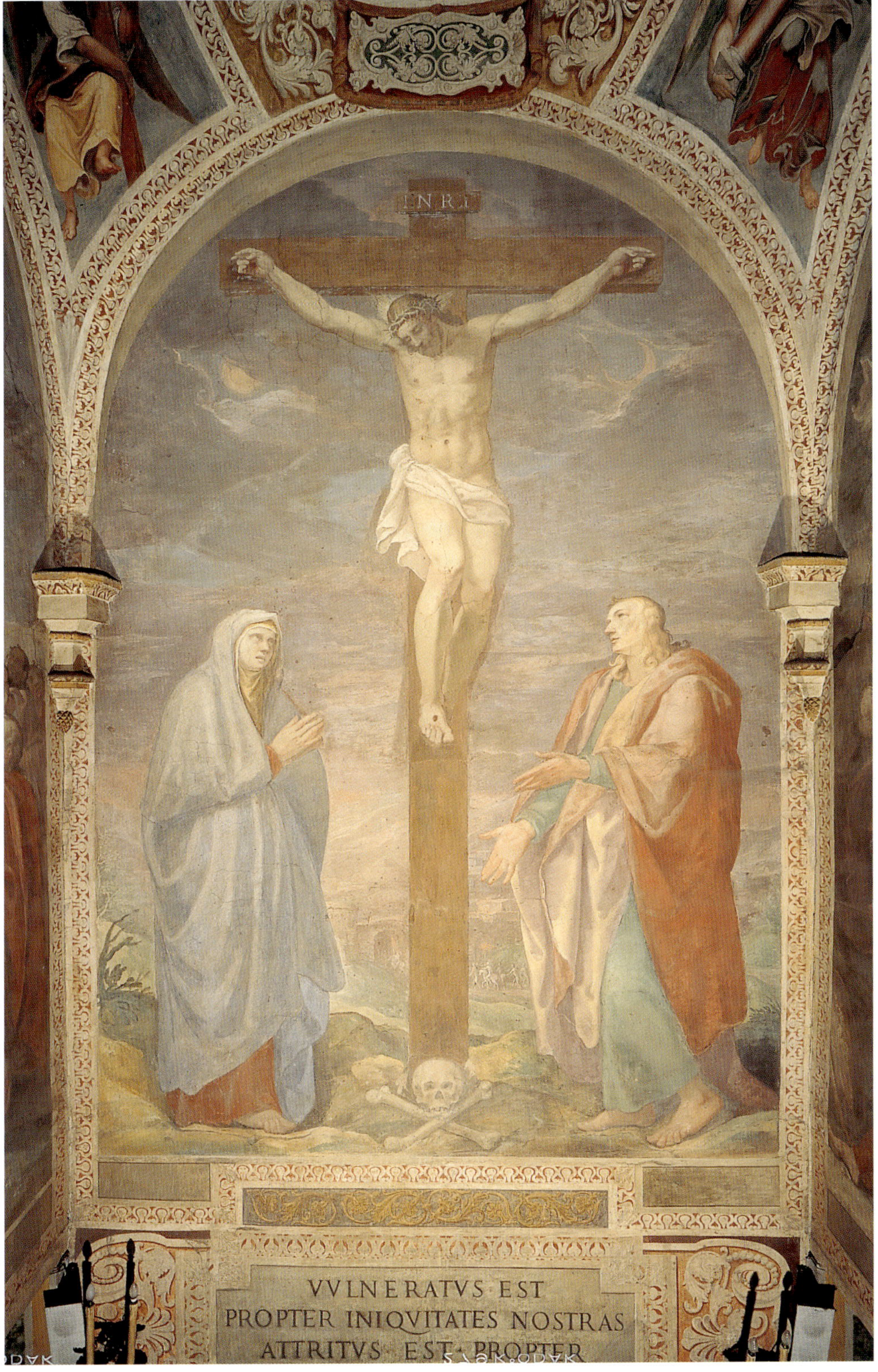

11

14. *Adam and Eve Banished from Paradise*, left wall

15. *Cain and Abel*, right wall (Ferraù Fenzoni)

16. *The Flood*, left wall

17. *The Drunkenness of Noah*, right wall (Giacomo Stella?),

18. *Abraham and Isaac Ascend the Mountain*, vault (Antonio Viviani)

19. *The Sacrifice of Isaac*, front wall at the top of the stairs (Giovan Battista Ricci)

20. *Jacob's Dream*, vault (Antonio Viviani)

21. *Jacob Dedicates the Pillar of Bethel*, right wall

22. *Jacob Wrestles with the Angel*, vault

23. *Joseph Cast into the Well*, left wall (Antonio Viviani)

24. *Moses in the Reed Basket*, right wall (Giovanni Baglione)

right staircase (from the top down):

25. *Samson and the Lion*, right wall

26. *Samson at the Gate of Gaza*, vault (Giacomo Stella)

27. *Jonah and the Whale*, vault (Paul Bril)

28. *The Whale Disgorges Jonah*, left wall (Paul Bril; figure of Jonah, Andrea Lilio?)

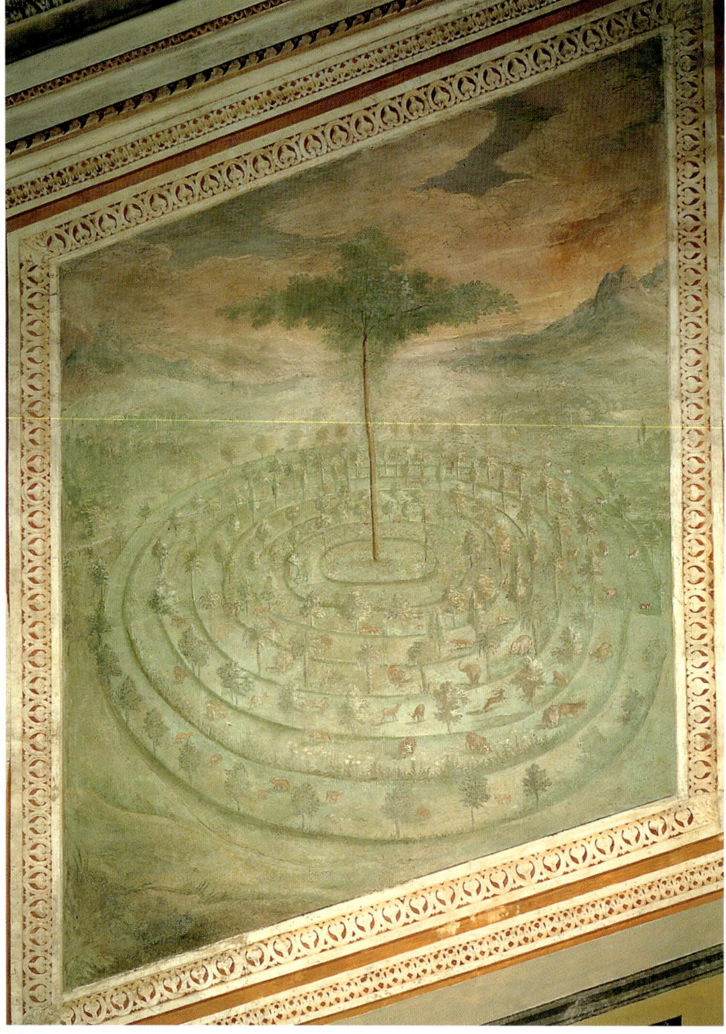

13

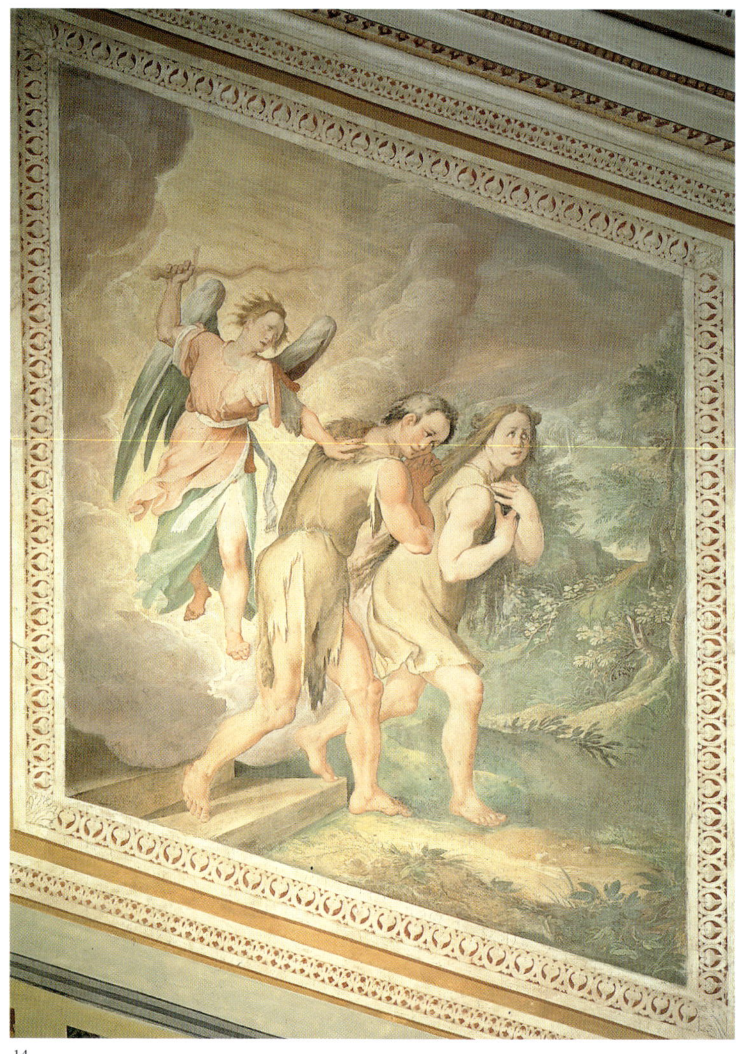

14

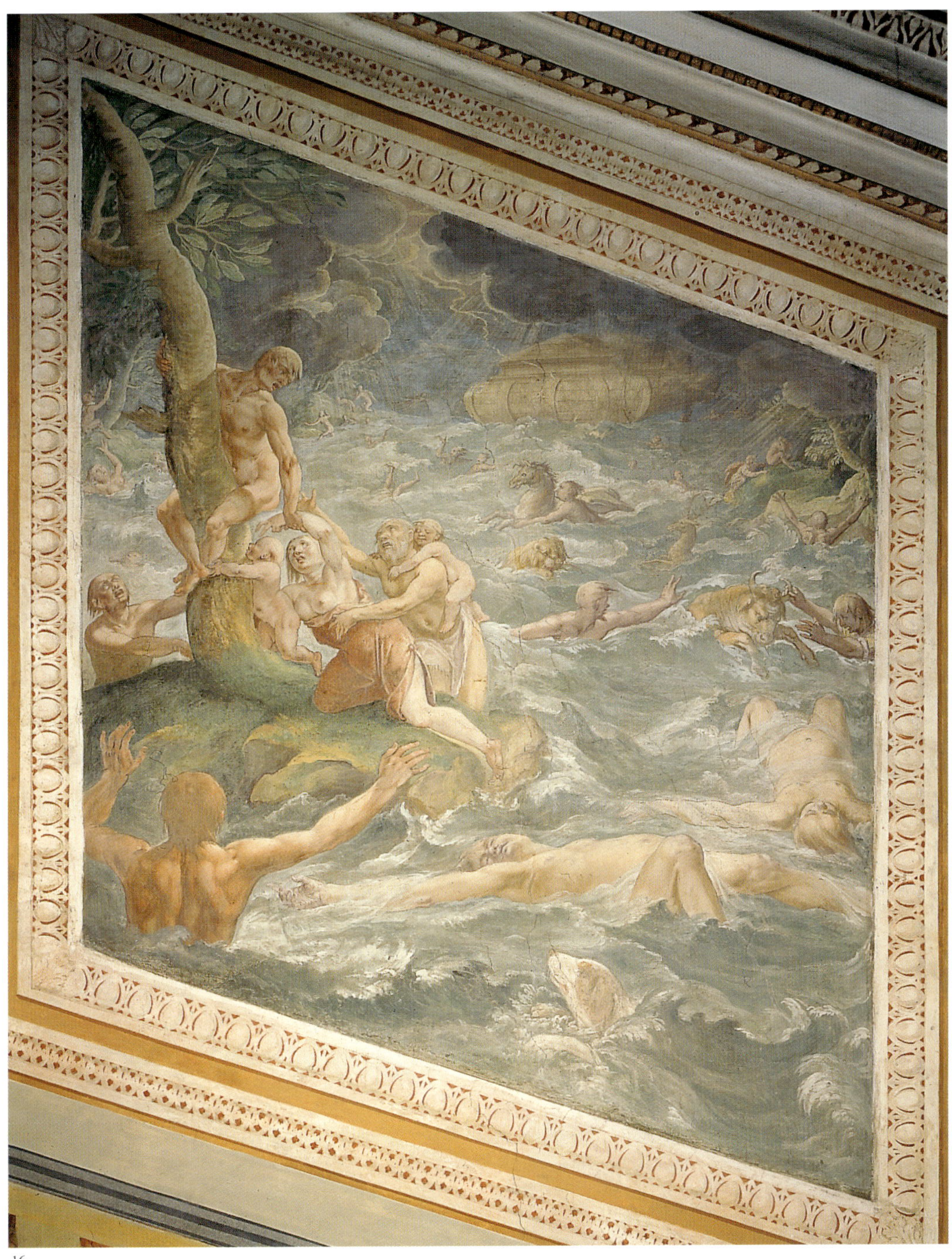

16

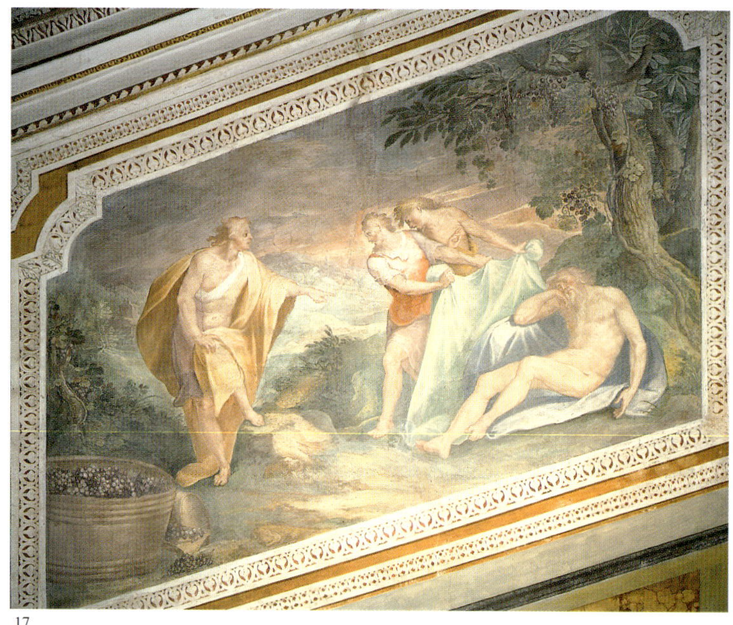

17

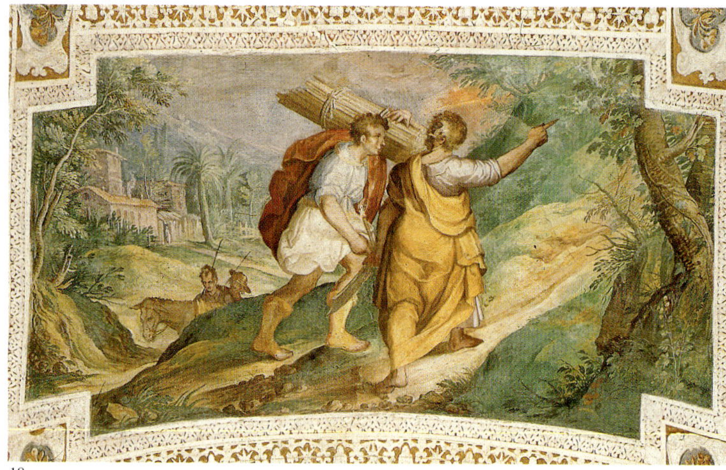

18

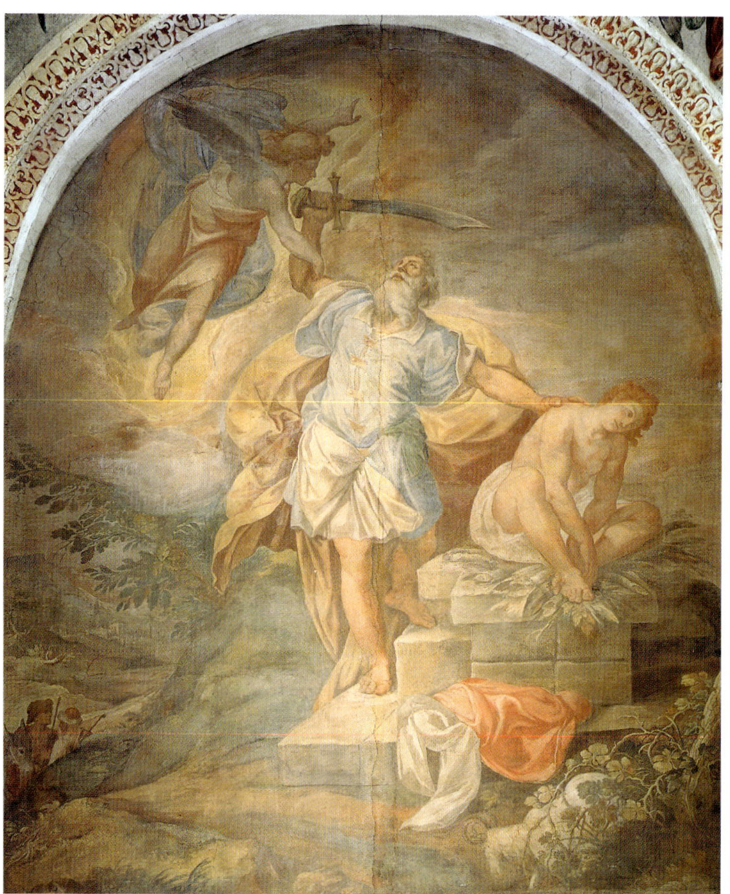

19

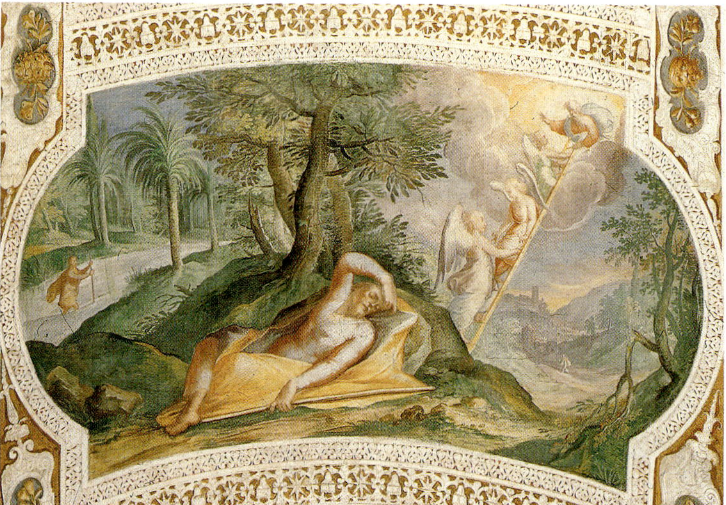

20

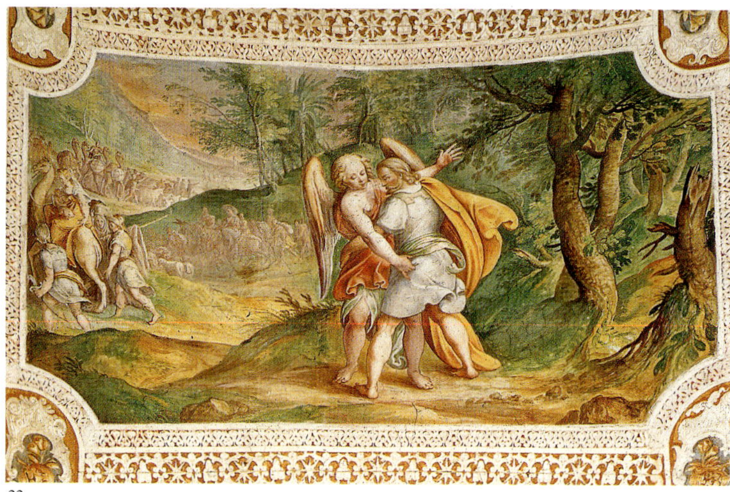

22

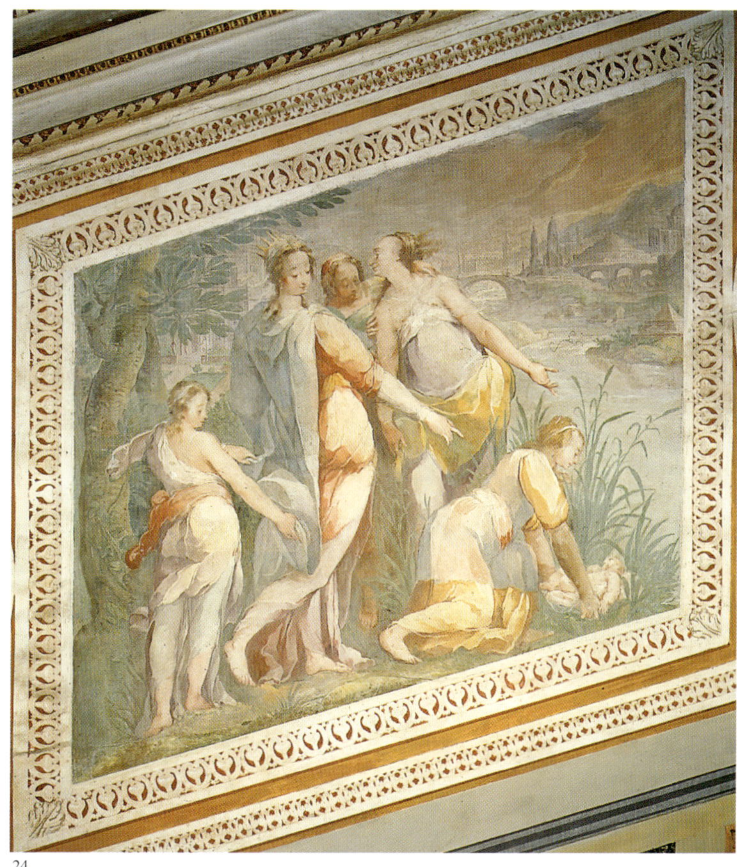

24

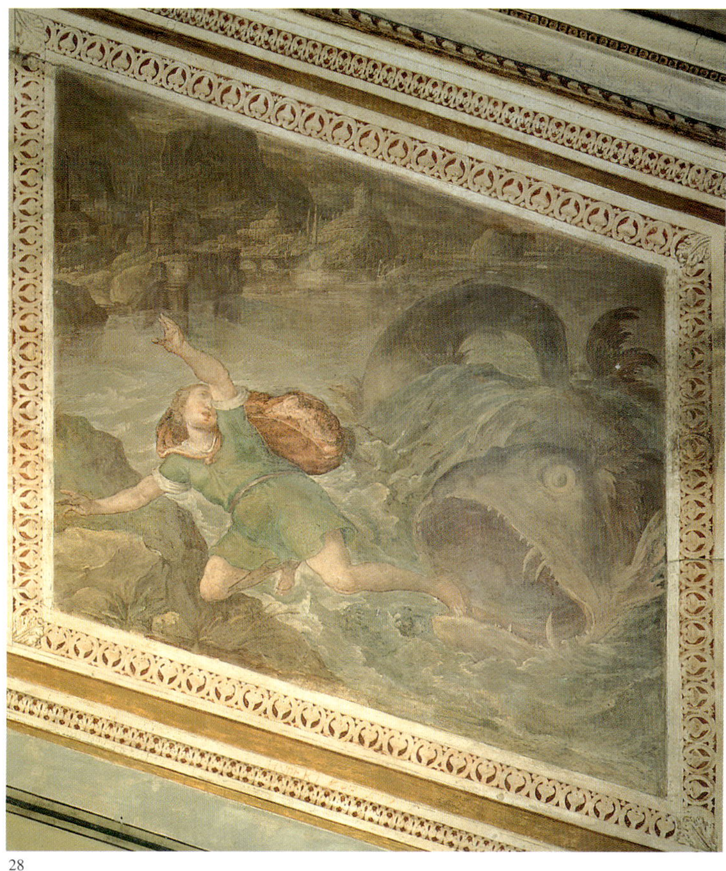

28

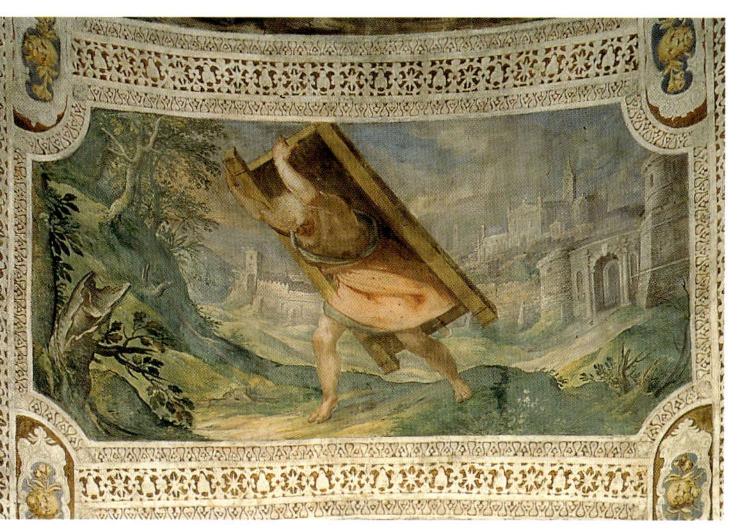

26

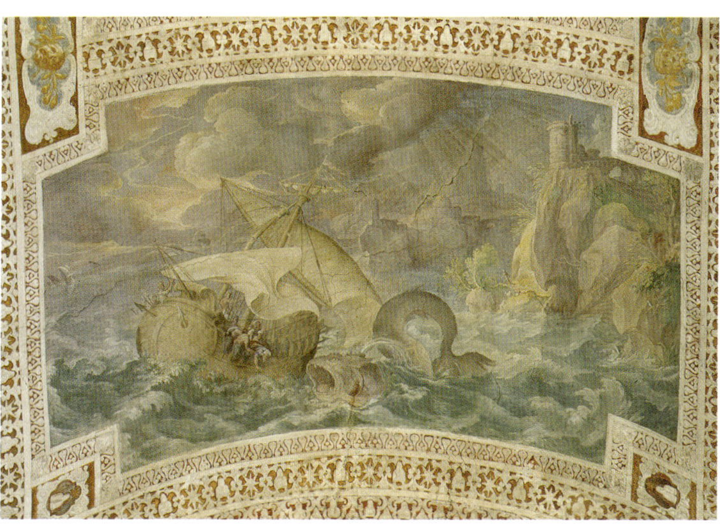

27

b.

Paul Bril
(supervision: Cesare Nebbia
and Giovanni Guerra)

Four landscapes, lunettes, fresco*
Commissioned by Pope Sixtus V

Datable 1589

1. *Rocky Landscape with Two Artists*
2. *Landscape with a Horseman
and Servant and Two Travellers*
3. *Landscape with a Beggar
and a Merchant*
4. *Landscape with a Man and a Mule*

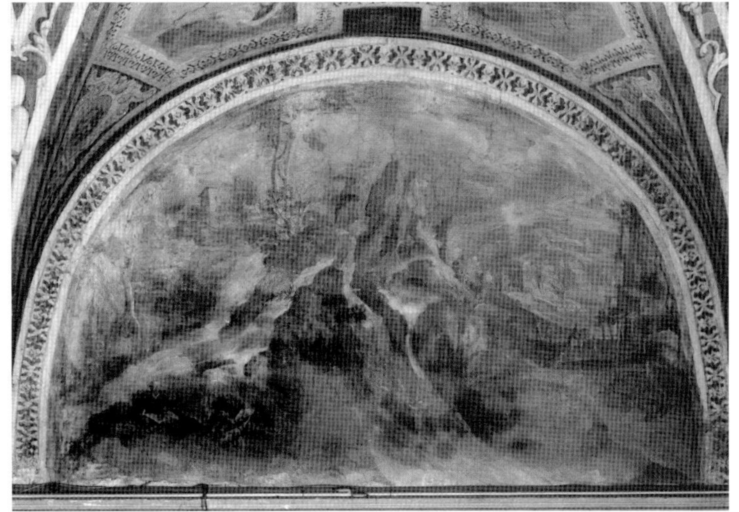

1

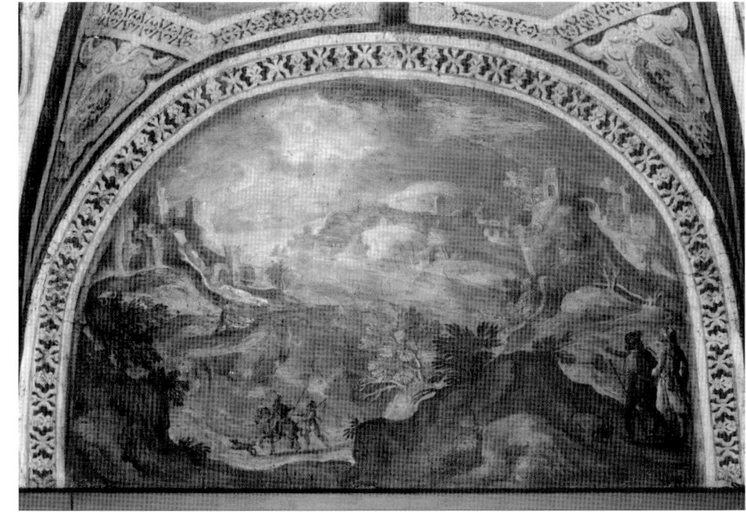

2

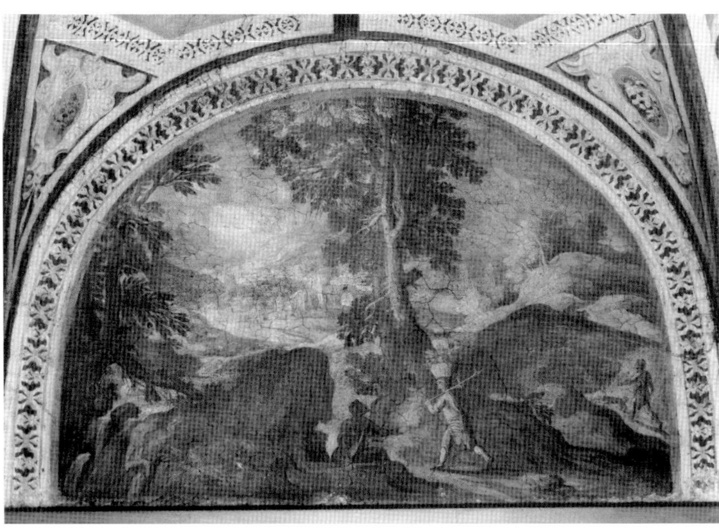

3

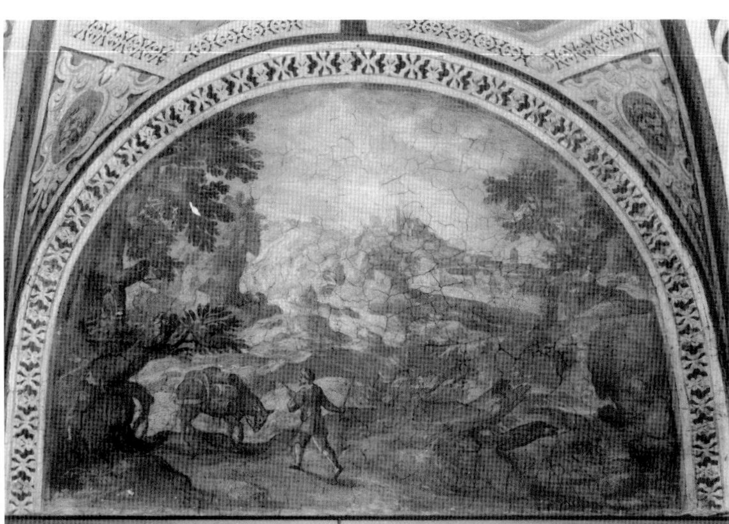

4

c.

Paul Bril
(ceiling decoration: Giovanni Alberti
and Cherubino Alberti; supervision:
Cesare Nebbia and Giovanni Guerra)

Three landscapes, vault and lunette,
fresco*
Commissioned by Pope Sixtus V

Datable 1589

vault:

1. *Landscape with Resting Figures*
2. *Landscape with a Walking Figure
and a Chapel on a Hill*

lunette:

3. *Landscape* (almost indiscernible)

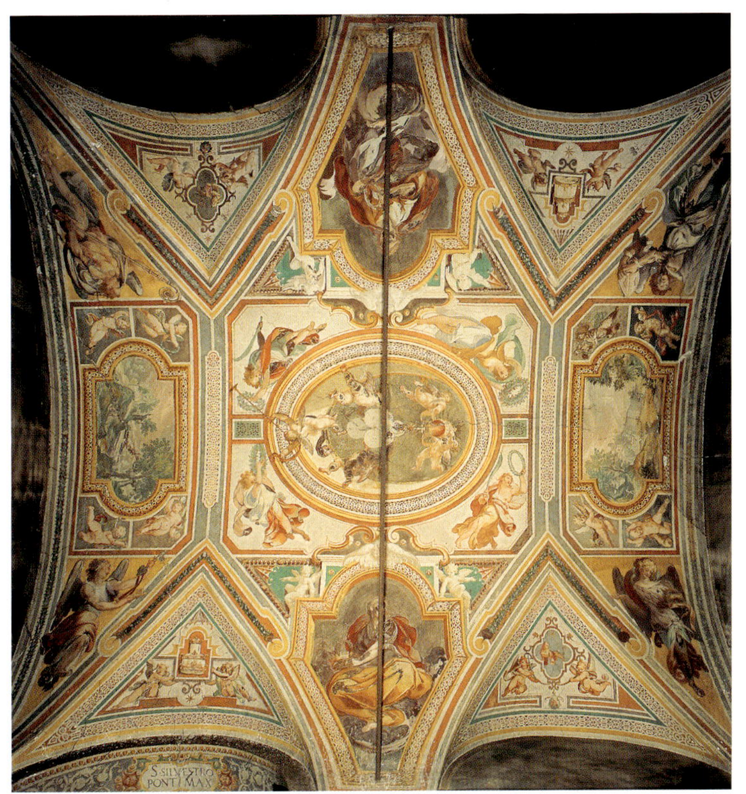

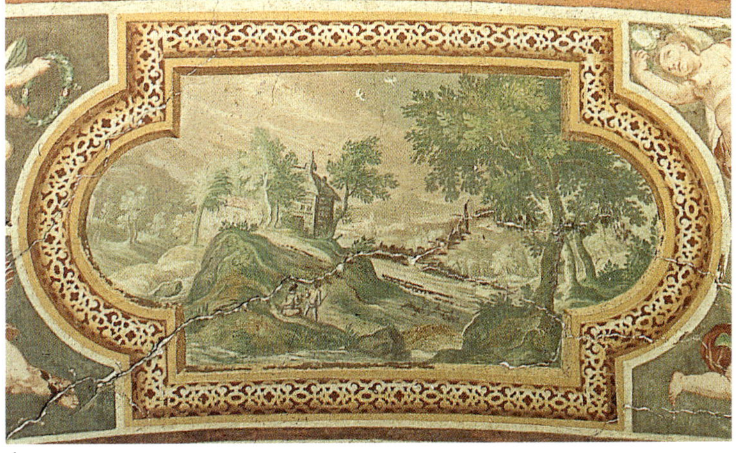

1

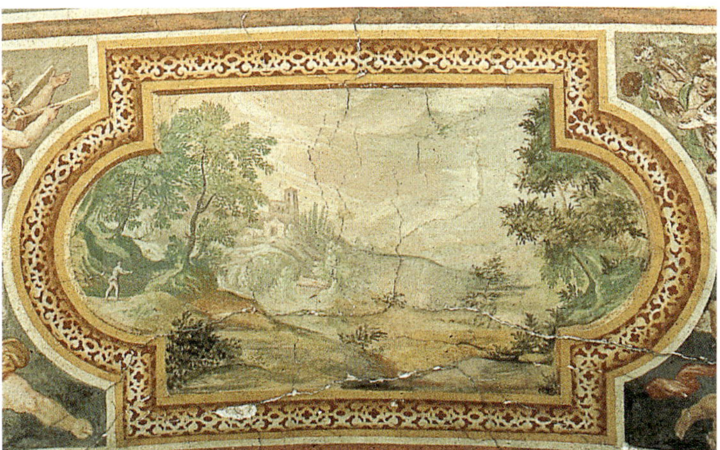

2

Courtyard

Paul Bril, Baldassarre Peruzzi

Landscape with St Bernard, fresco
Commissioned by the Theatine Order
Repaired in fresco. The original
was lost

Datable c. 1590 (?)

XIV. Villa Montalto Peretti

Loggia

Paul Bril and Gian Battista Viola

Four (?) landscapes, fresco*
Commissioned by Pope Sixtus V
Paintings destroyed (the villa was
demolished in the nineteenth
century)

Datable 1588

Page 6: Matthijs Bril, *Landscape* in *Domine Quo Vadis*. Palazzo Apostolico Vaticano, Galleria delle Carte Geografiche.

Page 10: Paul Bril, detail of *Summer*, Palazzo Pallavicini Rospigliosi, Casino dell'Aurora.

THE LIVES AND WORK OF MATTHIJS AND PAUL BRIL

Page 16: Matthijs and Paul Bril, *Landscape* in *The Hermit St Peter of Murano Receives Tidings of the Pope's Election*, Palazzo Apostolico Vaticano, Galleria delle Carte Geografiche.

1. Anonymous, *Portrait of Matthijs Bril*, oil on canvas. Rome, Accademia di San Luca.

2. Ottavio Leoni, *Portrait of Paul Bril*, drawing. Paris, Musée du Louvre, Département des Arts Graphiques.

3. Pier Leone Ghezzi, *Portrait of Paul Bril*, drawing. Lille, Palais des Beaux-Arts.

4. Matthijs Bril, *Landscape with the Sacrifice of Isaac*, fresco. Rome, Palazzo Apostolico Vaticano, Torre dei Venti, Room of the Old Testament Patriarchs.

5. Matthijs Bril, *Temple of Minerva in the Forum of Nerva*, drawing. Paris, Musée du Louvre, Département des Arts Graphiques.

6. Matthijs Bril, *Winter Landscape with Ruins*, fresco. Monterotondo, Palazzo Comunale (formerly Orsini), first floor, first room.

7. Paul Bril, *Landscape with the Temple of Sibyl*, oil on copper. Cologne, Wallraf-Richartz-Museum.

8. Paul Bril, *View of the Coast of Campania, River Landscape with Travellers*, print. Amsterdam, Rijksmuseum, Rijksprentenkabinet.

9. Paul Bril, *Landscape with the Temptation of Christ*, 1613, tempera on vellum. Enschede, Rijksmuseum Twenthe.

THE FRESCOES

Page 30: Matthis Bril, *Landscape* in *St Romuald Founds Camaldoli*, Palazzo Apostolico Vaticano, Galleria delle Carte Geografiche.

10. Matthijs Bril, *Nocturnal Landscape with Elephant*. Rome, Palazzo Apostolico Vaticano, Sala Ducale.

11. Matthijs Bril, *Rocky Landscape*. Rome, Palazzo Apostolico Vaticano, First Sala dei Foconi.

12. Matthijs Bril and Antonio Tempesta, *The Procession on the Bridge by Castel Sant'Angelo*. Rome, Palazzo Apostolico Vaticano, San Damaso Court, third Loggia.

13. Matthijs Bril, *Jacob's Dream*. Rome, Palazzo Apostolico Vaticano, Torre dei Venti, Room of the Old Testament Patriarchs.

14. Matthijs Bril, *View from the Viminale*. Rome, Palazzo Apostolico Vaticano, Torre dei Venti, mezzanino, Room with Topographical Views.

15. Matthijs Bril, *Esau Gives Jacob his Birthright*. Rome, Palazzo Apostolico Vaticano, Torre dei Venti, Room of the Old Testament Patriarchs.

16. Matthijs Bril, *View of a Coastal Landscape with Galleys*. Rome, Palazzo Apostolico Vaticano, Torre dei Venti, mezzanino, second room.

17. Matthijs Bril and Pomarancio (Niccolò Circignani), *Christ Calms the Storm*. Rome, Palazzo Apostolico Vaticano, Torre dei Venti, Sala Meridiana.

18. Matthijs Bril assisted by Paul Bril, *Landscape with Roman Ruins and a Fountain*. Monterotondo, Palazzo Comunale (formerly Orsini).

19. Matthijs Bril assisted by Paul Bril, *Hunting Landscape*. Monterotondo, Palazzo Comunale (formerly Orsini).

20. Antonio Tempesta, *Deer Hunt*, drawing. Paris, Musée du Louvre, Département des Arts Graphiques.

21. Cesare Nebbia, *Mathilda of Canossa Donates her Possessions to the Church*, drawing. Paris, Musée du Louvre, Département des Arts Graphiques.

22. Matthijs Bril, *Mathilda of Canossa Donates her Possessions to the Church*. Rome, Palazzo

Apostolico Vaticano, Galleria delle Carte Geografiche.

23. Paul Bril, *Seascape with Galleys and a Town in the Distance*. Rome, Santa Maria Maggiore, Cappella Sistina, Sacristy.

24. Paul Bril (with assistant), *Four Landscapes*. Rome, Palazzo Apostolico Laterano, Scala Pontificale (vault).

25. Paul Bril, *Seascape*, drawing. Stockholm, Nationalmuseum.

26. Paul Bril, *Coastal Landscape with a Man on Horseback, Hounds, a Cross, Herdsmen and Fishermen with a Town on a Bay*. Rome, Palazzo Apostolico Lateranense, loggias.

27. Paul Bril, *Seascape with Papal Galleys and a Fort and Town in the Distance*. Rome, Palazzo Apostolico Lateranense, Sala di Costantino.

28. Paul Bril, *Jonah and the Whale*. Rome, Scala Santa, Staircases.

29. Paul Bril (and Andrea Lilio?), *The Whale Disgorges Jonah*. Rome, Scala Santa, Staircases.

30. View of the Chapel of San Lorenzo. Rome, Scala Santa.

31. Paul Bril, *Landscape with Hunting Scenes*. Rome, Palazzo Caetani (formerly Mattei).

32. Paul Bril, *Landscape with Man and Woman on a donkey crossing a bridge*. Rome, Palazzo Caetani (formerly Mattei).

33. Paul Bril, *Maria Egyptiaca and Zozimos*. Rome, Santa Cecilia in Trastevere.

34. Paul Bril (with Cherubino and Giovanni Alberti), *Seascape with the Martyrdom of St Clement*. Rome, Palazzo Apostolico Vaticano, Sala Clementina.

35. Paul Bril, *Harbour View*, 1611, oil on canvas. Rome, Galleria Borghese.

36. Paul Bril, *View with a Boat on a River*. Rome, Palazzo Pallavicini Rospigliosi, Casino del Patriarca Biondo.

37. Paul Bril, *Winter*. Rome, Palazzo Pallavicini Rospigliosi, Casino dell'Aurora.

38. Paul Bril, *Rocky Landscape with a Bridge and Figures Walking*. Rome, Casino Ludovisi, Stanza dei Paesi.

BEFORE THE FRESCOES: THE DRAWINGS

39. Matthijs Bril, *Torre delle Milizie*. Paris, Musée du Louvre, Département des Arts Graphiques.

40. Matthijs Bril, *Ponte Sant'Angelo and Castel Sant'Angelo*. Paris, Musée du Louvre, Département des Arts Graphiques.

41. Matthijs Bril, *Cottage on a Hill*. Paris, Musée du Louvre, Département des Arts Graphiques.

42. Matthijs Bril, *Landscape with Monument*. Washington D.C., National Gallery of Art.

43. Paul Bril, *Bay with Galleys and a Town in the Distance*. Leiden, Prentenkabinet Universiteit Leiden.

44. Paul Bril, *Jonah and the Whale*. London, British Museum.

45. Matthijs Bril, *Tempest*. Paris, Musée du Louvre, Département des Arts Graphiques.

46. Paul Bril, *Landscape*. Paris, Musée du Louvre, Département des Arts Graphiques.

47. Paul Bril, *Landscape*. Paris, Musée du Louvre, Département des Arts Graphiques.

48. Paul Bril, *Landscape*. Paris, Musée du Louvre, Département des Arts Graphiques.

49. Paul Bril, *Landscape*. Munich, Staatliche Graphische Sammlung.

50. Paul Bril, *Landscape*. Dresden, Kupferstichkabinett.

51. Paul Bril, *Landscape*. The Netherlands, Art Market.

PAUL BRIL AND GUIDO RENI IN THE LOGGIA DELLA PERGOLA IN PALAZZO PALLAVICINI ROSPIGLIOSI

52. Overall view of the ceiling.

53. Anonymous, *View of the east side of Palazzo Borghese*, drawing, c. 1620. Vienna, Graphische Sammlung Albertina.

54. Guido Reni, *Putti Holding Two Monkeys*.

55. Paul Bril, *Deer Hunt*.

56. Paul Bril, *Landscape with Two Monks and a Village*.

57. Paul Bril, *View with Boats on a River*.

58. Paul Bril, *Marine Scene*.

59. Pietro Paolo Bonzi, *Mythological Scene*.

60. Pietro Paolo Bonzi, *Landscape with Two Women at a River*.

61-62. First bay and third bay of the pergola.

63. Direct engraving, revealed under raking light.

64-65. Details of a bunch of grapes.

66. Paul Bril, *Turkey*.

67. Paul Bril, *Bittern*.

68. Paul Bril, *Peacock*.

69. Paul Bril, workshop, *Peregrine Falcon*.

70. Paul Bril, workshop, *Owl Seizing a Magpie*.

Abromson 1978
Abromson, M.C., "Clement VIII's Patronage
of the Brothers Alberti", *The Art Bulletin*,
60 (1978), pp. 531-547.

Abromson 1981
Abromson, M.C., *Painting in Rome during
the Papacy of Clement VIII (1592-1605)*,
New York, London 1981.

Ackerman 1954
Ackerman, J.S., *The Cortile del Belvedere*,
Vatican City 1954.

Ago 1998
Ago, R., *Economia Barocca. Mercato e
istituzioni nella Roma del Seicento*, Rome 1998.

Amayden 1987
Amayden, T., *Storia delle Famiglie Romane
(circa 1610)*, ed. Carlo Augusto Bertini, 2 vols.,
Rome 1987.

Antinori 1993
Antinori, A., "Scipione Borghese, il Quirinale
e Frascati. Le vicende della residenza sulle
Terme di Constantino", *Rivista Storica
del Lazio*, 1 (1993), pp. 113-151.

Audin, Vidal 1918-1919
Audin, M., E. Vidal, *Dictionnaire des artistes
et ouvriers d'art de la France, Lyonnais*,
2 vols., Paris 1918-1919.

Baer 1930
Baer, R., *Paul Bril. Studien zur
Entwicklungsgeschichte der Landschaftsmalerei
um 1600*, Munich 1930.

Baglione 1649
Baglione, G., *Le vite de' Pittori, Scultori
et Architetti. Dal pontificato di Gregorio XIII
fino a tutto quello d'Urbano VIII*, 2 vols.,
Rome 1649, ed. C. Gradara, Velletri 1924
(reprint 1986).

Baldinucci 1681-1728
Baldinucci, F., *Notizie dei Professori del Disegno

da Cimabue in qua*, Florence 1681-1728,
reprint 1847, ed. P. Barocchi, Florence 1974.

Barbieri 1995
Barbieri, C., S. Barchiesa, D. Ferrara, *Santa
Maria in Vallicella. Chiesa Nuova*, Rome 1995.

Battisti 1954
Battisti, E., "Profilo del Gobbo dei Carracci",
Commentari, 4 (1954), pp. 290-302.

Bedoni 1983
Bedoni, S., *Jan Brueghel in Italia
e il Collezionismo del Seicento*, Florence,
Milan 1983.

Bensi 1990
Bensi, P., "La pellicola pittorica nella pittura
murale in Italia: materiali e tecniche esecutive
dall'Alto Medioevo al XIX secolo", in *Le pitture
murali. Tecniche, problemi, conservazione*,
ed. C. Danti, M. Matteini, A. Moles, Florence
1990, pp. 73-102.

Berger 1993
Berger, A., *Die Tafelgemälde Paul Brils*,
Münster, Hamburg 1993.

Bertolotti 1880 (1974)
Bertolotti. A., *Artisti Belgi ed Olandesi a Roma
nei secoli XVI e XVII. Notizie e documenti
raccolti negli archivi romani*, Florence 1880,
reprint Bologna 1974.

Bianchi-Cagliesi 1902
Bianchi-Cagliesi, V., *Santa Cecilia
e la sua basilica nel Trastevere*, Rome 1902.

Blankert 1978
Blankert, A., *Nederlandse 17e eeuwse
Italianiserende Landschapschilders*,
Soest 1978.

Böck 1988
Böck, A., *Das Dekorationsprogramm
des Lesesaals der Vatikanischen Bibliothek*,
Munich 1988.

Bodart 1970
Bodart, D., "Les tableaux de la succession
de Paul Bril", in *Mélanges d'archéologie
et d'histoire de l'art offerts au Prof. Jacques
Lavalleye*, Louvain 1970, pp. 1-14.

Boon 1992
Boon, K.G., *The Netherlandish and German
Drawings of the XVth and XVIth Centuries
of the Frits Lugt Collection*, 3 vols., Paris 1982.

Borroni 1970
Borroni, F., 'Gobbo dei Carracci', *ad vocem*
in *Dizionario biografico degli Italiani*, vol. 12,
Rome 1970, pp. 485-487.

Brown 2001
Brown, B.L. ed., *Il Genio di Roma 1592-1623*,
exhib. cat. (London/Rome), Rome 2001.

Brussels, Rome 1995
Dacos, N., B.W. Meijer, eds., *Fiamminghi
a Roma 1508-1608. Kunstenaars uit de
Nederlanden en het prinsbisdom Luik te Rome
tijdens de renaissance*, exhib. cat.
(Brussels/Rome), Ghent 1995.

Cappelletti, Testa 1994
Cappelletti, F., L. Testa, *Il Trattenimento
dei Virtuosi. Le collezioni secentesche di quadri
nei Palazzi Mattei di Roma*, Rome 1994.

Cennini 1992
Cennini C., *Il libro dell'Arte*, ed. F. Brunello,
Vicenza 1992.

Cerutti 1960-1961
Cerutti, F.F.X., *Gegevens over Bredase kunst
en kunstenaars in de 16e eeuw*, Breda 1960-
1961, vol. 1.

Chiarini 1973
Chiarini, M., *Disegni italiani di paesaggio*,
exhib. cat., Florence 1973.

Ciappi 1596
Ciappi, Marc'Antonio, *Compendio
delle Heroiche et gloriose attioni, et santa vita
di Papa Gregorio XIII*, Rome 1596.

Coffin 1979
Coffin, D.R., *The Villa in the Life
of Renaissance Rome*, Princeton (N.J.) 1979.

Cottino 1989
Cottino, A., in *La natura morta in Italia*, edited
by F. Zeri and F. Porzio, Milan 1989, vol. II,
pp. 698ff.

Cottino 1995
Cottino, A., in *Pietro Paolo Bonzi detto
il Gobbo dei frutti o il Gobbo dei Carracci*,
in *La scuola dei Carracci. I seguaci di Annibale
a Roma*, ed. by E. Negro and M. Pirondini,
Modena 1995, pp. 125-136.

Courtright 1990
Courtright, N.M., *Gregory XIII's Tower
of the Winds in the Vatican*, Ph.D. Thesis,
Institute of Fine Arts, New York University,
1990.

Courtright 1995
Courtright, N.M., "The Transformation
of Ancient Landscape Through the Ideology
of Christian Reform in Gregory XIII's Tower
of the Winds", *Zeitschrift für Kunstgeschichte*
58 (1995), pp. 526-541.

Delen 1938
Delen A.J.J., *Musée Plantin-Moretus. Catalogue
des Dessins Anciens: Ecoles Flamande
et Hollandaise*, 2 vols., Brussels 1938.

Della Pergola 1955-1959
Della Pergola, P., *La Galleria Borghese.
I dipinti*, 2 vols., Rome 1955-1959.

Delumeau 1979
Delumeau, J., *Vita economica e sociale
di Roma nel Cinquecento*, Florence 1979.

Doering 1896
Doering, O., *Des Augsburgers Patriciers Philipp
Hainhofer. Beziehungen zum Herzog Philipp II
von Pommern-Stettin*, Vienna 1896.

D'Onofrio 1969
D'Onofrio, C., *Roma nel Seicento. Roma ornata
dall'architettura, pittura e scultura
di Fioravante Martinelli*, Florence 1969.

D'Onofrio 1970
D'Onofrio, C., "Una grande scomparsa.
Villa Montalto", *Capitolium*, XLV, 2/3
(1970), pp. 59-63.

Emiliani 1962
Emiliani, A., in *L'Ideale classico del Seicento
in Italia e la pittura di paesaggio*, exhib. cat.,
Bologna 1962, pp. 321ff.

Faggin 1965
Faggin, G.T., "Per Paolo Bril", *Paragone*,
185/5 (1965), pp. 21-35.

Felici 1952
Felici, G., *Villa Ludovisi in Roma*, Rome 1952.

Felini 1610
Felini, M., *Trattato nuovo delle cose
meravigliose dell'alma città di Roma*,
Rome 1610.

Flaitz 1938
Flaitz, F., *Die Heilige Cecilia, Jungfrau
und Martyrin in Rom. Ihr Leben und ihre
Verehrung*, Vatican City 1938.

Fontana 1590
Fontana, D., *Della trasportazione dell'Obelisco
Vaticano et delle fabriche di Nostro Signore
Papa Sisto V*, I, Rome 1590; II, Naples 1604
(ed. A. Carugo, Milan 1978).

Forcella 1873
Forcella, V., *Iscrizione delle Chiese e d'Altri
Edifici di Roma dal secolo XI ai nostri giorni*,
14 vols., Rome 1873, vol. 3.

Frommel 1973
Frommel, C.L., *Der römische Palastbau
der Hochrenaissance*, 3 vols., Tübingen 1973.

Gambi, Pinelli 1994
Gambi, L., A. Pinelli eds., *La Galleria
delle Carte geografiche in Vaticano*, 3 vols.,
Modena 1994.

Gambi, Pinelli 1997
Gambi, L., A. Pinelli eds., *La Galleria
delle Carte geografiche in Vaticano. Storia
e iconografia*, Modena 1997.

Van Gelder 1970
Van Gelder, J.G., "Lambert ten Kate als
kunstverzamelaar", *Nederlands Kunsthistorisch
Jaarboek* 21 (1970), pp. 139-186.

Gerszi 1982
Gerszi, T., "Pieter Bruegels Einfluss
auf die Herausbildung der Niederländischen
See- und Küstenlandschaftsdarstellung",
Jahrbuch der Berliner Museen 24 (1982),
pp. 143-187.

Giustiniani 1981
Giustiniani, V. (ed. A. Banti), *Discorsi
sulle Arti e sui Mestieri*, manuscript before
1610, Florence 1981.

Van Goor 1744
Van Goor, Th.E., *Beschryving der Stadt
en Lande van Breda*, The Hague 1744.

Hahn 1961
Hahn, H., "Paul Bril in Caprarola; zur
Malerwerkstatt des Vatikans und ihren

Ausstralungen 1570-1590", *Miscellanea
Bibliotheca Hertzianae zu Ehren Leo Bruhns,
Franz Graf Wolff Metternich, Ludwig Schudt*,
Munich 1961, pp. 308-322.

Havermans 1652
Havermans, A., *Kort begrip en bericht
van de historie van Brabant*, Leiden 1652.

Herz 1974
Herz, A., *The Sixtine and Pauline Tombs
in Sta. Maria Maggiore. An Iconographical
Study*, diss., New York 1974.

Hess 1936
Hess, J., "Le logge di Gregorio XIII nel Palazzo
del Vaticano: i pittori", *L'Illustrazione Vaticana*,
VII (1936), pp. 161-166.

Hess 1954
Hess, J., "Tassi, Bonzi e Cortona a Palazzo
Mattei", *Commentari*, 4 (1954), pp. 303-315.

Hibbard 1964
Hibbard, H., "Scipione Borghese's Garden
Palace on the Quirinal", *Journal of the Society
of Architectural Historians* (1964), pp. 163-192.

Hibbard 1971
Hibbard, H., *Carlo Maderno and Roman
Architecture 1580-1630*, London 1971.

Hollstein 1949- in progress
Hollstein, F.W.H., *Dutch and Flemish Etchings,
Engravings and Woodcuts, ca. 1450-1700*,
Amsterdam 1949- (in progress), 61 vols.
published.

Hoogewerff 1912
Hoogewerff, G.J., *Nederlandsche schilders
in Italië in de XVIe eeuw: De geschiedenis
van het Romanisme*, Utrecht 1912.

Hoogewerff 1913
Hoogewerff, G.J., *Bescheiden in Italië omtrent
Nederlandsche kunstenaars en geleerden*, II,
Rome. Archieven van bijzondere instellingen,
The Hague 1913.

Hoogewerff 1917
Hoogewerff, G.J., *Bescheiden in Italië omtrent
Nederlandsche kunstenaars en geleerden*, III,
Rome. Overige bibliotheken, The Hague 1917.

Hoogewerff 1942
Hoogewerff, G.J., *Nederlandse Kunstenaars
te Rome (1600-1725). Uittreksels uit de
Parrocchiale Archieven* (Studiën van het
Nederlandsch Historisch Instituut te Rome, III),
The Hague 1942.

Howard 1988
Howard, S., "Carraccesque Landscapes
by Bonzi", *Gazette des Beaux Arts*, 1988,
pp. 227-249.

Incisa della Rocchetta 1979
Incisa della Rocchetta, G., *La collezione
dei ritratti dell'Accademia di San Luca*,
Rome 1979.

Jeudwine 1956
Jeudwine, W.R., "Old Master Drawings-VII:
Five Drawings from the Collection of Sir Bruce
Ingram", *Apollo* 64 (1956), pp. 191-193.

Jones 1988a
Jones, P.M., "Two newly discovered hermit
landscapes by Paul Bril", *The Burlington
Magazine*, CXXX (1988), pp. 32-35.

Jones 1988b
Jones, P.M., "Federico Borromeo as a Patron
of Landscapes and Still Lifes: Christian
Optimism in Italy ca. 1600", *The Art Bulletin*,
LXX, 2 (1988), pp. 261-272.

Jones 1993
Jones, P.M., *Federico Borromeo and the
Ambrosiana. Art Patronage and Reform
in seventeenth-century Milan*, Cambridge
(Mass.) 1993 (ital. ed. Milan 1997).

Letarouilly 1963
Letarouilly, P., *The Vatican Buildings
(Les Bâtiments du Vatican)*, 3 vols.,
London 1963, vols. 2, 3.

Limentani Virdis, Pietrogiovanna 1999
Limentani Virdis, C., "Flemish Winds
on the Roman Landscape: The Bril Brothers
and Other Painters in Rome at the Time
of Pope Gregory XIII", Part I;
M. Pietrogiovanna, "The Tower of the Winds:
Critical History and a Reading of the Scenes",
Part II, in *Fiamminghi a Roma 1508-1608.
Proceedings of the symposium held
at the Museum Catharijneconvent, Utrecht
13 March 1995*, Florence 1999, pp. 67-78.

Louvre 1978
Inventaire Général des Dessins Italiens,
III, *Dessins Toscans*, I, Paris 1978.

Lugt 1949
Lugt, F., *Musée du Louvre. Inventaire général
des dessins des écoles du nord. Ecole flamande*,
Paris 1949.

Macioce 1990
Macioce, S., *"Undique Splendent". Aspetti
della pittura sacra nella Roma di Clemente VIII
Aldobrandini (1592-1605)*, Rome 1990.

Madonna 1993
Madonna, M.L., ed., *Roma di Sisto V. Le arti
e la cultura*, exhib. cat., Rome 1993.

Malvasia 1844
Malvasia, G.C., *Felsina Pittrice. Vite dei pittori
Bolognesi*, con aggiunte di Gian Pietro Canotti,
Bologna 1844.

Manchester 1983
*The Draughtsman's Art: Master Drawings
in the Whitworth Art Gallery*, exhib. cat.,
Whitworth Gallery, Manchester 1983.

Mancinelli 1980
Mancinelli, F., and J. Casanovas, *La Torre
dei Venti in Vaticano*, Vatican City 1980.

Mancini 1621
Mancini, G., *Considerazioni sulla pittura*,
Rome 1621, ed. A. Marucchi, L. Salerno,
2 vols., Rome 1956-1957.

Mandel 1991
Mandel, C.L., *The Lateran Palace Fresco Cycle*,
Toronto 1991.

Mandel 1994
Mandel, C.L., *Sixtus V and the Lateran Palace*,
Rome 1994.

van Mander 1604
Mander, K. van, *Het Schilder-boeck*,
Haarlem 1604.

van Mander 1603-04
Mander, K. van, *Het leven der Doorluchtighe
Nederlandtsche en Hooghduytsche schilders*,
Alkmaar 1603-04.

van Mander 1973
Mander, K. van, *Den grondt der edel vrij
schilderconst*, 2 vols., ed. H. Miedema,
Utrecht 1973.

Marchetti 1984
Marchetti, B., "Il «Superbissimo Palazzo
Orsini» di Monterotondo", *Lunario Romano*,
14 (1984), pp. 185-198.

Martellotti 1996
Martellotti, G., *Note sulla tecnica esecutiva*,
in A. Negro, *Il giardino dipinto del Cardinal
Borghese. Paolo Bril e Guido Reni nel Palazzo*

Rospigliosi Pallavicini a Roma, Rome
1996, p. 137.

Martin 1990
Martin, J., *Vaticano sconosciuto*, Vatican City
1990.

Massimo 1836
Massimo, V., *Notizie Istoriche della Villa
Massimo alle Terme Diocleziane*, Rome 1836.

Mayer 1910
Mayer, A., *Das Leben und die Werke der Brüder
Matthäus und Paul Brill. Ein Beitrag
zur Geschichte der Landschaftsmalerei
um die Wende des Sechzehnten Jahrhunderts*,
Leipzig 1910.

Miedema 1994
Miedema, H., ed., *Karel van Mander. The Lives
of the Illustrious Netherlandish and German
Painters*, vol. I, Doornspijk 1994.

Miedema 1999
Miedema, H., ed., *Karel van Mander. The Lives
of the Illustrious Netherlandish and German
Painters*, vol. VI, Doornspijk 1999.

Mignosi Tantillo 1982
Mignosi Tantillo, A., *Un'antologia di restauri.
50 opere d'arte restaurate dal 1974 al 1981*,
exhib. cat., Rome 1982, pp. 124-125.

Negro 1996
Negro, A., *Il giardino dipinto del Cardinal
Borghese. Paolo Bril e Guido Reni nel Palazzo
Rospigliosi Pallavicini a Roma*, Rome 1996.

Negro in print
Negro, A., "Il giardino di Scipione Borghese
a Montecavallo, ovvero un percorso simbolico
verso l'esercizio della Virtù", in *Bernini
dai Borghese ai Barberini. La cultura a Roma
intorno agli anni venti*. Papers from the
meeting held at the French Academy in Rome
from 17 to 19 February 1999, in course
of publication.

New York 1968
The Great Age of Fresco. Giotto to Pontormo,
exhib. cat., The Metropolitan Museum of Art,
New York 1968.

New York 1986
*The Northern Landscape. Flemish, Dutch
and British Drawings from the Courtauld
Collection*, exhib. cat., The Drawing Center,
New York 1986.

Noack 1927
Noack, F., *Das Deutschtum in Rom seit dem
Ausgang des Mittelalters*, 2 vols., Stuttgart,
Berlin, Leipzig 1927.

Norgate 1919
Norgate, E., *Miniatura or the Art of Limning*,
ed. M. Hardie, Oxford 1919.
Norgate 1997
Norgate, E., *Miniatura or the Art of Limning*,
London ca. 1623-26, ed. J.M. Muller, J.
Murrell, New Haven and London 1997.

Ogden, Ogden 1955
Ogden, H.V.S., M.S Ogden, *English Taste
in Landscape in the Sixteenth Century*,
Ann Arbor (Mich.) 1955.

Orbaan 1911
Orbaan, J.A.F., *Bescheiden in Italië omtrent
Nederlandsche kunstenaars en geleerden*,
I, *Rome, Vaticaansche Bibliotheek*,
The Hague 1911.

Orbaan 1920
Orbaan, J.A.F., *Documenti sul Barocco
in Roma*, Rome 1920.

Ost 1978
Ost, H., "Die Cappella Sistina in Santa Maria
Maggiore", in *Kunst als Bedeutungsträger,
Gedenkschrift für Günter Bandmann*, Berlin
1978, pp. 279-303.

Ostrow 1987
Ostrow, S.F., *The Sistine Chapel at S. Maria
Maggiore: Sistus V and the Art of the Counter
Reformation*, Ann Arbor (Mich.) 1987.

Pagliara 1980
Pagliara, P.N., "Monterotondo", in *Storia
dell'Arte Italiana. Inchieste su centri minori*,
Turin 1980, pp. 235-278.

Partridge 1996
Partridge, L., *Renaissance in Rom: die Kunst
der Päpste und Kardinäle*, Cologne 1996.

Von Pastor 1927
Von Pastor, L., *Geschichte der Päpste
im Zeitalter der katholischen Reformation
und Restauration*, XII vols., Freiburg i. Br.
1927, vols. XI-XII.

Von Pastor 1958
Von Pastor, L., *Storia dei Papi dalla fine
del medio evo*, vols. X and XI: *Storia dei Papi
nel periodo della Riforma e restaurazione*

cattolica, Clemente VIII (1592-1605),
Rome 1958.

Pietrangeli 1991
Pietrangeli, C., ed., *Il Palazzo Apostolico
Lateranense*, Florence 1991.

Pijl 1995
Pijl, L., "Gezicht op Bracciano: Paul Bril
als veduteschilder", *Tableau*, vol. 17, n. 6,
(1995), pp. 36-40 with illustration.

Pijl 1997
Pijl, L., "Paul Bril getekend door Ottavio
Leoni", in *Album Discipulorum J.R.J. van
Asperen de Boer*, P. v.d. Brink, L. Helmus eds.,
Zwolle 1997.

Pijl 1998
Pijl, L., "Paintings by Paul Bril in collaboration
with Rottenhammer, Elsheimer and Rubens",
The Burlington Magazine, 140 (1998),
pp. 660-667.

Pijl 1999
Pijl, L., "Figure and Landscape. Paul Bril's
Collaboration with Hans Rottenhammer and
Other Figure Painters, in *Fiamminghi a Roma
1508-1608. Proceedings of the symposium held
at the Museum Catharijneconvent, Utrecht
13 March 1995*, Florence 1999.

Pliny 1961
Pliny, *Natural History*, (ed. Loeb),
10 vols., Cambridge (Mass.) 1961.

Procacci, Guarneri 1975
Procacci, U., L. Guarneri, *Come nasce
un affresco*, Florence 1975.

Pugliatti, M.T., "Pietro Paolo Bonzi", *Quaderni
dell'Istituto di Storia dell'Arte Medievale
e Moderna dell'Università di Messina*, 1975,
pp. 15-23.

Reinhard 1974
Reinhard, W., *Papstfinanz und Nepotismus
unter Paul V. (1605-1621), Studien und
Quellen zur Struktur und zu quantitativen
Aspekten des päpstlichen Herrschaftssystems*,
2 vols., Stuttgart 1974.

Reinhardt 1984
Reinhardt, V., *Kardinal Scipione Borghese
1605-1633. Vermögen, Finanzen und sozialer
Aufstieg eines Papstnepoten*, Tübingen 1984.

Richardson 1941
Richardson, E.P., "Paul Bril or Elsheimer?",
The Art Quarterly (1941), pp. 323-329.

Rombouts, van Lerius s. a.
Rombouts, Ph., Th. van Lerius, *De Liggeren
en andere historische archieven der Antwerpse
Sint Lucasgilde*, 2 vols., The Hague, s. a.

Ruby 1999
Ruby, L. Wood, *Paul Bril. The Drawings*,
Turnhout 1999.

Salerno 1977-1980
Salerno, L., *Pittori di paesaggio del Seicento
a Roma*, 3 vols., Rome 1977-1980.

Salerno 1984
Salerno, L., *Natura morta italiana. Italienische
Stillebenmalerei aus drei Jahrhunderten.
Sammlung Silvano Lodi*, exhib. cat.
(Munich/Berlin), Florence 1984, pp. 72-77.

Scavizzi 1959
Scavizzi, G., "Paolo Brill alla Scala Santa",
Commentari, 10 (1959), pp. 196-200.

Scavizzi 1960
Scavizzi, G., "Gli affreschi della Scala Santa
ed alcune aggiunte per il tardo manierismo
romano", *Bollettino d'Arte*, 45 (1960),
pp. 111-122.

Scavizzi 1961
Scavizzi, G., "Sugli inizi del Lilio e su alcuni
affreschi del Palazzo Lateranense", *Paragone*,
137 (1961), pp. 44-48.

Schwager 1961
Schwager, K., "Zur Bautätigkeit Sixtus V.
und S. Maria Maggiore in Rom", in *Römische
Forschungen der Bibliothecae Hertziana*, XVI,
Miscellanea Bibliothecae Hertzianae, Vienna
1961, pp. 324-354.

Sluijter-Seijffert 1985
Sluijter-Seijffert, N., *Bril, Paulus (Antwerpen /
Anvers 1554-1626)*, in J. Bolten, *Oude
Tekeningen van het Prentenkabinet
der Rijksuniversiteit te Leiden*, The Hague
1985, pp. 65-70.

Spezzaferro 1985
Spezzaferro, L., "Un imprenditore del primo
Seicento: Giovan Battista Crescenzi", *Ricerche
di Storia dell'Arte*, 1985, pp. 50-73.

Ternois 1976
Ternois, D., *Les Artistes de passage dans la ville
de Lyon aux XVIIe et XVIIIe siècle. Études
statistique* and *Peintres et Dessinateurs
Néerlandais à Lyon du XVIe au XVIIIe siècle.
Rapport de Mission aux Pays-Bas*, in *Le Rôle*

de Lyon dans les échanges artistiques. Séjours et passages d'artistes à Lyon (1500-1800), Équipe de Recherche associée au C.N.R.S., 2, Paris 1976, pp. 3-23 and 25-68.

Vaes 1928
Vaes, M., "Matthieu Bril (1550-1583)", *Bulletin de l'Institut Historique Belge de Rome*, 8 (1928), pp. 283-333.

Vitruvius 1991
Vitruvius, *De Architectura Libri Decem / Zehn Bücher über Architektur*, (ed. C. Fensterbusch), Darmstadt 1991.

Volpe 1964
Volpe, C., *La natura morta italiana*, exhib. cat., Naples 1964.

Waddy 1990
Waddy, P., *Seventeenth-century Roman Palaces. Use and the Art of the Plan*, Cambridge (Mass.), London 1990.

Waddy 1999
Waddy, P., *L'architettura del Palazzo a Montecavallo nel Seicento e nel Settecento*, in *Palazzo Pallavicini Rospigliosi e la Galleria Pallavicini*, texts by D. Di Castro, A.M. Pedrocchi and P. Waddy, Turin 1999, pp. 204-207.

Washington 1974
Recent Acquisitions and Promised Gifts: Sculptures, Drawings, Prints, exhib. cat., The National Gallery of Art, Washington D.C. 1974.

Weil-Garris, D'Amico 1980
Weil-Garris, K., J. D'Amico, *The Renaissance Cardinal's Ideal Palace: A Chapter from Cortesi's "De Cardinalatu"*, Rome 1980.

Witte 1998
Witte, A., review of A. Negro, "Il giardino dipinto del cardinal Borghese", *Journal für Kunstgeschichte*, 1998, 2, pp. 55-60.

Zuccari 1992
Zuccari, A., *I pittori di Sisto V*, Rome 1992.

Zuccari 1993
Zuccari, A., "Pittura come itinerario nella Roma sistina", in *Sisto V. I, Roma e il Lazio*, vol. I, Rome 1993, pp. 641-657.

Consulted Archives

Gemeentearchief, Breda
Stadsarchief, Antwerp
Archive of Accademia di San Luca, Rome
Archive of Santa Maria dell'Anima, Rome
ASR, Archivio di Stato, Rome
ASV, Archivio Segreto Vaticano, Rome
BAV, Biblioteca Apostolica Vaticana, Rome

Mander, Karel van, 13, 17, 20, 26, 27, 62, 68, 69, 70
Mascarino, Ottaviano, 116
Mattei, Girolamo, Cardinal, 26, 56, 83, 170, 171
Mattei (family), 62
Montalto Peretti, Felice, Cardinal, 48
Morelli, Francesco, 158
Muziano, Girolamo, 42, 60, 148, 150

Nebbia, Cesare, 40, 42, 44, 50, 55, 69, 70, 109, 110, 113, 148, 150, 158, 160, 182, 184, 190, 191
Nieulandt, Willem van (Guglielmo Terranova), 13, 20, 26, 28
Nogari, Paris, 56, 108, 180, 184
Norgate, Edward, 27, 29, 48, 52, 67, 69, 70

Orsini (family), 24, 36, 37
Orsini, Giordano, 102, 105
Ortelmans (also Wortelmans), Damiaen, 15

Paul V (Borghese), Pope, 26, 62, 63, 64, 67, 87, 166, 168, 169
Peretti, Felice, Cardinal (see Sixtus V)
Peruzzi, Baldassare, 192
Pliny the Elder, 34, 68
Pomarancio (see Niccolò Circignani)
Pomarancio (see Cristoforo Roncalli)
Pommern-Stettin, Duke Philip II von, 27
Ponzio, Flaminio, 64, 100

Raeff, Hendrik de (Corvinius), 20, 29
Raphael (Raffaello Sanzio), 11, 32, 62
Reni, Guido, 11, 29, 64, 67, 71, 83, 87, 89, 96, 98, 100, 173, 174
Ricci, Giovan Battista, 20, 180, 184
Roncalli, Cristoforo (called Pomarancio), 108, 170, 176
Rondanini, Alessandro, 21
Rubens, Peter Paul, 20
Ruckers (family), 27

Sabbatini, Lorenzo, 24, 116
Sadeler, Aegidius, 28
Sadeler, Jan, 28, 60, 70
Sadeler, Raphael, 28, 60, 70
Salimbeni, Ventura, 158
Santen, Jan van (see Giovanni Vasanzio)
Sbarra, Ottavia (see Bril Sbarra, Ottavia)
Scocchi, Clara, 17
Sfondrati, Paolo Emilio, Cardinal, 26, 60, 176
Simonetta of Treviso, Joanni Donato, 28
Sixtus V (Peretti), Pope, 19, 26, 27, 42, 44, 46, 50, 51, 55, 56, 57, 62, 69, 109, 110, 113, 158, 160, 182, 184, 190, 191, 192

Soens, Jan, 28
Spieringh, Karel Philips (Carlo Filippo Spiringh), 29
Stella, Giacomo, 158, 184
Stevens, Pieter, 84

Tempesta, Antonio, 32, 37, 67, 71, 89, 118, 174
Theatine, Order of the, 192

Udine, Giovanni da (see Giovanni da Udine)

Vasanzio, Giovanni (Jan van Santen), 64, 67, 100
Viola, Giovanni Battista, 48, 67, 92, 108, 192
Vitruvius, 34, 68
Viviani, Antonio, 184
Vos, Maarten de, 60, 70, 85

Wortelmans (also Ortelmans), Damiaen, 17, 27

Zampieri, Domenico (see Domenichino)
Zuccari, Federico, 20

Amministrazione Maria Camilla Pallavicini, Rome   nos. VIIIb (Abbrescia e Santinelli), fig. 37.

A. Angeli, Rome, courtesy of the Vatican Museums   no. VI l: 21.

Bibliotheca Hertziana, Rome   no. II, fig. 38.

British Museum, London   fig. 44.

M. Coen, Rome   fig. 1.

Documentation photographique de la Réunion des Musées Nationaux, Paris   figs. 2, 3, 5 (J.G. Berizzi), 20, 21 (Michèle Bellot), 39 (J.G. Berizzi), 40, 41, 45, 46, 47, 48.

Carla Hendriks, Rotterdam   nos. Ia, Ib, Vb: 1-15, VIf: 2, 3, 6, 7, 10, VIg: 2, 5, 7, 13, 15, 17, 19, 21, 23, VIh: 1, 1/2, VIi: 1, 2/3, 3, VI l: 7, 21 (detail), VIm: 3, 8, 13, VIo: 3, VIIa, VIIb, IX: 1, 2, 5, 6; figs. 6, 14-16, 18, 31-33.

Istituto Centrale per il Catalogo e la Documentazione, Rome   nos. XI: 1-3; fig. 23.

F. Marini, Rome, courtesy of the Vatican Museums   no. VIe: 1; fig. 17.

National Gallery of Art, Ailsa Mellon Bruce Fund, Washington   fig. 42.

Nationalmuseum, Stockholm   fig. 25.

Prentenkabinet Universiteit Leiden, Leiden fig. 43.

F. Ravà, Rome, courtesy of the Vatican Museums nos. XIIb.

Rheinisches Bildarchiv, Kattenburg (Cologne) fig. 7.

Rijksmuseum-Stichting, Amsterdam   fig. 8.

Rijksmuseum Twenthe, Enschede   fig. 9.

P. Rizzi, Rome   nos. VIIIa; figs. 36, 52-70; courtesy of the Vatican Museums: nos. VIr: 8, VIt.

Photo Scala, Florence   fig. 35.

Soprintendenza per i Beni Artistici e Storici di Roma. Gabinetto fotografico   nos. IX: 3, 4, 7-13.

Sotheby's, Amsterdam   fig. 51.

Staatliche Graphische Sammlung, Munich fig. 49.

Staatliche Kunstsammlungen, Dresden   fig. 50.

G. Vasari, Rome, courtesy of the Vatican Museums   nos. Va, Vb: 16, Vc: 1, 3, VIa, XI: vault, 4, 5, XIIa, XIIc; figs. 10, 24, 27-29.

Vatican Museums   nos. Vc: 2, 4, VIb (A. Bracchetti), VIc (A. Bracchetti), VId: 2, 4, 8, 9, 10 (P. Zigrossi), 1, 3, 5, 6, 7, VIe: 2-4, VIf: 1, 4, 5, 8, 9, 11, 12, VIg: 1, 3, 6, 8, 11, 24, VIh: 2, 3, 4, VIi: 2, 4, VIj, VIk, VIm: 1, 4, 6, 9, 16, 17 (D. Pivato), VIn, VIo, VIp (P. Zigrossi), VIq: 1, 2, 7 (P. Zigrossi), 3-6, VIr: 1-7, VIs, X (P. Zigrossi); figs. 4, 12, 13, 22, 26, 34.

F1 48868355
F   00000321
NORTHEN
LANDSCAPES ON
ROMAN WALLS
CARLA
HENDRIKS

CENTRO DI
EDIFIMI SRL